World Affairs in Foreign Films, 2nd edition

Roberta Seret

International Cinema Education

International Cinema Education, Org.
P.O. Box 363
New York, New York 10028

ISBN-13: 9780692656211
ISBN-10: 0692656219
Library of Congress Control Number: 2016903781
International Cinema Education, New York, NY

Library of Congress Cataloguing-in-Publication Data

Seret, Roberta
    Film
    Foreign Films
    International Cinema
    Global Education
    Human Rights
    World Affairs
    Current Events
    Cultural Education
    Geography
    Global History
    Global Economics & World Finance
    International Law
    Comparative Literature
    Religion
    Philosophy
    Critical Thinking
    Art
    Media Studies
    Technology

Cover Design: Kia Heavey
Cover Photos: Roberta Seret

<u>Praise from Students for *World Affairs in Foreign Films*, 1st ed.</u>

- "Part of the reason why I enjoy these movies, is because they are real. I learned that it is possible to change the world with a single voice and it inspires me to join in the effort to fight global problems. This program has helped me grow as a student and individual."

- "We got to travel to places we would never ordinarily go to. The idea of learning through film is the best part of the class. You're learning without realizing it. I had a lot of fun."

- "Taking this class is absolutely an eye opening experience. I felt that these movies helped me understand better than any teacher or person, what life is like in different countries. I started to understand issues that would otherwise go unnoticed."

- "I feel, at times, in school I'm never really challenged how I should be, but this program does it for me. It was a year full of challenges, new experiences and lessons that made us aware about the truth of what is happening around the world."

- "For the first time, my mind opened to foreign cultures and stimulated me to learn like I never did before. I got to express my opinions freely. I will remember this class forever."

- "All these films revolve around thematic struggles that strengthen the universal resilience of the human spirit. After viewing all these films and participating in activities, I better understand this."

- "I have become more informed in foreign affairs so I can listen to the opposing sides and remain neutral and unbiased. What I take away is a lesson on humanity. If we do not care for each other, then we cannot care for ourselves and will never grow to become better people."

- "Before taking this course, I was ignorant of the things going on around the world. I've learned more about global issues as well as historical events that have happened. I was able to see the events through the protagonists' eyes."

- "Throughout the year it has grown into a class that I really enjoy and love to come to. All these films revolve around thematic struggles that strengthen the universal resilience of the human spirit."

- "This program has been a gift to us."

From Their Teachers:

- "My students' thoughts and ideas enlighten the class and encourage thought-provoking discussion – the kind of discussion a teacher quietly observes and marvels at, while the students reason, reflect, and astonish you with their depth and curiosity. We want to build life-learners, and by teaching kids how to observe their surroundings, how to interpret and analyze images, we can foster awareness on so many levels. I am seeing such great results in my students and I am truly grateful to be a part of this program."

- "My students were moved and I believe forever changed because of these films. One of the most remarkable aspects of this program is that my students are learning so much, not only through the films, but also through their peers."

- "Our student population is submersed in visual imagery. Why not help students to see - see the people around them, see the world around them, see themselves?"

World Affairs in Foreign Films, 2nd edition

For my sons, Greg and Cliff,
and all you have given me

Other Literary Works by Roberta Seret

- **World Affairs in Foreign Films for Middle School,** (**International Cinema Education, 2015**) www.worldaffairsinforeignfilms.com.

- **Oxford University Press, 2014-15:**
  http://blog.oup.com/2014/12/artist-model-fernando-trueba-int-law-film-review-pil/;
  http://blog.oup.com/2014/10/timbuktu-film-review-abderrahmane-sassako-pil/;
  http://blog.oup.com/2014/07/poetic-justice-the-german-doctor-wakolda-pil/;
  http://blog.oup.com/2014/06/aung-san-suu-kyi-the-lady-film-besson-pil/;
  http://blog.oup.com/2014/06/hannah-arendt-and-crimes-against-humanity-pil/;
  http://blog.oup.com/2014/06/psychodrama-cinema-and-indonesias-untold-genocide/;

- "Film Review: Hannah Arendt and Crimes Against Humanity," **Journal of International Criminal Justice** (Oxford U. Press), **March 2014,**
  Film Review: "Hannah Arendt and Crimes Against Humanity."

- **World Affairs in Foreign Films: Getting the Global Picture,** (**McFarland, Publishers, 2011** www.worldaffairsinforeignfilms.com.

- **FILMeds© 2012-16,** www.internationalcinemaeducation.org.

- **The Gift of Diamonds** (work in progress), www.thegiftofdiamonds.com

- The Chronicle of the United Nations, **The United Nations As A Global Classroom, 2006,** www.internationalcinemaeducation.org

- The Chronicle of the United Nations, <u>A Picture is Worth A Thousand Words,</u> 2004

- **Welcome To New York,** 5th ed., AWS Press, 2001; 4th ed., AWS Press, 1993; 3rd ed, AWS Press, 1989; 2nd ed, Harper & Row Publishers, 1985; 1st ed., AWS Press

- **Justice American Style,** 1996

- **Voyage Into Creativity; the Modern Künstlerroman,** Peter Lang Publishers, 1992

In Appreciation

- To my dear Board members of International Cinema Education (I.C.E.): Richard Block, Esq., Judith Vogel, Lesley Leben, Vartges Saroyan, Esq., James McSherry, Will Nix, Esq., Linda Weinberger, Steve Talay, and Dan Heldridge;

- Contributors: Caron Knauer, Andreea Mihut, Aida Diaz Sola, Steve Talay, Kristina Kirtley, Serena Depero, Eileen Baker, Gabe Leben, Kyle Greenberg, and Kimberly Cionca;

- Staff of the United Nations and Department of Public Information, Lilli Schindler, Souad Fennouh Chalhoub, Ramu Damodaran, and Kathryn Good;

- Grantors: The Ford Foundation Good Neighbor Grants, and Dr. Robert C. and Tina Sohn Foundation;

- My diplomatic students at the United Nations with the Hospitality Committee with whom I look forward to our Tuesdays when we share the pleasure of discussing world affairs and foreign films;

- The Greenwich, Ct branch of the National League of American PEN Women; and

- My family: Michel, Gregory, Clifford, Hally, Arielle, Annabel, and Sam.

World Affairs in Foreign Films, 2nd edition

CONTENTS

INTRODUCTION

*W*orld Affairs in Foreign Films, *2ⁿᵈ edition* offers teachers and students of high school and college, as well as adults of all ages, the opportunity to experience foreign cultures through the power of film. The concept is to use film as a catapult to better understand international events and the diversity of people around the world.

World Affairs in Foreign Films serves as a guidebook to foreign film as well as a vehicle to visit unfamiliar countries and different cultures. Seeing is believing, and to be transported into the middle of a foreign country as it is today, and then to discuss it, offers students the opportunity to experience diverse ways of living and to better understand their own country in the global community. It allows them to experience exotic settings, ancient religions and witness uncomfortable rules of justice. Film has the power to show the relationship of geography with history, the interaction of economics and politics and the unifying message of the heart. Film has the power to connect us all.

Using film to teach is an outgrowth of the "Global Classroom" that I have created at the United Nations for students of all ages. I feel privileged to have access to such a venue, for what better classroom could exist than the U. N. where "the world" is part of its daily activities? And what better medium is there than film to teach students about world affairs and human feelings?

At the United Nations, we have screened dozens of films over the years and diplomats have become the teachers in post Q and A discussions. Foreign films have given thousands of students the experience of traveling beyond borders and limitations, and without a plane ticket or visa.

Film is a new art compared to literature, painting, sculpture and music. It is less than 150 years old, with a gamut of possibilities, and we are using it to teach. What is exciting to see is that after several minutes of watching a foreign film, we realize the protagonists are similar to us, despite their different language and customs. For film speaks a universal language that helps us understand what we share in common.

An essential element of using film to learn is to discuss what we have seen. In our "Global Classroom" and now in *World Affairs in Foreign Films*, I encourage our viewers to ask questions, open their minds to the unknown, and allow themselves to go beyond their limits.

In *World Affairs in Foreign Films, 2nd edition,* I have taken 14 films from Asia, Europe, Antarctica, Africa, and the Middle East that are representative of their global region and contain political issues. These films are just a sampling of possibilities. We all have our favorites, and my regret is that I could not analyze all of them in this book. But at the end of each film chapter, there is a bibliography that offers suggestions for further viewing and discussion. Of course the list continues, and I hope it does.

The structure I have chosen is to introduce a film and its country by analyzing each film from 9 inter-related, multi-disciplinary academic lenses: World History; Geography; Economics; Civics, Citizenship and Government; World literature; Media Studies; Philosophy /Critical Thinking; Art; and Technology. The questions and answers at the end of each academic section are for group activities to help reinforce skills in analysis, summary, problem solving, and synthesis – all skills that students need for success in school, career and life.

In the Media Studies perspective, I use film clips that target important scenes. By going directly to the film and discussing the specific scenes, students are able to analyze complex concepts that may initially have gone unnoticed. Activities at the end of this perspective, and for all 9 disciplines, are for group sharing.

For the Technology segment, I try to show how technology connects the dots from curriculum to job opportunities. Group projects are used to encourage students to work together to create videos, PSAs, power point presentations and blogs, while reinforcing their computer skills. With a Ford Foundation Good Neighbor grant, I have attempted to create an innovative approach to link technology with literature and interface the digital with the written, in the format of FILMeds© that are used for educational purposes. The 10-30 minute videos complement the films in the textbook and are posted on my NGO website:

(www.internationalcinemaeducation.org)

The specific goals of the 2nd edition of *World Affairs in Foreign Films,* are:

1. *Global Education:* Each film is divided into 9 academic inter-related perspectives to teach about one country and then to relate that country to its geo-political region and the world. Film is a vehicle to help us think critically about historical, political and economic events by applying concepts and information gained through visual and textual sources.

2. *Global understanding:* The foreign films chosen have young protagonists who are faced with problems to solve and overcome. By empathizing with these

protagonists and their challenges, we can relate to them and to others around us in a global understanding. We become inspired and motivated.

3. *General culture:* The book also introduces general culture by offering content about different religions, philosophies, customs, laws, art, literature, music, and foreign languages.

4. *How to think and learn:* The book and film used together, give the stepping-stones to the processes of learning, thinking critically, analyzing information, and collecting facts. We move from the unknown to the known by asking questions, and then on how to research and investigate these questions, as well as how to analyze and synthesize, how to evaluate and come to conclusions, and then on how to share, discuss and communicate ideas. These processes of thinking and reasoning serve as models for future learning.

5. *Promote Diversity:* The exposure to human diversity and the encouragement to absorb the validity of diversity, can make us better people and more productive. Diversity espouses tolerance, openness, creativity, and optimism – all strengths needed to reinforce our mental and emotional development. Foreign film has the ability to show diversity in a subtle way on the screen: the diversity of protagonists, societies, cultures, and thoughts.

As you read *World Affairs in Foreign Films* and screen films in your schools and homes, I hope they open up a window of understanding to the hearts of our young protagonists. It would be wonderful if these films can take you beyond any border to countries where you no longer see differences, but feel common areas where we can work together and create a better world. I wish you fun on your journey.

Roberta Seret, Ph.D.
President and Founder, International Cinema Education,
NGO/ United Nations, New York City

ASIA

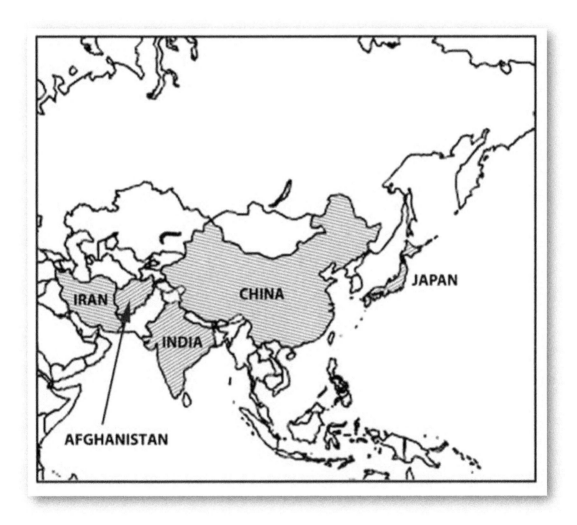

CHAPTER 1

LIFE OF PI (INDIA)

TITLE OF FILM: *Life of Pi*
YEAR OF RELEASE: 2012
COUNTRY: India.
DIRECTOR: Ang Lee
LANGUAGE: English (Tamil, French)
RUNNING TIME: 127 minutes
RATING: PG - 13
CURRICULUM THEMES:

A. HISTORY AND SOCIAL SCIENCE:

- **Chapter's Key Theme: The Will to Survive**
- **World History: European Colonization; Survival at Sea**
- **Geography: Partition of India; Pondicherry**
- **Economics: Imperialism; Emigration**
- **Civics, Citizenship, and Government: Bullying; Conditioning; Maslow's Hierarchy of Needs**

B. LITERATURE AND VISUAL ARTS:

- **World Literature: Gandhi, Hinduism, and nonviolence; Hinduism, Christianity, Islam, Sikhism, Jainism, Buddhism**
- **Media Studies: Film Clips and Scene Discussions; Documentary Style; Computer Generated Imagery**
- **Philosophy/ Critical Thinking: Existentialism; Narrative Conflicts; Aristotle and Catharsis; Platonic Approach; Unreliable Narration; Metaphors**
- **Music: Indian Music and Dance**
- **Technology: Mariana Trench and Google earth site (earth.google.com)**

Introduction:

Life of Pi was directed by Ang Lee; produced by Gil Netter and Ang Lee; edited by Tim Squyers; based on the screenplay by David Magee and on the novel by Yann Martel; music by Mychael Danna; cinematography by Claudio Miranda; and distributed by 20ᵗʰ Century Fox in 2012.

Pi Patel...Suraj Sharma
Adult Pi Patel..Irrfan Khan
Writer (Yann Martel)...Rafe Spall
Santosh Patel (father) .... Adil Hussain
Gita Patel (mother)..Tabu
Ravi Patel (brother) .... Vibish Sivakumar

Life of Pi tells the extraordinary story of Pi Patel, a sixteen-year-old Indian boy who survives at sea in a lifeboat with a Bengal tiger, alternating between fighting for his life and witnessing some of the most beautiful scenes nature can exhibit. In a unique twist that grants the audience an unusual degree of power over the narrative, Pi also offers a second version of his own story and lets his audience decide which to believe. The narrative derives its power from the combination of author Yann Martel's focus on the importance of storytelling and director Ang Lee's attention to the visual potential of such a message.

Pivotal Moments in the History of India:

- The Indus Valley Civilization was the first major civilization in South Asia, starting in 3300 B.C. Various empires ruled for thousands of years, the most significant being the Gupta Empire. This was the golden age of India.
- The first Europeans to come to India were the Portuguese in 1498, with explorer Vasco da Gama. The Dutch and the French also claimed land, but it was the English that ruled India from 1619 until 1947.
- As early as 1920, Mahatma Gandhi led non-violent protests again British rule. Thanks in large part to Gandhi, India achieved independence from British rule in 1947. At this time, India was partitioned into the mostly-Hindu Union of India and the mostly-Muslim Pakistan.
- In 1971, East Pakistan became independent and took the name of Bangladesh.

Pre-Screening Questions:

a. Who was Mahatma Gandhi and why was he important in the history of India?

- Mohanes Gandhi (2 October 1869 – 30 January 1948) was the widely admired and respected leader of the Indian independence movement. The honorific "Mahatma" that is often added to his name means "high-souled." He encouraged nonviolent methods of fighting oppression and led many peaceful but powerful protests. Gandhi was imprisoned for his actions several times, and he spent his time in prison reading widely and writing his memoirs, leaving his wisdom for future generations. A year after the British granted India its independence, Gandhi was assassinated in 1948. He is known as the father of the nation by many people in India.

b. What do you think you'd need in order to survive at sea? What are your priorities?

- *Do you think it's better to be lost at sea alone or as part of a group?*
- *How do your priorities change depending on whether you're alone or not?*

Suggested Activity:
Lost at Sea Team-building and Leadership Exercise:

- *Scenario: "You and your team have rented a yacht for a relaxing cruise in the Southern Pacific Ocean. As you sail, a fire breaks out and most of the yacht's contents are destroyed. Your location is unclear because your radio and navigation equipment have been damaged. You all look in your pockets to see what you can use to survive, and you manage to collect together the following 14 items.*
- *Rank them in order of priority in your quest to survive and be rescued:*

1. *A shaving mirror*
2. *Some mosquito netting*
3. *A can of water*
4. *A case of army food*
5. *Maps of the Pacific Ocean*
6. *A floating seat cushion*
7. *A 7 can of oil/ petroleum mixture*

8. *A small radio*
9. *Large plastic sheets*
10. *Shark repellent*
11. *Three bottles of rum*
12. *Rope*
13. *2 boxes of chocolate bars*
14. *A fishing kit*

After discussing the above questions as a group, you can individually rank the 14 items listed in order of priority. The rest of the activity and the answers may be given after the film screening.

Pivotal Moments in Film:

- In the film, Pi's father decides to sell his zoo and move his family to Canada because he is nervous about the political situation in India. This refers to real historical events. The film is set in 1977, two years after the start of what is known as "the Emergency." In 1975, unpopular Prime Minister Indira Gandhi was ordered to resign. Instead, she suspended constitutional rights and gave herself the power to rule by decree. In this period of economic and political turmoil, Pi's father speculates that Gandhi might try to take over his zoo. His subsequent decision launches the main plot of *Life of Pi*. The legacy of Indira Gandhi's rule is controversial. Although democracy and human rights were violated, the economy did improve and stabilize. In 1977, Gandhi called for elections, thus ending the Emergency.
- Pondicherry, the city in which Pi's family lives at the beginning of the film, was a French colony until the 20th century. French is still an official language there today, and many institutions have retained their French name. We see this influence in many instances in the film, for example when Pi is seen reading on three separate occasions and all three books have French titles, and with the fact that Pi's full name, "Piscine Molitor," is French for "the Molitor swimming pool."
- Pi himself can be said to represent India's heterogeneous composition in his approach to religion. He is raised as a Hindu, which constitutes India's oldest religion, but in his childhood embraces both Christianity and Islam. Religious tensions between Muslims and Hindus were the main driving force behind the

partition of India and Pakistan in 1947. Within Pi, however, the diversity of India's historical background and spirituality are made to coexist in harmony.

Post-Screening Questions:
History and Social Science:

a. *What have you noticed Pi doing that helped him survive at sea? What were his priorities? How would yours differ if you didn't have a tiger onboard with you?*

b. *Suggested activity: continued: Survival at Sea Team-building and Leadership exercise:*

* *"According to experts (United States Coastguard), there are basic supplies needed when a person is stranded at sea to attract attention and articles to aid survival until rescue arrives. Without signaling devices, there is almost no chance of being spotted. Furthermore, most rescues occur within the first 36 hours and a person can survive with only a minimum of food and water during that period. So, the following from the prior list is the order of ranking the items in their importance to survival:"*

1. *The shaving mirror would be critical for signaling.*
2. *The oil/ petroleum mixture would also be critical for signaling. The mixture floats on water and can be ignited with dollar bills and a match.*
3. *The water would be necessary for hydration.*
4. *One case of army rations would provide basic food intake.*
5. *The opaque plastic could be used to collect rain water and provide shelter.*
6. *The chocolate bars could provide reserve food supply.*
7. *The fishing kit is ranked lower than the chocolate since 'a bird in the hand is worth two in the bush', and there is no guarantee that you will catch any fish.*
8. *The rope could be used to secure people or equipment.*
9. *The floating seat cushion could be a life preserver if someone fell overboard.*
10. *Shark repellent.*
11. *The rum contains alcohol, which can be used as an antiseptic for any injuries.*
12. *The radio would be useless without a transmitter and you would be out of range of any radio station.*
13. *Maps of the Pacific Ocean would be worthless without navigation equipment.*
14. *The mosquito netting would not be necessary, as there are NO mosquitoes in the mid-Pacific Ocean.*

Post-Screening Questions:
Literature and Visual Arts

---

a. What are the two stories? Compare and contrast them. Which do you think is the
    true one? Which is the one you prefer? Watch the ending scene again:

    Film clip 1:56:12 – 1:59:14. What do you think Pi meant when he said "and
    so it is with God" when the writer said he preferred the story with the tiger
    over the other?

- Story 1: Pi is in a lifeboat with a zebra, a hyena, an orangutan, and a tiger. The
  hyena kills the wounded zebra and the orangutan and then the tiger kills the
  hyena. Pi learns to coexist with Richard Parker.
- Story 2: Pi is in a lifeboat with the sailor, the cook, and his mother. The cook
  kills the sailor and throws Pi's mother overboard and then Pi kills the cook.
  He survives alone on the boat.
- Connection: The zebra is the sailor, the hyena is the cook, and the orangutan is
  Pi's mother. Richard Parker is Pi; or it may be said that the tiger is the violent /
  evil side of Pi, which he learns to accept and live with, and which leaves him
  once he is rescued.
- The writer has no idea which of the two stories is the true one. Pi asks him
  which one he prefers and the writer tells him he likes the tiger story more. Pi
  then says "and so it is with God." That is, we also have two stories for our lives:
  one with God and one without God. We cannot know which one is the truth,
  so what is left is for us to choose the one we prefer and live accordingly. And
  that is the author's philosophical message of Existentialism.
- By creating the second story to survive, Pi uses Existentialism to the highest
  degree: he creates his own reality and defines himself by his actions by telling
  a story to survive the horrors he has experienced.

Curriculum Themes:
A. History and Social Science:

Chapter's Key Theme: The Will To Survive

a. The "will to survive" is not just a figure of speech. It is a documented psychologi-
    cal force that is considered one of the most basic human drives. There have been

many names for this force over the years. Sigmund Freud, for instance, described it in terms of the "pleasure principle" as an impulse toward pleasure and away from pain and death. Maslow's "Hierarchy of Needs," explained later in the chapter, is also based on the idea to survive. People have recognized the impulse to survive in life-threatening situations, but it also manifests in situations of symbolic survival, such as moments in which one's meaning or purpose in life is threatened or when one's central values or beliefs are challenged. The strength of this impulse in all of us is important because it can help us explain and understand the sometimes shocking lengths a person or a character may go to in order to survive.

Suggested Activities:
- *What measures can you think of that Pi takes in order to survive in the first story? Cite specific moments in the film and argue why they are examples of the will to survive. Share as a group your points.*
- *What additional examples of the will to survive does the second story have that the first does not? Think about the writer's reaction when Pi mentioned he has a family and a life – why do you think the author is surprised?*

Hints:
- Pi's life is in danger from two things: being lost at sea with limited resources; and Richard Parker. Some examples of what Pi does, which illustrates his will to survive are:
    - He eats fish, even though he is a vegetarian.
    - He takes up taming a wild tiger, despite his childhood experience with him.
    - He eats unknown roots on the island, because he starving.
    - He builds and sleeps on a dangerous raft, to avoid Richard Parker.
    - He sends messages in cans, despite the low likelihood that they will work.

The second story emphasizes the will to survive in the following ways:

- After seeing what the cook is capable of, Pi commits murder in order to outlive him. This is a darker example of the human will to survive.
- One interpretation of the film is that Pi's subconscious mind created the story with the animals in order to protect himself from a truth that would have horrified him too much to keep living: his killing another person, the cook, and witnessing his mother's death. Richard Parker's first appearance in the first story matches the moment when Pi kills the cook in the second; and Richard Parker disappears once Pi reaches Mexico and is saved. The tiger is Pi's violent / evil side, the one whose will to survive is so strong that

he commits murder. This denial, too, would be an example of the will to survive.

- Another possible example is the second story itself. The Japanese insurance investigators don't believe Pi. They threaten his need to be believed, so he comes up with a more believable story.
- Overall, Pi's narration of the first story, with the animals on the boat, is an example of storytelling, Art, which is the greatest form of survival: creating and imagining something else in order to survive.

1. World History:

a. European Colonization:

- Although most of India was under British rule from the 17th to the 20th century, various European powers asserted their influence over different parts of the country:
- Portugal: 1498-1961: The Portuguese, under explorer Vasco da Gama, were the earliest Europeans to come to India in 1498. Their main trading base was in Goa (western coast) until 1961.
- The Netherlands: 1605 – 1825: The Dutch established their main base at Ceylon (presently called Sri Lanka, southern island).
- Great Britain: 1619 – 1947: The British Empire included territories that are now Pakistan and Bangladesh. The saying, "The sun never sets on the British Empire" is very indicative of their Empire.
- France: 1673 – 1954: The French were in the south-eastern region. Most European territories were lost to the British, but Pondicherry remained a French outpost until 1954.

The most important factors for colonization were:

- Commercial: Portuguese King Manuel wanted to find a direct sea route to India in order to increase trade.
- Economic: The Industrial Revolution was beginning and European countries needed new markets and raw materials. By the mid-18th century, India had become one of Great Britain's most important colonies, especially as a source

of raw materials. The raw materials (tea, textiles, salt) from India went to the
UK, where they became manufactured goods, and sold both in the UK and in
India.

- Nationalism: There were strong nationalistic sentiments in Europe. Each
  country wanted to prove it was the strongest world power and started coloniz-
  ing new territory throughout Asia and Africa, to show it.

Suggested Activities:

- *In small groups, research a picture that is relevant to the topic of European colonization
  in India. Maybe it's a painting, an old photograph, a political cartoon, or a chart.
  Research who-what-where-when-why-how to discuss the following: Who are the people
  or what are the ideas being depicted? What is happening in the picture/ what event or
  fact does it refer to? Where is the setting of the picture? When did the event take place/
  when was the picture made or taken? Why is it important? How does it catch people's
  attention?*

b. Survival at Sea:

Pi survived 227 days at sea with a tiger in his raft.

Suggested Activities:

Your group can discuss:

- *Is it possible to survive 227 days at sea?*
- *Research some true stories of survival at sea. Answer the following questions: What is
  the name of the survivor or survivors? How long were they at sea? What kind of raft
  were they in? Did they have rations or water with them? What did they eat and drink to
  survive?*

Hints:

- Steven Callahan is a naval architect who got lost at sea in a boat he designed. He
  was rescued after 76 days. Director Ang Lee consulted Callahan for *Life of Pi*.
- Maurice and Maralyn Bailey are a British couple who survived 117 days at sea.
  In the first weeks they read and played cards on their rubber raft.
- Two Burmese men survived in an icebox for 25 days in 2009.

2. Geography:

a. Partition of India:

- After World War II, Great Britain announced that India was to become an independent nation. This sparked many religious conflicts about who should rule.

  It was Gandhi, the Father of Independence for India, who became the leader.
- On 15 August 1947, the British Indian Empire was split into the largely Muslim territory of Pakistan and the Hindu section of India. This is known as the Partition of India. During the partition, the largest mass migration in human history took place: about 14 million Hindus, Sikhs, and Muslims were displaced.
- Later in 1971, Pakistan further split into the Islamic Republic of Pakistan and the People's Republic of Bangladesh.

b. Pondicherry, India:

Pondicherry is the city that Pi is from. The French gained control of Pondicherry in 1674. Even though most of India became part of the British Empire, Pondicherry remained French. It gained its independence in 1954. The official languages of Pondicherry are Tamil and French. To this day, there are many institutions that have French names left over from the colonial period.

3. Economics:

a. Imperialism:

Imperialism is a policy of extending a country's power and influence by the economic and political control of other countries. Though the idea of imperialism dates back to Roman times, it reached its peak in what is now known as the "Age of Imperialism," lasting from the beginning of the 18th century to the mid-20th century, when many countries, including India, gained their independence. Most imperialist countries were European, e.g. Great Britain, Spain, Portugal, Netherlands, France, Germany. However, Japan, the Soviet Union, and the United States were also imperialist countries.

Suggested Activities:
- *Your group can locate on a map or globe the different Empires in Africa, Asia, South America, etc and exchange information and anecdotes about the colonized countries.*

b. Emigration:

Migration is the act of moving across national borders. Emigration (Latin, em means out of) refers to leaving one's native country in order to settle in another country and immigration (Latin im means into) the opposite, is the act of moving into a new country. Demographers, people who study population, explain migration as a combination of push-and-pull factors. Push factors are negative circumstances that push people away from their home country, while pull factors are positive circumstances that pull people to the new country.

Push factors:

- Political persecution
- Drought or flooding
- War
- Poverty
- Poor medical care
- Fewer job opportunities
- Pollution
- Crowded living conditions
- Infertile land
- High crime
- Gender discrimination

Pull factors:

- More job opportunities
- Political asylum
- More wealth
- Good climate
- Safer, less crime
- Religious freedom
- Fertile land

- Better living conditions
- Better medical care
- Better education
- High demand for labor

Suggested Activities:
- *When Pi's family left their home country, they became migrants. Today, we see millions of migrants fleeing Syria, Afghanistan, Iraq, Africa, the Middle East, and other countries. The 20th- 21st centuries have known many waves of migration after wars and strife. Examples of each movement can make a very dynamic discussion, personal as well as political.*
- *Include the push and pull examples as factors for today's migrants.*

4. Civics, Citizenship and Government:

a. Bullying:

Pi's story begins with an account of how he got his name (watch the clip: 3:58 – 9:29). He was named after a French swimming pool that sounded funny to the other students. His first attempts to get students and teachers to call him "Pi" were unsuccessful. Instead of giving up, Pi became more insistent and gave them something memorable that made his nickname stick.

Suggested Activities:
- *Many people sadly experience being bullied or bullying. To share these stories with members of the group could result in building group solidarity. What common elements or feelings tie these stories together? (For more information about bullying, refer to chapter ten with the film, In a Better World.)*

b. Conditioning:

- Pi constructed a raft that's tied to the lifeboat, so that he may be safe from Richard Parker. But he still needs to gain some control over the situation. One of the first things he does is try to make the tiger associate Pi's whistle with the motion of the boat rocking over the waves, so that in time the whistle alone would make him seasick. (Film clip: 1:00:04 – 1:04:12) This is called "classical conditioning", or "Pavlovian conditioning", and it is actually a proven psychological effect that works on humans as well as animals.

- Russian scientist Ivan Pavlov was the first to notice conditioning in the 1890s. Pavlov's dogs naturally started salivating when they saw food brought to them. Salivating is not a deliberate act, but a reflex. So Pavlov wondered if his dogs could learn to salivate in other conditions. He started to ring a bell every time he brought his dogs food. After some time, Pavlov's dogs would salivate whenever they heard the bell, even if there was no food in sight! They had learned to associate the bell with food, and so they produced the same reflex. Pi uses this same technique with his whistle when he tries to train the tiger.
- People are conditioned to make certain choices based on reflex behavior without even realizing it. For instance, pain plays a huge part in conditioning. Pain conditions us to avoid certain things that will give us pain.

Suggested Activities:
- *Ask your group to discuss why Pi's attempt to make Richard Parker seasick with the whistle failed? What else did Pi do to condition the tiger?*
- *Discuss what good can be done with the knowledge of how conditioning works?*

c. Maslow's Hierarchy of Needs:

Watch the film scene of 1:20:35 – 1:21:34, in which Pi talks about how he's come to appreciate the little treasures he has in his life and how "tending to [Richard Parker's] needs gives [Pi's] life purpose." Despite being lost at sea with only a dangerous carnivore for company and with limited resources, Pi actually seems to be happy, or at least at peace. How can this be? What is this telling us?

- In 1943, a psychologist named Abraham Maslow published his "Hierarchy of Needs" that he said all people needed to go through in order to achieve happiness. Maslow argued that we cannot move to the next level, find happiness, and/ or survive, without satisfying the needs from the level before: What are our needs: Physiological, Safety, Love/ Belonging, Esteem, and Self-actualization which brings happiness and satisfaction.

Suggested Activities:
- *Maslow's hierarchy can create diverse reactions because the terms he uses need to be abstract enough to work for everyone, despite the fact that people differ so much from each*

other. The group discussion can first begin by using Pi – did he have what he needed for a content life, despite his difficult beginnings?

- *A good way to continue the conversation is for each person to draw a pyramid or chart of their own Needs for Actualization and Happiness. Where does "purpose" fit? What does "love/belonging" mean? How could one measure "esteem" for oneself? How could someone determine people's "respect"? These needs do not have to be satisfied in a specific order or all at once in order to find happiness.*

5. World Literature:

a. Gandhi, Hinduism, and nonviolence:

'My life is my message.' -Gandhi

- Mohandas Gandhi (1869 – 1948) was the leader of the Indian independence movement against the British, whose nonviolent policies, inspired by his Hindu faith, have inspired many people all over the world. Gandhi was trained as a lawyer in London and practiced law in South Africa, both experiences helping him understand the power of nonviolent civil disobedience. When he returned to India in 1915, he began organizing peasants, farmers, and laborers in order to protest British taxes against India. One of his most famous campaigns was the peaceful 200-mile Salt March in 1930. It was in protest of a policy that forced Indians to buy salt for the British, so Gandhi led people to the sea where they gathered their own salt from the water. This march ended with the arrest of over 60,000 people including Gandhi himself. Another famous movement was Quit India in 1942, which encouraged noncooperation with British business and boycotted British-manufactured goods. For Gandhi, nonviolent resistance included boycotting British goods as well as strikes, marches, and protests.
- Gandhi's religion played a large part in the development of his values and nonviolent policies. Hindu teachings and writings gave shape to Gandhi's thoughts and influence.

b. Hinduism, Christianity, Buddhism, Islam, Sikhism, Jainism:

- One of the most powerful scenes occurs in the beginning of the film, when Pi talks about how he came to embrace Christianity and Islam in addition to his first religion, Hinduism (12:16 – 21:07). Pi's mother encourages him, but his father tells him he cannot practice three religions at once. These are the three biggest world religions. On the ship to Canada, Pi meets a young Buddhist boy, another major religion.

- India is characterized by a great diversity of religions. About 80% of Indians are Hindu, but there are significant groups of Muslims and Christians as well. Other religions that are practiced are Sikhism, Buddhism, and Jainism:

Hinduism

- Hinduism has is origins in India and has remained the dominant religion there until today. It has been called the oldest religion in the world.
- There is One Supreme Reality (Brahman) manifested in many gods and goddesses. Some of the most important ones are Vishnu, Shiva, Brahma, Krishna, and Ganesha.
- Other beliefs include reincarnation (upon death, one is reborn in another body and life until one reaches enlightenment), karma (if you do good, good things will happen to you and if you do bad, bad things will happen to you), mantras (repeated sayings or prayers that help one focus), and dharma (righteousness, or daily morality).
- More general Hindu values include honesty, mercy, purity, self-restraint, and celibacy.

Christianity

- Christianity was founded by Jesus Christ in Israel and became the largest world religion. Over time, different branches of Christianity have broken off, such as Catholic, Protestant, and Orthodox faiths. Chronologically, Christianity came after Judaism and before Islam.
- There is one God, who is composed of a trinity of Father, Son, and Holy Spirit. Jesus of Nazareth is the messiah that saved humankind from its own sins, and he is the son of God.
- Christians believe in judgment after death and which sends souls to either Heaven or Hell. Clergy are known as priests, ministers, pastors, or bishops; the house of worship is the church.

Buddhism

- Buddhism was founded by Siddharta Gautama (known as the Buddha) in India.

- Unlike most other religions, Buddhism does not claim the existence of any supreme beings known as gods. It is known as a non-theistic religion. Instead, Buddhism is a series of teachings and philosophy for how to live well.
- Some Buddhist concepts include Nirvana (a sublime state that is the ultimate goal of Buddhism), meditation (a silent contemplation of an object or idea until a tranquil state is achieved), Samsara (the cycle of birth, death, and rebirth that Buddhists seek to liberate themselves from).
- More general values include morality, mindfulness of thoughts and actions, wisdom, understanding, and liberation from earthly desires.

Islam

- Islam was founded by Muhammad in Saudi Arabia and has 1.3 billion adherents worldwide. There are two main branches of Islam: Sunni and Sufi (Shiites, Shias)
- There is one God (Allah). Unlike Christians and Jews, Muslims believe Muhammad a prophet.
- Other important beliefs include angels (messengers of God made of light that communicate revelations from God and that record every person's actions), Jannah (paradise) and Jahannam (hell), predestination (God has full knowledge and control over everything that happens, including our fates), Ramadhan (fasting from food and drink during daylight hours to encourage a nearness to God), and Sharia law based on the Koran.
- The clergy are known as imams and the house of worship is the mosque.
- For a chart of which countries are Sunnis or Shiites, see chapter fourteen with the film, *The Other Son.*

Sikhism

- Sikhism was founded by Guru Nanak in India and it is the fifth largest world religion, with 23 million adherents. Guru Nanak said that "realization of Truth is higher than all else. Higher still is truthful living."
- There is one God, Vahiguru, that is shapeless, genderless, timeless, and sightless.

Jainism

- Jainism was founded in eastern India and it has about 4 million worldwide adherents.

- There are many Gods that are organized in a complex hierarchy along with humans and all other living creatures.
- Other beliefs include the Five Great Vows (Non-violence, Truth, Celibacy, Non-Stealing, Non-Possessiveness), meditation, mantras, vegetarianism, and reincarnation.
- General values include harmlessness and renunciation.

Suggested Activity:
- *Religion is often a controversial subject. Why is that? One characteristic of religion is that not only is there great diversity among them, but even within the same religion people can have different interpretation and practices. Pi created his own religion by fusing three religions together. Have your group discuss Pi's concept. What would be some characteristics of religion if you had the ability to create your own? Perhaps your group can come together and create an "ideal" form of religion that appeals to all members of your group.*

6. Media Studies:

a. Film Clips and Scene Discussions:

- *Existentialism* is a theme that is used often in this film. From the beginning of the film, and as of eleven years old, Pi had to create himself. He was not happy with his name, Piscine, which means in French, swimming pool. He has to show his classmates that he is too intelligent to be bullied. (Scene: 07:28 –>09:18)

   The class can analyze how Pi took his fate into his own hands from the very beginning of the story: "When we returned the next for our first day of school, I was prepared. I am Piscine Molitor Patel. Know to all as "Pi." The sixteenth letter of the Greek alphabet. By the end of that day, I was "PI Patel," school legend."

   Discuss why the philosophy of Existentialism helped Pi survive being bullied? How does this philosophy explain why artists create? How does Art help man survive?

- *Survival.* This is a survival story, and Pi claims that the tiger, Richard Parker, helped him survive: (Scene 01:44–> 01:45)

   Pi's words tell us this: "I know Richard Parker's a tiger, but...I wish I had said: "It's over, we survived...thank you for saving my life. I love you, Richard

Parker. You'll always be with me. But I can't be with you. It's hard to believe, isn't it? It is a lot to take into figure out what that all means. No, if it happened, it happened. Why should it have to mean anything? See, I was the only one who survived the ship wreck."

How did the tiger help Pi survive? Was it the tiger? Or was it how Pi imagined the tiger to be?

- *Happiness:* (Scene: 01:53 –> 01:55)

Despite Pi's difficult situation, he has found a calmness due to his own actions. He is surviving and with the tiger. Pi has accepted his situation and has chosen to live by his actions. This is an expression of Existentialiem.

b. Documentary Style:

The style of the movie and the book is that of a "documentary," which refers to the recording of a truth in a form for later use – maybe to instruct, or to expose hidden truths. It is a kind of writing that bases itself on claims of truth, authenticity, and objectivity. Nonfiction forms that use this are journalism, news, and TV reporting. In the case of fiction, it is a stylistic choice that adds power to the message it's trying to send.

Suggested Activity:
- *Have your group find some films and books that combine fiction and non-fiction. Historical fiction, graphic novels, memoirs and biographies may fit into this category.*
- *A fun discussion is to read some passages or point out some cinematic scenes that combine both literary elements.*
- *Does a documentary film have a point of view? (POV). Is it completely objective?*
- *What is the difference between a feature film and a documentary film?*

c. Computer Generated Imagery:

- The tiger in the film *Life of Pi* looks and sounds so realistic, that it has come as a shock to audiences to find out that 86% of his scenes are made digitally with computer-generated imagery (CGI). Only the scenes in which Pi and Richard Parker were not in the same location (for instance, when the tiger is swimming in the ocean while Pi was on the raft) used images from four different real tigers. "We didn't want our actor to get eaten," explained Bill Westenhofer, the visual effects supervisor and Oscar winner for Best Visual Effects 2013.

- Making Richard Parker appear so lifelike required a bigger CGI enterprise than any that had ever been done before. It took a team of 40 animators and 120 other artists in the U.S. and India a year to get all the tiger scenes done. The special effects team spent a lot of time studying real tigers in order to determine how they would react and how to make them look real.
- But it wasn't just the tiger's surface that was difficult. Richard Parker was constructed by digital layers like a biology project. First the skeleton was animated, which controlled the tiger's basic movements. The second layer of muscles added extra movements, like muscle tightening or stretching. Skin and fur were layered on top, with even more movements, such as wind tugging on fur, the bounce of skin when he pounced, or how the light shimmered on him.

"It was these tiny things that, combined, made this really genuine, lifelike animal," Mr. Westenhofer said. "But if you look at the individual things by themselves, they seem insignificant."

Suggested Activities:
- *Many films today are done with the help of computers. A fun discussion could entail asking the following questions to analyze CGI: What other scenes in Pi were done with CGI?*
- *What does the expression "the whole is bigger than the sum of its parts" mean?*

Hints:
- The other animals were also mostly computer-generated. The flying fish were also done with CGI, as was the giant whale, the underwater imagery, and the fluorescent creatures.
- Sometimes when all the parts that make something up are placed together, the result is far greater than anyone could have imagined. For instance, teamwork: a group of people who can't individually solve a problem may be able to combine their ideas to come up with a solution. In this case, the CGI tiger was made by a huge group of people each working on a tiny detail and not seeing the big picture until they brought their work together.

7. Philosophy/ Critical Thinking:

a. Existentialism:

In the first part of the film when Pi is in India, we see him reading three different books. All are French versions of famous classics:

- <u>The Mysterious Island</u> (1874) by Jules Verne, a famous French writer known for his science fiction novels.
- <u>Notes from the Underground</u> (1864) by Fyodor Dostoyevsky, a Russian novelist. The novella, or short story, <u>Notes from the Underground,</u> is considered one of the first existentialist novels.
- <u>The Stranger</u> (1942) by Albert Camus, a French Nobel Prize-winning author born in the French colony of Algeria. The novel is about explaining and understanding a man named Meursault, who demonstrates emotional detachment from the events in his life, good or bad.
- All the above books have in common existentialist themes. "Existentialism" refers to a philosophical movement of the late 19th and 20th centuries. Its central argument is that in an absurd world that lacks meaning, every individual gives his/her life meaning through his/her actions. One of the central concepts, that "existence precedes essence," means that we are defined only by what we choose to be and to do. There is no predetermined meaning to our lives but what we choose as our purpose. Some major existentialist figures are:
- Soren Kierkegaard (philosopher, 1813-1855): "Life is not a problem to be solved, but a reality to be experienced."
- Fyodor Dostoyevsky (philosopher and writer, 1821-1881). His personal life was an example of Existentialism: "I used to imagine adventure for myself. I invented a life, so that I could at least exist somehow."
- Jean-Paul Sartre (philosopher, 1905-1980): "Man is condemned to be free; because once thrown into the world, he is responsible for everything he does." Man is rersponsible to create his own life and he is free to do so.
- Albert Camus (philosopher and writer, 1913-1960): "Basically, at the very bottom of life, which seduces us all, there is only absurdity, and more absurdity. […] You will never live if you are looking for the meaning of life."

Yet, for Camus, despite the absurdity of life, man must continue to live; for it is living that gives essence to our existence. Camus' protagonist Meursault is symbolic to Existentialism: Meur (to die) sault (alone). Before this happens, we must live life to its fullest. "There is not love of life without despair about life. There is scarcely any passion without struggle."

Suggested Activities:
- *Have the group discuss the quotes from above. Also, explore the word "existentialist" for clues about what it means. What is the root of the word?*

- *Existentialism is the constructive basis of this film. To analyze this structure, the film clip,(Scene: 01:53 –> 01:55) gives us insight.*
- *In order to survive, we create a meaning to life, and some people create a meaning to the universe and religion. Pi's words help us understand this: "Can I ask you something? Of course. I told you two stories about what happened out in the ocean...Neither explains what cause the sinking of the ship. And no one can prove which story is true and which is not. In both stories, the ship sinks, my family dies, and I suffer. So which story do you prefer? The one with the tiger. That's the better story."*

b. Narrative Conflicts:

- A "conflict" is any incompatibility between the goals of two or more characters or force. There are 7 main types of conflict found in fiction. Identifying conflicts can help you understand what you're reading and help you write clearly:

1. Person vs. Fate/God
2. Person vs. Self
3. Person vs. Person
4. Person vs. Society
5. Person vs. Nature
6. Person vs. Supernatural
7. Person vs. Technology

c. Aristotle and Catharsis:

- The ending of the book often comes when the conflict finds some resolution.

If there is a resolution, ideally there is also a "catharsis," a purging of emotions of pity and fear that are aroused as a viewer watched a tragic play. This is the basis of Aristotle's philosophy as he wrote in "Poetics" to describe Greek Tragedy. The concept is lnked to the psychological good and positive social function of Art – Poetics and Tragedy.

Suggested Activity:
- *When discussing the 7 types of conflict, which ones are used in the film?*

Hints:
The conflicts in the film serve to build character and plot development:

- Person vs. Nature. Pi is trying to survive the elements while out at sea and at the same time trying to survive a tiger.
- Person vs. Fate/ God. Pi's faith is tested and when the second storm hits he says he gives up to God, not to Nature.
- Person vs. Self. If Richard Parker is, Pi himself, as he tells the Japanese insurance men with the second story, the tiger represents the evil and violence in Pi.
- The family conflict at the beginning of the film is Person vs. Person. Pi wants to stay in India but his father wants to move to Canada.
- The relocation itself is Person vs. Society because of economic and political forces that Pi has to leave his home.
- The danger of the carnivorous island is Person vs. Supernatural.

d. Platonic Approach:

This form of learning is by questions. Plato encouraged in his teachings to have his students ask questions to him and to others in order to discuss and see different sides of a problem.

Suggested Activity:
- *Have a person in your group ask a question to a neighbor about Existentialism. In a round-robin format, continue this type of questioning and discussing.*

e. Unreliable Narration:

When we read a story from someone's point of view, we are trusting that they are being honest and sincere about events. But all people and all characters are flawed, so we may at some point realize that the story we are being told doesn't match reality. This is called unreliable narration, or we may say we have an unreliable narrator. Maybe he/she admits his memory is faulty, or we are directly or indirectly told he/she is biased. Maybe the character is guilty of something and is trying to mislead the audience into believing he/she is innocent.

Suggested Activity:

- *Discuss is Pi a reliable narrator? Watch the second story scene (Film clip at 1:49– 1:55). Notice Pi never says which story is true, only which one is "the better story."*

f. Metaphors:

A metaphor is a comparison between two unlike things without using "like" or "as." The purpose of a metaphor is to highlight a significant quality of one of the two ideas being compared. Which of the following is a metaphor?

1. This Oreo is like heaven.
2. This Oreo is heaven.
3. This Oreo is as good as heaven.

Metaphors can also extend over more than one sentence, in which case it is known as an "extended metaphor" or an "allegory." In *Life of Pi*, when Pi tells the second story, the animals can be considered metaphors: the zebra stands for the sailor, the orangutan for Pi's mother, and the hyena for the cook. Yann Martel also discusses in an interview how he thought of the whole story as a metaphor:

'And the main thing that struck me is the idea of a religious boy– because we have to say that Pi is a practicing Hindu, Muslim, and Christian– the idea of a religious boy in a lifeboat with a wild animal struck me as a perfect metaphor for the human condition. Humans aspire to really high things, right, like religion, justice, Democracy. At the same time, we're rooted in our human, animal condition. And so, all of those brought together in a lifeboat struck me as being… as a perfect metaphor.'

Suggested Activities:

Discuss the following metaphors:

- *Life is a rollercoaster.*
- *Time is money.*
- *The world is a stage.*
- *John's suggestion was just a Band-Aid.*
- *Jane's ambitions are a house of cards.*
- *He is a night owl.*

8. Music:

a. Indian Music and Dance:

- The film opens with Indian classical music playing while a series of beautiful images of Pondicherry roll by. Together, these two quickly create an atmosphere for the film. Words are not even necessary. Already we know that we are being told a unique story, set in a beautiful but strange world where tradition and nature play a huge role in people's lives. India has a long and varied history of music, and it has always played an important part in spiritual matters.
- Classical Indian dance has a history that is just as long as music. A dance is almost always also a story that the dancer acts out in gestures rather than words. The dance is considered a success if it manages to provoke a "rasa," an emotion, in the audience.

9. Technology:

a. Mariana Trench:

Before the storm sinks the ship that Pi's family is on, Pi mentions that they are sailing over the Mariana Trench in the Pacific Ocean. The Mariana Trench is the deepest part of all the world's oceans. It is one and a half thousand miles long and shaped like a half-moon, but very narrow, only 43 miles wide. The deepest part of the Trench is almost 7 miles. The Trench is completely dark and very cold. Despite this, scientists have found life there. Only a few people have made it to the very bottom of the Mariana Trench, and one of them was filmmaker James Cameron, director of *Titanic* and *Avatar*, also a proponent of CGI.

Suggested Activities:
- *Members of your group can use earth.google.com to help them with this map activity.*
- *Take turns placing the following on a chart or board where you think they belong after discussing them:*
  - *Deepest human scuba dive ever recorded. (1,044 ft)*
  - *Height of Mount Everest upside-down. (29,029 ft)*

   °   *Depth a nuclear submarine can go to before it collapses under pressure. (800 ft)*
   °   *Titanic's final resting place. (12,467 ft)*
   °   *The last rays of sunlight disappear. (3,300 ft)*

Hints:

In order, the answers are: 1,044 ft scuba dive; 29,029 ft Mount Everest; 800 ft nuclear submarine; 12,467 ft Titanic; 3,300 ft last sunlight.

Extracurricular Activites: Suggested Sample Curriculum:

Unit One: "Water," Gandhi, and an introduction to Imperialism

In this unit, we will explore the historical significance of Imperialism and its effects on various world cultures, specifically India. We will read different positions on imperial power and control and, through literature, we will explore India's struggle for equality and self-determination.

    Paired with this literature, we will watch and analyze the film, "Water," by Deepa Mehta, which tells the story of Chuyia, a young girl who is married and widowed by the age of seven. Having been sold by her parents, she is taken to an ashram, a traditional home for widows, where she must live out the remainder of her days in isolation.

Reading Materials:
Rudyard Kipling and Imperialism: "The White Man's Burden"
Derek Walcott's selected poems
Selected Indian Poems
Excerpts from Gandhi including his autobiography, <u>The Story of My Experiments with Truth.</u>

Unit Two: "Tsotsi," <u>Cry the Beloved Country</u>, and Apartheid in South Africa

In this unit, we will watch Gavin Hood's fascinating film "Tsotsi" which chronicles six days in the life of a young South African boy in a gang. This film will give us a glimpse into the aftermath of apartheid in South Africa and help us to understand why so many economic and social problems still exist in the country. We will also explore some of the writings of Nelson Mandela to understand his great influence on the abolishment of apartheid in South Africa.

In conjunction with this film we will also read Alan Paton's, <u>Cry the Beloved Country</u>, a novel that narrates the journey of a father in search of his lost son. It is steeped in the political and social anguish of apartheid South Africa and paints a despairing, yet beautiful portrait of life at the time.

Reading Materials:
Excerpts and Speeches by Nelson Mandela
<u>Cry the Beloved Country</u>, Alan Paton

Unit Three: "Osama," the Taliban, and Gender Discrimination

In this unit, we will be discussing the harsh reality of life under the Taliban rule in both Afghanistan and Pakistan. In the film, "Osama," by Siddiq Barmak, we will observe the treatment of women in Afghanistan through the eyes of a 12-year-old girl who disguises herself as a boy so that she may work to get food for her mother and grandmother.

We will also take a look into the cultural discrimination that has existed in Afghanistan through the novel <u>The Kite Runner</u>, by Khaled Hosseini. This story takes the reader through the political, social and emotional history of Afganistan from the 1930's to the Taliban's insurgency in the late '90s. It also tells the story of two young friends, one the son of a wealthy lawyer and the other the son of his servant.

Reading Materials:
<u>The Kite Runner</u>, by Khaled Hosseini

Unit Four: "Persepolis," the Islamic Revolution, and Human Rights

In this unit, we will read Marjane Satrapi's animated film and memoir, <u>Persepolis</u>, of her life growing up during the Islamic Revolution. While reading, we will research the cultural and political history of Iran and the Islamic Revolution as we encounter the author's struggles and resilience living under a fundamentalist regime.

We will also be reading excerpts from <u>Reading Lolita in Tehran</u>, a memoir by former professor of the University of Tehran, Azar Nafisi. In this memoir, Nafisi retells the story of how, despite all odds, she organized a secret book club with seven of her best female students in order to read literary classics that were banned by the Iranian government. This memoir stands as a testament to the power of literature and how it can, in many ways, be liberating.

Reading Materials:
Persepolis, by Marjane Satrapi
Reading Lolita in Tehran, by Azar Nafisi

Unit Five: "Sophie Scholl," Night, and the Holocaust

In this unit, we will read about and analyze the horrors of the Holocaust that took place during World War II under the rule of Adolf Hitler. Through the lens of the film "Sophie Scholl: the Final Days," by Marc Rothemund, and the memoir, Night, by Elie Wiesel, we will observe the devastating effects of genocide and the consequences for those who tried to stop it.

Reading Materials:
Night, by Elie Wiesel
Selected poems by Rainer Maria Rilke
Excerpt from Primo Levi's If This Is A Man

Unit Six: "Beijing Bicylcle," Balzac and the Little Chinese Seamstress, and China's Cultural Revolution

In this unit, we will learn about the academic and intellectual limitations that existed during Mao's Cultural Revolution (1966-1976) and the economic boom China experienced in its aftermath. The film, "Beijing Bicycle," by Wang Xiaoshuai is the story of two stubborn teenage boys, Guo from the country and Jian from the city. Both boys are engaged in a duel to claim ownership to the same bicycle. These two antagonists cherish the bicycle for their own reason: one for work, the other for fun. Symbolically, the bicycle becomes the symbol of old China in clash with modern China. The question is not only how will the country boy and the city boy resolve their problem, but metaphorically, how will the two worlds of China work together and coexist amidst their society's changes.

Together with this film, we will read the novel, Balzac and the Little Chinese Seamstress, by Dai Sijie, which tells the story of two young boys growing up in China during the Cultural Revolution who are exiled because they were considered "intellectuals," (any person who went to high school or wore glasses).

Reading Materials:
<u>Balzac and the Little Chinese Seamstress</u>, by Dai Sijie

_____

Sidebars:
_____

1. Public Response:

- Roger Ebert, just one of the many film reviewers, bestowed praise on *Life of Pi*: Ang Lee's *Life of Pi* is a miraculous achievement of storytelling and a landmark of visual mastery. Inspired by a worldwide best-seller that many readers must have assumed was unfilmable, it is a triumph over its difficulties. It is also a moving spiritual achievement, a movie whose title could have been shortened to "life."

2. Production:

- According to *Life of Pi* visual effects supervisor Bill Westenhofer, almost 86-percent of the scenes featuring Richard Parker use a computer-generated tiger, with the remaining scenes using one of the real tigers – usually when the story calls for the tiger to be in a completely different location (i.e., the water) from teenage actor Suraj Sharma, who plays Pi. In order to accomplish this, Lee and effects studio Rhythm & Hues needed to invest more than the usual time in the previsualization stage of production, mapping out every detail of where the tiger would be in each scene and exactly what he'd be doing. "The hardest [scenes to film] were when the tiger was in water and especially in the storm ..."
- Lee, Sharma, and the effects team also spent considerable time studying real-world tigers in order to determine how they might react to situations presented in *Life of Pi*.

3. Awards:

- Academy Awards, USA
  2013- Won- Best Director (Ang Lee), Best Cinematography ·Claudio Miranda), Best Visual Effects (Bill Westenhoffer), Best Original Score (Mychael Dana).

- Golden Globe Award:
  2013- Won – Best Original Score (Mychael Dana)

Bibliography of Films: Filmography
Further Global Study Resources through Film:

About India:

- *Fire* (India)
- *Earth* (India)
- *Water* (India)
- *The Middleman* (India)
- *Charulata* (India)
- *The Big City* (India)
- *Two Daughters* (India)
- *Monsoon Wedding* (U.S.A./India)
- *The Namesake* (India)
- *Lagaan* (India)
- *Embers* (India)
- *Zero Bridge* (U.S.A./Kashmir)

Bollywood Films:

- *Bride and Prejudice* (India)
- *Bollywood/Hollywood* (India)
- *My Bollywood Bride* (India)
- *Bombay Dreams* (India)
- *Rang De Basanti (Paint It Yellow)* (India)
- *Kaho Na Pyar Hai (Say You Love Me)* (India)
- *Saawariya* (U.S.A.)
- *The Mistress of Spices* (U. K.)
- *Jodhaa Akbar* (India)
- *Devdas* (India)

Famous Indian Film Director: Satyajit Ray

- *Pather Panchali*
- *Aparajito*
- *The World of Apu*
- *Goopy Gyne Bagha Byne*
- *Hirak Rajar Deshe*
- *Pratidwandi*
- *Seemabaddha*
- *Jana Aranya*
- *Sonar Kellea*
- *Joi Baba Felunath*
- *Parash Pathar*
- *Jalsaghar*
- *Devi*
- *Ghare Baire*
- *Sadgati*
- *Pikoo*
- *Shatranj Ke Khilari*

CHAPTER 2

BEIJING BICYCLE (CHINA)

TITLE OF FILM: *Shi Qi Sui De Dan Che (Seventeen-Year-Old's Bicycle)*
YEAR OF RELEASE: 2002
COUNTRY: China
DIRECTOR: Wang Xiaoshuai
LANGUAGE: Mandarin Chinese
RUNNING TIME: 113 minutes
RATING: PG-13
CURRICULUM THEMES:

A. HISTORY and SOCIAL SCIENCE:

- **Chapter's Key Themes: Ancient and modern China**
- **World History: China as an emerging capitalist nation**
- **Geography: Urbanization**
- **Economics: Money as a social barometer; BRICS countries and emerging markets; China's Global Bank**
- **Civics, Citizenship and Government: Social class differences vs. classless society; Conflict mediation and resolution**

B. LITERATURE and VISUAL ARTS:

- **World Literature: Social and political communication of fiction and film**
- **Media Studies: Film Clips and Scene Discussions; Cinematography and Techniques: symbols and character foil; Allegory; Historic cinema: Neo-realisim; Censorship in China**
- **Philosophy/Critical Thinking: Machiavelli; Polemic: China's Changing Legal System**
- **Music**

Introduction:

Beijing Bicycle was directed by Wang Xiaoshuai; screenplay by Wang Xiaoshuai; produced by Peggy Chiao, Hsu Hsiao-Ming and Han Sanping; cinematography by Liu Jie; edited by Liao Ching-Song; music by Wang Feng; and distributed by Sony Pictures Classic. (113 minutes)

Guei ....*Cui Lin*
Jian ....*Li Bin*
Friend, Mantis ....*Liu Lei*
Company Manager ....*Xie Jian*

Beijing Bicycle is a film that asks the question about China's transition into a Super power. The director presents the problem by using two seventeen-year-old boys and their relationship centered on a bicycle, the symbol of China. Both boys are of different social status, yearn for acceptance within their group, and are stubbornly determined to succeed.

In one of the concluding scenes, as a group of punks chase the two boys through an older section of Beijing, one boy says to the other, "What are you doing? This doesn't concern you." The other boy replies, "I don't know my way out." In today's new China, caught between the traditions of an ancient culture and the new urban reality, young people are having trouble finding their way.

Pivotal Moments in History:

- In the past forty years since Mao's Cultural Revolution (1966-1976), China has developed into an economically booming country. And yet, freedom and free markets have not paralleled as they do in other fledgling nations. Despite this, rapid economic growth persists in China under a communist one-party rule.
- Rising incomes in the large cities have created a middle class as we see in *Beijing Bicycle.* China has moved from a classless society where the majority of the population is poor, to a class society where money and tangible proofs of success are important indicators of a surging middle class.
- China is an example of a new type of Communism thriving side by side with a new expression of Capitalism. The state owns natural resources, land, real estate, banks, large companies, and joint ventures; yet, along side this are: individual enterprise, company ownership, and stock investments.

- With this move towards materialism and consumerism, comes urbanization where people from China's rural countryside leave their struggling farms and starving existence to strike it rich in the booming cities. With urbanization comes capitalism that gives birth to inequalities of income, educational opportunities, medical facilities and employment opportunities between the rural China of the past and the urban China of the future.
- The problem remains that China has a billion poor people who live in the countryside. The question this film poses is how can these two vast societies co-exist and co-operate to bring further growth and success to China?

Pre-Screening Questions:

a. *What means of transportation do you take to get to school? To visit your friends?*
b. *Do you work or did you ever work? How did you get to and from work?*
c. *Discuss how an urban environment and rural environment differ? Are people different in the city from those who live in the country? Why?*
d. *What do you know about China's changing society? How is it changing? In which areas? How is it staying the same?*

Pivotal Moments in Film:

a. Beijing Bicycle is a neo-realistic story, influenced by Vittoria De Sica's post-World War ll film, *The Bicycle Thief* (1947). This Chinese version, which is filmed and set in 2001, shares a similar psychological and economic time frame with its predecessor: a country's evolution towards modernization and consequently, the importance of work. The Chinese film is set against the backdrop of an emerging consumer culture in Beijing, a striving capital that still contains different classes in a once officially classless society.

b. Beijing Bicycle is the story of two stubborn teenage boys, Guei from the country and Jian from the city. Both boys are engaged in a duel to claim ownership of the same bicycle. These two antagonists cherish the bicycle for their own reason: one for work, the other for fun. Symbolically, the bicycle becomes the symbol of old China in clash with modern China. The question is not only how will the country boy and the city boy resolve their problem, but metaphorically, how will the two worlds of China work together and coexist?

c. Themes of: honor; saving face; rights of the child; friendship; family; violence; what is justice; materialism; consumerism; rural life vs. city life; changing values; and tolerance are interwoven into this mosaic of modern day Beijing.

Post-Screening Questions:
A. History and Social Science:

---

1. Social attitudes: How do the people in Beijing view the people from the countryside in the film?

Suggested Activity:
*   *Ask your group to discuss the following scenes where we see evidence of antagonism:*
    *   *At Guei's work, "Fei Da Express Delivery," the manager and female employers comment about the new recruits from the countryside.*
    *   *Guei's friend, Mantis, the shopkeeper, comments about the maid: "If I would have known she came from the countryside...." He also comments about the accountability and corruption of the delivery company.*
    *   *Jian's wealthy school friends bully Guei and have disdain for him because he comes from the countryside: the way he is dressed, his accent, his manners.*

2. In what ways are the characters and personalities of Guei and Jian shaped by their social background? Do they change by the end of the film?

B. Literature and Visual Arts:

---

1. How does the film reflect the importance of a job and money?
2. Why are the violent scenes in this film shown with such detail?
3. How is friendship depicted in the film? Refer to specific scenes.
4. How is courtship and dating depicted in the film? Refer to specific scenes.
5. Compare how the wealthy boys entertain themselves and the way their American counterparts would amuse themselves in their free time?
6. What is "machismo"? How is it depicted in the film? Refer to specific scenes.
7. What are the concepts of "honor" and "saving face"? How are they shown in the film? Several characters express this cultural value in a different way. Refer to specific scenes.

Curriculum Themes:
A. History and Social Science:

Chapter's Key Themes: Ancient and Modern China

a. Ancient and Modern China:

- In *Beijing Bicycle,* we see scenes of ancient China in the old, crowded *hutongs* (neighborhoods) of narrow streets and alleys: people are brushing their teeth and shaving outdoors for they don't have a bathroom; people are eating outside because they don't have a kitchen; and thousands of bicycles are used for all types of transportation. The camera also shows us the other side of China, the modern sections: Mercedes cars, taxis, traffic jams, skyscrapers, plush hotels, and spas.

Suggested Activities:
- *Ask your group to explain the points why China is considered an emerging "Super power"?*
- *Research when did China start changing into an economic society? What were the initial steps and signs?*

Hints:
- After World War ll, the Communist Party of China took control of mainland China under Mao Zedong. The opposing democratic, Kuomintang Party with Chiang Kai Shek as their leader, retreated to the island of Taiwan.
- In 1949 Mao Zedong declared the establishment of the "People's Republic of China" for mainland China. Foreign leaders referred to it as "Red China" – Communist China.
- In 1966 Mao and his allies took power and introduced the Cultural Revolution. This was a major purge of intellectuals in the city by killing them or relocating them to the countryside to "re-educate" them. They were considered dangerous and undesirable to the communist state because they read books, thought, asked questions and criticized the government. This purge and reign of terror lasted until Mao's death in 1976.
- In 1972, President Richard Nixon visited Chairman Mao and the People's Republic of China. This marked the first time an American president visited

China who at that time was an enemy country. Henry Kissinger, President Nixon's National Security Advisor, laid the groundwork for this visit as part of his political practice, *Realpolitik*. Both countries agreed to open trade and begin relationships.

- After Mao's death, the communist party loosened governmental control over the economy, turning China from a "planned economy" to open markets and granted some individuals the opportunity to create joint ventures (those who were family members of government leaders) with global companies and foreign countries.

- China is considered an emerging Super power because it is:
  - one of the 5 permanent members of the United Nation's Security Council;
  - member of the World Trade Organization;
  - the 1st-2nd wealthiest country in the world;
  - the 1st-2nd largest purchasing nation in the world;
  - the 2nd largest bank in market value in the world, after Citibank, which is the Industrial and Commercial Bank of China; As of 2014, they are creating their own China's Global Bank;
  - the 2nd largest research and development industry in the world;
  - a nuclear weapons country;
  - involved in global economic investments in Africa, South America, Asia, North America, and Europe;

1. World History:

a. China as an Emerging Capitalist Nation:

- *Beijing Bicycle* begins its story by showing that the western-style "Fei Da Express Delivery" company is recruiting teenage boys to work: "We want to help country boys fit into urban society," says the manager as he briefs a group of boys from different provinces. He explains how the shimmering silver bicycle can be theirs after one or two months and how after that, each boy will become a partner in the company. The boys are amazed by this concept of "Capitalism 101." It is this concept and the bicycle that catapults the story and unveils little by little, the major problem behind China's economic growth: how to introduce capitalism without tension? The film shows us what are the tensions: how materialism gives birth to stealing, lying, violence, dissolution of the family structure, and the Machiavellian principle that "the ends justify the means."

Suggested Activities:

- *Ask your group to divide into the following governmental groups and simulate a meeting to discuss a 5-year plan for China's growth: Ministry of Education (discuss the concept of private education as shown in the film); Ministry of Justice (discuss the concept of having lawyers and trials); Ministry of health (discuss such epidemics as SARS, AIDS and cancers related to environmental pollution); and Ministry of Finance (discuss the re-valuation of the yuan, volatile stock market, lack of transparency with corporate earnings, and China's trade surplus.)*
- *Divide into two groups to discuss and chart the positive and negative aspects of China's emerging into a capitalistic nation.*
- *Discuss Machiavelli's __The Prince__ and why is this philosophy taught in American graduate business schools? How is this concept related to the film?*
(For more information see Philosophical section of this chapter.)

Hints:

Characteristics of China's Emerging into a Capitalistic Nation:

- Today, China is a major global manufacturer in multiple industries. This is due to low overhead and a strong yuan, but also due to low salaries and the absence of labor unions.
- China invests heavily into South America, Africa, Asia, North America, and Europe where they have multiple joint ventures.
- China is investing in Europe to make money, to make *friends*, and to advance their companies in Europe as they go global. In Greece and Spain they are buying billions of dollars of government debt and bonds. In Italy they are expanding ports and building air terminals. In Poland and from Germany to Turkey, they are building new highways. In Greece they are enlarging ports and the cargo shipping industry. In Hungary, they are clearing the Danube River. In France they are buying airports. In Israel there are joint venture in irrigation and telecommunications, and in Germany and Macedonia, they are constructing railroads.
- Recently, the Chinese launched a rocket to Nigeria that will be used as a communications satellite to expand cell phones and Internet service in Central Africa. Chinese companies have invested $ billions in Africa. In turn, China imports 1/3 of its oil from Africa. China has also made a deal with Russia for oil and natural gas.
- Transportation has improved in major Chinese cities, with new constructions of subways and railroads. China has the 2nd largest number of highways in the world.

Negative Aspects of China's Emerging into a Capitalistic Nation:

- Increasing gap between the rich and the poor, urban dwellers and rural peasants.
- Lack of Human Rights. There is total government control of press, Internet and censorship.
- Increase levels of air pollution, environmental dangers, water shortage, water pollution.
- An example of negative industrialization can be found in Southern China's Fujian Province that has become the leading provider and exporter of seafood to the world. But that growth has been curtailed because of contaminated waters due to sewage and industrial waste. Concerns are centered that seafood from these waters have been "doctored up" by pesticides and drugs that have been determined to cause cancer and disease. Inspectors have imposed temporary export bans.
- Exporters of Chinese toys have had toys recalled back to China because of toxic paint and harm to children.
- Medical facilities are antiquated and inadequate to treat large public health problems related to air pollution and increasing cases of HIV/Aids. Western medicine is used jointly with Eastern medicine. For treating large populations, the latter is cheaper due to the use of herbs instead of medicines.
- China's growing trade surplus has worried U.S. and E.U. leaders who have been putting pressure on China to re-evaluate its currency; they devalued it in August 2015. China wants to have their currency, Renminbi, used as an international currency in business and trade. They have created their own international bank that may facilitate this.
- Construction sites are poorly built. Corruption exists for receiving building permits. Major accidents have happened because of this.
- The gyrations in their stock market has caused global disturbances and turmoil throughout international economic markets.

China Influences Global Markets:

- When China was growing rapidly, they needed natural resources and commodities. Markets around the world supplied the need, profited and developed their industries. China partnered with:
  - Chile, in the northern area of the Atacama for copper
  - Australia, where they increased their natural gas production 150+% and developed coal mines

  - ° Russia, who negotiated a favorable oil tariff to sell their own surplus
  - ° Canada, developed their oil sand fields
  - ° West Africa, opened up their iron ore mines
  - ° Peru, supplied copper and metals and tripled their production to do so
  - ° India, Myanma and Tajikistan built railroads and transportation arteries to expedite China's imports.
- When China's economy slumps, prices decline, leave partners with a surplus of goods and debt, decreases global growth, and precipitates a stock market sell off around the world. Mines that have been built, can't be unbuilt. The global economy suffers.

2. Geography:

a. Urbanization:

- Beijing represents half the title of this film as well as half the subject matter. The camera leads us through the city as if we are a modern "carrier pigeon" and we look at the bustling metropolis, with traffic, skyscrapers and hotels.
- We see middle-class youth who go to private schools, wear immaculate school uniforms and learn in small modern classrooms.
- We see middle-class youth who amuse themselves with bicycle competitions, video-games and by not working.
- We also see the tension between the poor country folk and the city slickers:
- Fei Da Express Delivery Company is not keeping proper accounts of Guei's right to own his bike. Is this an example of corruption?
- Maid is stealing clothes from employer and selling them.
- Female receptionist in Spa does not accept the mistake the establishment made.
- Who owns the bike? Will sharing resolve the problem?

Suggested Activities:
- *Ask your group to divide into pairs to research China's geography. They can include Hong Kong, Macau, Taiwan, and Tibet.*
- *Identify key areas as: 2008 Olympic Village, Tiananmen Square, silk market, parks, and university section.*
- *Beijing is the capital of China and its 2nd most populous city. There are also other cities in China that are rapidly developing. Yet, this developmet and construction have caused disasters. Discuss this. Why? Discuss also China's previous governmental policy*

of solving the population growth by installing a one-child family restriction. This, how-ever, has changed as of 2016. Why?

Hints:

- Beijing has a population of 21 million residents as of 2013. Shanghai has a population of 24 million residents. China has a population of more than 1.3 billion people.
- In the past 10 years, China's cities have expanded on the average of 10% annually.
- 80 to 120 million migrant workers work part-time in the major cities and return home to the countryside periodically with their earnings.
- China, over the decades, has tried to limit population growth by installing a one- child policy which was enforced until 2016. Prior to that, if a family had a 2nd child, they did not want to register that child for it was against the law. A penalty could be as much as a $45,000 fine. And by not registering the child at birth, the child lacked a *hukou* for life – which is a registration document that allows a child to go to a state school, receive health care, marry, open a bank account, buy a train ticket, get a passport.
- The question of limiting population growth was first initiated with Thomas Robert Malthus, a British demographer and political economist of the early 19th century. Malthus' theory of population states that productivity, agricultural or other forms needed for human survival, cannot keep up with the growth of population. He advocated that strong checks are required to control population increase. Malthus linked population growth to economics, political change and political violence.

3. Economics:

a. Money as a Social Barometer:

- There are several scenes in *Beijing Bicycle* which center around money as an indicator of China's new middle class:
  - Guei is always thinking and talking about money. He needs his bicycle for his job so he can make money.
  - Guei is preoccupied in how much he earns and when he will be the proud owner of his bicycle.
  - Jian steals money from his father so he can buy a stolen bicycle and show off to his girl friend.

    °   Jian's father saves his money prudently so he can send his daughter to private school. Clearly, China is a country where money is a tangible proof of one's wealth and is socially important. This strikes a discrepancy with traditional Communism.

Suggested Activities:
- *Ask your group to discuss what criteria constitute the middle class? Are there examples in the film? What defines class differences and divisions?*
- *Discuss and define a "consumer culture."*
- *China has moved in the past 35 years from a planned communist economy to a mixed "communist/capitalist" economy. Ask your group to discuss how they see China's future. What are some regions that are undergoing large development in China?*
- *What are the goals of China's new Global Bank?*

Hints:
- China has moved after Mao's death to a new type of economy never known before. We are seeing a market-oriented economy that is still within a rigid political framework under tight Party control but with openings for private enterprise and investment growth.
- The result of this has been a 6-fold increase of GDP since 1978. The government introduced the following reforms that have led to this creative economic style:
  - ° collective farms have been replaced with privatization of farmlands;
  - ° increase the responsibility of local authorities and industry managers;
  - ° allow small-scale enterprise;
  - ° encourage and promote foreign investment by relaxing investment laws;
  - ° relax price controls;
  - ° encourage consumer consumption.
- There still exists a disparity between the economic growth of the cities and rural sections as well as a difference between coastal regions and the inland of China. To address this, China has initiated several plans: the China Western Development strategy (2000); the Revitalize Northeast China Initiative (2003); and the Rise of the Central China Policy (2004) which are all centered on developing China's interior.

b. BRICS Countries and Emerging Markets:

- BRICS countries are a group of countries - Brazil, Russia, India, China, and South Africa - that have been considered to be at a similar stage of newly advanced economic development. They are characterized by a large land area (combined they represent 25% of the world's land coverage), large population (combined they have 40% of the world's population) and they hold a combined GDP of 15 trillion dollars. These five countries have been the fastest growing *emerging markets* for global investors in past years. However, once hailed as the building blocks of global growth, the BRICS nations' economic momentum is now crumbling. The concerted efforts made by Brazil, Russia, India, China and South Africa to intertwine their emerging economies are looking like increasingly risky ventures, and their economic volatility and currency devaluations have wreaked havoc on international markets.

Emerging markets for investors are presently Taiwan, due to their independence from mainland China, and South Korea.

c. China's Global Bank:

China is creating a multinational, multi billion-dollar bank to finance development and strength in Asia including to finance roads, rails and transportation. They aim to develop Asia's poor countries and consolidation wealth with China at the center. To achieve their goals, they would forgo environmental concerns, human rights, and anticorruption measures. The U.S. will not join this bank for it is in competition with the World Bank and the International Monetary Fund.

4. Civics, Citizenship and Government:

a. Social class differences vs. classless society:

- In *Beijing Bicycle*, the country boys who are employed by the courier company want to make money and join China's emerging middle-class. Guei's friend, Mantis, the shopkeeper, admires the bicycle and comments that one day Guei will be a rich man.
- Jian's father saves his money to give his step-daughter a private school education with the hope that she will have more opportunities in the future.
- The film represents something bigger than itself – the film is a picture of China's "market socialism economy" as the characters in the film are all

trying to leave their historical one-class society to be part of the new merging middle-class.

Suggested Activities:

- *Ask your group to research and define what constitutes class divisions in the U.S. and in China. Categorize and chart the differences.*
- *Give a presentation to compare different countries in different continents to learn how that country defines social class.*

Hints:

- Class is defined by the following components: level of annual income, occupation, education, residence, family background, and social connections. Social class is linked to history, for component parts change according to history. Social class is also linked to economy, to the degree that class contributes to consumer purchase power and behavior.
- In China, historically and traditionally prior to the 1970s, society divided workers based on the perceived usefulness of their work. Scholars ranked the highest. Under them were the farmers who produced useful food. Next were the artisans who produced useful objects. Merchants ranked at the bottom because they did not actually produce anything, while soldiers were sometimes ranked even lower because of the destruction they caused.
- The Chinese model was widely disseminated throughout east-Asia.
- After Mao's death, a turn in China's government opened the doors for an emerging middle class. Based on a report from the Chinese Academy of Social Sciences, there were 35.18 million middle class members in 2006 that is about 2.8% of the total population. However, the French bank, BNP Paribas, differs in their criteria and defines China's middle class as well-educated professionals with an annual income between 25,000 yuans ($3,010. US) to 30,000 yuans ($3,610. US) or household income between 75,000 ($9,040.US) to 100,000 ($12,050. US). This represents 13.5% of the total population. There are other reports with other criteria and opinion differs. But what is accurate is that most Chinese aspire to join this emerging middle class and social rank.
- According to the World Bank's more objective reports, only when urbanization is over 50% and a country's service sector accounts for more than 50% of the economy, is it possible for a country's middle class to become a mainstream reality.

- In South China, there has been a recent development of "running companies" similar to the courier service we see in the film. They are companies that specialize in rendering services: 15 yuan per hour for waiting in line for someone; 50-100 yuan per hour for saying sorry or declaring love; and 100-200 yuan per hour for delivering a rejection.

b. Conflict Mediation and Resolution:

- Guei and Jian symbolize the two opposing poles of present China: the rural countryside and the modern city. After fighting violently over who owns the bicycle, one of Jian's friends mediates between the conflicting boys and thinks of a compromise resolution. This is accepted.

Suggested Activities:
- *The group can discuss the progression of steps that led to this compromise resolution and the final scene. Are the steps of this mediation satisfactory for both boys? For the viewer? How does the last scene negate the compromise?*
- *Divide into small groups to simulate a geo-political problem China has with the U.S. and create a list of mediation-resolution possibilities. (Environment, pollution, balance of trade, valuation of yuan, human rights, Internet piracy, freedom of press and Internet, copyrights, Taiwan, Tibet, minorities, etc.)*
- *Pretend you are mediators and are called in by the school principal to solve: a case of bullying; teacher-student dispute; student caught cheating on an exam.*

Hints:
- What is conflict resolution? It is a way to resolve conflicts other than using violence or going to court. The process is usually confidential. Common forms of conflict resolution are:
    - Negotiation –two or more people discuss the problem with the aim of reaching an agreement.
    - Mediation – the parties create their own solutions and the mediator has no power over the outcome.
    - Arbitration – a neutral third-party person reviews evidence about the case and decides on how to settle the problem.
    - Peer mediation – young people or co-workers of a group, act as mediators to help resolve disputes.

B. Literature and Visual Arts:

5. World Literature:

a. Social and Political Communication of Fiction and Film:

- *Beijing Bicycle* is a portrait of a changing China. But to fully understand present and future China, it is important to understand its prior historical movement – Mao's Cultural Revolution. *Beijing Bicycle* does not show this. The camera does give us frames of "old" Chinese neighborhoods and ancient style of living, but to understand the political picture, the book, <u>Balzac and the Little Chinese Seamstress</u>, written by Dai Sijie is useful to read. The film is also directed by him.

Suggested Activity:
- *Ask your group to read the book, <u>Balzac and the Little Chinese Seamstress</u>. Divide the class into three groups and have each group write an essay together answering one of the following three topics:*
  - *This novel takes place in 1971 under the regime of Chairman Mao's Cultural Revolution when 2 teenaged boys are exiled from the city to the country because their parents are "intellectuals." In what way does the novel offer a more intimate portrait of life during this period than an historical account from a history book? Why did Mao want to re-educate people like the two boys?*
  - *In what ways does China under Chairman Mao resemble Afghanistan under the Taliban, or Iran, or other countries that strive to keep the modern world from influencing their citizens?*
  - *Do the events in the book change the two boys? Are they different in the beginning than they are at the end of the story? What is the irony of the story?*

Hints:
- In the novel, <u>Balzac and the Little Chinese Seamstress</u>, Luo and his friend, the narrator of the book, are taken from their homes and sent to a remote village to be "re-educated." During the "cultural revolution" all the universities were shut down and any boy or girl who was labeled an intellectual (which meant any child who went to high school or wore eyeglasses) was sent to be re-educated and to live the life of peasants. The two protagonists are sent into exile to the countryside and are forced to spend their days carrying buckets of excrement up and down a mountain to fertilize the fields.

- No one during the Cultural Revolution was permitted to read any book except the red book of sayings written by Chairman Mao. However, it is through chance that the boys obtain a book written by Balzac and discover the world of literature and ideas.
- They later meet the beautiful young seamstress, and, by sharing with her the stories of Balzac, they teach her how to read. She becomes as hungry for the books and ideas as the two boys. Her imagination has been freed and she has been more "re-educated" than the two boys.

6. Media Studies:

a. Film Clips and Scene Discussions:

- *Urbanization:* (Scene: 00:18–> 00:46 seconds)
  In the introduction of the film, the director of the Delivery service is recruiting young men from all provinces of China who have relocated to Beijing to find work. This is urbanization merged with capitalism as well as economic opportunities. The dialogue includes such questions from the chief as: "How old are you? Where are you from? What did you do back home? When did you arrive?"

  Break the group into pairs to discuss why these questions are important as an introduction to the film.

- *Country folk vs city folk:* (Scene: 06:09 –> 06:47 minutes)
  One of the important themes of the film is country folk vs city folk – how will the city (Beijing) create a unified and harmonious assimilation with all the people from different regions of China? The dialogue includes such questions between the two friends from the same small town in the countryside as: "Take a look. You see that? City folk... They're not even happy with a big house. She never smiles. If it was me, I'd eat dessert every day. And spareribs at every meal. Look, she changed dresses." How does this dialogue express the theme of assimilation?

- *Compromise:* (01:40: –> 01:42 minutes)
  The two boys decide to compromise and share the bicycle. The dialogue enforces the theme: "Leave him. Let's go. I didn't do anything. Give me back my bicycle. Give me back my bicycle. Give me back my bicycle. I didn't do anything. Give me back my bicycle. Stop breaking it, please. Don't break my bike."

The compromise of sharing the bicycle works for a while until the city boy's friends gang up against the country boy. Who wins this final struggle? How does this relate to the theme of the film? What is the director's message?

b. Cinematography Techniques:

1. *Symbols:*
- *Beijing:*
- The film is about a bicycle but is also about Beijing. Guei's search for the bicycle takes him into all corners of the city. With Jie Liu's magnificent cinematography, the city comes alive with modern roads of traffic and bicycles that are juxtaposed to mysterious old alleys where old men play board games and do Tai Chi, and two friends share a toothbrush.
- The capital symbolizes the potential future clash between the countryside and city; the fear of urban materialism effacing traditional Chinese values; and the lure of western culture influencing Chinese youth.

- *Bicycle:*
- The bicycle represents an escape for both boys from the competitive pressures of their lives. For Guei, it is a means of access to a job in the city, an income, and survival. For Jian, it is the pathway to being "cool" and being in the in-group, very similar to a teenager in a Western country who drives a sports car.

- *Cigarette:*
- This represents modern culture and is used several times in the film as a symbol of a sophisticated city dweller.

- *Red shoes and red dress:*
- In a minor plot, Guei and his friend, the shopkeeper, spend their free time observing Qin, a young attractive girl living in a nearby high-rise apartment, wearing red shoes and owning a lot of clothes. They believe she is a rich city girl but they notice she is not happy with her material possessions. Later, they find out that Qin is in fact a maid, also from the country, who dresses herself in her employer's clothes. Guei and Mantis's misconception about Qin's social status exemplifies their innocent nature of judging the superficial and admiring material possessions.

- The maid becomes a symbol of the negative aspects of what happens to the country girl who comes to the city. Her employer's clothes do not fit her and she sells them. It is not fortuitous that the shoes and dress are red. The color red is the symbol of communist China. Is the director telling us that the girl is destined to remain a communist and not be able to walk in capitalistic shoes that do not fit her?

c. Character Foil:

- Guei and Jian are character foils (opposites).
- Female protagonists are also used as antagonists (and city dwellers) in several scenes: Employees of Fei Da Express Delivery; Employees of hotel and spa where Guei gets lost; Wealthy girl in Jian's school and her circle of friends.

d. Allegory:

- Like Vittorio De Sica's *The Bicycle Thief* (1948), the stolen bicycle is central to the story, but here it is not about the hunt for the bike but about the consequences that follow from its recovery. The two boys are pitted against each other. Yet, a mutual need brings them together and allows them to work out a compromise by alternating days when they can use the bike.
- The last frame of *Beijing Bicycle* is the film's key message: we see Guei is carrying the broken bicycle on his shoulder. As he walks alone, we see the bustling city of Beijing behind him. This is the juxtaposition of the 2 words of the title coming together to give us a final picture of a wounded protagonist with his beaten-up vehicle in an unsympathetic city. But he has conquered the city and is proud of his achievement. The country boy is the future of a new China.

Suggested Activities:
- *Have your group analyze how each cinematographic technique is used to express the over all picture of a China emerging into a modern nation.*
- *Discuss what other scenes they would add to the film if they were the scriptwriter or director.*

e. Historic cinema: Neo-realism

- *Beijing Bicycle* is influenced by Italian post- World War II directors and neo-realists: Roberto Rossellini, Luchino Visconti and Vittorio De Sica. These directors show human suffering amidst a physical and moral degradation of a post war culture. The director of *Beijing Bicycle* shares similar points with the earlier Italian neo-realists:

- ○ Guei is a protagonist very similar to Italian personages after World War 11 of trying to rebuild a country.
- ○ Guei stands alone against a group of adversaries.
- ○ Guei's struggle is against the absence of human solidarity and against the indifference of modern society towards suffering.
- ○ Guei's story can be explained in a description of his emotions as it relates to plot.
- ○ Guei's story comes after Mao's Cultural Revolution, which can be defined as a war, not dissimilar to Italy after World War ll.
- ○ Protagonist struggles to survive.
- ○ Depicts a breakdown of social institutions and traditional values.
- ○ the use of local setting.
- ○ long camera takes with moments of silence to enhance tension.
- ○ natural lighting.
- ○ grainy black-and-white film stock.
- ○ the directors show the entire picture of a society and let the viewers decide what is important.

Suggested Activity:

- *An interesting activity is to view the Italian film, The Bicycle Thief, and discuss how the Chinese director used it for inspiration more than 60 years later.*
- *Have your group compare and contrast several key points of both films:*
  - ○ *Family's role;*
  - ○ *Crowd's role and the people who are enforcing justice;*
  - ○ *The ending of both films.*

Hints:

- Italian neo-realism is a Post World War ll film movement characterized by stories set among the poor and working class, frequently using nonprofessional actors.
- In the *Bicycle Thief*, De Sica portrays simple events in the life of a worker. The protagonist gets a job (at the time of the movie, 25% of the Italian workforce was jobless), and in order to go to work, the protagonist has to get his bicycle out of hock. In order to do that, he and his wife pawn their sheets and bedding (her wedding dowry). On his first day at work, the bike is stolen.
- Stylistically, Italian neo-realism is characterized by:

    °   avoidance of neatly plotted stories in favor of loose episodes that evolve organically;

    °   documentary tone; shows and reports without imposing a moral judgement;

    °   use of conversational speech of ordinary people, not literary dialogue.

f. Censorship in China:

- The film board of the Chinese State Administration of Radio, Film and Television, banned the screening of *Beijing Bicycle* in China after the director sent the film to the Berlin International Film Festival without first acquiring the board's approval. According to director Wang Xiaoshuai, he did submit the film to the Chinese committee for examination and the film board gave him some suggestions for revision. However, without doing the revisions, he abandoned the idea to get an official entry from the Chinese government, fearing that he would not finish the revisions in time for Berlin's deadline. Instead, he mailed a cassette directly to Berlin. At the festival he won praise and accolades and it was too late for the Chinese government to remove it from the festival. The Chinese government eventually lifted the ban in 2004, but with eight modifications to the film and a truncated title of *Bicycle*.

Suggested Activities:
- *Have your group research what is censorship, patents and copyrights, and discuss China's official policy in regards to these. How do these infringements of international law effect China's policies in global markets?*
- *Analyze the film, Beijing Bicycle with the eye of a Chinese censor and explain to the class why specific scenes should be edited out.*

Hints:
- There have been an increased number of Chinese cinephiles who travel to Hong Kong to see Chinese films in the uncut, uncensored, original version. These new type of tourists/moviegoers are comprised of China's new middle class who have money to travel and are interested in seeing political subjects and texts that are rarely seen in mainland China. These affluent urbanites are becoming accustomed to choices in their lives and resent deprivation because of censorship.
- Some Chinese movie fans have tried to sue the State Administration of Radio, Film and Television, which regulates the Film industry for deleting some films'

contents. Such a case was with Chinese film director, Ang Lee's award-winning film, *Lust, Caution* (2007). The lawsuit has been repeatedly rejected by Beijing courts.

- Still, many critics of China's censorship are semi-satisfied that even censored films are allowed. Before 2007, such films as *Beijing Bicycle* and *Balzac and the Little Chinese Seamstress* were not screened at all in mainland China. Presently, some films do pass through the authorities.

7. Philosophy/ Critical Thinking:

a. Machiavelli

- Niccolo Machiavelli wrote <u>The Prince</u> in Florence, Italy. Published in 1536, he describes how a ruler can keep political control. His main thesis is that force and prudence are needed to exist together. His concept, "the ends justify the means" substantiates the ruler's use of evil actions if it is done for a good purpose and if it is used as a means and not an end. Machiavelli defines the criteria for cruel action by emphasizing, "it must be swift, effective and short-lived." In order for a ruler to govern by political force, it is better for him to be feared than loved. In contemporary terms this philosophy has been incorporated into *Realpolitik,* real politics, and in business goals.

Suggested Activities:
- *Have your group divide into pairs to discuss Machiavelli's <u>The Prince</u> and why is this philosophy taught in American graduate business schools? How else can it be used? In what areas? How is this concept related to China, today?*

b. Polemic: China's Changing Legal System

- As the struggle between the 2 boys to determine who is the rightful owner of the bicycle continues for an extended period of time, the American viewer wonders why don't they go to the police or a lawyer and ask them to mediate? Instead the boys try to resolve the problem themselves and this escalates into violence. As they fight in the streets, the other citizens turn their head and ignore the altercation.
- In China, there is not a legal structure comparable to what we know in America.

Their legal apparatus is relatively new and the citizens are not accustomed to use it or do not have confidence in the law's judgment.

Suggested Activities:
- *Research China's past and present judiciary system. Include such items as: law school; lawyers; trials; judges; police; human rights; etc. Discuss if there is, or is not, a changing legal system in China. There have been numerous newspapers articles in our Press about this subject.*
- *Have your group simulate a trial to judge if Guei is the rightful owner of the bicycle. They can use the American system for this exercise. (To recreate this courtroom scene, you need to have, a judge, jury, witnesses, defense lawyer, and prosecutor.)*

Hints:
- The rule of "law" is a new concept in China. For thousands of years, China lived under the rule of one man, the Emperor, and later by a one-party communist rule. The concept that codified laws could protect individual rights was unheard of before the 1980s.
- Prior to the 1980s, a judge, legal defender or prosecutor in China did not need a formal legal education. Usually, they were "appointed" by the Emperor or the Party, regardless of qualifications.
- As of 1992, China has sought to create a legal system necessary for their market economy and global relations. To achieve this, they have done the following:
  ° Law schools have been created; the government has introduced basic laws regarding civil procedure, criminal justice and contracts.
  ° Citizens can hire private lawyers.
  ° Legal aid centers have been created to give legal assistance to the poor. It is mandatory that all lawyers perform a certain amount of legal aid per year.
  ° Since 1981, the number of lawyers in China have grown from 5,500 to 100,000.

- What is still needed in China:
  ° To raise the legal consciousness of the people and to influence citizens to fight for their rights and file complaints. (Throughout the country, there are slogans on public buildings to influence people to "respect" the law. *China Central Television* broadcasts a daily legal affairs program.)
  ° The government should enforce fairly the decisions from lawyers, courts, and judges. This is not always the case.
  ° Members of the jury should be fairly chosen and their judgments respected.

This is not always the case.

8. Music:

- *Beijing Bicycle* is a human odyssey that never loses its rhythm. There is little dialogue and the characters communicate mostly with body language, long silences and facial expressions. Music takes the role of filling in the silences and engaging us as we are caught up in the film's rhythm.
- The soundtrack is attributed to Wang Feng, the classical musician who is also China's first rocker. He began studying the violin at the age of 5 and started his own rock band when he was a student at China's Conservatory of Music.
- The film's musical theme becomes the rhythmic background that follows Guei on his bicycle as the camera takes us on a road trip through new and old Beijing.
- The musical theme is played by the Romanian naï, a shepherd's flute-like wooden instrument in the shape of a curved half circle. This folkloric instrument gives a cultural significance of the countryside; establishes historical context of the countryside in the city; and defines the country character, Guei. It is the music that accompanies Guei on his bicycle and becomes his theme.

Suggested Activity:
- *Have your group research on the Internet information about the Romanian* naï. *They can find a picture and compare it to an American flute, piccolo and clarinet, as well as a Peruvian flute and recorder. A famous Romanian musician of the* naï *is Zamfir. His music can be found on itunes.*

Extracurricular Activities:

1. Before screening the film, ask someone in your group to prepare a fact sheet with some information to better understand the film, eg:
   a. 6.3 Yuan = $1.00; or 0.15 US dollar = 1 Yuan (as of 2015)
   b. There are 10 million bikes in Beijing with a population of 21 + million people. (2016)
      Beijing has the 4th most population in the world after Tokyo (37 million), Delhi (25 million) and Shaghai (22 million).
   c. *Hutongs* are narrow streets or alleys, most commonly associated with Beijing, China. In Beijing, hutongs are alleys formed by lines of *siheyuan* to form a hutong, and then joining one hutong to another. The word hutong is used also to refer to such neighborhoods. People in these neighborhoods share

common kitchens, bathrooms, sinks, etc. We see both Guei and Jian live in such neighborhoods.

Prepare Discussion Questions:

- Describe Guei and list the adjectives.
- How do the city-people in Beijing view the people form the countryside? Where is the evidence of this in the film?
- How do country folk view the people in the city? What scenes reveal this?
- What makes up Guei's identity? Create an identity chart for him.
- What are the goals of the Fei Da Express delivery service?
- Do you think the process of Guei owning his bike is fair? Why or why not?
- Describe Jian and list the adjectives.
- What makes up Jian's identity? Create an identity chart for him.
- How do Jian's friends treat Guei?
- How is friendship depicted in this film?
- How are the characters of Guei and Jian shaped by their social background?
- How does the last scene negate the compromise of their mediation?
- What defines class differences and divisions? Find examples of these differences in the film.
- How does the film reflect the importance of a job and money?

2. Another way to introduce the film is: *Today's China: Capitalism 101*
   a. Character Foils: Guei from the country, and Jian from the city
   b. History of China since World War II: Mao (1966-76)
   c. Beijing Society: classless society to class differences; urban vs rural
   d. Chinese culture: saving face, honor, materialism, money
   e. Conflict resolution: nonviolence, judicial system, negotiations, mediation
   f. Themes and Symbols: bicycle, Beijing

———

Sidebars:

———

1. Current Debate:
How Things have Changed - or not- Since the Period Covered by the Film.

- Many Chinese filmmakers are obliged to work "underground" to avoid the government's rigid censorship bureau. Some filmmakers circumspect the regulations by having their films produced in Taiwan or Hong Kong. The films are then "technically" considered "not Chinese." Or they set up s small production company in mainland China with "accepted" filmmakers. To work "above ground" means that the filmmaker must submit a two-stage application of screenplay and rough-cut versions to the Film Bureau. Despite China's changing society, there is still censorship, repression and marginalization facing filmmakers in China.

- Children in poor rural areas of China, "the old China," are being recruited by unethical employment agencies, or even kidnapped to coastal cities, where they work 12-hour shifts for less than 25 cents per hour to produce much of the world's toys, clothes and electronics. There is evidence of wide spread violations of international child labor laws in China.

- China is involved in global development: In Africa, the Chinese government has joint ventures with many African companies, especially those rich in natural resources as petrol, gas, and minerals. The Chinese help the African leaders, legitimate or rogue, in clandestine activities to conquer niche markets. China has also contracted to receive billions of dollars of petrol from Iraq. They have also started sending oil riggers and equipment to help Brazil develop their newly-discovered oil fields off the coast of Rio de Janeiro. China has become a strong client for Brazilian soybeans. Venezuela has also become a trading partner with China and has tripled their oil exports as of mid-2008 to China. In 2010, China bought from Afghanistan their largest copper mine located outside of Kabul.

- In 2008, China was involved in a wide-spread crisis and scandal related to food contamination of their milk products. Due to the inclusion of high levels of the toxic chemical melamine in their dairy products, there were thousands of consumers who died.

- China has a problem with Tibet:
  - In 1950, China's Army under orders from Mao, took over Tibet, suppressing Buddhism, killing more than 1.2 million Tibetans, and setting up in the region factories and collective farms in Chinese-style.
  - At that time, the Indian Prime Minister, Jawaharlal Nehru, offered the Dalai Lama safe refuge in northern India, where India developed a Tibetan Buddhist center.
  - The Dalaii Lama is the Buddhist religious leader. The present Dalai Lama is the 14th Tibetan Dalai Lama, living in exile in northern India in Dharamsala since 1959. Prior to that, he and his predecessors lived in Lhasa, Tibet's capital, where they had their headquarters and center of followers. Not only is he the religious leader, but he is also the head of the Tibetan government.
  - In 1988, the Dalai Lama introduced the "Strasbourg Proposal" which called for Tibetan autonomy from China rather than independence. His

offer was refused by the Chinese who feared his influence and he had to remain in exile in northern India. But he was awarded the Nobel Peace Prize for his efforts.

°   Presently, Tibet's request for autonomy for Tibetans living under Chinese rule, is one of the major issues facing the Chinese government. To weaken the Tibetans, China has relocated millions of Chinese *Hans* to live and work there. They have also made it illegal for Tibetans to speak or read Tibetan, practice their religion, and have children learn in school about Tibet. (This is a strategy the Chinese used in Hong Kong, Macau and other areas where there is ethnic unrest.) The Dalai Lama has also requested autonomy in other regions of China that have significant Tibetan populations.

°   China's millions of undergraduate students are being educated to move the country toward a white-collar, middle-class economy; but that is not the reality. As of May 2010, there were 6 million undergraduates seeking jobs in large cities. Those students are trained in accounting, finance and computer; and yet, they cannot find jobs in Beijing and Shanghai. They are called the *ant tribe* for they are like ants searching for work. On the other hand, the young people who stay in the countryside find work easily as laborers in factories and farms, and their salaries have grown 80% in the past year.

2. Public Response:

•   *Beijing Bicycle* was produced in Taiwan with a Chinese Film company, so technically it was an approved Chinese production despite its not getting official approval for export.

3. Actors and Directors:

•   Wang Xiaoshuai has directed another film, *Drifters,* which was screened in Cannes in May 2007. The Chinese government was "dissatisfied" with the film.
•   Wang, along with his contemporaries, is part of the film movement called the "Sixth Generation." They are interested in showing *the here and now* of China's urban society. They prefer to write their own original screenplays, rather than work on literary adaptations. Most of their work is done underground to avoid censorship.
•   Lin Cui and Bin Li, who play the teenage boys, won international acclaim for their acting at the Berlin International Film Festival in 2001.

4. Awards:

- Berlin International Film Festival-
  2001- Won- New Talent Award – Lin Cui and Bin Li Won- Silver Berlin Bear – Jury Grand Prix – Wang Xiaoshuai

- Singapore International Film Festival
  2001- Nominated- Silver Screen Award, Best Asian Feature Film - Wang Xiaoshuai

---

Bibliography of Films - Filmography:
Further Global Study Resources through Film:

Chinese Martial Arts Films:

- *Crouching Tigers, Hidden Dragons* (China)
- *Come Drink with Me* (China)
- *Ashes of Time* (China)
- *Last Hurrah for Chivalry* (China)
- *The Karate Kid* (U.S.A.)
- *Blood Tues* (U.S.A.)
- *Teenage Mutant Ninja Turtles* (U.S.A.)
- *Tiger Claws* (U.S.A.)

About China:

- *Not One Less* (China)
- *Suzhou River* (China)
- *Balzac and the Little Chinese Seamstress* (France)
- *The Go Master* (China)
- *Raise the Red Lantern* (China)
- *Nanking* (China)
- *Lust, Caution* (China)
- *The Last Emperor* (U.S.A.)
- *Together* (U.S.A.)

- *Kundun* (U.S.A.)
- *Qiu Ju* (China)
- *Farewell My Concubine* (China)
- *Red Firecracker, Green Firecracker* (China)
- *Welcome to Destination Shanghai* (China)
- *My Father and I* (China)
- *The Days* (China)
- *Red Beads* (China)
- *Two Hearts* (China)
- *Sons* (China)
- *Two Hearts and Enter the Clowns* (China)
- *Summer Palace* (China)
- *Still Life* (China)
- *The Curse of the Chrysanthemum* (China)
- *Ashes of Time Redux* (China)
- *City* (China)
- *Xiao Wu* (China)
- *24 City* (China)
- *Still Life* (China)
- *The Little Flower* (China)
- *Petition* (China)
- *Mao's Last Dancer* (Australia)
- *The King of Masks* (China)
- *The Wedding Banquet* (China)
- *Pushing Hands* (China)
- *Eat, Drink, Man, Woman* (China)
- *In the Mood for Love* (China)
- *Chung King Express* (China)
- *Happy Together* (China)
- *Coming Home* (China)

About Tibet:

- *Kundun* (U.S.A./Tibet)
- *Free Tibet* (U.S.A./Tibet)
- *Dalai Lama: The Soul of Tibet* (U.S.A./Tibet)

CHAPTER 3

PERSEPOLIS (IRAN / FRANCE)

TITLE OF FILM: *Persepolis*
YEAR OF RELEASE: 2007
COUNTRY: Iran
DIRECTOR: Marjane Satrapi and Vincent Paronnaud
LANGUAGE: French
RUNNING TIME: 95 minutes
CURRICULUM THEMES:

A. HISTORY and SOCIAL SCIENCE:

- **Chapter's Key Theme: Totalitarian Government in Iran**
- **World History: Shah of Iran; Islamists/Fundamentalists; Iran-Iraq war**
- **Geography: Iran; Austria; France**
- **Economics: Poverty**
- **Civics, Citizenship and Government: Theocracy; Marxism; Human rights abuses; Immigration issues**

B. LITERATURE and VISUAL ARTS:

- **World Literature: Graphic novels; Coming-of-age-novel**
- **Media Studies: Film Clips and Scene Discussions; Cinematography Techniques: animation, voiceover, black & white, abstract characters, symbols; Manga and Anime; Avant-garde**
- **Philosophy/Critical Thinking: Heroes; Rebellion; Autobiography**
- **Art: Sculpture**
- **Technology: Internet in Iran**

Introduction:

Persepolis was directed by Marjane Satrapi and Vincent Paronnaud; produced by Tara Grace, Marc Jousset, Kathleen Kennedy and Xavier Rigault; edited by Stéphane Roche; production design by Marisa Musy; music by Olivier Bernet; and distributed by Sony Pictures Classic in 2007; (95 minutes)

Marjane .... *Chiara Mastroianni*
Mother .... *Catherine Deneuve*
Grandmother .... *Danielle Darrieux*
Father .... *Simon Abkarian*

What makes *Persepolis* unique is the blending of literature and cinema in the following:

- use of one art form (literary graphic novels) with another (cinematic animation);
- use of black and white in cinema, as in printed matter, to create images of ordinary people who can live in any country where political revolution is possible;
- use of film as a Bildungsroman: the story of a young girl's development in a novel;
- entwinement of storyline with the political story: Iran's political turmoil in the past 50 years (similar to the form and technique used by authors of historical novels);
- use of film as political opposition which allows viewer to become involved; cinema allows the viewer to *easily* observe revolution

Pivotal Moments in History:

- In 1921 Shah Reza Khan establishes a constitutional monarchy. During World War II he is pro-German.
- In 1941, Britain and the U.S.S.R. invade Iran and use the Iranian railroad for their war efforts. They force Shah Reza Khan to abdicate in favor of his son, Shah Mohammad Reza Pahlavi.
- As of 1941, Shah Mohammad modernizes Iran with American and British support, but also introduces a secret police and totalitarian form of government.

He denounces all opposition and sends the religious leader, Ayatollah Khomeini, into exile.

- In 1978 the Iranian Revolution (also known as the Islamic Revolution) begins with demonstrations against the Shah. (This is when the film *Persepolis* begins.) Marjane's intellectual, left-wing family denounces the Shah's abuses. They are delighted when the Shah is forced to flee the country and Ayatollah Khomeini returns from exile to become the Supreme leader.

- Marxists and Communists join together to overthrow the Shah and initially the Islamists allow them free reign to voice their opinions. But soon after the Islamists come into power, they solidify their control, introduce a theocracy, and arrest and execute the irreligious Leftists.

- In 1980 Saddam Hussein of Iraq invades Iran through the Kurdish area and kills 500,000 to 1,000,000 Iranians (including Kurds) with chemical warfare. He takes over the oil reserves and the Iranian-Iraqi war continues until 1988.

Pre-Screening Questions:

1. *Persepolis* is autobiographical. The author, Marjane Satrapi, begins her story when she is 9 years old in 1978 Tehran and dreams of being the last prophet of the Galaxy. We see all stages of her life until she is 25 years old, married, divorced and on her way to live permanently in Paris, France.

Suggested Activities:
- *Your group can discuss what motive an author has when he/she writes an autobiography.*
- *Divide into pairs to discuss the following possible answers:*
  - *to witness and document historical events;*
  - *to denounce a critical political period;*
  - *to immortalize the love and respect one has for family or country;*
  - *to purge oneself of a past so as to go forward to the future;*
  - *to immortalize one's ego.*

2. The title, *Persepolis*, means something.

Suggested Activities:
- *Discuss what and where was Persepolis? Does anyone recognize the suffix -polis? Look up the components Perse- and -polis and try to deduce what Persepolis means. Can you*

think of other words that end in –polis? Why does the author use this as the title for her film and graphic novels?

Hints:

- A *polis* was the name for a city in ancient Greece; *Perse* is a prefix for "Persia." Persepolis was the name of the Persian (Iranian) capital that dates from 500 B.C. It is situated 70 kilometers north east of the present city, Shiraz. Darius the Great built the palace, terraces, military quarters, treasury, reception quarters, and main buildings.
- Persepolis was built as a celebration of the Persian Empire's greatness and as a gathering site to celebrate special events.
- Today it is an archaeological site that has intact sculptures and bas-reliefs that tell the history of the Persians.

Pivotal Moments in Film:

- *Persepolis* is an animated film in black and white made by cartoonist, Marjane Satrapi, with fellow cartoonist, Vincent Paronnaud, based on four of Marjane's autobiographical graphic novels: "Persepolis 1," (2000) which recounts the story of her childhood. "Persepolis 2" is the story of her return to Iran from Vienna. "Persepolis 3 and 4" are the stories of her life in Iran during and after college.
- The structure of using graphic novels and putting their images into animated format in black and white with simple characters is a breakthrough in cinematic technique. The cartoons are viewed as abstractions but contain in their simplicity a great deal of emotion and dynamism. To adapt the graphic novel content into cinema animation, the art director and executive producer, Marc Jousset, created a special design that they did by hand.
- The film, in the format of a light comic book style, interjects deep thought and philosophical interpretations with a myriad of themes: political totalitarianism, religious oppression, teenage rebellion, cultural dissonance, war, exile, and immigration.
- *Persepolis* is based on Marjane Satrapi's memoirs of her first-hand experiences living in Iran under the Shah and the Fundamentalists, from the 1970s until 1994.

She recounts her teenage years as a student in Vienna, Austria; her return to a theocratic Iran; and her need again to leave the country, this time permanently.

- The film is part Iranian history lesson and part memoir, fused together, to show the viewer a family's experiences and lifestyle under drastic political changes. The lives of the characters parallel the history of Iran during this period. It is also the story of a rebellious, precocious child who grows up in a repressive society. It is the story of how an artist finds pleasure and meaning even when a fanatical government fights to prevent her from doing so. The books and film, *Persepolis,* are proof that despite struggle and opposition, the human spirit is indomitable and can turn around difficult experiences to bring forth "Art."

Post Screening Questions:
A. History and Social Science:

1. Who was Shah Mohammad of Iran? Why did Communists and Marxists denounce the Shah? Why did Islamists, who took power after the Shah, allow the Marxists and Communists to express their opinions and demonstrate? Why were they soon stopped?

Hints:
- Shah in Persian means King.
- The Communists and Marxists denounced the Shah's government for being imperialistic and being supported by the West, the U.S. and U.K.
- The Islamists were anti-capitalistic, anti-Imperialistic and anti-American; so initially they allowed the Communists and Marxists freedom to speak. However, once the Islamists were securely in power, the religious government began to restrict the Leftists.
- The Communists and Marxists were anti-religious and the Islamists could not accept such dissension under their theocratic rule. The Leftists were thus marginalized and exiled; those who remained in Iran were executed in 1988-89.

2. Discuss the following scenes or episodes that influence Marjane's political beliefs:
   a. Her uncle Anoosh is a Marxist and takes great pride in teaching her to carry on the family's Leftist tradition. There are several scenes with him.
   b. Marjane denounces a boy's father who works for the secret police. Then she tries to befriend the boy but is rebuked.
   c. Marjane opposes the religious teachers in her school in Tehran.
   d. The Iran-Iraq War takes place and Marjane sees for herself the horrors and destruction from war.

e. Her father is threatened by teenage government officials who threaten him with machine guns.

f. While in Vienna, she opposes a series of people from different social-political backgrounds.

g. She opposes the religious professors in her Iranian university.

B. Literature and Visual Arts:

- How do we identify with Marjane even though we come from different cultures? Take into consideration the following universal themes: her youth, her growing up, her likes and dislikes, her fears and ambitions, her rebellious spirit, her desire to be free, and her young womanhood. Use transition words to go from one topic to another.

Curriculum Themes:
A. History and Social Science:

Chapter's Key Themes: Totalitarian Government in Iran

- Author/director Satrapi shows the change of Teheran from a modern urbane culture with a tradition of democracy and independent thought (pre-Shah), to an Iran repressed by Islamic Fundamentalists who have converted the country back into a medieval society (post Iranian Revolution, 1979).
- Under Iran's totalitarian government, we see an omnipresent secret police; how intellectuals are suspected and arrested; and how common party supporters are rewarded. We view a scene in which the window washer becomes the chief hospital administrator and decides which patients can travel abroad for medical care. Marjane's uncle is such a victim, for he needs cardiac surgery in the U.K., but he is denied the right to leave and consequently dies.
- Under Shah Mohammad Reza Pahlavi's rule (1941-1979) there is a constitutional monarchy, but he rules with an iron hand supported by a tyrannical secret police that arrests and executes dissidents.
- After the Shah's rule, Ayatollah Khomeini returns from exile in France to Teheran and installs a theocratic constitutional Islamic rule (1979). He, too,

tyrannizes the population with his secret police, tyrannical arrests, and mass executions of dissidents. His theocracy is also a totalitarian form of government.

Suggested Activity:
- *Your group can discuss some of the rigid controls that the new Islamic government under the rule of the Ayatollah imposes on Marjane, her family and their society.*

1. World History:

a. Shah of Iran:

- In the first frame of *Persepolis* we are introduced to Marjane, a spirited nine-year-old child who is dressed like a karate kid and is running around the house yelling support for the Shah. But her parents don't agree with her political sentiment and they enlighten her that the Shah does not have divine power as she learned in school and he is not a superior creature with his secret police. She returns in the next frame by yelling in the same manner, "Down with the Shah."

Suggested Activity:
- *The opening frame introduces the personality of Marjane and also serves to place the setting in its historical context. Marjane, as a child, acts like the crowds in the streets, switching allegiance for and against the Shah within seconds. Your group can discuss who are the different groups in Iran at that time who are supporting and denouncing the Shah, and why? How are they represented in the film?*

Hints:
- In the 18ᵗʰ century, the Qajar dynasty ruled Iran. Unlike their neighboring countries, the Qajars maintained their sovereignty and were never colonized. However, they did lose territories to Russia and the British Empire in wars over 200 years.
- In 1921, Shah Reza Khan overthrew the weak Qajar dynasty. His power lasted until World War ll when his pro-German ties angered the U.K. and the U.S.S.R. Consequently, these two Allies invaded Iran. Shah Reza Khan was forced to abdicate in favor of his son, Mohammad Reza Pahlavi.
- This last Shah modernized Iran. Partnering with the U.S. and the U.K. in oil production, he used petrol profits to westernize Iran but he also became

corrupt and feared. He imposed a secret intelligence agency to suppress any opposition and maintained an autocratic and cruel government.

b. Islamists/ Fundamentalists:

- As the film's animated frames project, we hear Marjane's family accept the introduction of Islamists into power with the opinion, "It can't be worse than the Shah." Yet, as the storyline unfolds, we see it is.

Suggested Activity:
- *Discuss what is the significance of the scene in which the two female teachers dressed in black Hijabs reprimand Marjane for wearing a punk jacket, a badge of Michael Jackson and punk sneakers. How did Marjane feel and how can you tell?*

Hints:
- The Iranian Revolution, also known as the Islamic Revolution, began in 1978-79 with demonstrations against the Shah. He was forced to flee the country in 1979.
- Nationalists, Marxists and Communists joined with Islamic traditionalists to overthrow the Shah, but the government that came in next under Ayatollah Khomeini was no better.
- Ayatollah Khomeini had been imprisoned under the Shah and was sent in exile to Turkey, Iraq and France in 1979. He returned to Teheran to lead the revolution. He took power as the "Supreme Leader" and Iran became an Islamic Republic under a totalitarian style of government and theocratic constitution.

c. Iran-Iraq War:

- The scenes that depict the war between Iran and Iraq are not clearly portrayed. They are quickly presented without much dialogue, explanation or narration. And yet, they represent an important part of Iranian history.

Suggested Activities:
- *Your group can review and discuss the specific scenes that relate to the Iran-Iraq War.*
- *Research the American role during this war. What was the position of the Iranian and Iraqi Kurds during this period?*

- *Analyze the political significance of the Iran-Iraq War and what followed in Iraq and Iran. Discuss the role of the Kurds in northern Iraq and why they have received preferential support from the Americans during the U.S. occupation in Iraq.*

Hints:

- In 1980, the U.N. reported that Iraq, under the rule of Saddam Hussein, had attacked Iran, especially in the bordering Iranian-Kurdish area, by using mustard gas and chemical nerve agents. Saddam took advantage of Iran's weakened military that had been disbanded during the Islamic revolution of 1978-79. He sought to increase Iraq's access to the Persian Gulf and to the area's rich oil fields. The war continued until 1988 when Ayatollah Khomeini accepted a truce for Iranians that was mediated by the U.N. Iranian casualties were high in this "chemical war" with 500,000 to 1,000,000 deaths.

2. Geography:

a. Iran:

- In *Persepolis* we see urban landscapes of Teheran with grand mountains in the background surrounding the capital. Most of the scenes, however, are from inside Marjane's house or from the streets in her neighborhood. Perhaps this is done intentionally. Yet, we do get a feeling of Iran and Teheran as a cosmopolitan, active city.

Suggested Activities:

- *Your group can find a map of Iran with its bordering countries. For each country, include the capital, leading cities, important mountain ranges, and rivers.*
- *Discuss the influence of Iran's geography on its politics, religion, society, culture, agriculture, economy and environment.*

Hints:

- Iran's area roughly equals the size of the United Kingdom, France, Spain and Germany combined. Iran is the 18ᵗʰ largest country in the world.
- Its borders are with Azerbaijan and Armenia to the northwest; the Caspian Sea to the north; Turkmenistan to the northeast; Pakistan to the east; Turkey to the west; and the waters of the Persian Gulf and the Gulf of Oman to the south.

- Iran is one of the world's most mountainous countries in its region. The eastern part consists of deserts that are mostly uninhabited.
- There are small plains found along the remaining coast of the Persian Gulf, the strategic Strait of Hormuz and the Sea of Oman.
- Iran's climate is varied: subtropical along the southern coast of the Persian Gulf and Gulf of Oman with mild winters and hot summers; on the northern edge of the country (the Caspian coastal plain) temperatures nearly fall below freezing with snowfall; and the desert areas are arid with little rainfall, cold winters and hot summers. Due to the mountains surrounding the city, Teheran is built as if in a valley. Pollution is a major problem that the government has a difficult time controlling.
- Iran's economy is based on government controlled and state ownership of oil, gas and large enterprises. Iran ranks second in the world in natural gas reserves and third in oil reserves. Agriculture remains one of the largest employers, accounting for 22% of all jobs according to the last census. There are multiple co-operatives in the villages. Main products are dates, flowers and pistachios.
- The U.N. classifies Iran's economy as semi-developed. Unemployment is high.

b. Austria:

- In *Persepolis,* we see that Marjane angers her religious teachers for wearing sneakers, a punk jacket and a Michael Jackson pin. Her parents fear that their rebellious daughter will get into more trouble, even imprisoned, and they decide to send her to Vienna to attend the Lycée Français. Initially she lives with friends of her parents. However, at this school, which attracts wealthy international students, she has a series of other problems. Marjane is in Vienna from the age of 14-18 years old (1983-87), which is the period before the demise of Communism in Eastern Europe (1989).

Suggested Activities:
- *Your group can summarize what Marjane's daily life in Vienna is while she is at school.*
- *Debate the pros and cons of going to a boarding high school.*
- *Divide into 2 groups: one group to research and report on a description of Vienna, and the other group to research and report about Austria.*

Hints:
- Austria is a country in Central Europe. It borders both Germany and the Czech Republic to the north, Slovakia and Hungary to the east, Slovenia and Italy to the south, and Switzerland and Liechtenstein to the west.

- Austria became a member of the European Union in 1995 and retained its constitutional neutrality as other European Union members and Sweden.
- Austria is one of the 10 richest countries in the world in terms of GDP per capita and has a very high standard of living.
- Vienna is Austria's capital and main city with a population of about 1.7 million.
- It is the 10th largest city according to population in the European Union. The United Nations has offices there as the Organization of Petroleum Exporting Countries and International Atomic Energy Association. (IAEA)
- In the last census, 16% of people living in Vienna had nationalities other than Austrian. Religions of the Viennese population is divided as follows: Roman Catholic- 49.2%; Muslim- 7.8%; and Protestants- 35%.

c. France:

- Marjane returns to Teheran from Vienna. She is equally unhappy at home as she was away from home. Yet, after a period of time she readjusts, enrolls in art school at the university in Teheran and even falls in love. However, after one year of marriage, she divorces and decides to immigrate to Paris.

Suggested Activities:
- *Why is Paris a good choice for Marjane? Consider and discuss her language skills, her interest in art, and her political leanings as all being "in synch" with Paris.*
- *Immigration laws were restrictive in France when Marjane first went there. What does Marjane have to do to become a French citizen? Compare French requirements with American requirements for citizenship. Did Marjane have a problem getting a visa to study and live in France? How have these laws changed in the past few years?*
- *Your group can discuss issues of immigration and compare present American immigration laws with those of the European Union and present-day France with accepting migrants and political refugees, as of 2015.*

Hints:
- From a geographic perspective, France is bordered by Belgium, Luxembourg, Germany, Switzerland, Italy Monaco, Andorra, and Spain. It also has other territories (Outre Mer): St. Martin, Martinique, Guadeloupe, Tahiti, and French Guiana.
- During the years after the war (1945-1974), the country's reconstruction and steady economic growth led to a need for laborers from French territories (especially from former French colonies in Africa). France allowed these

needed workers to live and work in France with lax immigration restrictions. This led to 1.6 million French colonials from Algeria, Tunisia and Morocco who migrated to France in the 1960s. In the 1970s over 30,000 French colonials left Cambodia during the ferocious Khmer Rouge regime.

- In the past 35 years, France has ceased being a country that allows mass immigration. Immigrants who live in France are supervised closely to assure that they live and work according to French laws and immigration policies.
- As of 2015, the French national institute of statistics estimated that 4.9 million foreign-born immigrants live in France (8% of the country's population and to grow by 8% by 2030). This is a low rate of immigration compared to Germany.
- As of the 2000 Census, there are in France an estimated 6 million Muslims (registered), 1 million Protestants, 600-700,000 Jews, 600,000 Buddhists, 150,000 Orthodox Christians, and 181,312 Hindus.
- Marjane immigrates to France with a student visa to study art and a visa as a political refuge. Both visas would allow her to live in France for a period of time. Once there, she had to arrange specific citizenship papers to continue to live in France. Most likely this was not difficult for she became a very productive asset to the French society.

3. Economics:

a. Poverty:

- *Persepolis* shows us how a visiting Iranian student with little economic support, lives in western Europe. Marjane did go to the Lycée Français in Vienna that is a private institution and her parents did have to pay for tuition. But beyond that, she lived very frugally. She lived with friends or worked for her room and board. She did not have money to return home to Iran for Christmas or summer vacations. At the end of her 4-5 year stay, she was living on the streets, hungry, alone and sick with serious bronchitis.

Suggested Activities:
- *Discuss how would an American high school student finance his/her education if he/she attends a boarding school and could not afford the tuition. How can an American college student with little money finance his/her American college education? List the ways, using sequential transitions like "firstly," "secondly," "moreover," and "lastly."*
- *Research how a foreign student would finance going to the Lycée Français in Vienna, which is a private school. Look up some pictures of the Lycée in Vienna. What conclusions*

can you draw from the images? E.g. does it look like a big school? Does it look expensive and why?

Hints:

- Some costly boarding schools have rich endowments and alumni funds that they use to award scholarships to needy students. Scholarships can also include payment of books and personal computers. There are also work-study programs to help finance a student's education.

- For college students in need of scholarships, there are a number of ways to apply. Guidance departments in each high school have a list of suggestions as well as forms for specific grants, work-study programs and scholarships. There are also loans available and various programs to repay the debt after graduation. Individual colleges and universities also have their own scholarships and endowment programs. The Financial Aid department at each college is happy to provide this information.

4. Civics, Citizenship and Government:

a. Theocracy:

- In the guise of an animated film that appears light and amusing, we are given a history lesson about Iran. As a personage, Marjane serves as a vehicle and narrator, who shows us the politics and history of Iran's second half of the 20th century.

Suggested Activities:

- *Divide into groups to define and give examples of the following forms of governments: Democracy, Monarchy, Totalitarianism, Communism, Socialism, Fascism, and Theocracy.*
- *Create a chart that compares the characteristics of a democracy (as exemplified by the U.S.A), totalitarian government (as exemplified by North Korea), and a theocracy (as exemplified by Iran.)*
- *Analyze the governments of China and Russia that have their unique form of government.*

Hints:

- The word *theocracy* comes from the Greek, *theokratia*, which means "the rule of God." Theocracy is a form of government in which only God and his law is sovereign. The government claims to rule on behalf of God or a higher power, as specified by the nation's religion.

- In a theocracy, the civil leader is believed to have a direct personal connection with God. For example, Moses ruled the Hebrews and Muhammad ruled the early Muslims.
- Most observers consider Iran to be a theocracy with the Ayatollah as Supreme Leader. But Iranian authorities deny this and consider their government to be a "Theo-democracy" or "Religious Democracy." (Some people see this as a play on words to camouflage the restricted Totalitarian government that exists in Iran.)

b. Marxism:

- In *Persepolis*, uncle Anoosh is a Marxist. It is through scenes about him that we see the role Marxists had in Iran.
- During the Shah's regime, radical Left dissidents including Communists and Marxists, were anti-government because of the Shah's allegiance to capitalism and western nations. The Shah's secret police did not tolerate these dissidents and arrested them. During the Islamists, the radical Left were anti-religious. However, they were allowed relative freedom for they were also anti-West and anti-imperialistic. But after a while, the Leftists were rounded up, arrested and executed. Iran became more repressive and dictatorial.
- Marjane's parents, Tadji and Ebi, are politically active intellectuals with Leftist ideas. Uncle Anoosh is even more radical as he explains to Marjane about his escape to Moscow and his time spent in prison. He warns Marjan about the sacrifices of standing up for freedom and innocent people. She is deeply influenced by uncle Anoosh and her family's political leanings.

Suggested Activities:
- *Divide into small groups to discuss which scenes relate to politics in the film. Chart the progression of Marjane's political thoughts while she is in Iran and Austria.*
- *Discuss global politics during the time of this film, 1978-1994. Identify key events that caused demonstrations and anti-government protests in Eastern Europe and China in 1989.*

Hints:
- To understand Marxist political thought, one should be familiar with Karl Marx (1818-1883). He is famous for his political theories that espouse the downfall of capitalism and the emergence of communism.
- The Communist Manifesto (1848) written by Marx and Friedrich Engels, describes the history of all society as the history of class struggles. Marx

advocates the fall of the bourgeoisie (industrialists, capitalists, landowners) and the victory of the proletariat (the workers) to establish communist governments. The ideal state of government for him is a communist society in which human beings develop their nature in cooperative production. Private ownership and individual achievements run counter to communism. Marx predicts the Bolshevik Revolution and the spread of communism around the world when the capitalist system would succumb to a communist society. The last line of his book, is "Workers of all lands, unite."

- Political philosophy is influenced by economics, wrote Karl Marx in <u>Economic and Philosophical Manuscripts</u> (1844). The economics of a country determines the politics. First comes the economic situation of a country that in turn determines the political picture.

- Marx was anti-religious, believing that religion is the opium of the people. He advocated that the social function of religion is a way of coping with social inequality and thereby functions to maintain the status quo of alienating the workers.

- <u>Das Kapital</u> (1867) is an extensive treatise on political economy written by Karl Marx and edited in part by Friedrich Engels. The book is a critical analysis of capitalism and analyzes the capitalist process of production. Marx elaborates on his theory that capitalism exploits workers and leads to a falling rate of profit and the collapse of industrial capitalism.

c. Human Rights Abuses:

- *Persepolis* shows us that under the Shah we see scenes of arrests, escapes and executions. We also see similar scenes of massive human rights abuses under the Islamists:
  ○ No one can go to a party
  ○ No woman can be with a man who is not her husband
  ○ No one can drink alcohol
  ○ Women cannot wear the clothes they want
  ○ Dictatorial power of policemen
  ○ Existence of anti-Semitism – they bombed "Baba Levy's house."

Suggested Activities:
- *Divide into small groups to discuss the reactions about human rights from the following characters in the film: uncle Anoosh, Grandma, Marjane's parents, her classmates in Vienna, her friends in Tehran, her husband, and Marjane.*

- *Compare the laws of the Taliban in Afghanistan with those of Islamists in Iran.*
- *What is a charter? Can you think of any synonyms? Look up the charter of the United Nations, chapter 1, "Purposes and Principles." What does it say about Human Rights? What are other important purposes of the United Nations?*

Hints:

- In 1948, the United Nations adopted the Universal Declaration of Human Rights that established guidelines to assure all people in all countries with freedoms. These are standards that aim to protect the individual citizen from abuses. These rights include: freedom from slavery; freedom from torture; equal protection of the law; freedom of thought, opinion and religion; the right to education; the right to good health, shelter and food; the right to work and to form trade unions; freedom from arbitrary arrest; and the right to a fair trial.
- For more information about the United Nations Human Rights agency, visit their site: <www.un.org/rights>
- Chapter 1 of the U.N. charter can be found here: <http://www.un.org/en/documents/charter/chapter1.shtml>
- A charter is the document of an organization that outlines its purposes, its duty, and its authority. Some synonyms include: code, constitution, license, declaration, or mission statement.

d. Immigration Issues:

- In *Persepolis* the author/ director shows several examples of how difficult it was for her to be an immigrant:
- She is a victim in Vienna of people identifying her with the brutes and tyrants that she has fled. For this reason she tells the Austrians that she is French, not Iranian.
- When her husband tells her that he wants to leave Iran, she questions him, where to go? "In the West," she claims, "you can die on the street and no one would care." Marjane speaks from experience.
- The question of guilt for leaving one's country and family is very evident in the film. When she thinks of her grandmother and how she never saw her again when she immigrated to France, Marjane sadly comments, "Liberty has its price."
- Marjane realizes in Vienna and Paris, that to escape persecution and live as an exile, does not necessarily bring happiness. The outsider to the new society loses solidarity and shared experiences with the home group.

Suggested Activities:
- *In a round robin discussion, each person can discuss what he/she would do if they were Marjane and were a victim of Iranian politics.*
- *Point out scenes that depict Marjane's immigration by using a "cause and effect" principal.*
- *Discuss if Iranians have become "migrants" in the recent wave of immigration to European countries. Why? And who?*

Hints:
- Cause and effect is the relationship between two things when one thing makes something else happen. For example, in the film *Persepolis*, Marjane wears punk sneakers and clothes. That is the "cause." The "effect" is that she is interrogated by the school's director. Another effect is that her parents decide she should leave Iran and live abroad.

B. Literature and Visual Arts:

---

5. World Literature:

a. Graphic Novels:

- *Persepolis* is first introduced to the public through "graphic novels," which is a type of comic book. But it is different, for it has a complex storyline and is targeted to an adult reader. Marjane and her co-director, Vincent Paronnaud, have utilized the same style and literary genre in their film.

Suggested Activities:
- *Google and research Satrapi's 4 graphic novels and compare the film with her literature. Interesting discussions can be based on:*
  - *is the film loyal to the novels;*
  - *what are the different characteristics of both genres;*
  - *what is the effect on the audience with the different genres.*
- *Compare the graphic novels, <u>The Adventures of Tintin</u> and <u>Astérix</u>, with <u>Persepolis</u>.*
- *A fun activity is to write a graphic novel either in pairs or groups. Those who enjoy sketching, can draw the scenes. Others can write the storyline or storyboard.*

Hints:
- A graphic novel is typically bound in a longer and more durable format than familiar comic books. The graphic novel is sold in bookstores rather than at newsstands.

- In recent years, the definition of the *graphic novel* is not strictly defined. In Europe and Asia, it is a popular literary genre.
- It suggests a story that has a beginning, middle and end, as opposed to an ongoing series with continuing characters; and it deals with more mature themes. The term is commonly used to disassociate works from the juvenile or humorous connotations of *comics* and *comic book*, implying that the graphic novel is more serious or literary than comics.
- The French term is *bande dessiné* and in French the term applies equally to all kinds of comic strips in newspapers, magazines and comic books. (Satrapi has a syndicated column of *bande dessiné* in a French newspaper.)

b. Coming-of-age novel:

- The books and film of *Persepolis* take us from when Marjane is 9 years old until she's 25 years old. During this "voyage through youth" she is trying to understand the enigmas that surround her, especially those related to justice and government. Marjane concentrates on the subject of Iran for she lives there but the themes in her art can be described as universal. The books and film are part of the genre, "coming-of-age" novels, *Bildungsroman.* (And even more precisely, *Künstlerroman,* because she talks of her development into an artist.)

Suggested Activities:
- *Your group can identify situations in the film that are similar to events they experience as a young person growing up.*
- *Research the formal literary name for coming of age novels, Bildungsroman, and find examples of this type of literature.*

Hints:
- *Bildungsroman* comes from the German term of which the archetype example is, <u>Wilhelm Meister's Apprenticeship</u> by Goethe, meaning "bildung" (development, in German) and "roman" (novel, in German). The book's theme is the spiritual, moral, psychological, and social development of the protagonist. The period of time is the character's childhood to maturity/adulthood.
- These themes are often portrayed in films as well as in novels. The Bildungsroman usually contains specific and common elements:

     °   Journey motif and structure. The protagonist has a reason to go on this journey. It can be due to a loss or unhappiness that catapults he/she to travel away from the home or family.

     °   Struggle to define oneself, consisting of repeated clashes between the desires of the hero and judgments of the protagonist's society.

     °   The novel ends with an assessment by the protagonist of himself/herself and his/her new role in society.

     °   There are themes of exile or escape.

     °   Within the literary genre, is the Künstlerroman, when the protagonist is an artist (Künstler, in German is Artist) and the story ends when the artist-protagonist matures and emerges as an artist and produces a work of art.

- The following works fit into the genre of Bildungsroman or Künstlerroman. Can you think of any others?
  Harry Potter series by J. Rowling
  Portrait of the Artist as a Young Man by James Joyce
  The Adventures of Huckleberry Finn by Mark Twain
  Candide by Voltaire
  Persepolis by Marjane Satrapi
  Of Human Bondage by Somerset Maugham
  Siddartha by Hermann Hesse
  The Genius by Theodore Dreiser

6. Media Studies:

a. Film Clips and Scene Discussions:

- *Journey theme:* (Scene: 02:22 –> 03:15 minutes)
  Marjane's story is a "coming of age." She begins the narration as the adult in her remembers the way she was as a young girl: "Madame, your ticket and your passport. Marji, you've really grown up! Did you bring me a present? How is Paris? And the Eiffel Tower? Welcome to Teheran. You're here! I remember. Back then, I had a quiet life. A little girl's life."
  Growing up is a journey. And each journey is different, marked by experiences, thoughts, ambitions, people, places, etc. Members of your group can

discuss and share how their growing up, their journey, was affected by strong moments in their life.

- *Immigration:* (Scene: 00:35 –> 00:37 seconds)
  Multiple references to immigration issues are used as a theme in this autobiographical film. Marjane, our protagonist and author, reveals how difficult it is to leave one's country: "His heart is sick because his children are far away. Children always leave sooner or later. But being separated from your 13-year-old child because of war is absurd! It can break you heart for sure."

  In the past several years, millions of migrants and refugees have left their countries in the Middle East, Asia and Africa to find a better life in Europe. To leave one's country in order to find freedom and more opportunities, have a price. Your group can discuss the positive and negative points of immigration from the refugee's/ migrant's s point of view, as well as the pont of view of the host country, and the country that loses their educated people.

- *Freedom:* (Scene: 01:26 –> 01:28)
  The ending of the film summarizes the theme of freedom: freedom to live one's life as one chooses, freedom to create art, and freedom to be an artist: "Then, one day, the time to leave had come. My father cried, as usual. You're leaving forever. You're a free woman. Iran of today isn't for you. I forbid you to come back. I never saw my grandma again. She died a little later. Freedom always has a price."

  You can discuss all aspects of freedom as well as some thoughts of what freedom means to individuals in your group.

b. Cinematography Techniques:

1. Animation:
- Satrapi hand-drew all the cartoons and illustrations in her books and film. Computer technology was not used. However, instead of duplicating exactly the figures in her books for the film, she made the figures more fluid for the screen as befitting cinema's animation genre. The frames of one scene to the next are rapid. There is little background music or sound. The film is rather stark, mostly in black and white, with little décor, no perspective, and quite flat. Yet, there is great emotion and movement. The voices of famous actors give personality to the abstract characters and the storyline moves quickly.

- Satrapi and art director, Jousset, also created specialized studios for producing the animation: *Je Suis Bien* and *Pumpkin 3D*.

Suggested Activities:
- *Compare Persepolis with other animated films like: Ratatouille, The Bee Movie, Snow White and the Seven Dwarves, Life of Pi, Madagascar, and Spirited Away.*
- *Compare and contrast aspects like the main character's personality, what they struggle against, what they desire, and what is holding them back.*
- *Discuss the differences between the role of the viewer watching the film of Persepolis vs. the role of the reader with the book.*
- *Animation, as a cinematic style and technique, has become very popular in film schools and in film festivals. Why?*

2. Voiceover:
- is a direct vocal address to the viewers, that may come from a character, as in *Persepolis*, or the narrator in *March of the Penguins*. It is a storytelling technique that links the viewer to the character, be it human or animal.
- The characters' spoken voices in French are: Marjane: Chiara Mastroianni; Mother: Catherine Deneuve; Grandmother- Mami: Danielle Darrieux; and Father: Simon Abkarian.
- This device of using well-known celebrities for voiceovers is to enhance the personality and human quality of the characters. The term voiceover refers to a production technique where a disembodied voice (a voice coming from someone who cannot be seen) is broadcast live or pre-recorded in film, television, radio, or broadcasting.

3. Black and White:
- Ms Satrapi uses black and white for the characters. This format causes the characters to appear more general and universal. Perhaps it is also a style that reflects the author's philosophy of life: she sees the world in absolutes, with no shades of color and little compromise. Or, as Ms. Satrapi said in an interview, she did not want the characters to look foreign in a foreign country, but simply like any ordinary person in any country and to show how easily a country can become like Iran.

Suggested Activities:
- *Ms. Satrapi does not use color. However, on several occasions she uses red for Marjane's coat when she shows her protagonist as an adult. Identify several scenes when the director uses a red color (to indicate the present) and discuss. Why does she do this?*

- *Discuss how Ms. Satrapi's cinematographic style reflects her personality as depicted in the film.*

4. Abstract Characters:
- Ms. Satrapi has said that she made her characters abstract so they'd be more universal. In this way, the outline forms of the characters do not have specific characteristics. They could be a young girl anywhere in the world or the mother from any country, not necessarily Iran. We all remember scenes and images of our childhood that may be similar to Marjane's, even though we come from different social, political, religious, and cultural backgrounds.
- We realize that in this autobiographical genre, the memories are difficult for the author/director to share with the public, but having them in abstract form places the past faraway emotionally for Ms. Satrapi. This distance allows her a relative objectivity and ability to laugh at herself when she shows how wrong the young girl was in specific scenes and situations.

Suggested Activity:
- *Evaluate which situations are difficult for Ms. Satrapi to show the public and how she handles them.*

5. Symbols:
- a. Swan: Uncle Anoosh, a Marxist, gives Marjane two swans at different times of her life that he had made out of bread during his two imprisonments.

- b. Plastic key: During the Iran-Iraq war, young men were recruited to fight. The government gave them a plastic key and told the boys that this is their key to Paradise if they perform a suicide bombing and/or die fighting for their country.

Suggested Activity:
- *Compare the Iranian Fundamentalists' concept of dying for one's country and religion with present-day "suicide bombers" in the Middle-East and other Arab countries. Marjane talks about a "plastic key." In what context? What is her attitude?*

c. Manga and Anime:

- *Manga* is the Japanese word for "whimsical pictures." It's a style developed in Japan during the 19th century and modernized after World War ll. The modern form consists of comics and cartoons in printed book format. The literary genre includes a wide range of subjects: romance, sports, action-adventure, historical drama, science fiction, mystery, comedy, horror, sexuality, business, and many others.

- In Japan, people of all ages read manga. It represents a big business for their publishing industry, earning more than $3.6 billion per year.

- Manga is typically printed in black-and-white, although some full-color manga are printed. Often, manga are serialized with favorite characters presented in single events.

- Manga have been popular in Asia, especially in Taiwan, South Korea, China, Hong Kong and Japan.

- *Anime* is the shortened word for Animation in Japanese. Anime, like manga, has a large audience in Japan and recognition throughout the world.

- Distributors can release anime via television broadcasts, directly to video, or theatrically, as well as on the Internet. Anime is designed and produced from hand-drawn and computer animations.

- The earliest form of anime date from 1917 in Japan but it is as of the 1960s, with the works of Osamu Tezuka and Hayao Miyazaki, that anime has received global acclaim.

- Hayao Miyazaki's film, *Princess Mononoke*, was released in 1997 by Miramax and earned the Japanese director a celebrated international reputation as well as producing the highest-grossing film in Japan. His next film broke even more box-offices, *Spirited Away*, (2001) and was the first anime film to win an American Academy Award. (See chapter seven for more details of *Spirited Away*.)

Suggested Activity:
- *View one of Hayao Miyazaki's anime films and compare it to Persepolis. In France, "la nouvelle manga" has developed as a form of "bande dessinée."*

d. Avant-garde:

- Some critics have categorized this film as Avant-garde. Filmmakers of avant-garde use film as a medium for new creative exploration. The goal is to use film as a means of personal expression and to address important social and political issues.

- They are interested in exploring and expanding the use of technological capabilities of the film medium. They center on the "materials," as film, light and sound.

- These films often draw inspiration from photography, painting, sculpture, literature, music, and dance.

7. Philosophy/ Critical Thinking:

a. Heroes:

- It is a wonderful thing if while growing up, one's heroes are near. This was the case with Marjane, for she had her two heroes, uncle Anoosh and grandmother, as part of her family.
- Uncle Anoosh is the voice of the political Leftist and symbol of martyr and idealist. Mami is the symbol of wisdom and free-thinking. She is a woman before her time and role model for the young girl. Marjane resembles her grandmother: both of them are rebellious, out-spoken, liberal, and intelligent.

Suggested Activity:
- *Your group can make a chart and write some of the famous quotes that are spoken by uncle Anoosh and Mami. Analyze what they mean and how Marjane internalized these words during her life.*

b. Rebellion:

- If we were to coin one word to describe Marjane, we would use *rebellious*.
  In the film, we see several scenes that illustrate her personality:
- Marjane rebels against her peers who don't share her political beliefs.
- She is the ring-leader against a boy whose father works for the secret police.
- She does not want to wear her veil, *hijab*, as required by the Fundamentalists.
- She wears make-up and tight-fitting clothes and meets her boyfriend in public.
- She goes to parties, dances, and drinks alcohol.
- She smokes cigarettes and marijuana.
- She buys CD music on the Black Market.
- She wears punk sneakers, punk jacket and a Michael Jackson pin – all western symbols.

Suggested Activity:
- *Many times young people rebel as a way to avoid facing reality. This can become a lively discussion, personal as well as psychological and philosophical.*

c. Autobiography:

- *Persepolis* is based on four graphic novels that are memoirs of the author's early years. They cover the following periods:
  - ° Childhood, when Marjane lives in Iran and the Shah is in power, and then the Fundamentalists oust him and they take power.
  - ° Teenage years, when she is in boarding school at the Lyçee Français in Vienna.
  - ° Marjane's return to Iran and her years at the university in Tehran when she studies art.
  - ° Her marriage at 21 years old, divorce at 22 years old, and painful self-exile to Paris.

Suggested Activities:
- *Your group can choose and discuss one of the 4 chronological periods of the entire autobiography. If there is any one in the group who has been born in another country, or has passed their youth during a political movement, perhaps he/ she would like to share this with the group?*
- *Analyze how Ms. Satrapi uses the writing of her novels and the creation of her film as a "catharsis." In this way her art has not only become her "resolution" but her "homeland" for she must live in exile in Paris. An interesting point is to discuss, if you think she would have created her art if she had stayed in Iran?*

Hints:
- Autobiography is an intimate literary style where the author uses the first person. The aim may be to confess and/or to win the reader's confidence and support.
- Ms. Satrapi gives us a child's perspective of historic events, while as an adult she tries to understand injustice, truth, God, and government.

8. Art:

a. Sculpture:

- The treasures of Persian art that we have today, date to the 4th century B.C. Pottery and ceramics are the oldest art forms, followed by metal work that are characteristic of Persian silver gilded cups and dishes.
- But the greatest pieces of early Persian art are sculptures, carved mostly in stone and limestone. Popular subjects were human-headed bulls and kings fighting monsters. When the figure was human, the garment was carved in folds, in contrast to a straight-falling robe, popular with the Greeks of the same period. The largest series of Persian sculpture that exists from antiquity

are those found at the Palace of Darius in Persepolis. The subject of those sculptures is the glorification of the Kings that depict Persian history.

Suggested Activity:

- *Uncle Anoosh carves two sculptures for Marjane during his imprisonment. Discuss why he chooses the swan as his subject. Discuss why he chooses bread as his material. Does bread have a symbol? Does a swan have a symbol?*

9. Technology:

- Your group can explore to what degree Iranian students have freedom of the Internet. While you explore the web to get an answer, use epals to see if Iranian schools are allowed to communicate with American students to form pen pals. If yes, you can use the Diigo site to participate as a "pen pal." Explore the site audacity.sourceforge.net, a free audio editor, and wikis to post music and photos to post if you get an Iranian pal.

Extracurricular Activities:

- A fun group activity is to recreate an "Academy Awards" event and rate the films that you have screened from this book as well as from the cinema during the year by giving 1st prizes to several categories: Best Picture, Best Director, Best Actress, Best Actor, Best Supporting Actress, Best Supporting Actor, Best Musical Score and Best Adaptation from a Screenplay.

Sidebars:

1. Current Debate:
How Things Have Changed - Or Not- Since
The Period Covered By The Film.

a. Iranian International Relations:

- Western governments, the U.S., and the UN Security Council have all denounced Iran's uranium enrichment program that they believe Iran will use to for their nuclear weapons program.

- The U.N. Security Council has voted (in 2006 to 2014) to impose sanctions on Iran, freeze their assets, and stop them from enriching uranium for their nuclear program.
- Iranian officials retort that their nuclear ambitions are civilian, for electricity and energy, not for military purposes.
- Russia, under the government of Putin, has supplied Iran with nuclear fuel as of 2007 for Iran's light-water reactor and electricity program. Russia and the U.S. agree that the supply of nuclear fuel to Iran means that Iran will have no need to continue its own uranium enrichment program, a process that can provide fuel for a nuclear bomb or nuclear reactor.
- As of 2010, Russia is partnering with Iran to startup Iran's first nuclear power plant. The Russian company, Rosatom, will have their technicians move tons of low-enriched uranium fuel from a storage site into an Iranian reactor in the southern province of Bushehr, Iran. The joint venture is expected to be completed and functioning in 2011. Iran claims its nuclear program is for generating electricity and for medical purposes. Russia claims their partnership is a way to "control" Iran's nuclear activities for the U.N.'s International Atomic Energy Association (IAEA).
- As of 2015, Iran has agreed with the U.S. and U.N. in a mutually accepted treaty to stop their uranium enrichment facilities and their intentions to build a nuclear bomb. There will be regular inspections of their nuclear facilities to determine if they are being honest. If yes, 100-140 billion dollars of embargoed money will be returned to Iran for their co-operation in the beginning of 2016. Missile develement is an issue and was not part of this treaty.

b. Internal Problems:

- As of 2014, the Supreme Leader is Ayatollah Ali Khamenei and the President of Iran is Rouhani.
- On June 12, 2009 there was an election where the previous president, Ahmadinejad was re-elected. Millions of Iranians and opponents from the "Green Movement" went to the streets to demonstrate against what they called an illegal election. Violence unfolded throughout the country. Mr. Moussavi, the opposition leader, declared himself the winner and called for nullifying the election's results. Ayatollah Khamenei, the Supreme religious leader, declared the elections valid with President Mahmoud Ahmadinejad the winner. This was the worst crisis in Iran since 1979 when the Shah was forced out and the Islamic Revolution brought in the Ayatollah.

- American and world leaders have tried to topple the theocratic government and replace it with a democracy. Iranian students and the young are anti-government and have been actively demonstrating in the streets. 70% of the population of Iran is under the age of 30. 33% of the population of Iran lives in Teheran. 33% lives in large cities near Teheran. The future of Iran, and its politics, is in the hands of their young population.
- The Iranian Ayatollahs and clerics are part of the government's power structure and they are served by a strong, vicious corps of different type of Police: The *Basijs,* who number 3 million, but some sources claim as many as 11 million. During demonstrations, the *Basij,* ride on motorcycles and beat protesters with clubs and electric prods. The demonstrators force the *Basij* off their motorcycles and burn the motorcycles. Other groups from the government are: *Revolutionary Guards,* who number 120,000; the *Artesh* list as many as 430,000 enforcers. In addition, police from Lebanon's *Hezbollah* and Palestinan *Hamas,* come to help the religious police in Iran.
- In August 2010, Iran unmasked the completion of their first *drone* with the capacity to travel 620 miles. The entire state of Israel is within this area.
- As of the summer of 2010, the U.N. has approved new sanctions against Iran, but Russia and China have not voted in agreement with the U.N. Security Council. In protest, hundreds of detainees have been tortured and raped by guards and interrogators, often at secret detention centers. The Iranian government's crackdown on dissidents has been horrific.
- The divorce rate has soared in Iran as women defy tradition and seek employment outside the house. In the past decade, the number of divorce has tripled In Tehran; the ratio is 1 divorce for every 3.76 marriages. Nationwide in Iran, there is 1 divorce for every 7 marriages. Iranian women have initiated the divorces as early as in their first year of marriage. 20% of the women have entered the work force. More than half the student population at universities are women.

c. Increase in Human Rights Abuses:

- The Islamists and Fundamentalists have imposed harsher penalties. As of 2007, there has been an increase in death penalties by hanging for citizens convicted of murder and drug smuggling. Increase in double amputations of right hand and left foot as punishment.

2. Public Response:

- The Iranian government was angry about the success of *Persepolis*. In France, the Iranian Ambassador contested against the French Ministry of Culture for submitting this film as France's entry for the 2008 Oscar for Best Foreign Language Film. Iran claimed it depicts their country badly. France replied that most of the film takes place in Vienna and Paris, not in Teheran.
- The Iranian government organization, *Iran Farabi Foundation*, sent a letter to the French embassy in Teheran, stating that the Cannes Film Festival has chosen a film about Iran that has presented an unrealistic rendering of the glorious Islamic Revolution.
- The French government has integrated *Persepolis* into their high school history curriculum to teach students about Iran. In addition, the French educational system now uses Film and Art as studies for all students.
- Arab countries have criticized, even protested and violently demonstrated, against the film's use of an image of God who talks. Such an image of the face of God is not allowed in the Islamic religion.

3. Actors And Directors:

- In an interview for French "e-media," Ms. Satrapi commented how she sees her film: "It's a story about love, family, how changes in a country cause personal turmoil and how the individual finds his way. It's a film that shows a point of view that is personal, not a political tract."

4. Awards:

- Cannes Film Festival, France
  2007– Tied – Jury Prize – Vincent Paronnaud and Marjane Satrapi
  2007– Nominated – Palme d'Or – Marjanene Satrapi and Vincent Paronnaud

- Golden Globes, USA
  2008- Nominated- Best Foreign Language Film- France

- Academy Awards, USA
  2008– Nominated – Best Animated Feature Film – France. New York Film
  Critics Circle Award, USA
  2007– Won – Best Animated Film

Bibliography of Films: Filmography
Further Global Study Resources through Film:

Famous Iranian Film Directors:

Mohsen Makhmalbaf:

- *The Gardener*
- *Gabbeh*
- *The Peddler*
- *A Moment of Innocence*
- *The Cyclist*
- *Kandahar*
- *Boycott*
- *Marriage of the Blessed*
- *Once Upon a Time*
- *Cinema*
- *The Actor*
- *Bread and Flower*
- *Time of Love*
- *The Man Who Came with the Snow*

Abbas Kiarostami:

- *Close-Up*
- *Taste of Cherry*
- *Ten*
- *Five*
- *The Wind Will Carry Us*
- *Through the Olive Trees*
- *ABC Africa*
- *The Experience*

- *The Traveler*
- *Colors*
- *First Case, Second Case*
- *Where Is the Friend's Home?*
- *Life and Nothing More*
- *Shirin*
- *Certified Copy*

Jafar Panahi:

- *The White Balloon*
- *The Journey*
- *The Mirror*
- *The Circle*
- *Crimson Gold*
- *Offside*
- *This Is Not A Film*
- *Taxi*

Majid Majidi:

- *Children of Heaven*
- *The Color of Paradise*
- *Baran*
- *The Willow Tree*
- *Barefoot to Herat*
- *The Song of Sparrows*

Bahman Ghobadi:

- *No One Knows About Persian Cats*
- *A Time for Drunken Horses*
- *Marooned in Iraq*
- *Turtles Can Fly*

Samira Makhmalbaf:

- *The Apple*
- *Blackboard*

- *11 September*
- *5 in the Afternoon*
- *Two-Legged Horse*

Animated Films:

- *Up, dir Pete Docter* (U.S.A.)
- *The Bee Movie* (U.S.A.)
- *Triplettes of Belleville* (France)
- *Peanuts* (U.S.A.)
- *Ratatouille* (France)
- *Waltz with Beshir* (Israel)
- *Princess Mononoke* (Japan)
- *Spirited Away* (Japan)
- *Finding Nemo* (U.S.A.)
- *Ponyo* (Japan)
- *Sita Sings the Blues* (U.S.A.)
- *Avatar* (U.S.A.)
- *Madagascar* (U.S.A.)

CHAPTER 4

SEPARATION (IRAN)

1. **TITLE OF FILM:** *A Separation*
2. **YEAR OF RELEASE:** 2011
3. **COUNTRY:** Iran
4. **DIRECTOR:** Asghar Farhadi
5. **LANGUAGE:** Persian
6. **RUNNING TIME:** 123 minutes
7. **RATING:** Unrated
8. **CURRICULUM THEMES:**

A. HISTORY and SOCIAL SCIENCE:

- **Chapter's Key Themes: Theocracy: Religious Totalitarian Government**
- **World History: Iranian Revolution; Islamic Fundamentalism; Ayatollah Khamenei; President Rouhani; Iran's Nuclear Program**
- **Geography: Tehran; Iran's Neighbors; Sunnis and Shiites; the Reign of Terror; Strait of Hormuz**
- **Economics: Class struggle; Economic Sanctions**
- **Civics, Citizenship and Government: Divorce; Judicial System; Sharia Law; Human Rights Abuses**

B. LITERATURE and VISUAL ARTS:

- **World Literature: Graphic Novel: Persepolis**
- **Media Studies: Film Clips and Scene Discussions; Cinema as a reflection of politics: Hidden message, what is the truth; Censorship; Cinematography: Camera's Blocked Images**
- **Philosophy/Critical Thinking: What is the Truth? What is the Morality?**
- **Art: Carpets**
- **Technology: ePals; Diigo; wikis**

Introduction:

Separation was directed by Asghar Farhadi; screenplay by Asghar Farhadi; produced by Asghar Farhadi; cinematography by Mahmoud Kalari; edited by Hayedeh Safiyari; music by Sattar Oraki; released by FilmIran (Iran) and Sony Pictures Classics (U.S.A.); (123 minutes)

Nader .... *Peyman Moaadi*
Simin .... *Leila Hatami*
Termeh ....*Sarina Farhadi*
Razieh .... *Sareh Bayat*

Cinema has the power to transport viewers to worlds they may not be able to visit. In doing so, it becomes a visual vehicle for us to learn about a country and to discuss it. The goal is to bring to light an element of Truth. In *A Separation*, we are struck by the fact that both the storyline and the setting in Tehran are more about what is not said or shown than what is. We are continuously baffled on many levels as we prod through the film to find out what is the Truth.

There is a strong link between geo-politics and the film, which presents "separations" from multiple perspectives in present-day Tehran. The film shows a dehumanization and break-down of their society's pillars: family, marriage and religion.

The question the director asks is what happens to the individual in a totalitarian/theocratic government? Similar to human interaction under Communism, in theocratic Iran, the animal in man emerges in order to survive. "Every man for himself" dictates actions. Human dignity is disregarded and truth is blurred. When we leave the theater and discuss the film, we wonder if people in the West are any different from those in Iran. The politicians say one thing but the film, *A Separation*, shows another.

Pivotal Moments in History:

1502-1736	**Safavid Empire** established a great Iranian empire· and established Shi'a Islam as the official religion.
1925-1979	**Pahlavi Era** Reza Shah ruled for almost 16 years until 1941, when he was forced to abdicate during World War II for his pro-Fascist ideology. • He established an authoritarian government that valued nationalism, militarism, secularism, state censorship, state propaganda, and anti-communism.

	Iran was a vital oil-supply source. Reza Shah's son Mohammad Reza Shah Pahlavi, came to power during World War II with U.S. and U.K. help. He ruled until 1979 with a dictatorial government.
1979	**Iranian Revolution and the Islamic Republic** The revolution that transformed Iran from an absolute monarchy to an Islamic Republic under Supreme Leader Ayatollah Ruhollah Khomeini. The ideology of revolutionary government was populist, nationalist and most of all Shi'a Islam (Shiiites). Iran's prior modernization and capitalist economy was replaced by populist and Islamic economic and cultural policies. Much industry was nationalized, laws and schools Islamicized, and Western influences banned (the danger of "Westoxification")

1979-1989	1979-1981	**Khomeini Era** **Iranian Hostage Crisis (1979-1989):** Fifty-two Americans were held hostage for 444 days after a group of revolutionary Islamist students took over the American Embassy in Tehran. **Iran-Iraq War (19980-1988):** Iraq, under Saddam Hussein, took advantage of the chaos in Iran to invade. This prompted Iran to enter into negotiations with the U.S.
	1981-1989	**Khamenei Presidency** Ayatollah Khamenei served as president. The President is elected by the Ayatollah. Under his reign, Iran's regime is a Theocracy.
1989-present	**Khamenei Era** Ali Khamenei is elected Supreme Leader. 2009 – President Ahmadinejad beat his reformist opponent and protests broke out demanding a recount. The government supported Ahmadinejad and made many arrests during the protests. This demolished the legitimacy of the country in the eyes of its people and of the international community. 2013 – Hassan Rouhani becomes President. He has spoken of co-operating more with the West.	

Pre-Screening Questions:
History and Social Science:

1. Freedom House is an independent watchdog organization monitoring free-dom around the world. It classified Iran as a 6 (the scale is 1 to 7 with 1 being most free) for political rights and civil liberties. What does this say about Iran's

position in the world? Compare the implications of the Freedom House score with Mr. Farhadi"s representation of freedom in the film, *A Separation*: does fiction match reality?

2. The Islamic Revolution brought changes for the role of women and men in Iran. In what way did women gain more equality in Iran? In what way did they lose it?

Hints:

What women have gained:

- more than half college students are female;
- more than half doctors and government employees are female.

What women have lost:

- Judges interpret Sharia Law in favor of men;
- Divorce and custody laws favor men;
- Men can easily file divorce while women cannot.

3. What crucial social institutions are repressed, censored, or controlled in Iran? (e.g., political parties, newspapers, Internet, television, literature, cinema, labor unions, and other private organizations.) In groups, students can illustrate one on a poster without using words; other groups can try to guess what they represent, like in a game of charades.

Pivotal Moments in Film:

- *A Separation* begins by introducing us to our two main characters, the wife Simin and the husband Nader, who are presenting their case for a divorce in front of a judge. The wife wants to leave Iran with a visa she has recently secured for the family. The husband wants to remain in Iran to take care of his elderly father. We share in deciding "who is right or wrong" and "should a divorce be granted?" And if there is a divorce, who should have custody of their 11-year-old daughter, Termeh?
- The opposite of truth is not always a lie, and in the film, each person is right: everyone has logical reasons. Yet the characters give the truth in incomplete piecemeal; the director withholds visual scenes from his viewers; and vital

information is missing. What he does show just reinforces uncertainty. Words and actions become blurred.

- As the film unfolds, we become familiar with the couple's unraveling relationship as well as Iran's complicated legal proceedings. When we listen to the evidence, the director skillfully unfolds a series of *separations*. The human condition is deteriorating as symbolized by Nader's demented father who loses his dignity to disease – Alzheimer's. Next, dehumanization is presented by the secondary characters: the housekeeper, Razieh, who is hired to take care of the elderly father; and her unemployed, debt-ridden husband. They represent a schism in Iran's society: the poor and religious against the educated class. Iran's male-dominated society is also threatened by the two wives who make decisions without getting their husbands' consent. Tehran, itself, is breaking down as we see modern traffic chaos with cars targeting jaywalkers. Police stations and court-rooms are overwhelmed with confusion and injustice. Witnesses and neighbors no longer know if or when to lie. The director's scenes are relentless as he overwhelms us with shots of Iran's crumbling society until he reaches his goal: Iran's future. The 11-year-old daughter, Termeh, the director's own daughter, needs to know the Truth in order to respect her parents. And the parents, who truly love their daughter, wrestle with their responsibility and ability to tell the Truth.

- No one can judge what is True, neither the characters nor the viewers. At the end, there is no answer, just as we are not privy to the daughter's decision of which parent she chooses to live with.

Suggested Activities:
- *Ask your group to draw an alphabet chart to remind them of the story and plot. This is a way to recall the sequence of events and conflicts. Divide into small groups. Ask each group to list the letters of the alphabet from "A" to "Z." For each letter, they should write a key word or phrase from the film, e.g. for "A" they can list apartment house, automobile, accident, advisor on telephone, attorney, etc.*
- *It is always fun to discuss a film – to share ideas and questions enhances the film's message. An interesting comparison to* A Separation *is the American film,* Kramer vs. Kramer. *This American film is years old, but the message is more and more poignant each day as divorce rates become more costly to human relationships. After seeing both films, it makes a discussion more challenging.*
- *How did this film pass Iranian censorship? An interesting comparison can be made with director Jafar Panahi. He directed a series of award-winning films:* The Circle, Crimson Gold, Offside, This Is Not A Film, Taxi, Closed Curtain. *A debate can be made to discuss what role the artist has in a totalitarian government.*

- *In* A Separation *we see the actual city of Tehran, very unusual in Iranian cinema because of censorship. However, in a prior film,* The Song of Sparrows, *directed by Majid Majidi in 2009 – nominated for an Oscar – we see several scenes of Tehran. Is there a difference in a few years how Tehran is depicted?*

Post-Screening Questions:
History and Social Science:

1. Discuss the different social and religious backgrounds between the two couples: Nader and Simin; Razieh and her husband.

Curriculum Themes:
A. History and Social Science:

Chapter's Key Themes: Theocracy: Religious Totalitarian Government in Iran

a. The word theocracy comes from the Greek, *theokratia,* which means "the rule (*kratia*) of God (*theo*)." Theocracy is a form of government in which only God and His laws are sovereign. The government claims to rule on behalf of God or a higher power, as specified by the nation's religion.
b. Iran's Theocracy is defined by the government that is ruled by religious leaders who use the Book of Law of the country, the Koran from Iran, which contains the basic tenets of Religion and Law.
c. Most observers consider Iran to be a theocracy with the Ayatollah as Supreme Leader. But Iranian authorities deny this and consider their government to be a "Theodemocracy" or "Religious Democracy." Some people see this as a play on words to camouflage the restricted Totalitarian government that exists in Iran.
d. In Iran, there is a Guardian Council composed of clerics that approves all candidates who run for government office. The Ayatollah is the head of the government. The president is second to the Ayatollah.
e. Iranians are Muslims and a religious Muslim follows the "Five Pillars of Islam":

1. They believe that they should be a good Muslim.
2. They believe that God should be worshipped and that Muhammad is his Prophet.

3. There is a call to pray five times a day, always facing Eastward towards Makkah (Mecca). They should pray at least one time a day.

4. They donate money or pay a portion of their earnings to the poor.

5. They try to make a pilgrimage once in their life to Makkah (Mecca). This is called *hajj*.

Suggested Activities:

- *Ask your group to define and give examples of how Muslims worship: they can discuss the role of the mosque; why women wear head coverings; and what is the role of the Iman in the religion.*

Hints:

- The Koran (Qur'an) requires that women and men cover their head. Men wear a cap, the style and shape varies. Women wear head scarves (*hijab*) and sometimes they cover their entire body with a *burqa*, a long robe or cloak that covers their face

- American and world leaders have tried to topple Iran's theocratic government and replace it with a democracy. Not all Iranians are anti-west. Support comes from the following: 70% of the population of Iran is under the age of 30 years old. 33% of the population of Iran lives in Tehran. 33% lives in large cities near Tehran.

1. World History:

a. The Iranian Revolution:

- The Iranian Revolution also known as the Islamic Revolution, began in 1978 with demonstrations against the Shah. He was forced to flee the country in 1979.

- Nationalists, Marxists and Communists joined with Islamic traditionalists to overthrow the Shah, but the government that came in next under Ayatollah Khomeini was no better.

- Ayatollah Khomeini had been imprisoned under the Shah and was sent in exile to Turkey, Iraq and France. In 1979, he returned to Tehran to lead the revolution. He took power as the "Supreme Leader" and Iran became an Islamic Republic under a totalitarian style of government and theocratic constitution.

b. Islamic Fundamentalism:

- One of the most defining features of Islamic Fundamentalism is belief in the "reopening" of the gates of jihad.
- For Fundamentalists, the law is the most essential component of Islam, leading to an overwhelming emphasis upon jurisprudence.
- An important distinction can be made between mainstream Islamists and Fundamentalists, saying a Fundamentalist is "a political individual" in search of a "more original Islam," while the Islamist is pursuing a political agenda.
- Fundamentalists are more passionate and extreme in their opposition to the perceived "corrupting influence of Western culture," avoiding Western dress, "neckties, laughter, the use of Western forms of salutation, handshakes, applause."

Other distinctions are in:

- Politics and economics. Islamists often talk of "revolution" and believe "that the society will be Islamized only through social and political action. Fundamentalists are uninterested in revolution, less interested in "modernity or by Western models in politics or economics" and less willing to associate with non-Muslims.
- Sharia Law. While both Islamists and Fundamentalists are committed to implementing Sharia, based on the Koran, Fundamentalists are more extreme in interpretation.
- Issue of women. "Islamists generally tend to favor the education of women and their participation in social and political life: the Islamist woman militates, studies, and has the right to work, but while wearing a head scarf and/or veil. Islamist groups include women's associations." While the Fundamentalist preaches for women to return to the home, Islamism believes it is sufficient that "the sexes be separated in public."

c. Ayatollah Khamenei:

- Khamenei was involved in the Islamic activities of 1963, which led to his arrest. Upon release, he resumed teaching in religious schools and mosques. He then studied and graduated from the Peoples' Friendship University of Russia, but officially there is little mention of this. Instead, his biography states that he spent a "clandestine life" in Tehran from 1966 to 1967 after which he was arrested by the police and imprisoned.

- Ayatollah Khamenei was a key figure in the Iranian Revolution of 1979. In June 1981, he narrowly escaped an assassination attempt when a bomb, concealed in a tape recorder at a press conference, exploded beside him. He was permanently injured, losing the use of his right arm.
- In 1981, he was elected President and became the first cleric to serve.
- Khamenei helped lead the country during the Iraq-Iran War against Saddam Hussein, and developed close ties with the now-powerful Revolutionary Guards. As president, he had a reputation of being deeply interested in the military.
- After Khomeini's death in 1989, he was elected the new Supreme Leader, the Ayatollah.

d. President Rouhani:

- Hassan Rouhani is known as an intellectual man, educated in Scotland, receiving his Ph.D. in Law, and writing and speaking in English.
- In 2013 he was elected President, and he redefined Iran's relations with the world. He promised greater openness and to repair the country's international standing, offering greater nuclear transparency in order to restore international trust.
- He elected as foreign minister Zarif, a western educated man and experienced diplomat, who has been his ally in negotiating Iran's nuclear program for lowering of economic sanctions, which was achieved in 2016.
- The economic policy of Hassan Rouhani focuses on the long-term economic development of Iran. It deals with increasing economic growth, increasing purchasing power for the people, and improving the business environment in the short term.
- Rouhani believes that improving the economic conditions of the people should be accomplished by reducing the wealth gap, indirectly assisting low-income groups, and cutting down high unemployment.
- Nobel Peace Prize winner, Shirin Ebadi, has criticized the human rights record of President Rouhani. Ebadi highlighted a rise in executions since Rouhani took office and accused the government of lying about the release of political prisoners. Ebadi said Rohani may have a reputation as a moderate reformer but so far his government was sending "bad signals" on human rights.
- Rouhani is a supporter of women's rights. In a speech after he was elected as the President of Iran, he said, "There must be equal opportunities for women. There is no difference between man and woman."

- On 27 September 2013, a day after Rouhani's visit to New York and the U.N. General Assembly, the two countries' foreign ministers met. Also, Rouhani had a phone call with President Obama that marked the two countries' highest political exchange since 1979. However, due to this phone call Rouhani was protested by conservatives when he returned to Tehran.

e. Iran's Nuclear Program:

- Western countries, the United States, the European Union, and NATO have imposed economic sanctions on Iran to pressure them into terminating their nuclear program and halting production of centrifuges capable of enriching uranium. Iran has repeatedly denied that they have a uranium enrichment program to develop nuclear arms, stating that their nuclear development is for peaceful purposes of electricity and medicine.
- Iran's enrichment plants are numerous and installed underground in caves, deep under mountains and tunnels, making them difficult to detect or destroy.
- The nuclear program of Iran dates back to the 1950's under the Shah of Iran with the help of the United States, President Eisenhower, and western European countries as part of a joint "Atoms for Peace" program.
- In 1967, the Tehran Nuclear Research Center (TNRC) was established, run by the Atomic Energy Organization of Iran (AEOI). The TNRC was equipped with a U.S.-supplied, 5-megawatt nuclear research reactor, which was fueled by highly enriched uranium.
- In 1976, President Gerald Ford signed an agreement with Iran, offering the chance to buy a U.S.-built reprocessing facility for extracting plutonium from nuclear reactor fuel. At the time, Richard Cheney was the White House chief of staff and Donald Rumsfeld was the Secretary of Defense.
- After the Iranian revolution of 1979 deposed the Shah, the United States stopped fulfilling their contracts. Iran then continued independently to develop their nuclear program.
- Russia, under the government of Putin, has supplied Iran with nuclear fuel as of 2007 for Iran's light-water reactor and electricity program. Russia and the U.S. agree that the supply of nuclear fuel to Iran means that Iran will have no need to continue its own uranium enrichment program, a process that can provide fuel for a nuclear bomb or nuclear reactor.
- As of 2015, Iran has agreed with the U.S. and U.N. to stop their uranium enrichment facilities and their intentions to build a nuclear bomb. There will

be regular inspections of their nuclear facilities to determine if they are being honest. If yes, 140 billion dollars of embargoed money will be returned to Iran for their co-operation in the beginning of 2016.

2. Geography:

General Information:

- Iran's area roughly equals the size of the United Kingdom, France, Spain and Germany combined. Iran is the 18th largest country in the world.
- Its borders are with Azerbaijan and Armenia to the northwest; the Caspian Sea to the north; Turkmenistan to the northeast; Pakistan to the east; Turkey to the west; and the waters of the Persian Gulf and the Gulf of Oman to the south.
- Iran is one of the world's most mountainous countries in its region. The eastern part consists of deserts that are mostly uninhabited.
- There are small plains found along the remaining coast of the Persian Gulf, the strategic Strait of Hormuz and the Sea of Oman.
- Iran's economy is based on government control of and state ownership of oil, gas and large enterprises. Iran ranks second in the world in natural gas reserves and third in oil reserves. Agriculture remains one of the largest employers. Unemployment is high in other sectors.

Suggested Activities:
- *Your group can discuss how the geography of Iran has presented a major problem for its environment. Pollution is high and cars use diesel gas.*

a. Tehran:

- In *A Separation* we see the actual city of Tehran. This is unusual for Iranian cinema, which usually uses the countryside as the setting. In *A Separation,* Tehran is a reflection of the opposing couples and we see how they are part of the city in two opposing ways. One couple drives a car, one for the wife and one for the husband; while the housekeeper has to depend on the bus. How each character responds and functions to the flow of traffic in Tehran is important to note. The physical environment influences the individual, and this can change depending on the socio-economic class of the individual.

Suggested Activities:

- *Your group can form groups to discuss life in Tehran. Include the following topics: what do we know about the living conditions of the two families; how do the two daughters spend their time; what clues does the director give us about city sounds, traffic patterns, overcrowding, stores, friendships and relationships, government buildings, services to citizens, neighborhood of apartments. Does the director have a point of view – how he sees the city and how he wants us to see the city.*

b. Iran's Neighbors:

- Syria – What will happen? Will Assad remain the leader? Who will follow?
- Egypt – The "Arab Spring" and subsequent removal of dictator-leader Mubarak have brought in the Military for leadership with General Sisi as President. Sisi is trying to curtail the Muslim Brotherhood and Islamists in Egypt.
- Saudi Arabia – Leader, King Abdullah, in October 2013, rejected his country's "coveted" election to a non-permanent seat on the United Nations Security Council as a protest about developments in the Middle East. In 2015, King Abdullah died and was succeeded by King Salman.
- Iraq –Sunnis vs. Shiites with the threat of extremist Al-Qaeda, ISIS and Fundamentalists.
- Jordan – King Abdullah is an ally of the U.S. and maintains cordial relations with Israel. Jordan has 50% Palestinian refugees living in their country, and does not want the return of the West Bank from Israel to Jordan.
- Lebanon – Hezebollah's Shiite leader, Nasrallah, supports and helps arm, the governments of Syria, Iran and Iraq.
- Gaza Strip - Gaza is between Israel and Egypt. It is land that belonged to Egypt, but was seized by Israel after they won the six-day war in June 1967. Israel has allowed this territory to have an independent government. The government is Hamas, a terrorist group at war with Israel. Fatah and Hamas have joined forces.
- The West Bank – belonged to Jordan. It has an independent government, Fatah, previously known as the PLO's. Today, Palestine has a special status at the U.N.
- The Golan Heights - belonged to Syria. These territories were also seized by Israel after they won the six-day war in June 1967. Israel has not loosened its control.
- Persian Gulf Arab States: refer to the rich oil producing countries on or near the Persian Gulf. They are: Kuwait, Iraq, Bahrain, Oman, Qatar, Saudi Arabia and the United Arab Emirates.
- Who are the following?

- Fatah– previously known as the PLO's, with their Founding leader, Yasser Arafat until his death in 2004, maintains power in the West Bank. Abbas is the leader and has said that he will retire in 2016.
- Hamas – is the opposition Palestinian party, maintaining power in the Gaza Strip. The United States, Canada, the European Union, and Japan classify Hamas as a terrorist organization while Iran, Russia, Turkey, and Arab nations do not.
- Kurds – is the second largest ethnic group in the world, located in Turkey, Syria, Iran, and Iraq. This collective geographical area is referred to as Kurdistan, which the Kurds would like to have as an independent country.
- ISIS - what is a califate? Where do they have territories? How do they get their money? Are they Sunnis or Shiites?

c. Sunnis and Shiites:

- "The Islamic Religion is divided throughout the world into 2 branches: Shiites and Sunnis." (See the chart in chapter 14: *The Other Son*)
- There are more than a billion Muslims worldwide. 85-90% are Sunnis. 10-15% are Shiites, also pronounced as S*hia's.*
- Despite many common beliefs and their shared obedience to the Koran, their differences make co-existence difficult.
- What countries have a majority of Shiites? Iran, Iraq, Bahrain and Azerbaijan.
- What countries have a majority of Sunnis? Afghanistan, Algeria, Morocco, Tunisia, Egypt, Kuwait, Indonesia, Pakistan, Saudi Arabia, Syria, Turkey, United Arab Emirates and Yemen.

d. The Reign of Terror:

There are a dozen countries in North America, Europe, Asia, and the Middle East that have been involved, willingly or unwillingly, in terrorism and wars. For the millions of people in these countries, the threat and fear of terrorism has been no less frightening than it was 300 years ago in France during the Reign of Terror.

Which countries are involved today?

- *United States:* under President Obama, ISIS in Iraq and Syria, as well as the Taliban in Afghanistan and Pakistan, has the American government fully involved, despite the wish not to be.

- *Turkey:* is a key and pivotal player. And yet, Turkey, is more worried by the PKK, a Kurdish militant group on their own soil and the threat of a Kurdistan, than by other terrorist groups.
- *Iran:* a Shiite Muslim country, is involved battling Saudi Arabia, a Sunni Muslim country, in a power struggle for prominence in the Middle East, and as a competitor for exporting oil. Iran has been a key supporter of Bashar al-Assad of Syria.
- *Russia:* wants to reassert its military position on the Syrian coast where their fleets and military / naval base has access to the Mediterranean Sea for trading. Russia has propped up Assad as protection for their own spot on the Mediterranean.
- *Syria:* Assad has positioned himself to be a bulwark in the region against ISIS and rebel terrorist groups from taking over Syria.
- *Saudi Arabia:* is the Sunni country that's the birthplace of ISIS and Wahhabiaism. The monarchy is conflicted for they fear their own power can be usurped. They have been busy fighting Iran and Yemen, against the Shiitee Houthi rebels.
- *Iraq:* split by both Shiite and Sunni forces in the same country, they struggle to survive as a country. Their Sunni tribes and Kurds have helped the Iraqi government keep ISIS at bay.
- *Israel:* has been busy protecting itself from Hezbollah and Hamas. ISIS seems less a threat to Israel's stability.
- *Yemen:* a Sunni Muslim country that has been busy fighting Shiite Houthi rebels whom Iran supports and Saudi Arabia opposes.
- *France:* is the most involved European country fighting terrorist groups in Mali and Africa. They have also had the most attacks at home from their citizens who have been trained by terrorist groups.

e. Strait of Hormuz:

- The Strait of Hormuz is an important strait, a narrow body of water, located off the northern coast of Iran that connects the Persian Gulf and the Indian Ocean. It is strategically located and it is the only sea passage for shipping oil from the Persian Gulf. If Iran would close their area of the strait, the shipment of oil for many areas would be curtailed.
- There is no mention of this geographical straight in the film, but it is an example of what the western world questions about Iran's truthful intentions. The

Iranian government has repeatedly threatened to close the straight to shipping traffic.

Suggested Activity:
- *Your group can discuss the Strait of Hormuz: the United States had deployed troops and ships to this region during the Persian Gulf in 1991 when George Bush Sr. was president.*

Hints:
- The Strait of Hormuz at its narrowest is 21 nautical miles (39 km) wide. Around 20% of the world's oil, which is about 35% of seaborne traded oil, passes through the strait.

3. Economics:

a. Class struggle:

- Conflict between people can arise from differences in economic and social standing. Even when the majority of people in society are governed by a Theocracy and believe in the same religion, there is a difference in living conditions, educational level, job opportunities, hosing, and luxuries. This brings competition and human conflict. This is illustrated by the two opposing families: Nader-Simin and Razieh and her husband.

Hints:
- After the Iranian Revolution in 1979, the middle class population doubled from 15% to 32% in 2000. Social class in Iran is divided accordingly: upper (landowners, industrialists, financiers), middle, working class (factory workers,, mechanics, construction workers, carpenters, electricians, plumbers) and lower class. Education and degrees have become important marks of class separation in Iran.

b. Economic Sanctions:

- As of 2016, there has been the cessation of Iran's embargos from the U.S., E.U., U.N and NATO, for Iran's agreeing to stop their nuclear development. Iran will receive more than 100 billion dollars in back hold-ings. They have started to use this money to update their oil sites and petro production with the help of joint ventures with France, Spain, Italy and the Netherlands, to export oil at a very competive price and thus bring down the price of oil.

Suggested Activities:
- *Students can research and disicuss why the United States is not getting involved in such a lucrative opportunity to work with Iran's export oil industry?*
- *How will Iran's oil industry compete with Saudi Arabia? Russia? How will it help Europe and the E.U.? How will it not?*

4. Civics, Citizenship and Government:

a. Divorce:

- For the first time in an Iranian film, we see a separation of family and mar-riage. Although not prohibited, divorce is strongly discouraged in Islam and disapproved by Iranian culture. A religious saying (hadith) attributed to the Prophet Mohammad says, "Of all things permissible, divorce is the most reprehensible."
- The situation is aggravated because Islamic laws give men the right to custody of their children after age three in the case of sons, and after seven in the case of daughters. After the Islamic Revolution of 1979, this law was replaced by a Special Civil Court ruling that women could include a specific condition (work, travel abroad) that could change this ruling. A magistrate in Family Court could then rule custody of children to the mother.

Suggested Activity:
- *Simin, a professional modern woman, educated and from the upper middle class, has a visa to leave the country and wants to do so with her family. Simin does not want her daughter to grow up under the political situation in Iran. However, Nader does not want to leave his sick father. At the end of the film, in family court, their separation is made permanent and Termeh is asked to decide by the judge whom she wants to live with. Divide into two positions and discuss what you think the daughter will answer and why.*

Hints:

- The divorce rate has soared in Iran as women defy tradition and seek employment outside the house. In the past decade, the number of divorce has tripled In Tehran; the ratio is 1 divorce for every 3.76 marriages. Nationwide in Iran, there is 1 divorce for every 7 marriages. Iranian women have initiated the divorces as early as in their first year of marriage. 20% of the women have entered the work force.

b. Judicial System:

- The political system in Iran is one of a kind in that it blends theocracy with some form of democracy. There are institutions to represent both parts in government, but the theocratic part has clear superiority.
- Theocratic institutions: National Government with the supreme leader, Guardian Council, Expediency Council.
- Democratically-elected institutions: The President, Assembly of Religious Experts, National Assembly.

c. Sharia Law:

- Sharia Law is used to refer both to the Islamic system of law and the totality of the Islamic way of life. It is a code for living for Muslims. Sharia is derived from the *Koran,* which is believed by Muslims to be the word of God, as dictated to the prophet Muhammad by the angel, Gabriel, and illustrates the exemplary life of the Prophet, Muhammad. Some Sharia laws are:
- No sex outside a marriage
- No adultery
- No drinking of alcohol
- No stealing
- Specific laws for women who get divorced and women who inherit money and property.

Punishments are:

- Flogging (whipping)
- Stoning
- Amputation of a hand for stealing

d. Human Rights Abuses:

- The Islamists and Fundamentalists have imposed harsh penalties on their citizens that have been considered by western nations as "Human Rights abuses" -
- As of 2007, there has been an increase in death penalties by hanging for citizens convicted of murder and drug smuggling.
- Increase as of 2008 of double amputations of right hand and left foot that makes it almost impossible for the condemned to walk with a cane or crutches. Amputation has been a punishment in Iran since the Islamic revolution of 1979 but rarely did they have "double amputation."

Hints:
- In 1948, the United Nations adopted the Universal Declaration of Human Rights which established guidelines to assure all people with freedoms. These are standards that aim to protect the individual citizen from abuses. These rights include: freedom from slavery; freedom from torture; equal protection of the law; freedom of thought, opinion and religion; the right to education; the right to good health, shelter and food; the right to work and to form trade unions; freedom from arbitrary arrest; and the right to a fair trial;
- For more information about the United Nations Human Rights agency, visit their site, www.un.org/rights

5. World Literature:

a. Graphic Novel: Persepolis

- A graphic novel is typically bound in a longer and more durable format than familiar comic books. The graphic novel is sold in bookstores rather than at newsstands.
- In recent years, the definition of the *graphic novel* has not been strictly defined. In Europe and Asia, it is a popular literary genre.
- It suggests a story that has a beginning, middle and end, as opposed to an ongoing series with continuing characters; and it deals with more mature themes. The term is commonly used to disassociate works from the juvenile or humorous connotations of comics and *comic book*, implying that the graphic novel is more serious or literary than comics.

Suggested Activities:
- *Have your group research Marjane Satrapi's Persepolis as it appeared in 4 graphic novels and compare the film with her literature. Interesting discussions can be based on:*
- *is the film, Perseplois, loyal to the novels?*
- *what are the different characteristics of both genres, literature and film?*
- *what is the effect on the audience with the different genres?*
- *Your group can discuss the famous European graphic novels The Adventures of Tintin and/ or Astérix and Obelix and compare them to Persepolis.*
- *A fun activity is to write a graphic novel either in pairs or groups.*

6. Media Studies:

a. Film Clips and Scene Discussions:

- *Universalism:* (Scene: 01:36 –> 02:30 seconds)
  In many cultures, universalism is the quality ascribed to an entity whose existence is consistent throughout the universe, e.g. the human being.

  What makes this film special, is that it deals with universal human values, problems and emotions. And because of that, we realize that the Iranian people are similar to us. The opening scene sets the stage for this theme: "What you are saying are not good reasons for a divorce. If there is something else let me know. He won't come with me. If he does, I'll withdraw my request for a divorce. Will you come? No, I won't. My father. I can't leave him."

- *Truth. What is the Truth?* (Scene: 00:47 –> 00:49 seconds)
  The plot and action of this story is moved forward by a series of un-truths. One un-truth is the following: "Did you have a fight with that woman? What did she do? Tied the old man to the bed and locked the door. Went after her own errands. If I'd gotten there 10 minutes later I would've lost him. He had fallen off the bed. I don't know for how long he was like that. She said you hit her. Nonsense. Then why is she in the hospital? I just pushed her out of the house. The sister-in-law called and told me off. Saying that if she dies, her blood will be on your hands."

After the characters discuss what is true, what is a lie, we, the viewer, do not know anymore what is real. Is the director making a comment about Iranian politics or the

Iranian government? There are several situations throughout the story that confuse truth with non-truth. Your group can discuss these.

- *Justice:* (Scene: 1:01 –> 1:03 minutes)
  This scene is difficult for Americans. We wonder what is true and what is the punishment? "You have to post bail. What for? You're charged with murder. I can't let you leave. How am I going to post bail? I live at my dad's. He has Alzheimer's. If you don't you'll go to jail. I can't go to jail. I've left him at home to come here. I can't go to jail. It's not in my hands. It's the law."

  Such questions in America are discussed with the presence of lawyers, a jury, and/ or a judge. In Iran, justice is different.

b. Cinema can be a Reflection of Politics:

What is the "hidden message," and what is the Truth? The inner core of the film is "hidden." What is the Truth in this film? We wonder:

- Who stole the money that was in the apartment? And for what purpose?
- Did Nader push Razieh? Down the stairs or just away from the door?
- When did Razieh have a miscarriage?
- Did Razieh's husband take the money that was offered to him by Nader and Simin?
- Who will Termeh live with after the divorce?
- And above all, the hidden question that is never asked: a political truth, what is the extent of the many separations in Iranian society?

c. Censorship: Document-Based Question (D.B.Q.)

"Iran's Leaders Shut Down Independent Film Group" -
"http://www.nytimes.com/2012/01/12/world/middleeast/irans-leaders-shut-down-independent-film-group.html?_r=0 Full article, January 11, 2012

- *A Separation* was directed, written and produced by Mr. Farhadi, (independently financially) and therefore, it came out of Iran's Independent Film Group called the House of Cinema, which was "the only domestic organization that supports independent film" in Iran. Somehow, the censors let pass many controversial points of this film. To redress their sloppiness, Iran's Culture Ministry formally dissolved the House of Cinema in mid-January 2012, and moved to replace it with a committee that would not deviate from strict Islamic censorship guidelines.

- Founded 20 years ago, the House of Cinema has more than 5,000 members and is the parent group for a range of motion picture guilds in Iran. It has acted to protect their financial interests and creative rights, so the breakup of the organization, if not reversed, could fracture and silence Iran's last remaining autonomous outlet of visual artistic expression.

- Shirin Ebadi, an Iranian women's rights activist and Nobel laureate (2003), now living in exile in London, wrote in an open letter to the United Nations that the censorship and the closing of the House of Cinema, should be added to the list of Iran's human rights violations now under investigation.

- "Professional and civil institutions are the very tools of democracy," she wrote in the letter. Particularly since the 2009 election, she wrote, "several professional and civic organizations for journalists, writers, students, workers, bus drivers have been shut down, and the latest example is the House of Cinema."

D.B.Q

1. What political movement was the House of Cinema associated with?
   a. the Green movement
2. What argument did Iranian officials cite for the closing of the House of Cinema?
   a. an invalid license
3. Which of the following is NOT a role the House of Cinema had before its dissolution? Protecting the creative rights of several motion picture groups; producing films approved by the Supreme Leader himself; representing a tool of democracy; protecting the financial rights of smaller film groups.
   a. Producing films approved by the Supreme Leader himself.

Suggested Activities:

- *Cinema has the power to make political changes, even stir up rebellions and revolts. Examples of this are the films* Persepolis *and* A Separation. Persepolis *had a great power to stir up the masses in riots before political elections in Iran, 2011, as well before elections in Tunisia after the Arab Spring of 2011. A Separation had the power to cause alarm in Iran's Central government with the movement to exile the director, as well as in the Censorship department. Divide your group in half, with each half seeing the film, Persepolis and A Separation. The group should report on what the political implications of the two films are, and what was not recognized at first by the Censorship Bureau to allow A Separation to pass.*

- *How did this film, A Separation, pass Iranian censorship? An interesting comparison can be made with director Asghar Farhadi and Jafar Panahi. The latter, a little older and more acclaimed, directed a series of award-winning films: The Circle, Crimson Gold, Offside. He was tried, put in house arrest, and not allowed to direct films. A debate can be made to discuss what role does the artist have in a Totalitarian government?*

d. Cinematography: Camera's Blocked Images:

The director uses a hand-held camera and gives us a "fuzzy" shot at a time when he does not want us to see specifically what is happening. This occurs when he tells the servant to leave his apartment. For one minute, we are not sure if he pushed her as she claims, if he slammed the door on her, if he pushed her down the stairs, or if she did fall down the stairs. We get this blocked and fuzzy camera perspective also in the streets of Tehran when she is caught in a traffic jam and wants to cross the street. Is she hit by a car? The director does all this unclear filmmaking in order to confuse us and to get us to ask, what is True? The director has said that this film is more about relationships with people than politics. But again, it is difficult for us to know, what is the truth?

7. Philosophy/ Critical Thinking:

a. What is the Truth? What is the Morality?

- In the film, we are not sure if Nader caused Razieh to have a miscarriage because he pushed her out his apartment. A court is assigned to determine the cause of the miscarriage and Nader's responsibility for it. If it is proven that Nader has knowledge of Razieh's pregnancy and caused the miscarriage by his actions, he could be sentenced to one to three years imprisonment. Simin attempts to arrange a financial deal with Razieh and Houjat, who are very poor, to compensate them for the loss of their unborn child. In this segment of the film, the morality of all four characters is called into question as each one reacts in a different way to the truth of the situation and the offer for financial compensation.

Suggested Activity:

- *Ask each member of your group to take the position of one character, Simin, Nader, Razieh and Houjat, her husband. They can describe what they believe is the truth of the miscarriage and the monetary offer for compensation and link this position to match the character's moral code.*

- *Is the director trying to say something about Iran's political position related to Truth? In his film, About Elly, that was made before A Separation, but was released afterwards, the director shows his fascination, and obsession, about lies and disceptions— what some characters know but others do not, and how that discrepancy in knowledge sends shockwaves through their middle-class lives and families. About Elly opens with a group of Iranian college friends—among them three couples, two with children. A mystery story unfolds and the truth is manipulated. The only witnesse is a five-year-old girl. She wants to tell the truth to the police, but her parents manipulate her, and finally her parents teach her how to lie. This film can initiate a debate about what damage lies can cause and the relationship of Iran's culture to their politics.*

b. Separations in Iran and the United States:

- Iran is a country that is far away from the U.S. We have a different language, different government, different culture. But we do share, according to the director of the film, *A Separation,* common separations in both our societies. Discuss this concept within your group.

8. Art:

a. Carpets:

- Simin's and Nader's apartment in Tehran is very beautiful. It is obviously the home of upper class Iranians. The furniture is well chosen, especially the Iranian carpets.
- Iran is known for their beautiful Persian carpets. We see in their apartment several floor coverings of carpets. This Iranian art form began more than 2,500

years ago with nomadic tribes who used the carpets not for beauty but for practicality: to block the wind at the entrance of their hut when they did not have a door, and to cover the floor for warmth when they do not have heat. In the past hundreds of years, Persian carpets have become coveted treasures with many styles named after the areas of Iran and historical periods: Tabriz, Bukhara, Pazyrik, and Safavid.

- Carpets are woven on looms, from yarn of wool, knotted by hand, sometimes with 200 knots per square inch, with many patterns and designs, usually symbolic to express thoughts, feelings, personal relationships and values. Persian carpets have become so valuable that they are used as barter, gifts, wedding dowry, and government treasures.

Suggested Activities:
- *Have your group research Iranian (Persian) carpets. Discuss which cities in Iran are carpet centers. Share pictures of Persian carpets.*

Hints:
- During the period of the "Silk Road," nomads and merchants traded Persian (Iranian) carpets because they were easily transportable on the back of a camel. Centuries later, Persian carpets were shipped to Venice and then traded in western Europe as one of the most-sought after signs of wealth. It is said that Marco Polo was the first European to trade with oriental carpets.
- Carpet connoisseurs say that Persian carpets are special because of the quality of wool that is used and the tightness of the weave. Big centers are Shiraz and Tabriz. *Kilim* carpets, made from sheep wool, goat and camel hair, are characterized by geometric patterns. *Dhourri* carpets are made from cotton and also have geometric designs. They are even brighter in color.
- There are many books and websites for reference to learn more about Persian carpets. It is a very important, appreciated art form. Many museums have special exhibits and sections dedicated to the art of carpets.

9. Technology:

- Have your group explore to what degree Iranian students have freedom of the Internet. Have them explore if there have been any blogs, or Facebook postings about political situations in Iran? Discuss your findings.

Sidebars:

1. Awards:

- Academy Awards, USA
  2012– Won – Best Foreign Language Film of the Year, Asghar Farhadi

- Berlin Film Festival, Golden Bear, Germany
  2012– Won – Best Foreign Language Film of the Year, Asghar Farhadi

- Golden Globes, USA
  2011– Won– Best Foreign Language Film, Asghar Farhadi

- Cesar Award, France
  2012– Won – Best Foreign Language Film of the Year, Asghar Farhadi

Bibliography of Films: Filmography:
Further Global Study Resources through Film:

Famous Iranian Film Directors:

Mohsen Makhmalbaf:

- *The Gardener*
- *Gabbeh*
- *The Peddler*
- *A Moment of Innocence*
- *The Cyclist*
- *Kandahar*
- *Boycott*
- *Marriage of the Blessed*
- *Once Upon a Time*
- *Cinema*
- *The Actor*
- *Bread and Flower*
- *Time of Love*
- *The Man Who Came with the Snow*

Abbas Kiarostami:

- *Close-Up*
- *Taste of Cherry*
- *Ten*
- *Five*
- *The Wind Will Carry Us*
- *Through the Olive Trees*
- *ABC Africa*
- *The Experience*
- *The Traveler*
- *Colors*
- *First Case, Second Case*
- *Where Is the Friend's Home?*
- *Life and Nothing More*
- *Shirin*
- *Certified Copy*

Jafar Panahi:

- *The White Balloon*
- *The Journey*
- *The Mirror*
- *The Circle*
- *Crimson Gold*
- *Offside*
- *This Is Not A Film*
- *Taxi*

Majid Majidi:

- *Children of Heaven*
- *The Color of Paradise*
- *Baran*
- *The Willow Tree*
- *Barefoot to Herat*
- *The Song of Sparrows*

Bahman Ghobadi:

- *No One Knows About Persian Cats*
- *A Time for Drunken Horses*
- *Marooned in Iraq*
- *Turtles Can Fly*

Samira Makhmalbaf:

- *The Apple*
- *Blackboard*
- *11 September*
- *5 in the Afternoon*
- ***Two-Legged Horse***

CHAPTER 5

OSAMA (AFGHANISTAN)

TITLE OF FILM: *Osama*
YEAR OF RELEASE: 2003
COUNTRY: Afghanistan
DIRECTOR: Siddiq Barmak
LANGUAGE: In Dari with English subtitles
RUNNING TIME: 82 minutes
RATING: Unrated
CURRICULUM THEMES:

A. HISTORY and SOCIAL SCIENCE:

- Chapter's Key Themes: Gender discrimination; Children's rights
- World History: Major religion: Islam; War with Russia; Taliban
- Geography: Afghanistan; Pakistan
- Economics: Supply and demand: Drugs
- Civics, Citizenship and Government: Theocracy; Women's rights; Education

B. LITERATURE and VISUAL ARTS:

- World Literature: Historic fiction and historic film; Folktales: Arabic oral storytelling
- Media Studies: Film Clips and Scene Discussions; Cinematography Techniques: symbols, irony, light, color, character foil; Comparative media: Documentary; Cinema as a reflection of culture; Cinema as a reflection of politics
- Philosophy/Critical Thinking: Art imitates life; Policy paper
- Art: Carpets
- Technology: Currency; Power point presentation; Internet

Introduction:

Osama was directed by Siddiq Barmak; screenplay by Siddiq Barmak; produced by Siddiq Barmak, Julia Fraser and Julie Lebrocquy; cinematography by Ebrahim Ghafuri; edited by Siddiq Barmak; production design by Akbar Meshkini; music by Mohamed Reza Darwish; and released by United Artists in 2003. (83 minutes)

Osama.. *Marina Golbahari*
Espandi...*Arif Herati*
Mother.. *Zubaida Sahar*

The mark of an outstanding film is if it lives inside you long after you've seen it. Great films don't die, for they are not a victim of taste or time. They even have the power to predict the future. Such is the film, *Osama.*

Hillary Clinton showed *Osama* in November 2004 to members of the Senate when she was a Junior Senator from New York. She wanted to apprise her colleagues how the U.S. would support free elections in Afghanistan. Colin Powell, the American Ambassador to the United Nations, screened the film at the U.N's Dag Hammarskjold Auditorium on March 17, 2004 as he briefed all the Ambassadors why the United States will increase its military presence in Afghanistan. The film served as a visual briefing for politics and foreign policy. This is a reminder to viewers that cinema can have an impact to educate and encourage action.

Osama's mark as an important cinematic contribution is that the inner core of the film's human story is as strong as the outer level of technique. The film's message reflects how art and life intertwine. And in doing so, it transposes the viewer to another country and serves as a window to an unknown world. After such a journey, the viewer unravels the mystery of a different culture and tries to understand.

Pivotal Moments in History:

- As early as 1979, the Americans train the "Mujahideen" forces as part of the American Cold War strategy under President Carter. This group is trained in Pakistan and is comprised of discontented Muslims who oppose the atheism of the Russian Marxist regime in Afghanistan during the Russian occupation of Afghanistan, 1979-1989.
- As a result of the fighting between the Soviet Republic and Afghanistan, the Russians lose and are forced to leave Afghanistan; many Afghans escape to take

refuge in neighboring countries such as Pakistan, Iran, Iraq, and Tajikistan. However, in Afghanistan, fighting continues among the various Mujahideen factions, eventually giving rise to a state of warlords and feudal tribes. Mujahideen factions become a group of terrorist militants operating in Kashmir and Pakistan and are engaged in "Jihad" - war against Christians and Jews.

- When the Russians leave in 1989, the U.S. and its allies do little to help rebuild war-torn Afghanistan and the rebel Mujahideen forces return to Afghanistan and take advantage by staying in power.
- There are different factions of these Mujahideen rebels and in turn they fight with another group, the Taliban, who are mostly from the Kandahar region located on the border of Pakistan. The Taliban fight the Mujahideen from 1989 to 1996. The Taliban seizes the capital, Kabul, and rules Afghanistan from 1996 to 2003. At the peak of their power in 2000, the Taliban controls 95% of Afghanistan. Today, we see the Taliban forces still strong as they fight, interact, and sometimes discuss with Al-Qaeda, ISIS and other extremist groups about this war-torn country, where peace is still unknown.

Pre-Screening Questions:

1. The film, *Osama*, can be viewed as an example of gender discrimination. Discuss what that means.
2. During the Taliban's rule in Afghanistan, Afghan women experienced restrictions and violations of women's rights. What are some examples of these?

Post-Screening Questions:
A. History and Social Science:

1. What has happened in Afghanistan since September 11, 2001?
2. How was Afghanistan involved with the September 11th attacks on the United States?

Suggested Activities:
- *Ask your group to divide into pairs to do research on the Internet about Afghanistan's history. Include the country as part of Empires and even ruled by a King.*
- *Organize your research into a timeline highlighting important events and moments in Afghanistan's history leading up to September 11th, 2001.*

B. Literature and Visual Arts:

1. Discuss which scenes in the film show restrictions placed on women by the Taliban.
2. Was there any opposition by the characters in the film?

Suggested Activities:
- *Ask your group to discuss why such restrictions occurred.*
- *Split into groups with members taking an assigned scene that showcases a restriction.*
- *Analyze and evaluate the Taliban's motives behind such restrictions.*

Curriculum Themes:
A. History and Social Science:

Chapter's Key Themes: Gender Discrimination

a. Gender discrimination:

After the hospital scene, Osama returns with her mother to their house. The mother cries to the grandmother, "I wish I had a son and not a daughter so he can get food for us." The grandmother responds, "A woman with short hair looks like a man."

Suggested Activities:
- *Discuss why Osama is forced by her mother and grandmother to take on the role of a boy. What is Osama's attitude?*
- *Divide into small groups to discuss gender discrimination and the following headlines that have appeared in newspapers:*
    "Women in Iran want to attend a soccer match."
    "Women in Saudi Arabia want a Driver's License."
    "Property Inheritance Limited for Women of Pakistan."
- *Each group is then assigned a specific headline to discuss and do a comparative analysis of gender discrimination in other countries. Use as a contrast, the countries that have an advanced proponent of women's rights - Iceland, Finland, Norway, and Tunisia.*

b. Children's rights:

- One of the strongest scenes of *Osama* is the last scene. Osama, the child, is forced to become a woman. Under the Taliban, girls are sold when they are young, and often resold when their husbands tire of them. In the film, we see two scenes of child brides:

- Osama and her mother help their neighbor at a wedding ceremony and we see the bride's face as she moves her scarf. She is a mere child wearing lipstick.
- Osama's life is spared after her trial but is she truly saved? She is "sold" to Mullah Sahib.

Suggested Activities:

- *Ask your group to analyze and discuss this D.B.Q.:*
  The following document is from an article in "The Washington Post," December 13, 1997, Page A. 01. (The practice of forcing young daughters to marry older men has come under increasing assault when a 12-year-old girl killed her 30-year-old husband.)

DOCUMENT BASED QUESTION:
By Stephen Buckley
KORHOGO, Ivory Coast—
It is just after noon, and inside, in a steamy square room no larger than a prison cell, Aisha Camara is covered in a pink-and-white striped blanket. She briefly lifts a veil that hides her angular features. Her neighbors are celebrating her wedding day. The 10-year-old is not smiling.

Suggested Activities:

- *Ask your group to hold a round-table discussion about countries around the world that traffic girls as young as seven and eight years old, to be brides. (Include: India, Pakistan, Afghanistan, China, Indonesia, Vietnam, Saudi Arabia, Ivory Coast, and African countries.)*
- *Your group can use the Internet to research and find letters written by child brides or young girls who have been kidnapped and sold.*
- *Are there common themes found in the letters of these child brides, and/ or kidnapped young girls?*

1. World History:

a. Major Religion: Islam:

- Afghans are very religious. 99% are Muslims; approximately 74-89% are Sunnis; and 9-25% are Shiites. Taliban are Sunnies; Al-Qaeda are Sunnis.
- The scenes in *Osama* of the young boys being taught the Koran and Islamism at an early age, are scenes based on actual teachings in a religious school,

madrasah. We see how the students learn to pray, dress themselves with a white turban, and perform their ablutions, water purification. But as the boys pass through their religious lessons, we wonder what will happen to Osama?

Suggested Activities:
Ask members of your group to research the following:

- *What is a madrasah? What ages are the students? What subjects do they study? What countries have madrasahs? Do girls go to madrasahs? What do they do for an education?*
- *An interesting project is to study and compare the educational system in countries as Finland, Norway and South Korea that have shown such wonderful results. Why do they have a better educational system than we have in the U.S.? What is their philosophy about tests? Grades? Homework? Asking questions? How do they integrate sports and the Arts in their school day? What can we learn form these countries?*
- *Identify by timelines the spread of Islam throughout world history.*
- *Who were some leading Islamic individuals and the contributions they have made to social, political, economic and cultural fields?*

Hints:
- Islam began in Arabia in the 7th century under the leadership of Muhammad, the Messenger of God and final Prophet, who united the many tribes of Arabia under Islamic law. Muslims do not regard Muhammad as the founder of a new religion but as the restorer of the original monotheistic faith of Adam, Ibrahim and other prophets.
- Islam is the second largest religion in the world today, with an estimated 1.4 billion followers known as Muslims. Only about 18% of Muslims originate from Arab countries; 20% are found in Sub-Sahara Africa; 30% in the South Asian region of Pakistan and Bangladesh; and the world's largest Muslim community is in Indonesia.
- Islam is the second largest religion in many European countries, such as France, that has the largest Muslim population in Western Europe (more than 6 million documented), and the United Kingdom.
- There are a number of Islamic denominations; each one has significant theological and legal differences from each other but share common beliefs. 85% of the world's Muslims are Sunni and 15% are Shi'a (Shiites). (See chart in chapter 14)
- Muhammad wrote down his revelations and visions that were memorized by his followers and written in The Koran, the Muslim Bible.

- The Koran praises Muhammad the Great Prophet, the founder of Islam, and his teachings that are the basis of The Koran which is the first book written in Arabic. Muslims consider every word of The Koran to be inspired by Allah, God.
- A mosque is a place of worship for Muslims. The primary purpose of the mosque is to serve as a place of prayer. Nevertheless, mosques are also important to the Muslim community as a meeting place and a place of study. Today, most mosques have elaborate domes, minarets, and prayer halls, demonstrating Islamic architecture.
- "Jihad" usually refers to military exertion against non-Muslim combatants. In a broader sense, the term has both violent and nonviolent meanings. It can refer to striving to live a moral and virtuous life, to spreading and defending Islam by fighting injustice and oppression. The word "jihad" is often wrongly translated as "Holy War." The primary aim of jihad is not the conversion of non-Muslims to Islam by force, but rather the conversion by understanding. The Koran dose not encourage violence or war.
- One of the main tenets of Islam is that there is one God, monotheism, and there is no God but Allah. The concept of a monotheistic God has its origins in the religions of Judaism and Christianity, which are earlier religions.
- In Arabic the word, "Islam" means "submission to the will of Allah." The followers of Islam are called Muslims. The word "Muslim" means "one who has submitted."
- The following are leading Islamic individuals who have made major contributions in the following fields:
  Medicine:
  - Dr. Muhammad as-Razi (865-925) was the most important physician in Baghdad and wrote a medical encyclopedia called, <u>The Comprehensive Book,</u> and <u>Treatise on Smallpox and Measles</u>. Both books were translated into many languages (in Venice 1509 and in Paris 1528 and reprinted in 1745) and used for 1,000 years as the basis for medical teaching.
  - Dr. Ibu Sina (980-1037) known as Avicenna, wrote <u>The Canon Medicine</u> which served as an encyclopedia of diseases until the 18th century and served as the medical foundation for the School of Medicine at Louvain, Belgium, one of Europe's first medical schools.
  Mathematics:
  - Arab scholars used the concept of zero from India's mathematicians and established the Arabic number system that is the basis for algebra, geometry and trigonometry.

Astronomy:
° Using the basis of math, Arab scientists were able to calculate the Earth's distance to the stars, chart comets, planets and stars, observe the earth's rotation and calculate the circumference of the earth.

Navigation:
° Muslim explorers between 750-1350 opened the way for European traders, as Marco Polo (1254-1324). During this time, Muslim explorers introduced a network of international trade of fine carpets, silk, glassworks, leather, cotton textiles, leather, and steel between the Arab world, Italy and Europe.

Literature:
° <u>Thousand and One Arabian Nights</u>, the classical favorite is a collection of folk tales first compiled in Arabic during the 8th century. The work was collected over many centuries by various authors and in turn relied partly on Indian, Arabic and Persian oral elements.

Art:
° Calligraphy was first introduced in the Arab world as a way to write about the glory of Allah. Architects designed mosques, domes and geometric decorative patterns called arabesques. (An excellent example is the Alhambra Palace in Granada, Spain.)

b. War with Russia:

- Osama's mother laments the death of her husband. As she cries to the grandmother, we learn Osama's father was killed "in the Russian war."
- The Soviet Republic fought in Afghanistan from 1979-1989 and was forced to leave, defeated.
- 1989 marks a very crucial point in global history: the defeat of the Russians in Afghanistan; the demise of the Soviet bloc; and the emancipation of Satellite countries ruled by Soviet communism since post-World War II.
- Many historians point their finger at Russia's war in Afghanistan as a reason the U.S.S.R.'s lost control of their Satellite countries as of 1989. The war was very costly. At that point, Russia's economy fell and so did their politics.

Suggested Activities:
- *Discuss in small groups: What is the relationship of the Russians losing the war in Afghanistan in 1989 and the dismantling of the Eastern Wall in East Berlin in 1989? Discuss what comes first- Economics or Politics?*

- *What role did President Gorbachev of Russia play in this? Pope John Paul II? President Ronald Reagan? Prime Minister Margaret Thatcher of the U.K.?*
- *What is the domino theory?*
- *What is the relationship of the domino theory and terrorism today in the Middle East?*

Hints:

- The "domino theory" is a 20th century foreign policy theory, promoted by the government of the United States, that speculates if one land in a region comes under the influence of communism, then the surrounding countries would follow in a domino effect. The concept suggests that some change, even small, will cause a similar change nearby, which will then cause another similar change, and so on in linear sequence, by analogy to a falling row of dominoes. Later, the concept is used for other forms of governments coming under a pernicious influence and then succumbing to a disintegration that has profound influences.
- The domino theory has been extrapolated and used as an example and warning when referring to Extremist and Terrorist groups and the Middle East.
- An exercise to show this, is to take a box of dominoes, line them up at the front of the class, and then knock down one. The falling down of all the pieces is an example of the domino theory.
- During the Cold War, the term Soviet Bloc or Satellite countries was used to refer to the Soviet Union and the countries they dominated in Central and Eastern Europe as Bulgaria, Czechoslovakia, East Germany, Yugoslavia, Hungary, Romania, and Albania.

c. Taliban:

- In the opening scene, young Espandi warns the women and widows who are demonstrating that, "The Taliban is coming." The viewers begin to stiffen in fear. The Taliban soldiers spray the demonstrators with high-powered water hoses. The women run away.
- The Taliban are a Sunni Muslim Pashtun movement of fundamentalist insurgents who rage a terrorist, guerilla war. They are comprised of Afghans and Pakistanis and are recruited from madrasahs. They are recognized diplomatically only by three countries: Pakistan, Saudi Arabia and the United Arab Emirates.
- During the Taliban's official seven-year rule in Afghanistan (1996-2003), Afghan women experience restrictions on their freedom. Women are not

allowed to ride a bike. (In the film, the Taliban soldier reprimands Osama's mother that she is on a bike.) Women are supposed to cover their entire body in a burqa. (In the same scene, the Taliban soldier yells at Osama's mother that her toes are uncovered. She is wearing sandals.) Women are not allowed to earn money, for money gives power and power leads to political demands for rights. (Osama's mother hides as she takes money for helping in the hospital and during the neighbor's wedding celebration.)

- The principle of the Taliban is to rule the government according to Islamic law and The Koran. All western influence is considered illegal, un-Islamic and subject to severe punishment. No CD's, no music other than religious music, not even ringtones on cell phones, no DVD's, no television and no cinemas are allowed under the Taliban rule.

- Filmmaking is also not allowed during the Taliban's rule. At the beginning of the film, we see the young boy, Espandi, is receiving dollars from a filmmaker for his help. We see the filmmaker's camera and hand as he gives the boy the American dollars, but we do not see his face. At the end of the film during the trial, we see the same movie camera from the beginning of the film and we see the filmmaker for the first time. The judge pronounces his sentence: "Death." Someone in the crowd asks, "Where's the witness?" But there is no answer. Instead, as a response, we hear several gunshots. He was executed for making a film. That was the verdict and judgement.

- As of 2016, there is as much Taliban control in Afghanistan as during 2001 and the filming of *Osama*.

Suggested Activities:
- *The group can be split into two sections to debate the opposing and supporting views of the following: The United States government has a policy not to negotiate with terrorist groups or countries that harbor terrorists. However, this is not a rule that is shared by all countries, as Italy and others. And the U.S. as of 2015 has been changing this policy.*

- *What steps would you take, if you were members of the American State Department and your Nationals were kidnapped by terrorists from Afghanistan, Pakistan, Iran or Iraq? Should the U.S. government exchange prisoners and/or hostages in such a situation?*

- *Research recent cases and include in your discussion the case of the American journalist, Daniel Pearl, who was kidnapped and killed by terrorists in Karachi, Pakistan in 2002. (Bibliography: the book written by his wife, Mariane Pearl, and/or the film, A Mighty Heart (2007) starring Angelina Jolie, (Goodwill Ambassador for the UN.)*

Hints:

- In the past years, Muslim terrorist cells and groups have emerged in the Middle East, Asia, Africa and elsewhere. Linked to Al Qaeda, they terrorize the local population and neighboring countries as they engage in jihad. There are currently more than 40 organizations on the State Department's list of foreign terrorist organizations. Some are:
  ○ Ansar al-Islam (Iraq/Iran)
  ○ Hamas (Palestine)
  ○ Islamic Jihad (Palestine)
  ○ Hezbollah (Lebanon)
  ○ Islamic Revolutionary Guard Corps (Iran)
  ○ Dar-ul-Islam (Indonesia)
  ○ ISIS or ISIL or Daesh (Iraq, Syria and in neighboring countries)
  ○ Janjaweed (Sudan)
  ○ Jamiyat Islamiya (Pakistan)
  ○ Muslim Brotherhood (Egypt)
  ○ Al Qaeda Magreb (Morocco, Algeria, Tunisia)
  ○ Hizb ut-Tahir (United Kingdom and Europe)
  ○ Lashkar-e-Taiba (Pakistan/Kashmir)
  ○ Jaish-e-Muhammad (Pakistan/Kashmir)
  ○ Al Shabab (Somali, East Africa)
  ○ Haqqani Network and Tehrik-I-Taliban (Pakistan)

2. Geography:

a. Afghanistan:

- The capital of Afghanistan is Kabul. Another large city is Kandahar, and a sacred city is Mazar-I-Sharif.
- Excavation of prehistoric sites suggests that humans were living in what is now Afghanistan at least 50,000 years ago, and that farming communities of the area were among the earliest in the world.
- Official language is Farsi, spoken by 50% of the population. Farsi is also spoken in Iran and Tajikistan. The Pashto language is spoken by 35% of the Afghan population; and there are many other dialects like Dari.
- Afghanistan is a landlocked country in Central Asia with no access to the water. It is a dry, mountainous terrain with desert areas and plains in the north and

southwest. In many parts of the country there is little fresh water. Afghanistan has a continental climate, with hot summers and cold winters. The country is frequently subject to minor earthquakes, mainly in the northeast of Hindu Kush mountains at the Pakistani border. (An area where terrorist cells hide in caves.)

- It is smaller than Texas, surrounded by Pakistan in the south and east; Iran in the west; Turkmenistan, Uzbekistan and Tajikistan in the north and China in the far northeast.

- Afghanistan is a mosaic of ethnic groups. It has been an ancient focal point of trade and migration between the East and West as early as the 12th century. The region has seen many invaders and conquerors, including the Persian Empire, Alexander the Great, Muslim Arabs, Turkish Empire, Mongol nomads, Genghis Khan in the 13th century, the British Empire, the Soviet Union, and the United States of America. It has been said that no invader or country has been able to conquer Afghanistan.

- During the 19th century, following the Anglo-Afghan Wars of 1839-42 and 1878-80 and lastly in 1919, the U.K. tried to take Afghanistan as part of its Empire. The U.K. did exercise a great deal of influence, but it was not until King Khan acceded to the throne in 1919 that Afghanistan re-gained complete independence and annexed territories from Great Britain on August 19, 1919.

- The country's natural resources are gold, silver, lapis lazuli, copper, zinc, iron ore, petroleum and natural gas. Plans are underway to extracting them now. China began extracting copper in 2009 from a mine near Kabul as well as building hydroelectricity and transportation lines for trade.

- The longest period of stability in Afghanistan was between 1933 and 1973, when the country was under the rule of the Afghan King Zahir Shah.

- The film takes place in Kabul, the capital of Afghanistan. We see parts of the town and where people live and work, but we do not see the entire terrain of the country. Knowing and understanding the geography of Afghanistan is key in understanding present-day politics of this country in crisis as well as in the geo-political region.

Suggested Activities:

- *Describe the ways that present political and historical events have resulted due to Afghanistan's unique geographic factors.*
- *Research the caves and mountains as possible hiding places for Al Qaeda and Taliban members.*

b. *Pakistan:*

- In *Osama,* we hear about Pakistan when the young girl's boss does not open his store one morning. His neighbor explains to Osama that her employer went to Pakistan. Business was not good in Kabul.

- Pakistan, surrounding Afghanistan, on its southern and eastern border, has an ambiguous relationship with its neighbor. On one side, the Pakistani official government is theoretically allied with the U.S. to fight the Taliban and arrest them. Yet, on the other hand, Pakistani tribal Elders have clandestinely harbored the Taliban at key locations at the Pakistani-Afghan border and thus, allowing them to infiltrate deeper into Afghanistan. Pakistan is also aware that the Elders on their side of the border have set up training camps for terrorists groups in association with the Taliban and Al-Qaeda leaders, as well as sharing skills, and the Pakistani government has not stopped these activities. There is a strong "tribal culture" in both countries.

- The Inter-Services Intelligence (I.S.I.) has been accused of training and assisting militant groups. The Pakistani Taliban have allied themselves to the Afghan Taliban under the pretext that they want to block India from gaining a foothold in Afghanistan. The I.S.I. has also shown evidence of supporting the Pakistani Taliban for this reason. (India and Pakistan have a history of differences and animosity.)

- Western diplomats claim that Pakistan has not done enough to stop the Taliban and Al Qaeda. They voice the opinion that Pakistani government can do much more, in particular the powerful Inter-Services Intelligence (I.S.I.) and Military Intelligence, under the government and army.

- The I.S.I. created the terrorist group, Lashkar-e-Taiba, in the 1980s as a force against Indians in Muslim-dominated Kashmir. Since then, the group has trained with Al Qaeda and the Taliban and their relationship with the I.S.I. is murky. They have been accused of terrorist attacks in Afghanistan, Iraq and Mumbai in November 2008.

- The fear among leading Westerners is the danger that Pakistan has nuclear weapons as highly developed and bazaared under Dr. Khan, the "Father" of Pakistan's atomic energy program, and that Islamists and terrorists could possibly get their hands on this.

- As of 2009, American officials have reported that they see evidence that fighters linked with Al Qaeda, ISIS and other terrorist groups are moving from Pakistan and the border areas with Afghanistan, to Somalia and Yemen in

Africa. Some American officials say that this regrouping is due to American and NATO attacks on insurgents in Afghanistan by "drones."

- As of 2015, ISIS has infiltrated into Afghan areas, especially in the mountains at the Pakistani border, where ISIS and other extremist groups can move freely into Pakistan when it is necessary for their safety.

Suggested Activities:
- *Ask members of your group to divide into two sub-groups to debate the following: Is Pakistan doing enough to help the international world stop the resurgence of the Taliban and Al Qaeda in Afghanistan?*
- *Discuss the present role of ISIS in Afghanistan.*
- *Divide into small groups to study Afghanistan's problems and strategize what you would do if you were the leader of Pakistan and wanted to help Afghanistan achieve reconstruction and stability.*
- *Have each group present their strategies in a short presentation.*
- *Discuss the following problems in Afghanistan: the Taliban, Islamic extremism, terrorism, drugs, warlords, border control, and women's rights.*
- *Research and analyze the relationship of Pakistan's geography of the role of the "Elders." Discuss how the Elders have influenced present-day politics in Afghanistan and Pakistan.*

Hints:
- The Pakistani government claims that they are trying to control the Afghan/Pakistan border where Afghan terrorists and warlords are being sheltered by tribal Elders.
- In areas where there are clandestine crossings, they are putting up fences, similar to what they have in Israel at the Palestinian border. And yet, the Pakistani government claims that the border area is too long to prevent all people from crossing into Afghanistan.
- A solution to the problem is that as part of border control, the 300,000 Afghan workers who cross daily into Pakistan for work, will receive electronic ID's to document who is working and to facilitate border crossing.
- During the Russian occupation (1979-89), more than 3 million Afghan refugees crossed into Pakistan. The U.N. and the U.S. set up refugee camps in Pakistan that still exist for these people. However, the problem is that Taliban militants cross into Pakistan, enter these camps, mingle with the refugees and recruit terrorists from dissatisfied Afghans. Pakistan has been repatriating these Afghan refugees to return home.
-

3. Economics:

a. Supply and demand: Drugs

- In several scenes of Osama we see Taliban soldiers carrying rifles to intimidate and control the citizens. When Osama walks down the streets of Kabul the first day when she does not wear her burqa and she is a "boy," she is afraid. It is the first time she looks at her surroundings with eyes unmasked behind the net fabric of the burqa. At this moment, the camera serves as Osama's wide-opened eyes and we see her staring at all the Taliban soldiers carrying rifles.

Suggested Activities:
Discuss the following in small groups:

- *Where did all these rifles come from?*
- *Which country or countries have been supplying Afghanistan with arms?*
- *How can the American government stop the flow of money that terrorists use to buy weapons? Is there a source of money that the Taliban uses to finance their wars?*
- *Discuss and analyze the concept of supply and demand, using drugs and opium as examples, and work together as a group to create a chart that visualizes the important role that this concept plays in determining what is produced and distributed in a competitive market system.*
- *Research and discuss the concept of production, distribution and consumption of the opium poppy drug.*

Hints:
- Poppy plants are the sources of opium and heroin. White and pink poppy flowers have been planted in areas of Afghanistan since Alexander the Great. Today, Afghanistan produces 93% of the world's supply of illegal opium and heroin. To wipe out poppy as a profitable and desirable agricultural source, the U.N. and U.S. have promised economic alternatives to Afghanistan. But this is a slow process.
- Taliban forces have worked for years with Afghan drug warlords, kingpins, traffickers, and even government officials who are all involved in exporting Afghanistan's lucrative "poppy business." The $3 billion ı opium trade per year helps pay for the guns, vehicles, soldiers and bombs the Taliban and Al Qaeda insurgents have used against NATO and coalition troops.

- As late as 2016, Afghan government officials are directly involved in the opium trade, expanding competiton with the Taliban beyond politics and into a struggle for control of the drug traffic and revenue. Government and police all get their percentage from a poppy tax imposed on farmers from the government. Particluarly fertile are poppy fields between Helmand and Kandhar provinces south of Hindu Kush Mountains, also an area of intense guerilla fighting among Al Qaeda, Taliban, NATO and coalition troops. Perhaps, not a coincidence.

4. Civics, Citizenship and Government:

a. Theocracy:

- In the trial scene of Osama, we see before our eyes how a theocracy rules Afghanistan under the Taliban.
- The word theocracy originates from the Greek "theokratia" meaning the rule of God. In a theocracy, the leaders come from the dominant religion and the government claims to rule on behalf of God, as specified by the religion.

Suggested Activities:
- *Ask members of your group to analyze the courtroom scene, and discuss their impressions of the nature of theocratic justice.*
- *Hypothesize and discuss how the trial scene would be different in an American democratic courtroom. You can present two types of trials: American and Afghan —a democratic courtroom and a theocratic courtroom, using the principles of liberty, justice, equality, and the fair rule of law. Discuss Sharia Law.*
- *Does a theocracy have a constitution? What is the nature and purpose of a constitution? What is the place of law in the American constitutional system?*
- *Research and discuss which countries have a history of being a theocracy in the past and/or present. (Tibet, Iran and Nepal)*

Hints:
- A theocracy is a form of government in which the leader is seen as having divine power and governs as a representative of the religion of the country. The religious government therefore replaces the civil government. Those who do not follow the religious tenets are seen as non-believers and heretics, and thus, are punished.

- In Afghanistan, the Taliban established an Islamic state with the goal to return to the values of Islam and reject the values of the West. They used the ideas of Sunni Islam and imposed severe restrictions on citizens: men have to wear beards and the beards have to be as long as a fistful of hair; men have to have cleanly cut hair; no one can listen to music except for religious chants; no movie theaters; no one can dance; and women have no rights.
- A totalitarian government as it was during Fascist Germany and Italy and Communist Russia, is when the government controls every aspect of the citizen's life through a one-party dictatorship and the dictator is at the head of the government. There is a strong secret police to control the citizens and suppress any opposition. There are no civil rights, no freedom, no individual liberties.

b. Women's Rights:

- The opening scene of *Osama* introduces a group of Afghan women, dressed in blue burqas, who are demonstrating. They are carrying signs indicating their reason:
  - "We want work."
  - "We are widows."
  - "We are not political."
  - "We are hungry."

Suggested Activities:
- *Analyze the sequence of events of the first few minutes of the film, and discuss a timeline of the events.*
- *What is the purpose of the young boy (Espandi):*
  - *Who is giving him the dollars? Why?*
  - *Why does the director introduce this boy as a character?*
  - *Why is the boy carrying a metal can that has smoke?*
  - *What is the smoke's purpose?*
- *Ask members of your group to discuss where in the world women suffer from similar restrictions of freedom. Identify them on a map.*
- *Discuss whether similarities in geographical location and terrain might play an important role in the restrictions of women's freedom.*

Hints:
- There are many countries in the world that restrict women's freedoms. To address this problem, the United Nations arranges conferences related

to Women's Rights. The first "World Conferences on Women" was held in Mexico City in 1975 and called for changes in the status and role of women.

Their goals:
° Education should be equal for men and women;
° Increase women's participation in their country's economic sector;
° Increase women's participation in government;
° Laws should be made to improve women's employment and pay.

Suggested Activity:
- *Discuss the following as a group: Cause and Effect - Women's Rights*
- *Cause and effect is the relationship between two things. The first spurs the appearance/presence of the second. This is why we call the first thing, a cause, and the second, an effect; the first causes the second, and the second is the effect of the first.*
- *For example, in the film Osama, widows are not allowed to work under Taliban rule. This is the first thing; the "cause." The second thing, the "effect" is that Osama's mother forces her daughter to work as if she were a son, due to this rule.*
- *(As of 2006 in Afghanistan, there has been a resurgence of Taliban rule and widows cannot work again. This time the "cause" is the same, but now the "effect" is that sons look to make money for their family, and do so by joining the Taliban, ISIS and extremist groups. As extremist groups re-enter in Aghnaistan, there is a correlation with less women's rights.)*

c. Education:

- We see in *Osama* that the young Mullah (religious leader) goes into the store where Osama is stirring milk. Believing he is a boy, he takes Osama to school. Dozens of young boys of various ages are also being "rounded-up." Osama's friend, Espandi, tells the other boys, that this is where they will be prepared to "serve bin Laden."
- Under Taliban rule, girls are not allowed to go to school, and boys must attend a madrasah where they study Islam and The Koran.

Suggested Activities:
- *There are many countries around the world that do not encourage or allow girls to go to school. To counter this violation of women's rights, the United Nations' Food Program offers incentives to families and schools to allow girls to be educated. The World Food Program offers 4 liters of cooking oil to families whose daughters attend school at least 40 days a year.*

- *Ask members of your group to list possible incentives to families, schools and govern-ments, to allow girls in Third World countries to go to school.*
- *An interesting film and biography is about the teenager, Malala Yousafzai, from Pakistan, "He named me Malala." It shows how the Taliban tries to kill her for speaking out on behalf of girls' education. As a consequence, she emerges as a leading advocate for children's rights and the youngest Nobel Peace Prize Laureate.*

Hints:
- Western journalists have written articles about madrashas, in Afghanistan and Pakistan, where male students are trained to perform suicide bombings to support the jihad. Additionally, young boys are selected in the madrasha to be "chai" (tea in Arabic) boys for the Taliban. Chai boys are uncompensated, apart from receiving food and board. They live closely with Afghan command-ers. Journalists have reported that some of these boys are apprentices, others are valets, and some suffer sexual abuse.

B. Literature and Visual Arts:

5. World Literature:

a. Historic fiction and historic film:

- In 2003, the same time that *Osama* takes place, Afghan-American author, Khaled Hosseini published The Kite Runner which, though a work of fiction, captures much of the history, politics and culture experienced in Afghanistan from the 1930s to the time period of the film, Osama.
- With the historical background of the novel, the reader learns about the final days of Afghanistan's monarchy and the beginning of the atrocities of the Taliban. The fictional aspect is the story of friendship between a wealthy Afghan boy and the son of his father's servant.

Suggested Activities:
- *Some members of your group might enjoy reading Mr. Hosseini's follow-up book, A Thousand Splendid Suns (2007) and compare how he presents Afghan women as a theme similar to the theme of Osama.*
- *Other members of the group might enjoy reading The Kite Runner and discuss the following:*

  ○ *What are the historical elements in the novel that are related to Afghanistan?*
  ○ *Discuss how the changing politics of Afghanistan affect each of the characters in the novel: Babba, Ali, Amir and Hassan.*
  ○ *Why has this film not been shown in Afghanistan?*
  ○ *What is kite flying? How is it used by the author as a symbol? How does the symbol relate to the film, Osama?*

Hints:

- During Spring in Kabul, there are many kite flying festivals. These festivals are contests that contain risk and danger.
- The object of this contest is to slice your opponents' string with yours and cause the kite to spiral downwards. The winner is the person who has the last kite flying.
- To achieve their goals, the kite flyers use string that can cut the string of rival kites. Those with money can buy string containing cotton twine with finely grounded glass; or string made with Pakistani nylon that resembles very sharp fishing line; or even razor-sharp wire from China.
- The better kites are made of a thin bamboo frame that has invisible joints and is very sensitive to the slightest tug of the owner.
- In the streets are crowds of people following the winning kites.
- Young boys who are too poor to buy their own kites, are the kite runners for others.

Suggested Activities:
- *It might be fun to start a kite-flying contest.*

b. Folktales: Arabic oral storytelling

- Osama's grandmother loves her dearly. Several times she tells Osama's mother, "What would I do without her?" When Osama cannot sleep because she is worried about her fate as a boy, her grandmother tells her a story. This reminds us of the Arabic storytelling tradition of folktales that can be traced to the famous collection of tales in the <u>Arabian Nights: Tales from a Thousand and One Nights.</u>

Suggested Activities:
- *Ask members of your group to practice oral tradition of telling a story in a round-robin format. Each person narrates part of a tale for several minutes and then the next person continues.*

- *Is the director making a parallelism between Scheherazade and Osama in the film, and the King and the Mullah Sahib in the story? If so, what is the parallelism?*

Hints:

- Folktales, or folklore, includes tales, legends, oral history, proverbs, popular beliefs, children's rhymes, riddles, jokes, ghost stories, and customs within a particular population comprising the traditions of that culture or group.
- The aim of these folktales is to record and preserve the traditions, identity, and customs of groups of people, and to pass them from one generation to another. Folktales usually concern the mundane traditions of everyday life, but sometime they include religious and mythological elements. Often the folktales are in the form of oral narrative storytelling, but they are also in written format or in different art mediums, like music and dance.
- The collection of stories in the Arabian Nights are derived from this original tale: The king, Shahryar, upon discovering his former wife's infidelity had her executed and then declared all women to be unfaithful. He begins to marry a succession of virgins only to execute each one the next morning. Eventually his assistant cannot find any more virgins. The assistant's daughter, Scheherazade, offers herself as the next bride and her father reluctantly agrees. On the night of their marriage, Scheherazade tells the king a tale, but does not end it. The king is thus forced to keep her alive in order to hear the conclusion. The next night, as soon as she finishes the tale, she begins, but only "begins" another tale. And so she continues for 1,001 nights.

6. Media Studies:

a. Film Clips and Scene Discussions:

Women's Rights: (Scene: 2:04 –> 3:05 minutes)
The film begins with Afghan women demonstrating for the right to work, a right that is non-existent under the Taliban and religious extremists: "Come see the revolution. It's not for political reasons! We're hungry! We need jobs. The Taliban are coming to bring hell! WE ARE WIDOWS. Run! The Taliban are coming! Run! You'll get killed. Run! Don't lock us here! Heretics!"

Ask members of your group to discuss why the Taliban and religious extremists in Afghanistan do not allow women to work. What have women in Afghanistan tried to achieve in the past ten years? Compare this with the achievements of women in Icleand, Finland and Tunisia.

Justice under the Taliban: (Scene: 01:04 –> 01:08)

Religious justice, rules made by the Taliban and enforced by their leaders, is a judicial system based on Sharia Law. The scene of judging the filmmaker, foreign nurse and Osama, reveals how justice is enforced under the Taliban: "Death is the punishment! Judge ordered the death penalty for him... This unfaithful woman was swearing. The judges decided that stones must be thrown at her until she dies. Where is the witness? Only God knows. Bring the girl that pretended to be a boy. Whoever does this, will conclude like him. In our Holy Islam has never happened anything like this. We have seen many bad things... in Kabul like we see today. I forgive her. May your life and faith go on forever. This orphan girl doesn't have anyone. I marry her to you...legally and in a religious way. Do you accept? I accept. Judge, don't give me to him, please, I want my mother. Bring me my mother. They forgave her and Molah Sahib took her. Now justice has prevailed."

Ask your group to discuss which countries base their judicial system on these rules? How are the judgments enforced? Can the accused appeal the decision? Your group can re-create a crime as it is declared and judged under Sharia Law and then re-create the same scene as it would be tried in an American court.

- Compare the progressive judicial systems in Portugal, Norway and Sweden with that of Afghanistan and the United States.

b. Cinematography Techniques:

1. Symbols:

Burqa:

- All women in Osama wear a burqa. A burqa is a full robe that covers a Muslim woman's entire body and face save for a small slit at the eyes, which is covered by a concealing net. In Turkey and Iran the burqa is black. In Afghanistan it is light blue, brown, green, or black. In Pakistan and India, the burqas may expose the face or eyes. Its purpose is to make sure that women behave modestly in public as dictated in The Koran.
- Before the Taliban took power in Afghanistan, the burqa was infrequently worn in cities. But during the Taliban's reign, women were required to

wear a burqa whenever they appeared in public. Presently, it is not required under the present Afghan regime, but local warlords still enforce it outside Kabul. Due to political instability in these areas, women who might not otherwise be inclined to wear the burqa must do so as a matter of personal safety.

- When Osama changes her identity to a boy, she no longer wears the traditional burqa. When she walks in the street free of the restraints of her gender, she clutches her mother's arm. She feels "exposed" and naked.
- Discuss the concept of the burqa and/ or veil in Tunisia, Morocco, Algeria, Turkey, Indonesia and France.

Flower pot:

- When Osama's hair is cut, she plants a lock of her hair in a pot filled with earth. She waters it with the I.V. her mother took from the hospital. Clearly, she hopes her hair will be free to grow and be beautiful.

Jumping rope:

- The image of Osama jumping rope appears several times as a leitmotif. This image unfolds before Osama's imagination at key moments when she feels life is hopeless. It is her escape, her fantasy, her wishful thinking that she is free to be a child and enjoy the simple pleasure of jumping rope.

Ablution:

- According to The Koran, before a man offers prayer, he must be in pure condition. It is necessary that he cleanse the parts of his body that are generally exposed to dirt or dust or smog. This performance is called ablution. This rite is shown two times in the film which correspond to the two other times the male must cleanse himself:
- At the madrasah when Mullah Sahib teaches the boys how to become clean "after they have a wet dream or night discharge." And the last scene of the film when Mullah Sahib is cleansing himself after he made love.

Locks and chains:

- In the film, these are not used to protect a home from criminals but to "reign in" a woman's freedom.

Suggested Activities:
- *Work in small groups; each group member interpret how each symbol is used:*
  - ° *to describe the main protagonist, Osama;*
  - ° *to represent a theme;*
  - ° *and to accelerate the plot's progression.*

2. Irony:

- Irony is saying or showing one thing and meaning another thing. Irony is used often in literature and cinema as a technique to enhance a theme or develop a character. In Osama, director Siddiq Barmak uses irony often by twisting a symbol so it has two interpretations. His use of irony becomes the symbol's flip side.

Suggested Activity:
- *The same group can interpret the symbols from the opposite point of view so that the symbols now express irony, eg the times when Osama jumps rope with the desire to be free.*

3. Light:

- In Osama, light is used by the director as a cinematographic technique as well as a symbol. He uses natural light rather than artificial light. This device is reminiscent of Scandinavian filmmakers who are members of the "Dogme" school led by Danish filmmaker, Lars von Trier, "Dancer in the Dark." (See chapter Ten for Oscar-winner director, Susanne Bier, is part of this film school.)
- In key interior scenes, Mr. Barmak uses the light from the one kerosene lamp. This enhances realism, for that is the actual way Afghans live. In addition, the darkness symbolizes their life. The director, therefore, uses the concept of light and dark as symbols.
- It is not coincidental that when Mullah Sahib is leading Osama to his house by wagon, when night is approaching. The darkness, which is symbolic and foreboding, takes over the screen and fills the audience with tension.

4. Color:

- Most of the color in Osama is monochromatic with shades of brown to reflect the desert terrain of Kabul. However, when there are key moments, the director highlights the screen with color:

- The film opens with a group of women in blue burqas, the color of the sky. When they run, the light fabric opens up in folds like they are birds, or birds of prey.
- When Osama is being "prepared" for Mullah Sahib, she is dressed in a purple and red scarf and one of the wives applies red lipstick to her lips.
- Saturation refers to the strength of a hue and color. Desaturated colors are less pure. They contain more white than saturated colors and appear on the screen as grayish. Most of Osama is filmed in desaturated colors to emphasize the dreariness of the characters' situation.
- Chiaroscuro (named after the Italian painter de Chirico) is a technique of arranging both light and dark colors in the same frame and composition. It evokes an element of trauma and drama at a tense moment.

Suggested Activity:
- *Identify the scenes where colors take over and discuss the way, in which color and light are used to highlight a scene, or character.*

5. Character Foil:

- Osama's friend, Espandi, is a boy and is Osama's character foil regarding gender. He is the only one who knows she is a girl. He even tries to blackmail her: "I recognize you. Pay me or I'll denounce you." But he also protects her. (Again the double-edged interpretation.)

Suggested Activity:
- *Describe when and how Espandi changes his attitude toward Osama. What is the significance of his changed attitude?*

b. Comparative media: Documentary

- The term documentary was not coined until 1926. It was used initially by the French to refer to any nonfiction film medium, including travelogues and instructional films. It tends to "document" reality and it is a filmmaking process that has expanded to include video and digital productions.
- In recent years, the documentary as an art form has become very popular and creative in its format. Often, it is difficult to tell when fiction stops and nonfiction begins. The challenge is to understand the political background and the director's point of view. (POV)

c. Cinema as a reflection of culture:

- The film, *The Kite Runner,* was delayed from its scheduled release of October 2007 due to the possibility that the three young Afghan actors would be punished in Afghanistan by the Taliban. Acting, filmmaking and movie theaters are outlawed by the Taliban. In addition, the boys acted in the film's rape scene that was condemned by the Taliban. Paramount Studios felt obliged to protect the young actors and their families from possible retribution. Paramount arranged for them to relocate to the United Arab Emirates and found schools for the boys and work for their parents/ guardians.

Suggested Activities:
- *This is an unprecedented legal case that can be analyzed and discussed based on cross-cultural ramifications.*

Hints:
- The boys were casted to act in *The Kite Runner* in 2006 when the Taliban's presence in Kabul was not as strong as in 2007 when the film was scheduled to be released. In addition, the film studio and Afghan and American officials fear the movie could aggravate smoldering enmities between the politically dominant Pashtun people, depicted by one young protagonist, and the oppressed Hazara people, depicted by another protagonist.

d. Cinema as a reflection of politics:

- The film, *Kandahar* (2001), directed by Mohsen Makmalbaf is a poignant portrayal of life in Kandahar, a border-town where the Taliban fought bitterly and presently still controls. The story is about an Afghan journalist, living in Canada, who returns to her native city in search of her sister. We witness with her how the Taliban tragically affects everyday life. Her journey is truly a struggle into human suffering and terror, regardless of gender, age or status. The director designed Kandahar for Western eyes with the aim to expose an oppressive regime that built its power upon the despair of an entire national population, and to shame the West for its complacency.

Suggested Activity:

- *Some members of your group can watch the film, Kandahar. Compare/ contrast through discussion the film's central themes to those of Osama.*

Hints:

- The director of *Kandahar* is Iranian Mohsen Maklalbaf, one of the most respected directors in Iran and in world cinema. He has several children and has schooled them at home. His children and wife are also directors of cinema. His daughter, Samira, at the age of 17, won Cannes' Camera d'Or prize for Best First Feature Film for *The Apple*.

7. Philosophy/Critical Thinking:

a. Art imitates Life:

- The story of Osama is based on reality. There are no statistics on how many girls are masqueraded as boys by their families. However, the practice has been done for generations.
- These children are not addressed as "daughter" or "son" but "bacha posh," which means in Dari, "dressed up as a boy." Afghan parents may pretend their daughter is a son for economic reason so the girl can work, or to create a son within a family of all daughters.
- When the girl reaches puberty, she changes back to her female clothes and prepares to get married.

Suggested Topic of Discussion:

- *The philosophical question - Does art imitate life, or does life imitate art? - has been attributed to the Greek philosophy of "Mimesis," imitation, as articulated by the Greek philosophers, Plato, in Book II of "The Republic" (380 B.C.) and Aristotle, in "The Poetics" (335 B.C.). Both philosophers advocate that Art imitates Life. However, famous British playwright Oscar Wilde, advocates the opposite, that life imitates art in his essay, "The Decay of Lying" (1889). Life has an imitative instinct and that it is Art that offers the form that Life then imitates.*
- *You can choose which side of this philosophical question that you'd like to advocate and in your group debate the question through analyzing scenes, drawing conclusions on the motives of main characters, and citing evidence from the film, Osama.*

b. Policy paper:

- On the 2nd day of Osama's work, she goes to the store but finds it closed. The neighboring shopkeeper tells her sadly, "No business here."
- Since 2003, the U.S. and the European community have tried to rebuild Afghanistan's economy, but this is a slow process.
- And yet, the country does have the potential to move out of poverty and become an economically stable country. According to the U.S. Geological Survey and the Afghan Ministry of Mines and Industry, Afghanistan may be possessing up to 36 trillion cubic feet of natural gas, 3.6 billion barrels of petroleum, and up to 1,325 million barrels of natural gas liquids. Energy exports could generate the revenue needed to modernize the country's infrastructure and expand economic opportunities. In addition, Afghanistan is rich in gold, copper, coal, iron ore, and semi-precious stones like lapis lazuli.

Suggested Activities:
- *Ask members of your group to research, and define, "What is a policy paper?"*
- *Form small groups and write a policy paper describing the steps you would take if you were members of the U.S. Government's Department of Treasury and State Department rebuilding Afghanistan's economy. Perhaps you can submit this as an Op-Ed or article in your community newspaper? Or for your school?*
- *How would 'micro-financing' be part of the financial strategy?*

Hints:
- One of the theories why terrorism is spreading in poor countries is because young people are uneducated and unemployed. Without future prospects, they remain poor and become resentful, making them easy prey to be recruited by terrorists. In addition, their families receive payment and/or a free house, if they become a suicide bomber. Terrorists are also trying to do the same in Pakistan, Iraq, Palestine, Egypt, and India.
- One of the main drivers for economic recovery in Afghanistan is the return of over 4 million refugees from neighboring countries and the West, who bring with them entrepreneurship and wealth-creating skills as well as much needed funds to startup businesses and to teach the young people and women.

8. Art:

a. Carpets:

- During the trial scene, we see the "judge" is sitting on an Afghan carpet. He is the only person on this carpet – a symbol of importance – while the dozens of men attending the public hearing are sitting on the dirt floor. His carpet stands out also because it is multi-colored.
- Afghanistan is known for its beautiful carpets. Before the Taliban, the carpet industry was Afghanistan's third export after oil and fruit (grapes, apricots, melons).
- During the 12th -15th centuries, Afghan carpets were shipped from Afghanistan to Venice and then traded in western Europe as one of the most-sought after signs of wealth. It is said that Marco Polo was the first European to trade Afghan carpets in Europe.

Suggested Activities:
- *Ask members of your group to research Afghan carpets; share the pictures.*
- *Report which cities in Afghanistan are carpet centers.*
- *What makes Afghan carpets different from Persian (Iranian) carpets?*

Hints:
- Carpet connoisseurs say that Afghan carpets are special because of the quality of wool that is used and the tightness of the weave. Unfortunately, this is often achieved at the toil of a child laborer. Kilim carpets, made from sheep wool, are characterized by geometrical figures.
- A major carpet center in Afghanistan is in Herat, a western city near the Iranian border, where many of Afghanistan's finest carpets are made. Herat has a history of over 2,500 years and was once occupied by Alexander the Great, and subsequently invaded by Mongols led by Genghis Khan in the 13th century. Herat was considered part of the Persian Empire, and the Persian influence in carpet making is still seen in Herat, today.
- The material used for making Afghan carpets is derived from what they have at their disposal: wool from their sheep, goat hair, and camel hair that is especially prized for smaller prayer carpets.

9. Technology:

a. Currency:

- Afghans, to purchase goods, to travel, to do business transactions, convert their money into dollars or Euros. This is a good opportunity for your group to get involoved in currency transactions as well as how to recognize counterfeited money.

b. Power point presentation and the Internet

Suggested Activities:
- *Research the U.S.S.R.'s war in Afghanistan and present your findings in the form of a power point presentation.*
- *You can research Afghanistan's geography by using resources, data and tools as aerial photographs, satellite images, geographic information systems (GIS), map projections, and cartography.*
- *Create a Google map of Afghanistan and include: key cities, mountains, plateaus, deserts, and bordering countries.*
- *You can do the same for Kabul and recreate the city of Osama. Include Osama's route through Kabul as seen in the film. Use google.earth.*
- *Some members of your group can analyze, interpret, and organize in a chart the interrelationships of Afghanistan's physical, political and cultural patterns, such as religious cities and where the Elders live at the Pakistani border.*

Extracurricular Activity:

- As a way to introduce your group to different types of religion, you can visit a mosque, synagogue and church. Perhaps you can arrange with the laymen and directors to talk to your group about their religion(s).

Sidebars:

1. Public Response:

- Iranian government ministers donated hugely to the production and editing of *Osama*. We wonder, "why?" Perhaps, it is because the Iranians are Shiites, and the Taliban are Sunnis? Also, both countries share a common language – Farci.

2. *Actors and Directors:*

- The actress, Marina Golbahari, who plays twelve-year-old Osama, is not a professional actress. She was discovered by the Afghan director in the streets of Kabul. As payment, she received a house, but the director legally set up ownership of the house in the girl's name, even if her parents and siblings live in the house with her. This represents the first time that a woman is allowed to own property in Afghanistan and can have it registered in her name.
- During the time of the Taliban in Afghanistan, director Siddiq Barmak was barred from filmmaking in Afghanistan and was sent in exile. The scenes of the filmmaker in *Osama*, who is filmmaking and then condemned, is autobiographical. However, Mr. Barmak was the first director who was allowed to return to Kabul in 2003 at the time when the Taliban influence had been weakened. He was financed and helped by the internationally-acclaimed Iranian filmmaker, Mohsen Makmalbaf, who made the film Kandahar in 2001. Mr. Makamalbaf, an icon in Iranian cinema, gave Mr. Barmak $100,000 in funding, as well as 35 mm cameras with equipment and his personal cinematographer and crew.
- Mr Barmak filmed two endings and decided on the one that we have now. The other ending, shows Osama walking through a rainbow. This brings the film back to a circle when in the beginning of the story, her grandmother is telling her the story of how a boy walked through a rainbow and became a girl.

3. *Awards:*

- Golden Globes, USA
  2004– Won- Golden Trailer- Best Foreign Language Film- Afghanistan

- Cannes Film Festival, France
  2003– Won- Best Director –Siddiq Barmak

- London Film Festival
  2003– Won – Sutherland Trophy – Siddiq Barmak

Bibliography of Films: Filmography
Further Global Study Resources through Film:

Gender Discrimination:

- *Baran* (Iran/Afghanistan)
- *Offside* (Iran)
- *The King of Masks* (China)
- *Whale Rider* (New Zealand)
- *The Merchant of Venice* (U.K.)
- *Moolaadé* (Senegal)
- *Bend It Like Beckham* (U.K.)
- *Camille Claudel* (France)
- *Milk* (U.S.A.)
- *Philadelphia Story* (U.S.A.)
- *Billy Elliot* (U.K.)
- *Zanzibar Soccer Queens* (Zanzibar)
- *The Stoning of Soraya M* (U.S.A. /Canada)
- *4 Months, 3 Weeks, and 2 Days* (Romania)
- *Made in Dagenhaum* (U.K.)

Children's Rights:

- *Water* (India)
- *Central Station* (Brazil)
- *Pixote* (Brazil)
- *Children Underground* (U.S.A./Romania)
- *A Time for Drunken Horses* (Iran/Iraq)
- *Turtles Can Fly* (Iran/Iraq)
- *Child Soldiers in Sierra Leone* (Sierra Leone)
- *Kolya* (Czech Republic)
- *The Italian* (Russia)
- *Crows* (Poland)
- *Born Into Brothels* (India)
- *Salaam Bombay* (India)

- *The Chorus* (France)
- *Slumdog Millionaire* (USA/India)
- *Nobody Knows* (Japan)
- *War Dance* (Uganda)

About Afghanistan:

- *Fire Dancer* (U.S.A.)
- *Lions for Lambs* (U.S.A.)
- *Massoud, L'Afghan* (France)
- *Opium War* (Iran)
- *Charlie Wilson's War* (U.S.A.)

CHAPTER 6

THE LADY (MYANMAR / BURMA)

TITLE OF FILM: *The Lady*
YEAR OF RELEASE: 2011
COUNTRY: Myanmar / Burma
DIRECTOR: Luc Besson
LANGUAGE: English, Burmese
RUNNING TIME: 135 minutes
CURRICULUM THEMES:

A. HISTORY AND SOCIAL SCIENCE:

- Chapter's Key Themes: Military Dictatorship; student demonstrations
- World History: Colonialism; World War II and General Aung San
- Geography: The Golden Land; Southeast Asia
- Economics: Relationship with China
- Civics, Citizenship and Government: National League for Democracy (NLD); Unitary Presidential Constitutional Republic; Parliament; Ethnic Groups

B. LITERATURE and VISUAL ARTS:

- World Literature: Biography; Manifesto; Letters
- Media Studies: Film Clips and Scene Discussions; Cinematography Techniques; Emphasis by contrast
- Philosophy/ Critical Thinking: spiritual strength; moral dilemma; political symbol
- Art: Oriental Music
- Technology: Computer Use

Introduction:

The Lady was directed by Luc Besson; produced by Virginie Besson-Silla, Andy Harries, and Jean Todt; edited by Julien Rey; music by Eric Serra and Thierry Arbogast; and distributed by EuropaCorp (France), Entertainment Film Distributors (UK), Cohen Media Group (US), and Golden Scene Company Limited (Hong Kong) in 2011.

Aung San Suu Kyi.. *Michelle Yeoh*
Michael Aris..*David Thewelis*
Alexander Aris..*Jonathan Woodhouse*
Kim Aris..*Jonathan Raggett*

The mark of a hero is a person who has the courage and conviction to sacrifice everything for a Belief or Vision and act as we ordinary mortals do not dare. Such is the Lady, the protagonist of the film and the real-life icon, Aung San Suu Kyi, of Myanmar. She never gives up fighting the injustices of Burma's military junta that has been in power since 1958. Despite numerous attempts of assassination, imprisonment and house arrest of more than 15 years, Aung San Suu Kyi defies the Burmese Generals with patience and non-violence, winning adoration from her people.

The film's release came propitiously at the time of the first democratic elections in Myanmar in 2012. The Lady was allowed to lead her party, the National League for Democracy (NLD), and won 43 seats in Parliament. Her courage has inspired not only the Burmese but all people around the world who believe in Freedom. In 2015, she went on to win majority vote and her party's victory in Parliament.

Pivotal Moments in Burmese History:

1886-1920s:

- After three wars between Great Britain and Burma over a period of 60 years, the British successfully colonized Burma in 1886. Burma became a province of British India, with Rangoon as its capital.
- The British created divisions within Burma by favoring some ethnic minorities over others, for example by giving them positions in the military and in local rural administrations. These ethnic divisions affect Burma even today.

1920s-1935:

- The leaders of the anti-colonial movement were intellectuals (especially law students who had studied abroad), students, and Buddhist monks.
- The Students Union at Rangoon University was at the forefront of the movement by 1935. Aung San, a young law student, emerged as a leader, organizing strikes at the university and gathering the support of the nation.

1940-1945:

- Aung San and 29 others, known as the Thirty Comrades, underwent military training in Japan, and in 1941 they fought alongside the Japanese who invaded Burma. The Japanese promised Burma's freedom if they defeated the British.
- When it became clear that the Japanese did not plan to uphold their deal, General Aung San renegotiated with the British.

1947:

- In January, Aung San reaches agreement with the British granting Burma total independence.
- In July, Aung San's party draft new democratic constitution. General Aung San and his cabinet are assassinated by an opposition group.

Jan. 4, 1948:

- Burma officially granted independence from Great Britain.

1948-1958:

- Constant challenges to the new regime by communists and ethnic groups that felt underrepresented. This was a period of civil war. The economy was weak.

1958-1960:

- General Ne Win took control of the country in order to "restore law and order" to Burma, in 1958. In 1960 he stages a coup and became Burma's military dictator.

1960-1988:

- Isolation ideology: Burma retreated from interaction with the international community; there were few visitors from outside the country, and the ones that came were restricted to the capital, Rangoon.

1988:

- Democracy: Summer of August 1988, known as 8888, Ne Win announced he was giving up his position. Demonstrations broke out in Rangoon. The following month, troops began a four-day massacre, killing at least 10,000 civilians.
- This happened to be the year that Aung San Suu Kyi returned from abroad to care for her mother. In an attempt to pacify the international community, the government decided to hold elections; Suu and her colleagues founded the National League for Democracy (NLD), which rapidly gained support.

1989:

- In July, Suu was placed under house arrest for the first time, for a period of six years.

1990:

- With Suu under house arrest, the government held elections as promised. The NLD won with 82% of the vote. The State Law and Order Restoration Council (SLORC) refused to acknowledge the results.

1997:

- The SLORC was replaced by the State Peace and Development Council, but human rights violations continued to be reported. Both the U.S. and the E.U intensified sanctions against Burma.

2000:

- Suu was placed under house arrest again for two years.

2003:

- Suu once against placed under house arrest, in the middle of reconciliation talks with the government.

2007:

- There was a powerful wave of anti-government protests; the immediate cause was the decision of the government to remove fuel subsidies, which led to the skyrocketing of gas prices. Many protests were led by Buddhist monks, called the Safron Revolution. The government dealt with these protests harshly.

Pre-Screening Questions:

1. Instead of imprisoning or assassinating Aung San Suu Kyi when she was rapidly gaining power and support, the government placed her under house arrest. She was in and out of house arrest from 1989 until she was released in 2010.

Suggested Activities:
- *Your group can brainstorm the thinking behind the Military's choice to place Suu under house arrest rather than other forceful methods. What does house arrest mean? Is house arrest a milder or worse punishment than imprisonment? What made Suu different from other political enemies?*

Hints:
- House arrest is a legal penalty in which a person is confined to his or her home, often without the possibility to travel. It has often been used against political dissidents in authoritarian regimes. There is no access to communication, whether with other people or electronically.
- While the death of General Aung San did halt the pro-democracy movement, it had an unexpected effect on the people – they united under him as a symbol. The Military generals feared if they killed Suu, she, too, would become a martyr.
- Suu, having studied abroad at Oxford, and having her family in England, could attract unwanted international attention against Burma's military. This was the thinking behind Michael's attempt to get Suu nominated for the Nobel

Prize; anything that made her famous would protect her, because the military government would not risk international disfavor.

2. In one scene, Suu shares a quotation: "You may not think about politics, but politics thinks about you." Suu frequently makes attempts to emphasize the "human aspect" of politics, to reclaim the term from corrupt politicians and make it for the people, and about the people.

Suggested Activities:
- *Your group can make a list of possible reasons why Suu gained support from the people so rapidly.*

Hints:
- Her father, General Aung San, was already a symbol of democracy and respect; as his daughter, Suu, too, became a symbol, taking up her father's mantel. Also partly thanks to her father's influence, Suu had a network of like-minded colleagues ready to help her. The movement did not start from scratch, as it would have if she were a new figure.
- She spoke of politics not as something only a certain elite can understand, but as something that affects every person and that gets its power from the people.
- Having studied abroad at Oxford, lived in a democracy and worked at the United Nations for two years, Suu had a practical knowledge of how democracy works.
- Her devotion to her country and her determination inspired many people. She was granted permission from the government many times to leave Burma but the knowledge that she wouldn't be allowed back in the country kept her from leaving.

Suggested Activity:
- *In your group discuss the ways in which long-term colonialism weakened Burma, rather than strengthened it.*

Hints:
- The British favored certain ethnic groups over others, giving them government and military positions. This created tension between Burma's ethnic minorities as each of them vied for favor and for their own independence.

Burma has 135 ethnic groups; each one speaking a different dialectic and having different religions. Some examples are the Kachins, Karans, Kayans, and Rohingyas (Muslims). Tensions still remain today.

- Other cultural changes were made that fractured society. The British forcefully separated religion from state; but after independence, Buddhism (Theravada format) became an important aspect of Burmese life.

- Having the British in main positions of government meant that it was harder for the Burmese to rule their own country when it was returned to them in 1948.

- Many intellectuals had the opportunity to study abroad during colonialism, like Aung San Suu Kyi, and many settled in that country. Thus, there was an exodus of Burma's potential leaders. This caused a "brain drain" effect on their present society.

Pivotal Moments in Film:

- Suu not only gathered support from the people of Burma, but she also gave hope and courage to her people by her example to sacrifice everything for freedom.

- In 1988, she returns to Burma to visit her sick mother, and witnesses first-hand the cruelty of the military regime. With remarkable spirit, determination, and knowledge, as well as the love of her family and country, Suu becomes a democracy fighter herself. *The Lady* is the biography of Burma's freedom fighter gifted with a great capacity to love, following her through imprisonment, the winning of the Nobel Prize, and the eventual choice between family and country.

Post-Screening Questions:
History and Social Science:

1. What steps did the government take against Aung San Suu Kyi to try to stop her influence?
2. What steps did the government take in general to stop criticism and uprisings from the general population?

Hints:

- Government oppression generally involved force: uprisings and riots were put down often with gunfire and arrests. They took many political prisoners and silenced anyone whom they saw as a threat. We see evidence of this in an early scene in the film, in which Suu is witness to indiscriminate violence at the hospital where her mom was being treated.
- As time passed, however, the tactics of the military government changed and gained more subtlety. In the film we see Suu and Michael watching TV when the general declared upcoming elections. This was to create the illusion of a conciliatory government. However, as shown later in the film, they never intended to loosen their hold on the country or to allow anyone else any influence in politics. Suu was placed under house arrest as soon as she was declared the winner of the election in 1988-89 by a large margin.

Literature and Visual Arts:

---

1. What conflicts does Suu confront? How do they change her?
2. What is the significance of the title *The Lady*?
3. Love for her country and people are the main reasons that Suu succeeded. Consider the opening scenes of the film, and compare to the rest of the film. Why is the setting made to be so idyllic and beautiful? Why does it begin with the story that General Aung San tells his daughter?
4. What was the significance of the scene in which Suu faces the gun of a military man head on, paralleling the scene of her father's death?

Curriculum Themes:
A. History and Social Science:

Chapter's Key Themes: Military Dictatorship

a. On March 2nd, 1962, General Ne Win led the Burmese military in a coup d'etat. Almost all aspects of society were nationalized under the military's slogan: "Burmese Way to Socialism." In reality, the Socialism became a dictatorial military rule. Several aspects of this policy were:

- Nationalization in the style of the Soviet Union 1974 Constitution ensuring a one-party system. The "Burmese Way to Socialism" is the ideology of the government after 1962.
- The treatise sought to reduce foreign influence in Burma and to expand the role of the military. Over time, this policy turned Burma from one of the richest Asian countries (as the General tells his 2-year-old- daughter) to one of the poorest in the world, as shown by the crowded conditions of the hospital.

Suggested Activities:
- *Have your group research the features and the effect of the Burmese Way to Socialism. Include the following:*
  - *Extensive dependence on military*
  - *Extreme nationalism*
  - *Marxist/socialist, anti-Western; xenophobia and a policy of isolationism*
  - *Emphasis on rural population over urban growth*
  - *Extensive visa restrictions for Burmese citizens especially to go to the West; yet, the government sponsored travel to Russia and Eastern Europe*
  - *Negatively impacted the economy, educational standards, living conditions*
  - *Freedom of expression severely limited*
  - *Foreign language publications and newspapers prohibited*
  - *Press Scrutiny Board was established to censor publications*
  - *Nationalization (owned by the military) of industries such as trade, banking, mining, jade, gold, sapphires, rubies, oil, timber, teak wood, rice,*
  - *Black market thrived, representing about 80% of the national economy during the Socialist period*
  - *Ne Win was overthrown in a military junta. His family was imprisoned and was put under house arrest at his home on Inya Lake in Yagoon, on the opposite bank, facing the Lady during her house arrest*

Suggested Activities:
- *Your group can identify some scenes in the film that illustrate the political policies and military dictatorship of the country as described above.*

Hints:
- Nearly every time Suu talked to someone on the phone, the line was interrupted. Interference in a person's private life is a key characteristic of authoritarian regimes.

- The violence at the hospital scene, where Suu witnessed military men shooting people.
- The imprisonment in inhumane conditions of Suu's colleagues. To protest this, we see Suu refuse to eat while under house arrest.
- Suu being placed under house arrest after her party's 1990 success in elections.

b. Student Demonstrations

- The most noteworthy wave of demonstrations came in 1988-1989, when unrest over economic and political mismanagement led to widespread pro-democracy movements known as the 8888 Uprising. This is because the protest began in Rangoon on 8/8/1988. This was the period in which Suu came to Burma to visit her sick mother.
- The Inya Lake riots were among the first of the 8888 Uprising. Inya Lake, the largest lake in Rangoon, is located right next to Rangoon University. Students marched, demanding an end to one-party rule and were met violently by soldiers who clubbed many students to death.

1. World History:

a. Colonialism (1824-1948):

- Though the film is set after independence, the ties to the British are still felt. Suu herself studied abroad at Oxford; her and Michael's network of British professors is solid; and it helped her in the quest to the Nobel Prize. Furthermore, when Michael goes to print pro-democracy pamphlets, he is helped by the British Ambassador in Burma.

Suggested Activities:
- *Your group can do some research and then create a three-way Venn diagram, organizing the changes that colonialism brought to Burma as political, economic, or social.*

b. World War II and General Aung San:

- General Aung San, the Lady's father, was at center stage pre-, during and post-World War II:

- In October 1938, Aung San left his law classes and entered national politics. At this point, he was anti-British. He helped organize a series of countrywide strikes. He also became the founder and secretary-general of the Communist Party in Burma in1939.
- In 1940 he went to Japan with 29 colleagues, where they learned military training to support Japan and the Axis during the War. Aung San was presented with the Order of the Rising Sun by Japanese Emperor Hirohito.
- On 1 August 1943, the Japanese declared Burma to be an independent nation. Aung San was appointed War Minister. The war turns, the Axis in Europe begin to lose, and he becomes skeptical of Japanese promises of independence for Burma and of Japan's ability to win the war.
- The British Government had announced its intention to grant self-government to Burma within the British Commonwealth. General Aung San met with Lord Mountbatten in Ceylon (Siri Lanka) in September 1945 to solidify the agreement.
- On 27 January 1947, Aung San and the British Prime Minister, Clement Attlee, signed an agreement in London guaranteeing Burma's independence within a year; Aung San had been responsible for its negotiation.
- On 19 July 1947, a gang of armed paramilitaries of the former Prime Minister broke into the Secretariat building in downtown Rangoon during a meeting of the Executive Council and assassinated Aung San and six of his cabinet ministers.
- At the trial that followed, a number of middle-ranking British army officers were implicated in the plot; they also were tried and imprisoned. Several British officers had supplied weapons to the assassins. Perhaps Britain or some Burmese did not want Burma to become independent?

Suggested Activities:
- *Your group can research the consequences of an independent Burma without a democratic leader.*

Hints:
- Ethic groups became stronger, fighting for their independence.
- Russia sold arms and weapons to the Burmese military government so they could suppress conflicts with ethnic groups. The Chinese did the same.
- Military leaders became corrupt with unlimited powers. They formed joint ventures with Chinese officials who eventually took over Burma's wealth: ruby mines, gold, ivory, oil, forests. Over the years, China stripped Burma of its wealth.

- China has used factories in Myanmar to produce chemical weapons in secret. China has used these weapons against their Muslim population as Myanmar does against their belligerent ethnic groups.

2. Geography:

a. The Golden Land:

- The film opens with an idyllic scene and a background of gentle, oriental music. General Aung San tells his 2-year-old-daughter about their country as it was before the arrival of the British – a place of beauty, wilderness, and peace. He calls it "Golden Land" because of the diversity and value of the natural life in Burma. It also refers to the fact that gold is their most loved metal, used in pagodas, monasteries, etc.

Suggested Activities:
- *Your group can research the basic elements of Burma's geography. You may want to research: What is the total area of the country? The population? What is the topography like? Where are mountains, hills, and valleys located? How much of the surface area is water? What is the climate like? Who are its neighbors? What is the capital?*

Hints:
Capital: Naypyidaw (since 2005)
Largest City: Yangon (since 2005, previously known as Rangoon)
Population (2010): 60,280,000 people
Area: 676,578 km2 (3.53% water)
Land is rimmed in the north, east, and west by mountain ranges forming a giant horseshoe. Enclosed within the mountain barriers are the flat lands of Ayeyarwaddy, Chindwin and Sittaung River valleys, where most of the country's agricultural land and population are concentrated.
Country bordering Myanmar in the north is China; in the south is Thailand; in the east are China, Laos, and Thailand; in the west are India and Bangladesh.

b. Southeast Asia:

- India's presence was felt strongly when Burma and India were part of the British Empire. The British delegated soldiers from India to enforce law and order in Burma because there were not enough British soldiers to take charge. The British were not comfortable in Burma due to the hot and humid weather. On the other hand, the Indians shared a comparable climate. The Burmese were not happy with Indian enforcers. After the Burmese received independence from the U.K., the military junta under General Ne Win, forced many of the Indians who were living in Myanmar, to return to India. Yet, there are still some Indians who have remained in Myanmar. They are Muslim, from Bangladesh, and are part of the persecuted group, the Rohingyas.

- The Chinese presence in Myanmar is very strong. They represent a wealthy class who are engaged in business with neighboring mainland China. They have created many joint ventures with the military and trade agreements. Oil and gas pipelines are presently being erected from the Bay of Bengal to the border with China. The "Road to Mandalay" is owned by the Chinese. They receive tolls from trucks and cars; they maintain the road; they have young Chinese workers, female teenagers and male youngsters to maintain the road and facilitate Chinese trucks shipping teak wood and teak trees, bamboo, fruits as strawberries, pineapples, watermelons, vegetables and products from the ruby, sapphire, jade, gold, and silver mines and pearls and coral. When the U.S., United Nations and European countries placed embargos and sanctions on Burma for their lack of Human Rights, the Chinese stepped in as uncontested business partners. They have remained.

- One of Michael's concerns for Suu is that the international community would never know of her struggles in Burma; her anonymity was a danger to her life and her fame after the Nobel Prize protected her. This relative invisibility of Burma in the international community came as a result of decades of the government policy of isolationism. Furthermore, this choice to retreat from deep international relations, agreements, and trade was largely unchallenged by the international community; they had little interest in Burma that had become a very poor country.

Suggested Activities:
- *Study the map of Burma and its neighbors. Think about its location strategically. What potential do you see for agreements, trade, and other international interactions? How could an empowered and technologically advanced Burma benefit the whole of Southeast Asia?*
- *Your group can research what recent attempts have been made to strengthen Burma. Which countries have shown the most interest in Burma? Why and how?*

Hints:
- Burma has the power to unite S.E. Asia. It is located between China and India, and so may act as a conduit of trade and cooperation between the two powerful countries.
- India's landlocked northeast, separated by Bangladesh from the rest of the country, is also in a position to benefit from a connection to the outside via a stable and strong Myanmar.
- The Chinese are constructing pipelines for oil and natural gas transport, from Africa and Burma-dominated Bay of Bengal across Burma and into China, thus avoiding the Strait of Malacca and saving time and money. The pipelines will also benefit Myanmar, providing a route to export their plentiful reserves of natural gas.
- India is building an energy terminal to carry resources at Sittwe, along Myanmar's coast. This pipeline will potentially connect Burma, Bangladesh, and India, in one fluid, organic continuum.
- The important fact here is that both India and China, while pursuing personal interests in Burma, may in the process boost Burma as well.
- China's Geopolitical Interest: China has long benefited from Myanmar's abundance of resources (oil, natural gas, coal, zinc, copper, timber, hydroelectricity, etc.); after the isolation of Myanmar following the 1962 coup, China remained a significant player in Myanmar because of its need for its resources.
- The remarkable point is that interests in the region generally coincide; while China may yet benefit from ethnic strife in Myanmar, in the long run, Myanmar's economic development is good for China, India, and the rest of Southeast Asia. The economic and commercial potential may be reason for regional cooperation.

3. Economics:

a. Relationship with China:

Burma's relationship with its powerful neighbor, China, has been very deep. China provides Burma with extensive military and economic aid while exploiting the country's natural resources.

Suggested Activities:
- *It is an interesting discussion to research and discuss the following points:*

○   *Background: How did this relationship between Burma and China develop? When did it develop, and why is it still so strong despite American and foreign competition? What will happen now with democracy in Burma?*

○   *Trade and Commerce: What resources are traded? Does trade benefit one country more than the other or is it mutually beneficial? What countries are Burma's trading partners?*

Hints:

- Background: Burma was the first non-communist country to recognize the People's Republic of China after its foundation in 1959; they established diplomatic relations a year later. Relations began to improve even more in the 1970's and in 1988 they signed a major trade agreement that also started military trade.

- Trade: Bilateral trade with China is over $1.4 billion. China's imports are generally natural resources like wood, oil, coal, zinc, copper, rubber, etc. China is helping Burma with its infrastructure as well as dams, roads, bridges, and ports.

- Strategic: China supplies Burma with military tools such as jet fighters, naval vessels, and armored vehicles. Access to Burma gives China considerable power, with access to the strategic Bay of Bengal, the Indian Ocean, and the rest of Southeast Asia.

- Myanmar's business partners are members of the 10 ASEAN member nations: Indonesia, Laos, Malaysia, Myanmar, Philippines, Singapore, Thailand, Brunei, Cambodia, and Vietnam. This is a group of countries that represents a population of more than 620 million people and a collective economy of $2.4 trillion, the 3rd largest in Asia behind China and Japan.

Suggested Activity:

- *Your group can research what achievements the U.S., U.N. and the E.U. have made in Myanmar. Are these significant or just token gestures? What will happen now as democracy grows in Myanmar?*

Hints:

- The U.S. was the first to restore diplomatic relations with Burma in 2010. The U.S. used their influence to get Myanmar elected as the President of the ASEAN nations in 2014, to encourage their move toward democracy and economic growth.

- Other nations, particularly those in close geographic proximity such as Thailand, India, and Vietnam, urged the U.N. to get more involved with its support in developing the education and health sectors, reducing poverty, and improving the general well-being of the population, and to continue discussions with the government, encouraging it at every turn to "broaden political space and address socio-economic conditions."

- United Nations Development Programs (UNDP) has been very active in small villages in building medical clinics, hospitals and schools. Prior to 2010, these remote and isolated towns had no elementary or middle school. Today, the U.S. has offered grants for Education and there is an increased activity in school construction and attendance as well as computer literacy. Local government is encouraging students to finish middle school and then they are giving scholarships for eligible students to go to the nearest city for high school and college.

- As of Spring 2012, UNDP will have a principal office in Nepadaw and Yagon to co-ordinate international aid to Myanmar. In addition, the International Monetary Fund, World Bank and Asian Development Bank will widen their economic support in Banking, credit, investment and funding.

- The European Union also welcomed the reforms taking place and has announced plans to further assist the country and make sure the changes are irreversible. The E.U. is deeply committed with financial assistance. It announced plans to help reduce poverty, all the while encouraging big players like the World Bank and the International Monetary Fund to also get engaged.

- The E.U. and U.N. have also declared its commitment to helping ethnic groups in their struggles for peace and Human Rights.

4. Civics, Citizenship and Government:

a. National League for Democracy:

- Aung San Suu Kyi's party, National League for Democracy, NLD, was founded in 1988, in the aftermath of the 8888 Uprising and Suu is the President of the Party. In 1990, the NLD won a majority in Parliament but the government refused to recognize the result and placed Suu under house arrest.

- In 2012, the NLD party won 43 of the possible 45 seats open for election to Parliament. In 2015, she won overwhelmingly and has moved her party to rule Parliament and work to change the Constitution that had been established by the Military that opposes her from becoming the actual President. However, in 2016, she and her party elect the President who will be a "proxy" leader under her. As of 2015, the Constitution states that 25% of the 664 seats in Parliament are occupied by the Military. To ratify the Constitution, 75% of Parliament members are needed to vote, which she has due to her victory in 2015. For Suu Kyi to become President, a change in the Constitution is needed.

Suggested Activities:

- *Your group can research other rules why Suu cannot become President under the Constitution. However, her goal for 2016 is to wield power with a proxy President. Discuss this strategy. Is it a good idea? In 2016, she became Minister of Foreign Affairs and is chief of Parliament.*
- *What are the priorities that Suu as leader of the NLD must address:*

Hints:

- NLD Party platform for change in Constitution
- Non-violent movement toward democracy
- Human rights including freedom of speech
- Rule of law
- Release of political prisoners
- Freedom of Press
- Independence of the judiciary
- Increased social benefits

b. Unitary Presidential Constitutional Republic;

- When Burma first gained independence in 1948, the British left it with a system similar to their own in place: Burma had a president (as opposed to the UK's head of state, the Queen) and a prime minister (head of government) and a bicameral legislature. But despite this democratic form of structure, the Military took over and ruled as a dictatorship until 2015.
- When Aung San Suu Kyi was released from house arrest, the president was Thien Sein, who is a product of Burmese Military for he has been educated as a lawyer at the Military's School of Law. Myanmar's Constitution states that in order to be the President, that person has to come from the military elite.
- For most of his career he was a loyal enforcer in one of the world's most brutal military regimes. But since March 30, 2011, when he was elected president of Myanmar, Thein Sein has been leading his from military dictatorship to democracy that they finally achieved in 2015.
- There are no easy and clear reasons why Mr. Thein Sein, had decided to shake up one of Asia's poorest and most isolated countries. The question still remains

what will be Myanmar's relationship with the military that still controls some sections of the government like police, security, and lucrative economic relationships with China.

- President Sein did release Aung San Suu Kyi from house arrest and paved the way for Democracy.Some people have called him Myanmar's Mikhail Gorbachev.
- In 2014, Myanmar took on the chairmanship of the Association of Southeast Asian Nations (ASEAN) a tribute of confidence to President U Thein Sein. And encouragement to Myanmar to develop economically with their South East neighbors. In 2016, Thien Sein has retired from government.

Suggested Activities:
- *What is "freedom of the press"? Students can research new developments related to Myanmar's government that allow journalists freedom of press.*

c. Parliament:

- There are 664 seats in Myanmar's Parliament that meets in the capital, Naypidaw. There is a very strict composition of who can occupy these seats.
- To amend the Constitution, 75% of the houses need to approve a law before it passes. As of the 2015 elections, the Lady's party has this. Also the Constitution states that: the President has to come "from the Military," and cannot have been married to a foreigner or have foreigners in the family. This seems to have been written specifically to exclude the Lady from any chance to be elected President. Unless, if she can change the Constitution? She has the power to nominate the President of the country, which she did, for her party has majority rule and she is their leader.

Suggested Activities:
- *Is there freedom of the press in Myanmar today? Your group can research new developments related to Myanmar's government and journalists.*

Hints:
- In July 2014, a provincial court sentenced the head of a weekly newspaper and four of its journalists to 10 years in prison and hard labor for publishing a report that said a secretive and vast government factory was designed to produce chemical weapons for China and for Myanmar's military. Chinese workers were reported to be seen at the factory site.

d. Ethnic Groups and Conflicts:

- There are 135 ethnic groups in Myanmar.
- Ethnic divisions and tension began during British colonialism, and escalated after independence in 1948. Further oppressive policies by the military regime starting in 1962 intensified conflicts. One of the earliest and largest insurgencies was by the Karen National Union (KNU), who wanted large parts of lower Burma to become independent. The situation then worsened when Buddhism became the official religion, leaving in question the rights of many Muslim and Christian ethnic groups (Chin, Kayan, Pao, Kachin, Rohningya). Many ethnic minorities then broke out in rebellion in the 1960's after the central government refused to consider a federal government. In 2013-2014, escalation of tribal war was targeted against the Muslim group, Rohingyas, who are Muslims and have been called by the U.N. as the group that has been persecuted the most in the world.
- There is continued fighting in resource-rich Northern Myanmar against the Kachin group.

Literature and Visual Arts:

5. World Literature:

a. Biography:

- The film is presented in the form of a bio-pic, about the life of Aung San Suu Kyi. Film Biographies, however, consist of more than the facts of someone's life. They include more intimate details, presuming what is the protagonist's thoughts and feelings, personality, weakness and strength, and the importance of certain events in the historical context.

Suggested Activities:
- *For each of the scenes below, identify whether the scenes are based on historical fact or artistic interpretation, or both. Is it always easy to tell?*
  - *The story General Aung San tells his daughter at the beginning of the film.*
  - *The hospital riot.*
  - *The government's decision to place Suu under house arrest.*
  - *The phone call between Suu and Michael when she offers to come home.*

b. The Manifesto:

- In the film, we learn that there were opposition parties in Burma even though the same military-backed party was always in power. The strongest, most prominent of the opposition parties was Suu's party, the National League for Democracy. The NLD published a manifesto, presenting their ideology and goals.
- A manifesto is a written public declaration of intention. The word "manifesto" comes from the Latin "manifestum" that means "clear" or "conspicuous." Therefore, the purpose of a manifesto is not to be a complex outline of how the government would be conducted, or a document full of specialized terms; it is a basic statement meant for the general public.

c. Letters:

- In the film, we see Suu's love of her country through her determined and relentless pursuit for democracy. In one scene, she travels to different villages to talk to people, and we get a glimpse of the diversity of culture in Burma. In the collection of letters that Suu wrote, "Letters from Burma," published in 1997, Suu talks in depth about her country.
- In the introduction to "Letters from Burma," Irish editor Fergal Keane quotes an old man who was standing with many others, in the rain outside her house, on the day that she was released from house arrest: "We come here because we know that we are the most important thing in the world to her. She cares about us."
- Suu speaks fondly of every part of the political process of her Party – even the signs and logo: "These signboards [of the NLD], brilliantly red and white, are a symbol of the courage of the people who have remained dedicated to their beliefs in the face of severe repression, whose commitment to democracy has not been shaken by the adversities they have experienced."
- And she writes about the "humaneness of politics": "Politics is about people... love and truth can move people more strongly than any form of coercion."

Media Studies:

a. Film Clips and Scene Discussions:

- *Military government (Scene:* 11:15 –> 12 minutes)

The main action is introduced by television, while the Lady and her husband are watching BBC's reportage of students demonstrating in Burma against the Military dictatorship; "Eye witnesses at the incident claimed that hundreds of students taking part in a peaceful demonstration at Inya lake, were shot and killed by soldiers at point black range, many more protestors sustained serious injuries. They are demanding an end to the military dictatorship that has ruled the country with an iron fist since a coup in 1962. Burma's government is known as one of the world's most oppressive regimes. But despite the authorities' determined attempts to crush this uprising, it appears that the student's movement, is rapidly gaining massive popular support."

Divide into small groups to discuss other forms of totalitarian governments. What countries today are ruled by these governments? How are they different from democracy? How are they all similar?

- *Independence for Burma* (Scene: 1:46 –> 1:48)
  Aung San Suu and her husband, both agreed to fight in their own way for Burma's independence from Military control: "Michael, if you should ever wish to be free... To start again. I want you to know that I will understand completely. I won't deny this prolonged separation has been very hard. Not just for me, for the boys, too. But I want to make something clear. Throughout everything, from the very beginning, we have always shared a common dream for Burma. And far from being an obstacle, I have always considered it to be the very thing that bound us... That was the last time I saw her."

Discuss the choices that both Suu and Michael made? Ask each person in your group if he/ she could have made such sacrifices?

b. Cinematography Techniques:

- The director uses an innovative technique to structure his film: strong scenes that are used like building blocks to develop the main protagonist. It is as if Luc Besson was an architect and his scenes are constructed in a specific tangible form. What are some of these scenes:
  ○ In one scene, Suu is playing the piano while under house arrest and a soldier is instantly on guard. Michael explains with humor that it is "music". In a following scene, Suu is alone in her house after winning the Nobel Prize. She's

playing the piano alone, while the camera cuts to England where everyone is celebrating her. The same soldier that had earlier been so hostile to her piano-playing is shown smiling and explaining to his colleague what music is. Music, often portrayed as expression of soul and beauty, touches even Suu's enemies.

- ° In another scene, Suu is shown taping poster paper with various inspirational quotations all over her house. She begins talking to a reticent and stiff guard and shows him one of the posters: "You may not think about politics, but politics thinks about you." She tells him it's "food for thought", and leaves him looking thoughtfully up at the quotation.

- ° In another scene, Suu is alone in her house during house arrest while the Nobel Peace Prize was being presented in her name. Suu listens to the award ceremony on a radio as her elder son, Alexander, makes the acceptance speech. The orchestra plays the award's anthem while she plays along on her piano, thousands of miles away, in isolation, and in unity with her family.

Suggested Activities
- *After her release from house arrest, she went to Oslo's City Hall to personally accept her Nobel prize on June 16th, 2012. Her acceptance speech is online and offers the possibility to discuss what the prize meant to her politically and personally.*

Hints:
- According to Alfred Nobel's will, the Peace Prize will go to a person who:
  - ° is committed to nonviolent methods
  - ° qualifies as a person and sustained contributions to peace in such areas as justice, human dignity, and the integrity of the environment
  - ° possesses a world view rather than a parochial concern, with potential for a global rather than a limited impact.

c. Emphasis by Contrast:

- Aung San Suu Kyi's strength and will to remain in Burma despite the threat to her life and family is due to an enormous dedication to her home country. Such capacity for love does not have an easy source. The film tries to suggest this, by showing us Burma through Suu's eyes. How does Suu see the country? How would she describe her people? The government?
- One important image is the juxtaposition of Burma to Oxford. In the first scenes of the film, General Aung San tells Suu the story of Burma, with

beautiful images of the golden land and a background of gentle Oriental music. The camera then moves to Oxford which is filmed in gray colors- the concrete, the cars, the identical houses. Throughout the film, whenever we have an image of Oxford, we get the same curved driveway; meanwhile, Burma is represented by changing images, different colors and different scenes. What does this contrast reveal about Oxford and Burma?

7. Philosophy/ Critical Thinking:

a. Spiritual Strength:

- Aung San Suu Kyi has said in several interviews that meditation and her belief in the teachings of Buddhism helped her through her time under house arrest. Meditation is an introspective process that helped Suu build strength of character and purpose.
- The powerful scene in which Suu faces head on the line of armed military officials with the same calm and acceptance as her father had at the beginning of the film is a highly symbolic moment. By practicing the Buddhist belief in inner peace, she becomes more than a person; she becomes an idea and ideas are immortal. Is this why General Ne Win did not want to kill her or put her in jail?

Suggested Activities:
- *Your group can identity scenes in the film when Suu's spiritual strength helped her perform difficult actions that most people would not be able to do.*

Hints:
- 90% of Burmese people are Theravada Buddhists. (This is a form of Buddhism that also exists in Sri Lanka, Thailand, Cambodia, and Laos.)
- Muslims do live in Myanmar, formerly from India and Bangladesh, especially from the Rohingya Ethnic Group. The Muslims have mosques in every city. In 2012, the Burmese government has ruled that no new mosques can be built. However, they are allowed to increase their size, but in the same location.
- Monks and monasteries: Every boy is obliged to spend at least one week during his lifetime in a monastery as a way to learn about his religion. Girls are also encouraged and they join the Nunnery. Boys and males wear maroon robes in Myanmar; girls wear pink robes. The ceremony is called *novitiation,* and follows a traditional ceremony. Boys and girls, as young as 5 years old, are dressed

in white. Girls are heavily made-up, both boys and girls wear flower necklaces. They are placed in a horse cart that is decorated with bells and flowers, and is accompanied by a cart behind them with drummers and musicians. They all proceed through town and go to the monastery or nunnery where their hair will be shaved and they will leave their parents for a week. Teenagers stay longer.

b. Moral dilemma:

- A lot of people relied on Suu for different reasons and she had to fulfill multiple roles at once. To her husband, she played the role of wife; to her children, she played the role of mother; to the citizens of Burma she played the role of icon; and to the government she played the role of politician. Often times, these roles were in conflict with each other: for instance, when her husband was sick he insisted that she remain in Burma and fulfill both of their dreams, while her children begged her to come back home. This is an example of her role as a mother conflicting with her role as wife, icon, and politician.

Suggested Activities:
- *Your group can make a list of expectations of Suu for all four roles (wife, mother, icon, politician). Where do these roles conflict with each other? What choices did Suu make in each case? Would you have made a different choice?*

c. Political Symbol:

- When Suu returned to Burma, there were already people ready to amass behind her. A political base can take decades to form, but colleagues and friends of Suu's father united quickly behind her. He was a hero, a symbol of freedom and democracy to the Burmese people. Suu also becomes a similar political symbol over the course of the film.

Suggested Activities:
- *Your group can discuss the following moment in the film and its significance: How do these moments show the power of symbols?*

Hints:
- When General Aung San was assassinated, he faces the gun without fear. The film is suspended for a few seconds as Aung San faces off his would-be

murderer. There is no music, only Aung San's calm face accepting death. Later on in the movie, Suu faces a parallel moment as she walks toward a line of military men, facing death just as calmly. In this moment, Suu becomes her father, taking on his ability to inspire and change things, and she continues the fight for democracy where he left off. She believes that is her Fate.

- When the military leader goes to see a fortune-teller asking whether to kill Suu or not, she tells him a ghost is more dangerous than a person. Her rising status as a political symbol protects her life.

8. Art:

a. Oriental Music:

- The music used in the film is part of the director's insistence to recreate the authenticity of home and country. The Lady is shown playing the piano in several scenes but the background music to the film, is oriental.
- Traditional Burmese music is related to Chinese and Thai music, as well as the music of other countries in the vicinity. Some uniquely Burmese instruments are:
  - ° the kyam: a crocodile-shaped wooden instrument with three strings
  - ° the hne: an instrument with a wood body with 7 holes and a bell on top
  - ° the pat waing: a set of 21 drums in a circle played with bare hands
  - ° the ploong: an instrument of pipes

9. Technology:

a. Computer Use:

- Authenticity was a major concern for director Luc Besson. Despite the fact that the cast and crew of *The Lady* were not allowed to film in Burma, authenticity was an important part of the filming process. This meant creating an extensive atmosphere to reflect Suu's home on Inya Lake. Considering that she is under house arrest for more than 15 years, and the film centers on this theme, the reconstruction of her house was essential. The crew rebuilt a 1:1 model of Suu's house using Google maps and Google Earth, as well as hundreds of family photos.

- The scene where the Lady is campaigning in remote areas where different ethnic tribes live was filmed in the Golden Triangle, where Myanmar meets Laos and Thailand, on the Thai side. (Golden because this is the site of a profitable poppy industry.)

Suggested Activities:
- *Ask the group to use the websites of Google Earth and clustrmap to recreate a house in the Golden Triangle where the Karen tribe lives. Include a school and a market place.*
- *The life story of Aung San Suu did not end with Luc Besson's film. What has happened since? You can use the websites Fanfiction for some interesting stories.*

Sidebars:

---

1. Public Response:

Myanmar has criticized Luc Besson's film about *The Lady*. One critique is: the General was shot by machine guns; in the movie they show he was shot by a gun in the head.

- Actress, Michelle Yeoh, is Chinese, not Burmese. Although she studied the Burmese language, the criticism is that her acting did not get all the nuances of the protagonist.
- The Lady is shown as the only child in the family, while there were two older brothers. The elder brother was drowned at a young age and the next brother was a doctor living abroad, now retired in Pagan.

2. Director's/ Actors' Role:

- The initial title for *The Lady* was *Freedom from Fear*, a mark of the relentless spiritual and psychological strength that Aung San Suu Kyi championed in her quest for democracy in Burma. The title was changed partly as a result of the casting of Michelle Yeoh as Suu; the original script told the story solely from Michael Aris' point of view, but then Yeoh brought the full effect of Suu's vision of her home country.
- Screenplay creator Rebecca Frayn and her husband, producer Andy Harries, visited Burma in the early 1990's, inspiring the project. Dedicated to

authenticity, Rebecca Frayn constructed the script based on testimonies from Suu's confidants, interviewed mostly anonymously for their own protection.

- Authenticity was also a major concern for director Luc Besson. Refused entrance into Burma for filming, Besson entered as a tourist and filmed locations in disguise. The crew also rebuilt a 1:1 model of Suu's house using Google maps and hundreds of family photos. Besson's dedication came from an ambition to present a real-life heroine, whose mighty weapons were those of human virtue, strength and complexity.

3. Awards:

- Cinema for Peace Award, USA 2012 – Won – International Human Rights Award
- Satellite Awards, USA 2011 – Nominated – Satellite Award

Bibliography of Films: Filmography
Further Global Study Resources through Film:

Self Determination Category:

- *The Whistleblower* (Bosnia)
- *Incendies* (Canada/ Lebanon)
- *Red Gloves* (Romania)
- *In the Land of Blood and Honey* (Bosnia, Croatia and Serbia)
- *In a Better World* (Denmark/ Sudan)
- *No Man's Land* (Bosnia)
- *Force Maajeure* (Sweden)
- *The Artist and the Model* (Spain)
- *Pray the Devil Back to Hell* (Liberia)
- *Persepolis* (Iran)
- *Balzac and the Little Chinese Seamstress* (France)
- *Timbuktu* (Mali)
- *The Act of Killing* (Indonesia)
- *Leviathan* (Russia)
- *Chico & Rita* (Spain/ Cuba)

Gender Discrimination and Women's Rights:

- *Baran* (Iran/Afghanistan)
- *Offside* (Iran)
- *The King of Masks* (China)
- *Mulan* (USA)
- *Whale Rider* (New Zealand)
- *Moolaadé* (Senegal)
- *Bend It Like Beckham* (United Kingdom)
- *Camille Claudel* (France)
- *Milk* (USA)
- *Philadelphia Story* (USA)
- *Billy Elliot* (UK)
- *The Stoning of Soraya M* (USA and Canada)
- *4 Months, 3 Weeks, and 2 Days* (Romania)
- *Made in Dagenhaum* (UK)
- *The Flowers of War (China)*
- *In the Land of Blood and Honey* (Bosnia, Croatia and Serbia, Balkan War)
- *The Circle* (Iran)
- *The Day I Became a Woman* (Iran)
- *Rabbit Proof Fence* (Australia)
- *The Magdalena Sisters* (Ireland)
- *Ida* (Poland)
- *Winter Sleep* (Turkey)
- *Mustang* (Turkey)

Bio Pictures:

- *Lula* (Brazil)
- *Gandhi* (India)
- *Anne Frank* (Great Britain)
- *Hannah Arendt* (Germany)
- *The Last King of Scotland* (Uganda)
- *Sophie Scholl* (Germany)
- *A Mighty Heart* (USA)
- *Erin Brockovich* (USA)

CHAPTER 7

SPIRITED AWAY (JAPAN)

TITLE OF FILM: *Spirited Away*
YEAR OF RELEASE: 2001
COUNTRY: Japan
DIRECTOR: Hayao Miyazaki
LANGUAGE: Japanese
LENGTH OF TIME: 125 minutes
RATING: PG
CURRICULUM THEMES:

A. HISTORY and SOCIAL SCIENCE:

- Chapter's Key Themes: Environmentalism; Coming of Age (work, love, bravery, know thyself)
- World History: Globalization; Shinto Religion; Japanese Folklore (yōkai; shikigami; kami; Reikai)
- Geography: Map Study; Disputed Islands and China
- Economics: Lifetime Employment; Zaibatsu; Infrastructure
- Civics, Citizenship, & Government: Post-WWII Constitution; Group Identity; Simplicity; Relocation

B. LITERATURE and VISUAL ARTS:

- World Literature: Pillow Books; Haiku Poetry
- Media Studies: Anime and Manga; Film Clips and Scene Discussions
- Philosophy/ Critical Thinking: Honne and Tatemae; Proverbs; Allegory
- Music and Art: New Japan Philharmonic; 'Always With Me' ('Istumo Nandodemo'); ukiyo-e prints
- Technology: Studio Ghibli; Computer Generated Imagery (CGI) and Computer Graphics:

Introduction:

Spirited Away (千と千尋の神隠し) was written and directed by Hayao Miyazaki; produced by Toshio Suzuki; edited by Takeshi Seyama; production design by Norobu Yoshida; cinematography by Atsushi Okui; music by Joe Hisaishi; and distributed by Toho in 2001; (125 minutes)

Chihiro Ogino/ Sen...Rumi Hiiragi
Haku...Miyu Irino
Yubaba/ Zeniba..Mari Natsuki
Kamagi..Bunta Sugawara

Unusual as it is for a film to achieve a certain level of richness, depth, and complexity in either external events or internal experience, *Spirited Away* manages both. The world of spirits that Miyazaki created out of a combination of traditional Japanese mythology and his own imagination is one of constant surprises and delight. At every step we meet fascinating creatures, as: a six-armed man running the boiler room of a bathhouse, a giant but benevolent radish spirit, three disembodied hopping heads, a giant baby that gets turned into an adorable gerbil, a young boy that can turn into a ferocious dragon, and so much more.

Yet, this constant stimulation of the external senses does not in the least detract from the core of the story, which is a young girl's emotional journey from a soul overwhelmed by fear of the unknown to a soul that knows love, compassion, trust, bravery, and the value of work. Young audiences can easily identify with Chihiro's uncertainty when it comes to moving to a new home and new school. With this empathy and identity, viewers of all ages, undergo the emotional journey with her. It is a story that crosses barriers of country, culture, genre, and age. And this can be seen from its extraordinary success all over the world.

Pivotal Moments in History:

- **794 A.D. – 1185:** The Heian period is the golden age of classical Japanese culture. During this time, there was a strong centralized government with the imperial capital at Heian-kyo (modern-day Kyoto). Buddhist art and religion flourished.

- **1185 – 1603:** After the Heian period, political power started being decentralized and civil war claimed the country. Each domain fought with their own samurai warriors.

- **1603:** Tokugawa Leyasu unified Japan and was appointed shogun. This marked the beginning of the prosperous and peaceful Edo period, in which Japan cut off all ties to the outside world.

- **1860s:** The period of rule by Shogun (i.e. the Shogunate) came to an end, and power was once again returned to the emperor.

- **1868 – 1912:** The Meiji period ended feudalism and reopened contact to the outside world. Japan became a world power that followed Western models.

- **1894 – 1895:** The first Sino-Japanese War was fought between Meiji Japan and the Qing dynasty in China over control of Korea. Japan's victory shifted regional dominance in East Asia to them from China.

- **1931:** Japan invaded Manchuria, China and thus becomes an imperialistic nation.

- **1933:** Japan resigns from the post-WWI alliance called the League of Nations due to heavy criticism for its military aggressions in China.

- **1937:** Japan's terrorization of China culminated in the second Sino-Japanese War, and the fighting lasted throughout WW-II.

- **1940:** Japan joined the Axis powers in WWII, allying with fascist Germany and Italy in Europe. The pact through which they agreed to cooperate with one another was called the Tripartite Pact.

- **1941, December 7:** Japan attacks Pearl Harbor, the U.S. naval base in Hawaii. The next day, the U.S. declares war on Japan.

- **1945, August 6 and 9:** Japan refuses to surrender to the Allied Powers (U.S., Great Britain, France, Russia, and China). In response, the U.S. military drops atomic bombs, on Hiroshima and Nagasaki. Five days later, Emperor Hirohito surrenders to the Allies and Japan loses World War II.

- **1945 – 1952:** Japan is occupied by the United States. A new constitution is drafted, turning Japan into a parliamentary monarchy.

- **1952 – present:** Japan becomes an economic powerhouse, especially in engineering, automobiles, and electronics. Japanese people have a high standard of living and the highest life expectancy in the world.

- **2011:** The most powerful earthquake Japan has ever seen hit the coast, and was followed by a tsunami. In addition to extensive damage to life and infrastructure, three nuclear reactors experienced meltdowns. Humanitarian relief came to help from 116 countries and 28 international organizations.

Pre-Screening Questions:

a. What is an allegory?

- An allegory is a story, poem, picture, character, or idea that can be interpreted as having a hidden meaning and being a symbol for something bigger. For example, the animal characters in a fable are usually allegories of human traits. Allegories have also been popular in repressive political regimes, since authors could subtly criticize the government without getting into trouble.
- Another way to define an allegory is as an extended metaphor. Metaphors, which are comparisons between two objects or ideas without the linking words "like" or "as," are usually limited to one sentence or clause. E.g. "you are my guardian angel," "she is a walking dictionary," "his home was a prison." If the metaphor is continued or broadened, it becomes an allegory. Often this involves the creation of a figure, person, or creature that stands for an abstract idea.

b. In Japanese mythology, what is a 'yōkai'?

- In Japanese folklore, 'yōkai' is a class of supernatural creatures or monsters. There is no direct translation into English, so they are variably called demons, spirits, apparitions, or monsters. Yōkai often have animal characteristics but some have human forms with only one or two animal characteristics like animal ears or fangs. Though most yōkai are either dangerous or mischievous, some are said to bring good luck.

Pivotal Moments in the Film:

a. As the film begins, ten-year-old Chihiro and her parents are driving to their new home in the countryside, when Chihiro's father takes a wrong turn. Their exploration takes them to a theme park abandoned, like so many others, in the wake of the Japanese economic bust of the 1990s. In the decades before, Japan's economic development and success was a modern-day miracle.

   But when that economic bubble burst in the 1990s, not only were many establishments and buildings abandoned but they also evolved in a sense of nostalgia for a time gone by and for what might have been. It is this feeling that populates the abandoned theme park in *Spirited Away* with creatures of the spiritual realm, invisible to humans.

b. When her parents become stuck in the Spirit World, Chihiro accepts the help of a mysterious boy named, Haku, in order to rescue them. She sets out to get a job at the bathhouse owned by the witch, Yubaba. Thus, Chihiro is thrown into a world straight out of Japanese mythology: she encounters countless yōkai, ranging from the scary but benign Radish Spirit, to the powerful and benevolent River Spirit, and to the mysterious and dangerous No-Face Spirit. She also encounters the tiny spy spirits called shikikami that help Yubaba's twin sister Zeniba, as well as director Miyazaki's personal invention, the susuwatari coal spirits that look like fuzzy black balls with legs and eyes. With the help of her friends and her incredible bravery, Chihiro saves her parents and returns to the Human World, ready to face the difficulties of moving to a new home and school.

Post-Screening Questions:
A. History and Social Science:

1. The stinky Slime Monster that sluggishly came into the bathhouse turned out to be a River Spirit. How can this be? What was it that the thorn plugged in its side released, when Sen noticed it and Yubaba ordered everyone to help her remove it? What does the incident say about the pollution of our rivers?
2. It is revealed that Haku, too, is a River Spirit, the spirit of the Kohaku River in which Chihiro nearly drowned as a little girl. Compare Haku to the other River Spirit. Can you find any similarities that foreshadowed Haku's true identity?
3. How can the bathhouse be a metaphor for globalization?
4. Brainstorm scenes in which Chihiro's actions are determined by her loyalty to a group she belongs to, e.g. family, friends, workers, humans.

Hints:

*   When the bathhouse workers managed to pull out the thorn in the River Spirit's side, a flood of trash spewed out. The River Spirit had been weighed down by the trash. Finally free, it thanks Sen (Chihiro's new name) and then flies away happily and weightlessly, but only after leaving her a treasure – the healing dumpling. The spirit is a metaphor for the pollution of rivers. The

message of the scene is that rivers cannot flow freely and give us that precious clean water that we all need if they are polluted.

- When the River Spirit flew away, its shape was that of a long, sinuous dragon that greatly resembled Haku's dragon form. The slimy slug in Haku causes him sickness in a way similar to how the trash polluting the River Spirit made it sick.

- The bathhouse is home to a great diversity of spirits, living and working in harmony. Sharing cultures and finding harmony in diversity is what globalization does as well.

B. Literature and Visual Arts:

1. *Spirited Away* is a specific kind of Japanese animation called "anime." What differences did you notice between this film and other animated film you've seen, such as those by Pixar or Dreamworks?
2. Why did Haku help Chihiro?
3. What do you think was Zeniba's purpose in turning Yubaba's Bo into a small animal? How did it help him escape his mother's protective grasp? When Sen asked Zeniba to lift the spell off him, she said the spell had long worn off and he could change back if he wished; why do you think Bo didn't want to change back?
4. If you came across a restaurant with delicious foods in plain display but no owner or waiter in sight, would you do as Chihiro's parents did? Although they ate greedily without asking, the food was out in the open and they did promise to pay afterwards. Do you think their punishment was too harsh? Why or why not?
5. No-Face is probably the most mysterious of all the spirits that Chihiro encountered. Do you think he is good or evil, neither or both? What qualities or ideas do you think No-Face represents?

Hints:
- Possible differences your group may notice between Japanese anime and American animation may be:
  ◦ darker themes like No-Face's monster form or Chihiro's constant terror
  ◦ differences in the texture of the animation, e.g. bigger eyes, "Ghibli tears"
  ◦ cultural differences, e.g. sleeping in groups on the floor of bare rooms, the way the characters are dressed, etc.

- Haku recognized and helped Chihiro out of instinct. When Chihiro was younger, she fell into the Kohaku River. But she was carried carefully to safety by the spirit of the river. This love remained in Haku, even though he could not remember the incident or Chihiro herself, and he instinctively wants to save her again. This time, however, Chihiro is older and she saves Haku; thus forming a powerful mutual bond of friendship, protectiveness, and love.
- Yubaba did not recognize Bo after he was turned into a small animal, and this allowed Bo to escape his mother's over protectiveness and venture out into the world. One thing you may speculate is that Bo would feel safer as a small, unnoticeable animal than as a big, obvious baby.

Curriculum Themes:
A. History and Social Science:

Chapter's Key Themes:

a. Environmentalism:

- Environmental damage and pollution are very important themes in the film, expressed allegorically in several different instances:
  - Chihiro's first customer is a creature that Yubaba calls a Slime Spirit. It is big, muddy, slow moving, and smelly. It is such a horrible creature that everyone in the bathhouse – workers and guests alike – stop what they're doing to watch what happens. While Sen draws the Slime Spirit a bath, she discovers a thorn in its side and tells Yubaba about it. Yubaba immediately realizes the thorn is plugging something up, and everyone helps Sen remove the thorn. Suddenly, a flood of trash and broken objects flows out of the Slime Spirit, filling the bathhouse with garbage. It wasn't a Slime Spirit after all! It was a River Spirit that had become so polluted with trash that it was unrecognizable.
  - In gratitude, the River Spirit gives Sen a small dumpling. She uses it twice. Once she heals a very badly wounded Haku with it, and it helps eliminate from within him Yubaba's controlling slug. She gives the remaining dumpling to a maniacally greedy and consuming No-Face, who immediately begins purging himself of all that he had eaten. The River Spirit's dumpling is a healing object that has the power to eliminate everything that is dirty and foreign from inside characters. This in itself is an anti-pollution

metaphor. But it is also important to consider that this dumpling is something the River Spirit could only create after it had been cleaned. An unpolluted environment gives back to us; it offers truly powerful gifts in return.

 ° Chihiro finally remembers that as a small child she had fallen into the Kohaku River and was returned safely to shore. Haku was the spirit of that river, and he was the one who saved her. She also tells him that the river doesn't exist anymore, and Haku finally understands the reason he has been unable to return home.

Suggested Activities:

- *Members of your group can conduct eco-friendly activities for recycling bins in your school and residences.*
- *Very often, the reason people don't recycle is because they are not sure whether their item fits in a recycling category or not. You can research this and make a list of common objects that fall under different recycling categories (paper, plastic, metal), and put signs on the bins.*

Hints:

- Paper recycling: cardboard, printed paper without your name, milk cartons, construction paper, magazines, newspapers, brown paper bags, torn books you want to throw out, etc.
- Plastic recycling: (look for the recycle symbol to make sure it can be recycled); plastic liquid bottles, yogurt/ milk/ sour cream containers.
- Metal recycling: soft drink cans and other aluminum cans, aluminum foil, tin cans, soup cans
- Glass recycling: glass beverage bottles, some coffee containers, emerald glass, light bulbs, plastic caps
- Batteries contain metals like lead and mercury that can harm the soil and contaminate groundwater, so it is important that they are disposed of carefully. Batteries may be recycled at a nearby electronic store like Best Buy.

b. Coming of Age: (work, love, bravery, know thyself, don't be greedy)

Over the course of the film, Chihiro learns several important lessons. We can see the impact of these lessons if we compare her character at the beginning of the film and at the end:

 ° Comparing fear is one example. When her story starts, she is a very fearful young girl. In the family's symbolic encounter of the unknown – an abandoned tunnel and theme park – Chihiro's parents are eager to explore, while Chihiro herself tries desperately to hold them back and only follows out of fear of being left alone. At the end of the film, however, when Chihiro's father says that it is scary moving to a new place, Chihiro confidently and wryly says, "I think I can handle it."

    ◦ Over the course of the film, Chihiro becomes more mature, independent, and confident. This type of character development story is known as a "coming of age."

- Some of the lessons the film explores are:
  ◦ *Work*. Haku tells Chihiro that in order to be allowed to stay in the Spirit World, she must work. Furthermore, it is her responsibility to insist on working, no matter what Kamagi or Yubaba say. The theme of work is a recurring one. For example, Kamagi tells Chihiro that unless the soot balls work, they turn back into lifeless soot; work is necessary for their very existence. Another example occurs when Sen starts sweeping the bathhouse floor with several other workers, and she falls behind while everyone else acts in perfect synchronization: Lin derisively asks her if she's ever worked a day in her life.
  ◦ *Love*. The film director, Miyazaki, has spoken famously about the relationship between Chihiro and Haku: "I've become skeptical of the unwritten rule that just because a boy and girl appear in the same feature, a romance must ensue. Rather, I want to portray a slightly different relationship, one where the two mutually inspire each other to live – if I'm able to, then perhaps I'll be closer to portraying a true expression of love." Both Chihiro and Haku in turn demonstrate a very profound love for each other. Haku does not remember his own name, but he remembers Chihiro's; he does not remember where he met her; and he does not know why she is important to him. But the love that he has for her ever since he was a river spirit who saved her life, is so profound that his protectiveness and willingness to risk everything for her have become pure instinct. In turn, Chihiro defeats her fears for Haku. She faces heights to reach him; she risks Yubaba's wrath; and she volunteers to go on an unknown journey to Zeniba's home in order to save him. The love between them is so strong that both Kamagi and Zeniba observe that it was "pure love" that helped Chihiro destroy the slug Yubaba' place inside Haku. Furthermore, Chihiro is also motivated by her love for her parents and her desire to save them.
  ◦ *Bravery*. Chihiro has to defeat her fears regularly throughout the film. She must trust Haku when she finds herself in an unknown world. She must face the spirits in the Reikai even when she wishes she was dreaming. She

must defeat her fear of heights in order to get to the boiler room. Later, when she needs to face heights again in order to reach an injured Haku, she does so with no hesitation. She must defeat her fear of Kamagi to speak to him and ask for a job. She must venture into the unknown on the train in order to save Haku. Finally, she must face her fear of not being able to recognize her parents as her last test from Yubaba. Overarching everything is the story of how Chihiro manages to defeat her fear of moving and of facing the unknown.

○ *Know Thyself.* Yubaba takes away Chihiro's name and gives her another- Sen. When Haku reminds her of her real name because she needs it to leave the Sprit World, she realizes with horror that she had almost forgotten it. Can you imagine forgetting your own name, especially in only a short period of time like Chihiro almost did? Names are magical in this film; they have power and they hold someone's identity within them. Without their name, characters are lost to the Spirit World. For instance, Haku only becomes free of Yubaba when Chihiro tells him his own true name. Over the course of the film, Chihiro's relationship with her own name is symbolic of her coming of age: at first, Yubaba easily takes away her name – her identity – without her consent; then, although she knows her name, she goes by Sen and keeps her real self hidden. Finally, she freely offers her real name to Zeniba, which means she is at last confident in and in control of her own identity.

○ *Don't Be Greedy.* Chihiro's parents find a restaurant full of food and before they even find whoever owns the restaurant they begin to eat greedily. The punishment for such greed is that they are turned into pigs who can neither speak nor save themselves. Luckily for them, Chihiro was not greedy, so she remained human and eventually managed to save her parents. Chihiro's ability to resist greed is tested several more times over the course of the film. No-Face is an allegorical character for greed in two ways: he preys on the greed of other characters, and he represents greed himself. The conflict between No-Face and Sen is that No-Face is trying very hard to give Sen an overly abundant amount of what she wants. First, he notices that she needs a bath token and so steals all the bath tokens and offers them to her. Sen, however, humbly says she does not need so many. Again, when No-Face observes that everyone else in the bathhouse is willing to take the endless amount of gold he can create, he only wants Sen to accept the gold. But once more Sen tells him she does not need gold, and No-Face is disappointed. But if No-Face thrives on the greed of others, he is a slave to it as well. He has no voice, "noface," and no identity of his own; he can only speak with the voice of the spirit he eats. He becomes huge and bulging with everything he greedily consumes. The bathhouse, a luxurious place, is a very bad place for No-Face to live. In Zeniba's humble home where he is not poisoned by greed, however, No-Face finds friends and a purpose – spinning.

1. World History:

a. Globalization:

- In its fantasy setting, *Spirited Away* celebrates diversity; the constant introduction of creative new spirits gives the film its sense of enchantment. We meet frog spirits and radish spirits, nearly human-looking spirits like Lin and Kamagi, tiny black soot balls, hopping green heads, a giant baby, and so many more. All these different spirits live in harmony in the bathhouse. The bathhouse is a symbol and allegory of globalization, which brings people from diverse backgrounds and cultures together.
- Globalization is a term that refers to the spreading and integration of political, economic, and cultural trends across the world. This includes material resources, as well as intangible resources such as world views, knowledge, ideas, cultures, and languages.
- Some of the main reasons that have created modern globalization are:
  ○ Advancements in rapid transportation- air travel and cross-country railroads
  ○ Westernization of countries around the world
  ○ Improvements in communication technologies, e.g. Internet, cell phones
  ○ Increased media availability, such as music, film, television, social media.

Suggested Activities:
- *Determine the meaning of "globalization" by examining its components. Are there prefixes or suffixes that help define the word?*
- *Divide your group into smaller groups and ask each group to discuss reasons for globalizationas in the above. Ask each group to debate the above topics as being the most important factor for globalization.*

Hints:
- Examples of words ending in *–tion*: action, adoption, ambition, caution, civilization, collection, declaration, election, function, infection, location, operation,

personification, prediction, reaction, reflection, selection; transportation. The Latin suffix *–tion* is used to form abstract nouns from verbs. They can express an action, a process, a state, or a noun.

b. Shinto Religion:

- Shinto is practiced by about 80% of the Japanese population. Unlike most monotheistic religions of the world (Christianity, Judaism, Islam), Shinto is dedicated to the worship of numerous kami, a term that is often translated as gods or deities, or any divine or sacred essence in the world. Shinto is an action-centered religion, meaning it focuses on ritual practices.

Suggested Activities:
- *Ask your group to find pictures of Shinto shrines. What do they have in common?*

c. Japanese Folklore: (yōkai; shikigami; kami; Reikai)

- In order to create the Spirit World that Chihiro stumbled into, author Hayao Miyazaki borrowed from Japanese folklore, a rich and complex world with a very long history.
- Japanese mythology embraces Shinto, Buddhist, and agriculture-based religious traditions.
- One important role of mythology has been to provide a creation story that attributed divine origins to the Japanese Imperial family, assigning them godhood and therefore the right to rule. The Emperor is called "tenno" which means "heavenly emperor."
- Japanese folklore involves uncountable creatures, both terrifying and humorous.

2. Geography:

a. Map Study:

- Japan is a country formed of an archipelago of about 2,500 small islands. The four largest islands, sometimes called the "Home Islands," account for 97% of Japan's total land area. From north to south, these are Hokkaido, Honshu (the mainland), Shikoku and Kyushu. The remaining 3% of the land area is in small islands, some inhabited and others not. This includes the Ryukyo Islands and Okinaway, a chain of islands south of Kyush .

- Most of the islands are mountainous. A mountain range runs through each of the main islands. However, some land is volcanic; for instance, Japan's highest peak, Mount Fuji, is a 3,776-meter tall volcano dormant since 1707.
- Located along the Pacific Coast of Asia, Japan has the Sea of Japan on its western side. Nearby countries are South Korea, North Korea, Mongolia, China, and Russia. Japan has had differences with all these countries regarding territorial rights of islands.
- Japan's name (Nippon or Nihon) literally means "sun-origin." This is because it lies to the east of nearby countries, especially China. Japan is sometimes referred to as the "Land of the Rising Sun."
- Japan has the world's 10th largest population, with over 127 million people. Tokyo, its capital, is the largest city in the world, with over 30 million residents. Meanwhile, it is ranked 62nd in terms of total area. This means Japan has an unusually high population density in their cities.
- About 70% to 80% of the country is mountainous or forested, and is therefore unsuitable for agricultural, industrial, or residential use. Japan has to import their rice.
- The climate varies from cool temperate in the north to subtropical in the south. Although widely variable, it can be said that Japan is generally a rainy country with high humidity. Seasons are very distinctive, with variation such as the blooming of spring cherry blossoms and fall foliage colors that are celebrated in art. Summer and early autumn bring typhoons.
- Japan is prone to undersea earthquakes which puts the coastline in danger from tsunamis and tidal waves. The devastating 9.0 earthquake on March 11, 2011 was the largest Japan has ever recorded and the fourth largest seen in the whole world.

Suggested Activities:
- *Ask members of your group to make a vocabulary worksheet related to geography. Vocabulary words can include the following: archipelago, to inhabit, temperate, subtropical, foliage, typhoon, tsunami, tidal wave.*
- *In pairs, label a blank map of Japan with the four major island names and the names of Japan's neighboring countries.*
- *Japan's relationship with its neighbors is very tenuous in the present. Members of your group can discuss Japan's relationship focusing on territorial disputes but also considering economy and trade, with: South Korea, North Korea, Mongolia, China, and Russia.*

Hints:

- Japan is currently engaged in several territorial disputes with its neighbors: with Russia over northern islands called the Kurile Islands by Russia and the Northern Territories by Japan; with South Korea over islands in the Sea of Japan called the Dokdo Islands by South Korea and the Takeshima Islands by Japan; and with China over the southern islands known as the Diaoyu Islands by China and the Senkaku Islands by Japan.
- Additionally, Japan faces an ongoing dispute with North Korea over its abduction of Japanese citizens and its nuclear weapons program. Relations with Mongolia are improving, with Japan loaning Mongolia money for the construction of a new airport.

b. Disputed Islands and China:

- The Senkaku Islands are a group of 8 uninhabited islands currently controlled by Japan and located in the East China Sea. They are known as the Diaoyu Islands in China and as the Diaoyutai Islands in Taiwan. Their rocky history has led to ownership disputes between the three states. Japan had ownership of the islands from 1865 until its surrender at the end of World War II in 1945. The islands passed to the United States until 1971, when the U.S. returned ownership to Japan. However, China has laid claim to the discovery of the islands in the 14th century. Despite the conflict between Taiwan and China, both governments agree that the islands are a part of Taiwan. Japan does not acknowledge either claim.

Suggested Activities:
- *Research the following to understand better the Senkaku islands:*
  - *What is the total area of the islands?*
  - *Why are the islands so important to both China and Japan?*
  - *Which state, Japan, China, or Taiwan, is the closest to the islands?*
  - *If Japan and China come to war, whom would the U.S. support and why?*

Hints:
- The islands have a total area of approximately 7 square miles.
- In the 1970s, the Senkaku Islands were discovered to be potential sources of oil. In the present, they are also important because they are close to important shipping lanes and offer rich fishing grounds. Their position also makes it strategically important for military dominance in the Asia-Pacific region.

- The islands are about 400km from Japan, 330km from China, and 170km from Taiwan.
- If military force becomes needed, the U.S. would have to back Japan. This is because of a security alliance, sealed between Japan and the U.S. after World War II, called 'The Treaty of Mutual Cooperation and Security between the United States and Japan.'
- In 2012, the Japanese government bought three of the islands from their private owner, which brought the issue to the forefront of public debate and prompted large-scale protests in China.

3. Economics:

a. Lifetime Employment:

- Work is a very important theme in the film. In order to be able to stay in the Spirit Realm and at the bathhouse to try to rescue her parents, Chihiro is told that she needs to get a job. One of her first interactions with the Spirit Realm was with Kamagi and the soot balls carrying coal: with good intentions, Chihiro helped a struggling soot back carry its burden; but once she does, all the other soot balls start dropping their coal in order to receive help, and Kamagi tells her she can't just take away someone else's job. Once she signs the job contract, she is protected from Yubaba. Throughout the film, Sen learns how difficult it is to work.
- Similarly, work is very important in Japanese culture. Japan is sometimes called "the land of lifetime employment." Businesses take pride in their resistance to lay off workers, even in competitive economic climates. Workers, in return, pledge devotion to their corporate employer.
- The idea of lifetime employment ("sh shin koyō") existed as far back as 1910, but it was at its most widespread and powerful in the period of economic growth following World War II (until the year, 2000).
- Although mass layoffs are restricted legally and are socially taboo, this does not mean that individual jobs are secure. In recent years, almost all lifetime job employees are susceptible to replacement by temporary workers, as companies try to save costs and stay afloat in a competitive global marketplace. From 2001 to 2008, the proportion of Japan's part-time workforce increased by 6%, to make up nearly one-half of all workers – the highest proportion of part-time workers among all industrialized nations.

Suggested Activities:
- *Divide your group into pairs to discuss the value of lifetime employment. One group may consider the point of view of businesspersons reducing labor costs by ending lifetime employment; another, that of businesspersons against repealing the lifetime employment policy; the third, the point of view of lifetime employees whose lifetime employment guarantees have been taken away; and the fourth, that of part-time foreign workers. As a group, come up with a statement and arguments from the point of view of the people whom they are representing.*

b. Zaibatsu:

- "Zaibatsu" is a Japanese term referring to industrial and financial business corporate conglomerates whose influence and size allows for control over significant parts of the Japanese economy.
- Traditionally, zaibatsu were large family-controlled vertical monopolies consisting of a holding company on top, with a banking subsidiary providing finance, and several industrial subsidiaries dominating specific sectors of a market. The zaibatsu were the heart of economic and industrial activity within the Empire of Japan, and held great influence over Japanese national and foreign policies.
- By the start of World War II, 4 big zaibatsu had direct control over more than 30% of Japan's mining, chemical, metals industries, almost 50% control of the machinery and equipment market, a significant part of foreign trade, and 60% of the stock exchange. These 4 are Mitsubishi, Mitsui, Sumitomo and Yasuda.

Suggested Activities:
- *Your group may want to research the following business terms: market, industry, supply and demand, corporate conglomerate, monopoly, vertical monopoly, horizontal monopoly, etc.*

Hints:
- *market:* an abstract place ruled by supply and demand, where buyers and sellers meet to exchange goods or services; the "market" is what determines prices in a democratic economic system.
- *industry:* any particular business field, including its manufacturers and sellers e.g. agriculture industry, auto industry, tourism industry, textile (clothing) industry.

- *supply and demand:* supply is how much of a product exists, and demand is how much of that supply people actually want. These determine the price of products: if there is high supply but low demand, the object will be cheap; if there is low supply but high demand, the object will be expensive (e.g. diamonds are rare, but a lot of people want them, so they are very expensive.)
- *corporate conglomerate:* a corporation is a group of people recognized by law as a company; a conglomerate is a combination of two or more corporations in different industries, usually with a parent company at the top and many helping companies called subsidiaries.
- *monopoly:* a situation in which only one producer controls a whole industry. For instance, is H&M became so popular that people only bought clothes from them, all other clothes sellers would go out of business, and H&M would have a monopoly. This is generally considered bad, because H&M can control supply and demand, and make things very expensive for people. If other clothes sellers exist, prices would be lower because they would be competing for customers.

c. Infrastructure:

- Chihiro's father explains the presence of the abandoned theme park by explaining that, when the economy went bad in the 1990s, a lot of such theme parks ended up being emptied and abandoned.
- Japan had an isolationist approach to interaction with the Western world. After the horrible devastation that the atomic bombs caused in Nagasaki and Hiroshima, and Japan's subsequent surrender in World War II, no one could ever have anticipated the economic boom that followed. The period from the 1960s to the 1980s is sometimes referred to as the Japanese post-war economic miracle. Overall economic growth was 10% in the 1960s – an extraordinary amount. This was a period of conspicuous consumption: lavish spending on cars, alcohol, and real estate.
- However, in 1991, prices began to stagnate and the economic bubble burst. Just as Chihiro's father says, a lot of buildings had to be abandoned. The 90s are known as Japan's Lost Decade. Prices remained at the same level, but wages fell, which meant that products and services were suddenly too expensive for people. The Japanese government tried several techniques to revive the economy with little success. In recent years, Japan's economy has started growing again.

4. Civics, Citizenship, & Government:

a. Post-WWII Constitution:

- The first constitution of Japan was the 1889 Constitution of the Empire of Japan, or the Meiji Constitution. It provided for a limited monarchy. Theoretically, the emperor was supreme ruler, leading the Prime Minister and his cabinet. In practice, however, the emperor was more of a symbolic ruler (head of state), and the Prime Minister was the actual head of government. Neither was directly elected by the people.
- The current constitution was enacted on May 3, 1947, following Japan's defeat at the hands of Allied Powers.
- The new constitution allows for a bicameral legislature (similar to the American system, with two houses elected by the people). Human and civil rights are guaranteed, and the symbolic status of the Emperor is solidified. But by far the most controversial provision was Article 9 – the renunciation of war. This was intended to prevent Japan from becoming an aggressive military power again.
- Despite the role of the U.S. in drafting this constitution, within a decade the U.S. was pressuring Japan to rebuild its army in Asia after the Korean War and defend their territories in the South China Sea.
- In 2014, a reinterpretation was approved, despite protests. Japan would be allowed to exercise military action if one of its allies were to be attacked or if self-defense is necessary. Military troops have served abroad for U.N. peace-keeping operations and hundreds of troops are sent abroad for reconstruction, humanitarian, election monitoring, and water-purification missions around the world.
- Due to flexible interpretation of their Constitution and limits placed on building up their military, the Japanese government has focused on restoring their military, which now has the 7th largest military budget in the world.

b. Group Identity:

- The soot balls Chihiro meets in Kamagi's boiler room can only carry a tiny piece of coal alone, but they work together to keep the whole bathhouse operating well. They are not the only ones that exhibit group identity. Once Chihiro becomes employed at the bathhouse, she joins Lin and her group of female spirits. As part of this group, Chihiro's individual identity becomes secondary to her group identity. They wear the same clothes and sleep in rows in the same room. One scene demonstrates the power of group identity: in perfect synchronicity, several workers each push a brush across the floor, thus finishing the job much faster than if only one worker had been doing it. Sen struggles to keep up; that is, she is doing her best to become part of the group.

- Japanese culture is group-oriented rather than individual-oriented. This means:
  - ° They yield their personal rights and individual feelings to the group.
  - ° They are willing to sacrifice themselves for father, family or country.
  - ° Inclusion in the group is very important. To be excluded or shunned is a major misery.
  - ° "Individualism" and "equality" and "freedom of expression" are alien concepts.
  - ° To be or think differently from the group is considered anti-social.
  - ° Group loyalties last a lifetime in Japan.

- Some important terms include:
  - ° The goal of groupness is *"wa"* – harmony. In daily life, this means maintaining a comfortable atmosphere of acceptance and respect at all times. Confrontation is avoided. Respect for other people's feelings is a priority.
  - ° Group loyalty is measured by *"giri"* – obligations and duty – which are part of their motivation whenever they do something. This includes reciprocating in buying a present from someone to fulfilling their duty to their company.
  - ° Consensus in management style – *"ringi"* – is very important in business.

- This emphasis on the group rather than the individual has implications for the functioning of virtually every aspect of culture and politics.
- *In philosophy:* The Confucian ethic, which still governs in Japan, demands unanimity. In order to respect the rights of the minority, the majority will compromise on almost every issue until a consensus is reached.
  - ° *In school and education:* A Japanese person is part of a group, first and forever. The first group is family, where the child learns loyalty and vertical hierarchy. As one grows older, the group is applied to a school, club, organization, and later company and country. Excessive individualism is an ethically unacceptable thought for Japanese.

○ *In business:* Group consensus in negotiations is opposed to American individualism and the individual's power to make a decision. Americans find this process slow.

○ *At work:* Employees identify so much as a team player in their company, that, when they introduce themselves, they often give their company name before their own.

○ *In infrastructure:* Japan had offices designed as open space as early as the 1970s, when all employees at every hierarchical and management level worked as a group in an open environment.

COMPARISON OF CROSS CULTURAL PRACTICES:
U. S. and JAPAN

United States	Japan
Direct approach and bluntness, straight and open	Indirect approach, ambiguous replies
Individualism	Group identity, collectivism
"Yes" is yes, frank opinion	*Hai* (yes) does not necessarily mean yes; it can avoid personal confrontation
Melting pot society, heterogeneous, immigrant culture	Homogenous society, 99% are Japanese
Mobile society, "rags to riches" possibility	Closed society; *gaijin* (foreigner) are outsiders, assimilation is difficult
Short term business goals, immediate gains and profit	Long range planning, long-term profits
The end results are most important, less important are the means (Machiavelli's influence)	Smooth relations and *wa* (harmony) are most important
Informal personal relations	Formal relationships
Free expression of anger and negative emotions	Self-control, hiding emotions, *Nintai* (endurance)
Giggles and smiles caused by happiness	Giggles caused by embarrassment or self-deprecation
Self-assertion; to stand out is an asset	Humble, modest, deferential

Suggested Activities:

- *How does Chihiro demonstrate her loyalty or her belonging to her groups? Are there any groups that present clashing interests for Chihiro? Which does she choose?*

- *In pairs, a fun time is to write and perform a skit that illustrates the cultural differences between Japanese and Americans. Consider cultural differences and miscommunications that that can range from being funny to having serious consequences.*

Hints:
Chihiro's actions are defined by her inclusion in a group:

- *Family:* Chihiro follows her parents even though she is very scared, and she remains in the Spirit world in order to save them when they become pigs.
- *Bathhouse workers:* Sen becomes an important member of the bathhouse workers. She works hard for their interests in pleasing guests. Her belonging to this group is symbolized by the moment when everyone forms a line to help her remove the thorn in the River Spirit's side; they work as a unified whole and they are stronger because of this.
- *Female workers:* Sen sleeps with them in neat, identical rows.
- *Friendship:* At first, this group includes only Haku, but it soon grows to include Lin, Kamagi, Bo, the little Yubaba bird, No-Face, and Zeniba.

c. Simplicity:

- The bathhouse is a place of luxury that easily becomes victim to greed. We saw as much when No-Face, the spirit that grows as it feeds on the greed of others, quickly became a huge monster. As a direct contrast we have Zeniba's home, a much smaller and cozier place. There, No-Face is able to find satisfying and non-dangerous work. This is the power of simplicity.
- Simplicity is beautiful in Japanese culture. Shibui (adjective) and shibusa (noun) refer to an aesthetic of simple, subtle, and unobtrusive beauty; that is, the opposite of flashy or visually overwhelming objects. This term can refer to a wide variety of subjects: art, sculpture, fashion, interior design, writing, etc.
- Although shibui objects outwardly present themselves with economy of form and thus appear simple, they include subtle details such as textures or tiny designs. This balance of simplicity and underlying complexity ensures that one does not tire of a shibui object, but constantly finds new meanings and new reasons to appreciate its beauty.
- Shibui colors range from pastels to "muddy" colors, such as grays and browns.

- Other Japanese aesthetic principles are related to the idea of simplicity:
  - ◦ Expression in a plain, simple, and natural manner; clarity in thinking and the exclusion of the nonessential.
  - ◦ Naturalness, or the absence of artificiality or pretense.
  - ◦ Tranquility, calm, stillness, balance. This is a feeling you may have when walking through a Japanese garden or another natural scene; it is the opposite of clutter, noise, and disturbance.

d. Relocation:

- The film starts with Chihiro lying on the backseat of a car, her parents driving to their new home. We see immediately that Chihiro is sad and scared about moving. Her parents, in contrast, are excited and relaxed. We see their contrasting attitudes toward the unknown when they get out of the car: Chihiro's parents want to go forward and explore the unknown, while Chihiro herself tries to hold them back, and follows them only reluctantly. Although Chihiro develops into someone who is no longer afraid of the unknown throughout the film, her caution is not entirely misplaced. The Spirit World turns out to be dangerous for humans. Her parents are far too bold and they get stuck as pigs in the Spirit World. Therefore, the message of the film is to be brave when entering the unknown, but not to abandon caution and common sense.
- The film has a circular literary structure: it begins and ends with Chihiro and her parents in their car driving to their new home. This highlights Chihiro's change. After managing to survive in the Spirit World, moving to a new home is a piece of cake!

Suggested Activities:
- *The development of Chihiro's attitude towards relocation and the unknown are a main theme of the film. Compare the following two relocations: Chihiro at the beginning of the film, being introduced to the Spirit World, her new job, and her fellow workers; and Chihiro when she decides to take the train to Zeniba's in order to save Haku. How does her attitude change? Why has it changed?*
- *Compare the following synonyms for subtle differences in meaning: relocation, migration, deportation, displacement, journey, shift, and move.*

B. Literature and Visual Arts:

5. World Literature:

a. Pillow Books:

- The literary genre known today as "pillow books" began in the 11th century with *The Pillow Book* by Sei Shōnagon. *The Pillow Book* is a collection of observations and thoughts that Shōnagon wrote during her time as court lady to the Empress Consort Teishi, during the Heian period in Japan. In it she included lists of personal thoughts, interesting events in court, poetry, and some opinions about contemporaries.
- More generally, a pillow book is a collection of notes and fragmented ideas written and compiled in order to showcase a period of someone or something's life.
- While it is mostly a personal work, Shōnagon's writing and poetic skill make it valuable as a work of literature and as a historical document. Shonagon's Pillow Book was first translated into English in 1889 by T. Purcell and W. G. Aston.
- *Spirited Away* embodies some aspects of the style of pillow books. E.g. authors often write of observations in daily life as representative of wider social issues. *Spirited Away* also introduces the importance of work and love for Chihiro's life in particular as exemplary of the more general importance of work and love in everyone's life.

Suggested Activities:
- *Ask your group to research and read passages from The Pillow Book by Sei Shōnagon and discuss the style. How is a given section structured? What literary devices can you identify?*

b. Haiku Poetry:

- A haiku is a very short poem that, in English, usually has three lines following a pattern of 5, 7, 5 syllables per line. More specifically, haiku consist of

17 "moras" or "on", which are Japanese sound units. Although English haiku use syllables, the two concepts are not equivalent: e.g. the word "Tokyo" is perceived as having three syllables in English (To-ky-o) but four moras in Japanese (To-o-kyo-o).

- A haiku traditionally contains a "kigo," a defined word or phrase that symbolizes or implies the season of the poem. E.g. the word "kawazu" literally means "frog," but it implies springtime, when frogs emerge into the paddy fields; the word "shigure" means rain shower and implies late autumn or early winter, when there are rain showers in Japan. Therefore, language and culture intermix in haiku.

Suggested Activities:
- *Ask your group to practice writing their own haiku. This process may be split up into steps: first think of a moment in your life in which you admired a natural setting; then identify two related images (e.g. animals, flowers, trees, light, rocks, etc.); for each image, choose a carefully-selected adjective, and/or select at least two different senses to use.*
- *Write a haiku about an unexpected subject.*

6. Media Studies:

a. Anime and Manga:

- 'Anime' refers to animated Japanese productions with a specific visual style, usually characterized by colorful graphics, vibrant characters, and fantastic themes. Although it is often assumed by Westerners to be a genre of animation specifically aimed at children, anime productions actually belong to wide ranges of genres and therefore have wide ranges of audiences.
- 'Manga' is Japanese for 'whimsical images' or 'comics.' It is a style of drawing that corresponds visually with anime. Manga developed out of a mixture of ukiyo-e and Western styles of drawing. In Japanese and its English translations it is read from top to bottom and from right to left, so a manga book opens from the opposite direction compared to a Western book.
- Anime and manga are related modes of storytelling. The relationship between the two is sometimes summarized by defining anime as the animated version of popular manga series or books; ie. manga comes first and the anime is made afterwards. *Spirited Away* is an example of an original anime film.

- Unlike animation and comics in the United States that are assumed to be "for kids," a lot of anime is unsuitable for children. Japanese Anime and manga can be very dark and explicit. They can focus on heavy themes such as death, sex, and violence. Therefore, the intended audience of much anime and manga in Japan are young adults or adults.

b. Film Clips and Scene Discussions:

- *Environment:* (Scene: 00:34 – 00:40 minutes):
  Yubaba has little respect for humans. She tells Chihiro, "You humans always make a mess of things. Like you parents who gobbled up the food of the spirits like pigs."

    What other examples from the film demonstrate the damage that humans do to nature and to the spirit world?

- *Influence of Stress on Health.* (Scene: 00:42 – 00:43 minutes)
  Sen begins to feel physically sick. Strong emotions can have physical effects. All the fear and doubt of the past few hours begin to take their toll on Sen as she settles in for the night. She tells Lin she doesn't "feel so good," and crouches over as though her stomach were in pain.

    Have you ever felt emotions so strong they had a physical effect? What is the best way to handle this situation?

- *The theme of Love:* Scene: (01:52 -01:55):
  The director symbolizes the idealistic form of love between Sen and Haku by showing how two people come together to help each other fulfill their potentials.

    Haku remembers who he is with Sen's help. We can see the joy in Haku's eyes as he is given back his name and his memories, but we see in this scene that Sen/ Chihiro is just as full of joy, crying tears of happiness. Throughout the film, she has had plenty of reasons to doubt Haku. But she trusted her instincts, and they have proven trustworthy. "I knew you were good!" she says. Why is this scene important for Chihiro's character development? What is the significance of the fact that at the beginning of the scene Haku is carrying Sen, but at the end they are flying together, hand in hand?

7. Philosophy/ Critical Thinking:

a. Honne and Tatemae:

- When Sen sees Haku in public for the first time, he seems to be a completely different person than the one she knew. The Haku she knew was willing to defy Yubaba; the public Haku obeys her fully. Haku betrays no indication whatsoever that he knows Sen. Confused, Sen asks Lin if there are two Hakus.
- *"Honne"* refers to a person's true emotions, feelings, and desires. It is who someone is on the inside. These emotions may be contrary to what is expected by society or what is required according to one's position and circumstances, and so they are often kept hidden, except with one's closest friends.
- *"Tatemae"* means literally, "façade." It is the exterior behavior and opinions one displays in public. Tatemae is what is expected by society and required according to one's position and circumstances, and these may or may not match one's honne.

    The honne and tatemae dichotomy is considered to be of paramount importance in Japanese culture. The Japanese go to great lengths to avoid conflict, especially within their group. To achieve this, they show their outer self and not their inner self. They show what society expects to see and not what is true. It is very important in Japanese culture that everyone fulfill their role in society. The form is more important than the essence, the outer more than inner.

Suggested Activities:
- *Ask your group to identify moments in the film in which the division between honne and tatemae is demonstrated. An easier way to think about this is to identify moments in which a "poker face" is important.*
- *Are there moments in which characters do not observe the strict separation of honne and tatemae?*
- *Discuss the position of us as viewers, as related to different characters. Do we see Chihiro's honne or tatemae? Do we see things other characters do not? What do you think of this type of philosophy and practice?*

Hints:
- When the Slime Spirit arrives at the bathhouse emitting a horrible smell, Yubaba warns Sen not to insult their guest. They both have pained smiles stuck

on their face, attempting to uphold their tatemae – their role as gracious hosts of the bathhouse – while dangerously close to exposing their honne.

- In her first moments in the Spirit World, Chihiro meets Haku, who makes his desire to help her obvious. He makes sure she eats food from the Spirit World so that she will not fade, he tries to keep her invisible to all the other spirits, and he tells her exactly what she needs to do to save her parents. But when Chihiro sees Haku in public, he give no indication whatsoever that he knows her or cares about what happens to her. As Yubaba's servant, he must not show favor to anyone or act outside her knowledge. This sharp contrast between his honne and tatemae prompt Chihiro to question who is the real Haku?

- Chihiro does her best to hide her fear of the situation in which she is from most other characters. She hides her crying into her sheets as everyone else sleeps. She puts up a front of determination when she asks Yubaba for a job and she seems to be reluctant. But before other characters, she does not hide. She does not hide her fear in the first part of the film, when her parents keep insisting on exploring further, and she does not hide her fear from Haku.

- We, as viewers, see Chihiro's honne. This means we do not count as "the public"; rather, we are more like Chihiro's friends. By extension, we see both Haku's honne and his tatemae, which makes him our friend too, through Chihiro.

b. Proverbs:

- Proverbs are concise and precise sayings that express a culturally-held truth. Nothing defines and reflects a culture as distinctly as its language, and the simplest element of language that best encapsulates a society's values and philosophy, is its proverbs.

- Japanese proverbs give us a window to their culture. Some examples are:
  - "The pheasant that flies too high gets shot down."
  - "The one who yells the loudest, loses."
  - "Smart hawks hide their claws."
  - "If one sits on a rock for 3 years, it will heat up."
  - "Even the best have their failures."
  - "I was drunk at the time."

Suggested Activities:

- *Ask your group if anyone speaks another language. Ask them if similar proverbs as those above exist in their language? If yes, do they have the same cultural interpretation?*

c. Allegory:

- An allegory is a story, poem, picture, character, or idea that can be interpreted as having a hidden meaning. For example, the animal characters in a fable are usually allegories of human traits, so the animal which loses in the fable is the personality trait that is condemned and the animal that wins is the human characteristic that is celebrated. Allegories have also been popular in repressive political regimes, since authors could subtly criticize the government without getting into trouble.

SOME FAMOUS EXAMPLES OF ALLEGORIES ARE:

- George Orwell's *Animal Farm.* All animals stand for different aspects of society during and after the Russian Revolution and the rise of the dictator Joseph Stalin.
- Aesop's *Fables.* Usually, fables are allegorical by definition. They involve personified animal characters that represent certain personality traits that people may have, and they teach a lesson about those traits.
- Plato's *Allegory of the Cave:* A group of people have lived in a cave all of their lives, facing a blank wall. They watch shadows projected on the wall by things passing in front of a fire behind them and begin to ascribe forms to these shadows, using language to identify their world; e.g. they use the word "book" to describe a shadow of a book, not realizing that there is more to the concept. The shadows are as close as the prisoners get to viewing reality. One day, someone turns around and sees the actual objects that produced the shadows. He tries to tell the people in the cave of his discovery, but they do not believe him because the shadows are all they have ever known. This allegory is about a philosopher perceiving the true nature of reality while others understand only approximately what has happened. It is also an allegory about human ignorance and closed-mindedness.

SPIRITED AWAY HAS MANY ALLEGORICAL FIGURES;
- The whole Spirit World may be said to be an allegory for the unknown. Chihiro is afraid of what moving will bring, and she is forced to face all her fears in this fantasy world. She learns that whatever may come, she can handle it. The Spirit World may also be an allegory for the progression from childhood into maturity in life: what you need to survive is a job, friends, family, and bravery.

Suggested Activities:
- *Ask members of your group to find some fables to share and then discuss it. What lesson does the fable teach? Do you agree? How is it an allegory? What human traits are allegorized in the fable and how? Some fables that may be used are:*
  ° *The Tortoise and the Hare*
  ° *The Ant and the Grasshopper*
  ° *The Lion and the Mouse*
  ° *The Wolf in Sheep's Clothing*
  ° *The Boy Who Cried Wolf*

8. Music and Art:

a. New Japan Philharmonic:

- The New Japan Philharmonic is a symphony orchestra founded in 1972 and currently based in Tokyo, Japan. In the summer of 2004, an offshoot project called the World Dream Orchestra was launched, which aimed to appeal to a more diverse audience with programs that pushed genre boundaries. They are well-known for their video game performances and their film soundtrack productions. The following are some of the video games, anime, and films to which they contributed:
  ° Super Smash Bros.
  ° Resident Evil
  ° Kingdom Hearts
  ° Final Fantasy
  ° Neon Genesis Evangelion
  ° *Spirited Away*
  ° *Howl's Moving Castle*

b. 'Always With Me' ('Istumo Nandodemo'):

- Youmi Kimura is a Japanese singer and lyre performer originally from Osaka, Japan. Although she rose to fame in 2001 song with her song for *Spirited Away*, 'Always With Me,' she and Miyazaki knew each other for several years before. Kimura was so moved by his 1997 film *Princess Mononoke* that she wrote to him and enclosed her album. Miyazaki in turn was very impressed. Kimura composed 'Always With Me' with her lyricist, Wakako Kaku, for Miyazaki's *Rin the Chimney Cleaner,* but the project was eventually scrapped. Later, as Miyazaki began to work on *Spirited Away,* he would listen to Kimura's song repeatedly. The song about inner peace fit the coming of age story perfectly.

Suggested Activities:
- *Ask your group to find this music and to choose a few lines they can interpret.*

c. ukiyo-e prints:

- Ukiyo-e translates literally to "pictures of the floating world." It is a genre of woodblock prints and paintings that flourished in Japan from the 17th to the 19th centuries (Edo period, 1603 – 1867). The audience aimed for was the prosperous merchant class in newly urbanizing areas.
- Popular human subjects were geishas (traditional female entertainers and art performers), kabuki actors (classical dance-drama performers), and sumo wrestlers. Other subjects include scenes from history and folk tales, travel scenes, landscapes, flora and fauna, and erotica.
- The tradition of ukiyo-e is not dead. It has inspired many descendent traditions in the 20th and 21st century in Japan, and it has influenced the work of many Western artists as well.

Suggested Activities:
- *<http://ukiyo-e.org/> is a website where you can search many of the largest ukiyo-e collections in the world. It is organized chronologically, and then by artist.*
- *To discuss these prints, you may want to think about:: What characterizes prints in this time period and how are they different from other time periods? What colors are used? What are the main subjects – humans, landscapes, animals? Is there any writing? Are the drawings abstract or realistic?*

9. Technology:

a. Studio Ghibli:

- Studio Ghibli was founded in 1985 by Hayao Miyazaki, Isau Takahata (director), and Toshio Suzuki (producer). This happened following the success of Miyazaki's *Nausicaa of the Valley of the Wind*. Headquarters is in Tokyo, Japan. The name "Ghibli" was the name of an Italian aircraft that referred to a Mediterranean wind, the idea being that the studio would "blow a new wind through the anime industry."
- Since then, this Japanese animation film studio has had extraordinary success. 8 of Studio Ghibli's films are among the 15 highest-grossing anime films made in Japan. *Spirited Away* tops that list. 4 films were nominated for an Academy Award in the United States, and *Spirited Away* won an Academy Award for Best Animated Feature Film in 2003.
- *Nausicaa of the Valley of the Wind* was heavily edited for its U.S. release, which brought about the studio's "no-edits" policy when licensing their films abroad. A popular rumor is that when Mirimax co-chair Harvey Weinstein suggested editing *Princess Mononoke*, a Studio Ghibli producer sent an authentic Japanese sword with the simple message of "no cuts."

Suggested Activities:
- *An interesting topic for discussion is can a good book be turned into a good film? What differences and similarities between the two can be identified? Which contains more information? What advantages or disadvantages does each have compared to the other? If it helps, think of a story that is told both as a book and as a film (e.g. Harry Potter, The Fault in Our Stars, The Hunger Games, The Life of Pi, etc.) to compare. The topic may also be related to the difference between anime (film) and manga (writing).*

b. Computer Generated Imagery (CGI) and Computer Graphics:

- Miyazaki has used traditional animation, though computer generated imagery was employed with *Princess Mononoke* to give "a little boost of elegance." He used a balance between the two and calls his animation "2D." However, in his 2008 film, *Ponyo*, Miyazaki went back to traditional hand-drawn animation for everything, saying "hand drawing on paper is the fundamental of animation."

Sidebars:

1. Public Response and Directors:

- On July 11, 2012, Roger Ebert reviewed the film:
  "I was so fortunate to meet Miyazaki at the 2002 Toronto film festival. I told him I love the "gratuitous motion" in his films; instead of every movement being dictated by the story, sometimes people will just sit for a moment, or sigh, or gaze at a running stream, or do something extra, not to advance the story but only to give the sense of time and place and who they are.

  "We have a word for that in Japanese," he said. "It's called 'ma.' Emptiness. It's there intentionally." He clapped his hands three or four times. "The time in between my clapping is 'ma.' If you just have non-stop action with no breathing space at all, it's just busyness. What really matters is the underlying emotions–that you never let go of those. And to follow the path of children's emotions and feelings as we make a film. If you stay true to joy and astonishment and empathy you don't have to have violence and you don't have to have action. They'll follow you. This is our principle."

2. Awards:

- Berlin International Film Festival- 2002- Won - Golden Berlin Bear – Jury Grand Prix – Hayao Miyazaki
- Academy Awards, USA 2002- Won- Best Animated Feature Film
- New York Critics Circle Award: 2002- Won- Best Animated Feature Film
- Japan Academy Prize for Picture of the Year: 2002- Won – Hayao Miyazaki

Bibliography of Films: Filmography
Further Global Study Resources through Film:

Famous Japanese Film Directors:

Hayao Miyazaki (Manga and Anime):

- *Princess Mononoke*
- *The Castle of Cagliostro*

- *Castles in the Sky*
- *Nausicaa*
- *Gulliver's Travels Beyond the Moon*
- *Anima Treasure Island*
- *Ali Baba and the 40 Thieves*
- *Panda! Go, Panda!*
- *Howl's Moving Castle*
- *I Lost My Little Boy*
- *Ponyo on a Clif*
- *My Neighbor Totoro*

Kiyoshi Kurosawa:

- *Cure*
- *Kairo*
- *Retribution*
- *Bright Future*
- *Doppelganger*
- *Charisma*
- *Barren Illusion*
- *Séance*
- *Licence to Kill*

Akiro Kurosawa:

- *Stray Dog*
- *Rashomon*
- *To Live*
- *Record of a Living Being*
- *Spider Web Castle*
- *The Lower Depths*
- *The Bodyguard*
- *Heaven and Hell*
- *Dersu Uzala*
- *The Shadow Warrior*
- *Ran*
- *Dreams*
- *Rhapsody in August*
- *Not Yet*

Yasujiro Ozu:

- *I was Born But*
- *The Only Son*
- *Brothers and Sisters of the Toda Family*
- *There was a Father*
- *The Flavour of Green Tea Over Rice*
- *Early Spring*
- *Floating Weeds*
- *Late Autumn*
- *An Autumn Afternoon*

About Japan:

- *Departures*
- *The Taste of Tea*
- *Mishima*
- *Nobody Knows*
- *Tokyo Sonata*

EUROPE

CHAPTER 8

THE COUNTERFEITERS (AUSTRIA)

TITLE OF FILM: *Die Fälscher*
YEAR OF RELEASE: 2007
COUNTRY: Austria
DIRECTOR: Stefan Ruzowitzky
LANGUAGE: German
LENGTH OF TIME: 98 minutes
RATING: (not rated)
CURRICULUM THEMES:

A. HISTORY and SOCIAL SCIENCE:

- Chapter's Key Themes: Holocaust
- World History: Fascism; Nationalism and its negative global effects
- Geography: Austria; Berlin; Concentration camps
- Economics: Operation Bernhard; Relationship of economic and historical movements
- Civics, Citizenship and Government: Religious Intolerance: Anti-Semitism; Human rights; the Final Solution

B. LITERATURE and VISUAL ARTS:

- World Literature: Holocaust literature
- Media Studies: Film Clips and Scene Discussions; Cinematography Techniques: character foil, circular style and flashback, symbols, color
- Philosophy/Critical Thinking: Moral dilemma; What does it take to survive; Personal voice: memoir and diary
- Music: Argentine tango; Classical music
- Technnology: Banking in Iceland

Introduction:

The Counterfeiters was directed by Stefan Ruzowitzky; screenplay by Stefan Ruzowitzky and Adolf Burger; produced by Josef Aichholzer, Nina Bohlmann and Babette Schröder; cinematography by Benedict Neuenfels; edited by Britta Nahler; music by Marius Ruhland; distributed by Universum Film AG and Sony Pictures Classic. (98 minutes)

Sorowitsch, "Sali"... *Karl Markovics*
Adolf Burger...*August Diehl*
Sturmbannführer Herzog ....*Devid Striesow*
Kolya.. *Sebastian Urzendowsky*

The Counterfeiters retells the true story of the Germans' World War II "Operation Bernhard" of destroying the Allies on an economic battle-ground. Their aim was to destabilize the British treasury by forging English bank notes and then continue to do the same to the American one-hundred dollar bill. The leader of the group of counterfeiters in Sachsenhausen concentration camp is Sali, a complex character of many shades and stripes of grey.

Pivotal Moments in the History of Austria:

- World War I was started by the assassination of the Serbian Archduke Franz Ferdinand in Sarajevo in 1914. This also led to the end of the Austro-Hungarian Empire that was soon afterwards dismantled and its territories became independent states.
- Austria remained independent until 1938 when German troops occupied the country. At that time, Austria was incorporated into the Third Reich and ceased to exist as an independent country.
- Hitler was born in Austria and was an Austrian citizen. During the war, many Austrians joined the German Fascist party and the Nazi army, especially the section of the Wehrmacht.
- One month before the end of World War II in April 1945, Vienna fell to the Soviet offensive and occupation. After the defeat of Germany, Austria, like Germany, was divided into 4 zones: American, British, French, and Russian.
- On May 15, 1955, Austria regained full independence and several months later Austria was declared neutral.
- In 1995 Austria became a member of the European Union.

Pre-Screening Questions:

a. *Discuss and share information about concentration camps. Who were Kapos and Sonderkommandos?*

- *Kapo* was a term used for certain prisoners who worked inside Fascist concentration camps during World War II for the Germans in various ways. For their services, they received privileges as food.

- *Sonderkommandos* were also prisoners who worked for the Nazis in forced labor camps, concentration camps, Pogroms, Ghettos, and extermination camps. They also directly assisted the German soldiers in the exterminating process and killing of other inmates. However, *Sonderkommandos* did not participate directly in the killing, which was reserved for the Fascist SS guards. The primary responsibility of Sonderkommandos was to dispose of the corpses. They accepted to do this morally and ethically compromised work, because it meant they would have a few more days or weeks of life, as well as better living conditions compared to the other prisoners. They would sleep in their own barracks, receive extra food, medicines and cigarettes. In the film, *The Son of Saul,* we see them at work and learn that they were not kept alive by the Germans for more than 4 months, so they would not be able to reveal the secrets about the gas chambers and concentration camps.

b. *What countries were occupied by Germany during WW II?*

- Poland, East Prussia, Lithuania, Latvia, Czechoslovakia, Austria, Hungary, Romania, Yugoslavia, Bulgaria, Greece, Belgium, Luxembourg, France, Spain, Italy, Norway, Finland, Denmark, Netherlands, Algeria, Tunisia, Morocco, and Libya.

c. *What countries were Allied Forces during World War II? Who were their leaders? What countries were Axis Powers during World War II? Who were their leaders?*

Allied Forces: United States - Franklin Roosevelt
United Kingdom - Winston Churchill
Soviet Union – Joseph Stalin
Republic of China - Chian Kai-Shek

Axis Powers: Germany - Adolf Hitler
Italy - Benito Mussolini
Japan - Hideki Tojo

d. Define the following terms:
*   Gestapo, Wehrmacht, SS Army, Third Reich, Aryan race, swastika, air raids, bomb shelters, Final solution, safe houses, neutral countries, ghetto, forgery, underground, resistance groups, Gypsies, concentration camps, labor camps.

Pivotal Moments in Film:

a. The chronology of the film, *The Counterfeiters* begins in 1936 Berlin, where we are introduced to the main character, Salomon Sorowitsch, known as Sali, a gambler, loan shark and master forger. Living the good life in Berlin as a Russian Jew, Sali's business is to forge passports and currency, and to use both to pay for his life-style. But his carefree days are discontinued when he is arrested by Herzog, a Nazi police officer, who sends him to a forced labor camp in Mauthausen.

b. Sali uses his wits and talents to survive the concentration camps by working for the Nazis as a portrait painter. After a few years, he is transferred to another concentration camp, Sachsenhausen, where Herzog has become the officer in charge. Sturmbannführer Herzog heads a secret effort to destabilize the Allies' economy by issuing counterfeit British pound notes and American dollars. Herzog remembers that Sali is the best forger and installs him in a special barrack of the concentration camp to head up a group of 142 hand-picked Jewish inmates who are artists, printers, typesetters, and bankers.

c. The prisoners are coerced to co-operate with the Nazis or succumb to the gas chamber. From 1942-1945 they work as a group to reproduce 134 million pounds of forged British bank notes.

d. The story of *The Counterfeiters* is based on reality and is an adaptation from Adolf Burger's autobiography, <u>The Devil's Workshop.</u> The book and film explore the conflict of conscience that the counterfeiters felt. They knew their talents would save their lives as long as they were needed and they would live better than their fellow inmates who were being exterminated in gas chambers. And yet, they knew that their producing counterfeit money prolonged the war in favor of the Germans. They were torn between sabotaging or acquiescing. The moral question is as compelling as their forgery.

e. Herzog, the German Nazi in charge of Sachsenhausen concentration camp, is based on Major Bernhard Krueger, a German Fascist textile engineer who learned how to match the paper, printing and design of the British pound note. He located the 142 forgers from several concentration camps with the assistance of Heinrich Himmler, Hitler's associate. The aim was to pass off the forged pound notes to use as currency to pay for petrol, food, arms, and espionage activities for the German army.

Post-Screening Questions:
A. History and Social Science:

1. How would you describe Sali's moral conflict? What are some scenes where he conceals or expresses his conscience? How does Adolf Burger oppose Sali? Why?
2. How did the Nazis envision that forging British and American currency would serve as an economic weapon during World War II? Did it work? How?
3. How would you define "genocide"?

Hints:

- Genocide is "any of the following acts committed with intent to destroy, in whole or in part, a national, ethnic, racial or religious group by the following means:"
  - ° Killing members of the group;
  - ° Causing serious bodily or mental harm to members of the group;
  - ° Deliberately inflicting on the group conditions of life, calculated to bring about its physical destruction in whole or in part;
  - ° Imposing measures intended to prevent births within the group.

4. What other countries have experienced genocide?

Hints:

- *Armenia* – During World War I, 1 million Armenians in Turkey's Ottoman Empire (1915-1917) are victims of genocide. The Armenia massacre is considered the first genocide in the 20ᵗʰ century. In April 1915, the Turks order the deportation of nearly 2 million Armenians to the deserts of Syria and Mesopotamia. Along the way, almost 1 million die of starvation or are killed by Turkish soldiers.

- *Holocaust* - During World War II, 6 million Jews are killed in Europe because the Fascists, led by Adolf Hitler, want to wipe out the Jewish race for they are considered inferior to Aryan Germans and because they, or their grandparents, have been born Jewish. The Holocaust is a systematic destruction of more than two thirds of the prewar Jewish population of Europe.
- *Cambodia* – Under the ruthless leader, Pol Pot, in 1975-1979, the Khmer Rouge kill 1.7 million people in "Killing Fields" which represents 25% of Cambodia's population.
- *Former Yugoslavia:* Bosnia-Herzegovina, Serbia, and Croatia (1991-95). The war in Bosnia and Herzegovina is a bitter armed conflict due to ethnic hatred. The number of deaths reached more than 100,000 and 1.8 million people are displaced. Most Bosniaks and Croats claim that the war is due to Serbia's aggressions.
- *Iraq* – Kurds vs. Sadam's Bath Party of Sunnis (1988) In October 1988, Sadam and his Bath party spray Kurdish mountain villages in northern Iraq and Kurdish parts of Iran with chemical and lethal gas in order to wipe out the Kurds.
- *Rwanda* – Hutus vs. Tutsis: Hutus massacre more than 1 million Tutsis during a period of 100 days from April 6 to mid July 1994 because of ethnic hatred.
- *Sudan* – Darfur. Since 2003 the western Sudan area, Darfur, has been at war, fueled primarily by a government-supported militia recruited from local Arab tribes. They are called *Janjaweed.* The genocide in Darfur has claimed more than 500,000 lives and displaced over 2 1/2 million people. The Darfur region is home to racially mixed tribes of settled peasants, who identify as African and Arabs, and nomadic herders. The majority of people in both groups are Muslim. Since February 2003, the Sudanese government in Khartoum and the government-sponsored Janjaweed militia have used rape, organized starvation, displacement, threats against aid workers, and mass murder. Violence, disease and displacement continue to kill thousands of innocent Darfurians every month.

    As of 2016, there have been attempts to make peace.

Curriculum Themes:
A. History and Social Sciences:

Chapter's Key Theme: Holocaust

- Many of the prisoners in the concentration camps knew what was going on in Europe as the Allies fought against the Axis powers. They were also aware of what was Germany's Program of "the Final Solution."

Suggested Activities:

- *How did the Sachsenhausen concentration camp fit into the Fascist plan of "The Final Solution"?*
- *Which characters in the film give us information about the Holocaust?*
- *What was life for a Jew during this time?*
- *Research and discuss what the German population knew as of 1942 that there was a "Holocaust" going on in Europe?*

Hints:

- All the members of the counterfeiters are aware of what is happening inside their concentration camp as well as outside. As the film progresses, these prisoners give us bits of information similar to a Greek chorus. One character tells us at the end of the film that the bombing they hear is from Berlin and the allies are destroying Berlin. Burger is aware and says, that the war is ending. Herzog prepares to leave the camp just before the Allies liberate the prisoners. He even prepares his expected post-war trial by having Sali sign a letter that Herzog had saved the group of 142 Jews. He hopes this will exonerate him as a war criminal. (In reality, after two years of being incarcerated in England and one year in France, Herzog is set free because of these testaments.)

- The Final Solution was Nazi Germany's plan and execution of the systematic genocide of European Jews during World War II, resulting in the most deadly phase of the war – to systematically kill millions of Jews by mass extermination in selected concentration camps equipped with gas chambers. This was implemented as of 1942. Heinrich Himmler was the chief architect of the plan and the German Nazi leader, Adolf Hitler, termed it, "the final solution of the Jewish question." (*Die Endlösung der Judenfarge,* in German)

1. World History:

a. Fascism:

- *The Counterfeiters* begins its storyline in Berlin 1936 and ends in 1945 when the Fascists are defeated. These 9-10 years represent the duration of Fascism in Europe that was master-minded by Hitler and the Nazi army. We see how Sali is arrested and how he, as well as other Jewish prisoners, are treated as victims of the Fascist goal of exterminating all European Jews.

- There are strong scenes when SS soldiers arrest Jews, beat them up, shoot them, and humiliate them. The prisoners are afraid and do not fight back. They realize Fascism is the law during this heinous period of history and there is nothing they can do. *Hier ist nein warum.* (Here is no why.)

Suggested Activities:
- *Compare the democratic political system of the United States during the 1930s and 1940s with the Fascist political system of Germany. Include ideology, structure of government, decision-making processes, and court systems.*
- *Have your group create a time-line that shows dates and events that indicate the rise and fall of Fascism. Include the causes and consequences of its birth and decline.*

Hints:
- Fascism is a form of *totalitarian* state in which one leader controls every detail of the citizen's life from birth to death through a one-party dictatorship. Hitler's one party government was called the *Third Reich.* We see them in action during the film. This became one of the most ferocious and inhumane dictatorships in the world.
- Fascism is a term used to exalt the nation, or race, or culture with the intent to promote unity and strength. At the same time, this political ideology denigrates an opposing nation, or race, or culture of opponent groups. (Jewish race)
- Fascists promote a type of national unity that is usually based on ethnic, cultural, national, racial and/or religious concepts.
- The term *facismo* was coined originally by the Italian Fascist dictator, Benito Mussolini who ruled Fascist-controlled Italy from 1922 to 1943, in his *Doctrine of Fascism.* He defined fascism as a collective ideology in opposition to democracy, liberalism, individualism and even socialism. The word is derived from the Italian word *fascio,* which means "bundle" or "union" and suggests strength through unity.
- In a government of *Fascism,* the dictator has complete totalitarian control by suppressing all opposition by the use of secret police (the Gestapo), suppressing personal rights and freedoms, promoting a policy of racism, and disregard for human rights and justice.
- *Nazism* is the "policy" of ruling associated with the German dictator, Adolf Hitler, of the National Socialist Party based on the principles of extreme nationalism and military racism: the Aryan race should rule and all minorities like Jews and Gypsies should be exterminated.

- *Adolf Hitler* (1889-1945) was Germany's Chancellor and leader of the Nazi Party from 1933-1945. His goal was to conquer all Europe during World War II and kill all Europeans who were born Jewish or who had Jewish parents or grandparents.
- Fascism existed not only in Germany but in Italy as well under the dictator, *Benito Mussolini,* called *Il Duce* (The Leader). He allied Italy with Germany (Rome-Berlin Axis) during World War II.

b. Nationalism and its Negative Global Effects:

- Throughout the film, there are scenes when Sali, Burger and other characters disclaim the Third Reich's nationalism. The repetitive scenes of the counterfeiting workplace when Herzog tells the group that Himmler is not happy with their progress are full of tension. We are afraid for the Jewish inmates. We realize that Himmler, chief of Police and Interior, will have the final word. Herzog, as well as the other SS men, are carrying out orders of *Nationalism,* a negative form of nationalism.

Suggested Activities:
- *Each member of your group can represent one of the 28 countries of the European Union and report: What has their country done post-World War II to help encourage positive nationalism and religious tolerance? Has their country been involved in events about religious or ethnic intolerance? Discuss the country's present-day policy about "migrants" using as examples some of the 28 countries in the European Union.*

Hints:
- Nationalism is the feeling of patriotism and pride in one's country. However, when nationalism is twisted to the extreme, it causes negative results: international disagreements, conflicts, wars, and dictatorships.
- We see the negative aspects of extreme nationalism in Germany during the 1930s that led to justify the dictatorship of Hitler and the rise of Fascism in Italy and Germany.
- We see the negative aspects also of nationalism in Africa when countries tried to free themselves from colonial rule and assure their national heritage and rights. Often independence came at a high human price.
- An example of negative nationalism is the Rwandan genocide that was a result of a long-time hatred between Hutus and Tutsis and their competitive clash to become nationalistically superior.

- Violence in Chechnya against Russia is another example of negative nationalism from both perspectives.
- The continuous fighting in the Middle East, Syria, Libya, and Iraq illustrate further the negative aspects of zealous national pride.

2. Geography:

a. Austria:

- *The Counterfeiters* is made by Austrian director, Stefan Ruzowitzky, the only Austrian film to ever win the Oscar for Best Foreign language. The director felt the story of the Holocaust was Austria's history as well as Germany's. Hitler was born in Austria and many Austrians shared Hitler's anti-Semitic beliefs and volunteered to join the Fascist Army, as did Ruzowitzky's paternal grandfather.

Suggested Activity:
- *Members of your group can form smaller groups to report on a description of the city of Vienna and report on the country Austria, as it was pre-World War II, post, and today.*

Hints:
- Austria is located in Central Europe. It borders both Germany and the Czech Republic to the north, Slovakia and Hungary to the east, Slovenia and Italy to the south, and Switzerland and Liechtenstein to the west.
- Austria became a member of the European Union in 1995 and retained its constitutional neutrality like another E.U. member, Sweden.
- Austria, today, is one of the 10 richest countries in the world in terms of GDP per capita and has a very high standard of living.
- Vienna is Austria's capital and main city with a population of about 1.7 million. It is the 10th largest city according to population in the European Union. The United Nations has offices in Vienna as the Organization of Petroleum Exporting Countries and the International Atomic Energy Agency (IAEA).
- In 2010, only 16% of people living in Vienna had nationalities other than Austrian. The religions of the Viennese resident population is divided according to the 2010 census as follows: Roman Catholic- 49.2%; Muslim- 7.8%; and Protestants- 35%.

b. Berlin:

- On January 30, 1933, Hitler and the Nazi Party came to power and the Fascist government began to arrest members of Germany's Jewish community.
- On November 9, 1938 Hitler's gangs attacked Jewish property with an organized outbreak of violence against Jewish inhabitants. This was *Kristallnacht*, Night of Broken Glass. In one night, German soldiers throughout Germany, destroyed with sledgehammers 1574 synagogues (constituting nearly all Germany had); burned Jewish houses; desecrated Jewish cemeteries; and broke the glass windows of more than 7,000 shops and 29 department stores owned by Jews. The streets of Germany were covered with broken glass. More than 30,000 Jews (one fourth the male population) were arrested and taken to concentration camps. This marked the beginning of the Holocaust.
- The events in Austria were no less horrendous, and most of Vienna's 94 synagogues were partially or totally damaged on the same night.
- During the war, large parts of Berlin were destroyed in the 1943-45 air raids when the Allies were bombing the city.
- At the end of the war in 1945, the victorious Allied powers divided Berlin into four sectors, similar to the occupation zones into which Germany was divided. The sectors of the Western Allies (the United.States, United Kingdom, and France) formed West Berlin while the Russian sector formed East Berlin and went to communist rule until 1989.
- In 1961 the city was divided by the construction of the *Berlin Wall*. Any East German who attempted to cross the Wall into democratic West Germany was shot.
- The separation of the two German states into communist-controlled East Germany and democratic West Germany, and Berlin into East Berlin and West Berlin, increased Cold War tensions. West Berlin was surrounded by East German territory. East Germany, however, proclaimed East Berlin (which it described only as "Berlin") as its capital. Although half the size and population of West Berlin, it included most of the historic center of the city.
- In Berlin, it was possible for Westerners to pass from the eastern part of the city to the western part only through strictly controlled checkpoints, as *Checkpoint Charlie*. For most Eastern Europeans, travel to West Berlin or West Germany was impossible.
- The Berlin wall was demolished by East Germans on November 9, 1989. This historical event marked the demise of Communism in Germany and the end of the Cold War between Russia and the United States.

- On October 3, 1990, the two parts of Germany were reunited as the Federal Republic of Germany, and Berlin became the German capital according to the unification treaty. In 1999, the German parliament and government made Berlin their capital.

Suggested Activities:

- *Ask members of your group to divide into two groups to discuss the importance of the date, November 9th in Germany's history: the date that began Fascism and the date that ended Communism. How should this day be celebrated – or not- in Germany today?*
- *Discuss what is the responsibility of the German nation in regards to history? What is "collective guilt"?*
- *Discuss if the priority of history or human responsibility has changed today in Germany? Is this memory of history important to Germans today? What have Germans done to exonerate themselves from their past?*

Hints:

- *Kristallnacht* was the result of a 5-year planned Nazi program to destroy the Jewish population in Germany during one night on November 9, 1938. It marks the beginning of the Holocaust.
- Events began before on October 28,1938, when 17,000 Polish Jews who lived in Germany, had been gathered without warning in the middle of the night and were deported from Germany to Poland.
- Herschel Grynszpan, a seventeen-year-old German Jew who had fled to France, received a letter from his family describing the horrible conditions they experienced in this deportation. Seeking to alleviate their situation, he appealed repeatedly over the next few days to Ernst vom Rath, secretary of the German Embassy in Paris, who apparently had no intention of being helpful. In retaliation, Grynszpan shot and killed vom Rath, who died two days later on November 9th.
- Within hours, Vom Rath's assassination served as an excuse for the Nazi government to organize a planned outbreak of violence against Jewish inhabitants in Germany and Austria. This was *Kristallnacht.*

c. Concentration Camps:

- In the film we are shown Sachsenhausen concentration camp. This was based on the same plan as dozens of other concentration camps that the Nazis set up in

Europe during the 1940s to separate Jews and Gypsies from the population and to place them in a fenced area similar to prisons where they were starved, mistreated, forced to work, and ultimately killed. Some of the concentration camps under the Nazis were "extermination camps," where there was an intricate system of gas chambers and crematoria to murder large numbers of innocent civilians.

Suggested Activities:
* *Discuss what a concentration and extermination camp looked like. Use the Internet to study the location of some of the camps.*

Hints:
Major concentration camps and extermination camps located throughout Europe were:

Austria: Mauthausen (near Linz)
Germany: Dachau, Sachsenhausen (near Berlin), Bergen- Belsen (near Hanover), Dora-Miltenbau and Bucherwald, Flossenbürg, Dachau (near Munich), Ravensbrück (near Berlin), Neuengamme (near Hamburg)
Poland: Auschwitz- Birkenau (near Krakow), Gross-Rosen (near Breslau), Chelmo (near Lodz), Plaszow (near Krakow), Belzec, Majdanek, Sobibor, Treblinka, Stutthof (near Gdansk)
France: Natzweiler (near Strasbourg)
Czech Republic: Theresienstadt (near Prague)
Lativa: Kaberwald (near Riga)
Belarus: Koldichevo (near Minsk)
Ukraine: Janowsla
Slovakia: Sered (near Bratislava)
Romania: Odessa (Transnistria)
Netherlands: Westerbork
Croatia: Jasenovac

3. Economics:

a. Operation Bernhard:

* Operation Bernhard was the code name for the secret counterfeiting scheme named after Bernhard Krueger, a textile engineer who was able to match the

paper, printing, ink, and design of the British notes. This plot was launched by the Nazis in 1942 which had as its goal to flood international money markets with fake Bank of England pound notes of 5, 10, and 20 as well as $100 American bills. To organize this scheme, the Nazis hand-picked 142 Jewish graphic artists, printers, typesetters, typographers, and bankers from several concentration camps and relocated them to Sachsenhausen concentration camp where they lived in relatively comfortable barracks. Unlike the other prisoners, they ate regularly, slept in beds with white sheets instead of straw, had sanitary bathrooms, and worked while listening to classical music that drowned out the atrocities and yelling coming from inmates in other barracks.

- Bernhard Kruger was the Sturmbannführer in Sachsenhausen concentration camp, very much like Herzog in the film.

Suggested Activities:
- *Ask members of your group to discuss how forgery was used during World War II by other countries other than Germany.*
- *Analyze the scenes in the film that show how the Nazis tested the authenticity of the British pound notes before they put them into circulation. For what purpose did the Nazis use this counterfeit money? What happened to this money after the War?*

Hints:
- The Allies as well as the Axis were involved in forging stamps and banknotes: The British counterfeited the currencies of France, Italy, Morocco, the Netherlands, Norway, Germany, and Japan. The United States reproduced stamps of enemy countries as well as the currencies of Burma, Japan, China, France, Indochina, and Thailand.
- We see in the film how the Nazis used a ploy to test a batch of British banknotes by showing them directly to experts at the Bank of England and Swiss Bank. A German spy agent went to the directors of the Banks and said he had been given the pound notes and was not sure if they were fake, and if the Bank would examine them for him. Once they were diagnosed as authentic, the Nazis began to circulate more than 130 million British pound notes before the end of the War. Then they started to produce American 100 dollar bills.
- The original plan was to circulate the British forged notes by dropping the notes from airplanes in England, under the assumption that the British would

collect the money falling from the sky and spend it; thus triggering inflation. But the German Luftwaffe did not have enough planes to implement this plan. Instead, much of the money was taken to a hotel in northern Italy, in the Tyrol area, and used by the German government.

- From 1942 to 1945 the Germans used the money to buy war equipment, arms, petrol, and to finance their espionage service. The Nazis had 100 German agents abroad who used the currency for their own expenses. At the same time, they put the fake notes into circulation in Allied countries.

- A great deal of the counterfeit money landed n Argentina (under Peron), Paraguay (under Stroessner), Chile and Brazil, where Nazis fled, hid, took other identites, and perhaps used the counterfeit money to live.

b. Relationship of Economic and Historical Movements:

- In the film, we see and experience with our characters how the soldiers of the Nazi party were transporting Jews to concentration camps and forced labor camps. Based on an economic system, Germany used cheap labor and forced the labor of humans as their economic source to work rather than to transport them all to death camps. The German phrase, "ARBEIT MACH FREI" (WORK MAKES FREEDOM) was the slogan printed at the front door entrance to the work camps.

- The Nazi camp system expanded rapidly after the beginning of World War II in September 1939, as forced-labor became important in war production. Labor shortages in the German war economy became critical after German defeat in the battle of Stalingrad in 1942-1943. This led to the increased use of concentration camp prisoners as forced laborers in German armaments industries. Especially in 1943 and 1944, dozens of concentration camps were established in or near industrial plants.

Suggested Activity:
- *Compare other labor camps in history, e.g. the Gulag in Siberia, Russia, with the German labor camps during World War ll. An interesting literary source are the works of Aleksandr Solzhenitsyn (The Gulag Archipelago, Cancer Ward, The First Circle) and Vaclav Havel, who wrote some of their works when they were political prisoners. The film, Schindler's List shows how such a forced labor camp was run.*

4. Civics, Citizenship and Government:

a. Religious Intolerance: Anti-Semitism

- There are numerous scenes in this film when the SS soldiers beat up Jewish prisoners and denigrate them by calling them with the derogatory term *"Juden."* (Jews) One of the most powerful scenes is when the SS soldier urinates on Sali and the latter does nothing to defend himself. He has no choice but to control his temper and pride. When Sali sees Kolya being shot by the same soldier, we see how much Sali suffers but again he says and does nothing. We, as the audience, would like to fight for Sali. This was all done to dehumanize the Jews and destroy them morally.
- There are also numerous scenes when Sali and the other Jewish prisoners identify themselves by number and not name. The SS made sure that the prisoners would be stripped of all human dignity and individuality. They began with their name not counting.

b. Human Rights:

- In the scene when Sali meets Kolya for the first time as they are being transferred to the concentration camp, Kolya resembles a starving animal. We are horrified at the stark image. In contrast, it is Sali's humanity that can possibly save Kolya.
- Throughout history human rights (that all people are born free and equal in dignity and rights, and they should not be discriminated against because of their nationality, ethnicity religion, race, gender, political opinion, wealth, health, or age) have not been respected.

Suggested Activities:
- *Ask members of your group to discuss the roles of citizens and their responsibilities. How did the counterfeiters fulfill their responsibilities?*
- *Research the United Nations Declaration of Human Rights (written in 1948 as a result of World War II's deaths) and specify where Adolf Hitler's theories went against this document.*

Hints:

- During the 20th century, we have seen examples of human rights violations in many countries: in South Africa with Apartheid; with the Untouchables in India; with Muslims in Bosnia; with Kurds in Iraq; with Tibetans by the Chinese; and with many others. After World War II, the United Nations was created to provide to their member countries a means of solving world problems and organizing a forum where nations could meet and discuss international problems and how to avoid war and the loss of human rights.

c. The Final Solution:

- This decision to systematically kill millions of European Jews was made at the Wannsee conference, which took place in Berlin, in the Wannsee Villa on January 20, 1942. During the conference, there was a discussion held by a group of German Nazi officials to decide on the *"Final Solution of the Jewish Question."* The records and minutes of this meeting were found intact by the Allies at the end of the war and served as valuable evidence during the Nuremberg Trials to convict war criminals.
- In November 1941 the first extermination camps were built as a way to get rid of the dead bodies of thousands of Jews. As early as the 1930s there were concentration camps built but they did not have facilities of crematoria and gas chambers to kill masses of human beings as Auschwitz.

Suggested Activities:

- *Define the following terms: Gestapo, Wehrmacht, SS Army, Third Reich, Aryan race, swastika, air raids, bomb shelters, Final solution, safe houses, neutral countries, ghetto, underground, resistance groups, Gypsies, and* <u>Mein Kampf.</u>
- *Divide your group into two and compare the totalitarian states, Fascism and Communism. Then analyze the government of China.*

Hints:

- A totalitarian state is when the government controls every aspect of a citizen's life through a one party dictatorship. This existed in Nazi Germany under Hitler's Fascism; in Fascist Italy under Mussolini during

World War II; and in Communist Russia beginning with Lenin when he seized power after the Bolshevik Revolution in 1917 until 1989 when Gorbachev, the dictator in Russia at that time, introduced *Perestoika* and *Glasnost*, and precipitated the fall of Communism in Eastern Europe's satellite countries.

- The totalitarian system of Fascist government in Germany during World War II's Third Reich, had unlimited power, used secret police to control the people, and suppressed all opposition with the Gestapo. Children were forced to join Youth groups and devote their life to Hitler. This form of government ended in 1945 when Germany lost World War II.

- Karl Marx (1818-1883), German born, is famous for his political theories preparing for the downfall of capitalism and the emergence of communism. In his literature he popularized the theories that introduced communism:

a. The Communist Manifesto (1848) Marx wrote this work in conjunction with Engels, where he describes the history of all society as the history of class struggles. Marx advocated the fall of the bourgeoisie (industrialists, capitalists, landowners) and the victory of the proletariat (the workers) to establish communist governments. The ideal state of government for him was a communist society in which human beings develop their nature in cooperative production. Private ownership and individual achievements run counter to communism. Marx predicted the Bloshevik Revolution and the spread of communism around the world when he prophesized, that the capitalist system would succumb to a communist society. The last line of his book, was "Workers of all lands, unite."

b. Political philosophy is influenced by economics, wrote Marx in Economic and Philosophical Manuscripts (1844). The economics of a country determines the politics. Labor under capitalism alienates the worker and labor divides social classes which in turn causes class struggle.

c. Philosophy of Religion, was another treatise written by Marx where he states that religion is the opium of the people. He claims that the social function of religion is a way of coping with social inequality and thereby maintaining the status quo of alienating the workers.

d. Das Kapital (1867) analyzes the capitalist process of production. Marx elaborates on his theory of capitalists exploiting workers that would lead to a falling rate of profit and the collapse of industrial capitalism.

B. Literature and Visual Arts:

---

5. World Literature:

A. Holocaust Literature:

- Holocaust literature represents writings in poetry, prose and/or drama, of works related to the experiences of prisoners and victims of Germany's Third Reich and Fascist regime. The majority of works have been written by those individuals who were prisoners and survived Nazi concentration camps. Learning about their sufferings gives us insight into the horrific practices of the German Nazis during World War II.
- The story of *The Counterfeiters* is based on the autobiographical memoir written by Adolf Burger, The Devil's Workplace. Burger was one of the experts of the group of 142 counterfeiters. He was a Slovakian Jew who had been trained as a printer. In 1938, Hitler invaded Czechoslovakia and the population became pro-Fascist. Burger was working in a printing plant in Bratislava where he was forging birth certificates, passports and citizenship papers for underground communists. He was arrested, sent to Auschwitz as was his wife, and then he was sent to Sachsenhausen to work with Operation Bernhard.

Suggested Activities:
- *Research and discuss what is Holocaust memoirs.*
- *Discuss how the German Army knew which Jews to assemble from other concentration camps to work in Operation Bernhard at Sachsenhausen concentration camp.*

Hints:
- Jews in Europe were singled out, beaten up, arrested, forced into labor camps and concentration camps, and killed only because they, or one of their grandparents, were born Jewish. Those who survived have documented their eyewitness accounts to show how human beings, in the absence of ethical or moral law, can treat other human beings.

- For some survivors, the need to write their torturous experiences began as soon as the war ended; for others, it is their advancing years that have created the need to publish their personal testimonies. These memoirs have become a vast body of knowledge for the rest of the world. Topics include: Jewish home and community life before the war, the establishment of ghettos, acts of resistance, hidden children, the help given by non-Jews, the stories of individuals, the deportations, camps, death marches, and liberation.

Some Holocaust memoirs can be found in <u>Holocaust Memoir Digest.</u>
Others are:

<u>Anne Frank: The Diary of a Young Girl</u>, by Anne Frank
<u>The Devil's Workplace</u>, by Adolf Burger
<u>Night; Dawn,</u> by Elie Wiesel
<u>Auschwitz</u>, by Dr. Miklos Nyiszli
<u>Children of he Flames,</u> by L.M. Lagnado and S.C. Dekel
<u>The Garden of the Finzi-Continis</u>, by Giorgio Bassani
<u>Sophie's Choice,</u> by William Styron
<u>Is This a Man</u>, by Primo Levi
<u>Man's Search for Meaning,</u> by Viktor Frankl
<u>Krueger's Men: The Secret Nazi Counterfeit Plot and Prisoners of Block 19</u>, by Lawrence Malkin
<u>The Odessa File</u>, by Frederick Forsyth
<u>Nazi Counterfeiting of British Currency during World War II: Operation Andrew</u> and <u>Operation Bernhard</u>, by Bryan Burke
<u>Counterfeit Reich: Hitler's Secret Swindle</u>, by Arturo Delgado

- After Adolf Burger was liberated in 1945, he returned to live in Prague and wrote his first book, <u>Number 64401</u>. This was the number tattooed on his arm.

- *How did the Germans register the prisoner's occupation?*
  When each prisoner was arrested, he/she was registered with an IBM punch card containing pertinent information: name, date of birth, city of residence, city of imprisonment, occupation, tattooed number. The Nazis used this data for their records as well as to identify who would be a good candidate for clandestine activities as counterfeiting.

6. Media Studies:

a. Film Clips and Scene Discussions:

German Rule (Scene: 25:33 –> 26 minutes)
Under Hitler, Fascists were able to rule over Jews as they wished and with impunity. One of the Jewish prisoners of the counterfeiters comment on what is happening at Sachenhausen concentration camp: "Where are they all running to? The shoe-testing squad. They make the prisoners run in a circle...to test the shoes. Test them? How? It's a punishment. The shoes are too small, sandbags on their backs. Many of them die."

Discuss the dates and history when German Fascists who were part of the Final Solution were arrested and convicted of their crimes as at the Nuremberg trial, Eichmann trial, and Frankfurt trial.

Genres Mix: Documentary and Feature Film (Scene: 27-28 minutes and 39-40 minutes)
The story line is taken from the book, <u>The Devil's Workshop,</u> by Adolf Burger. This counterfeiting operation is considered the best in history. The key to their success is the discovery that British money is made from rags. "Our main problem is the paper. It has the wrong feel. The English paper has the same structure as a kind of Turkish linen. We've experimented with various chemicals, but the results remain unsatisfactory... Rags! The English use rags! Fibers, torn and abraded thousands of times! We're not just trying to slip a few notes past a shop assistant. We intend to flood and destroy Britain's economy."

Ask members of your group to categorize the factual and fictional elements of the film.

b. Cinematography Techniques:

1. Character Foil:
- Adolf Burger serves as Sali's opposite in regards to their moral attitude about working for the Germans and being part of Operation Bernhard. Burger, whose wife was interned in Auschwitz and then learns that she has been exterminated in Birkenau, believes the group should sacrifice their life to sabotage the counterfeiting scheme. Burger and Sali are presented as foils; they argue constantly about the concept of sabotage. Sali refuses to go against German policy. He wants to survive the war and tells Burger that all he wants is to live

one more day. Sali also takes professional pride in counterfeiting the U.S. dollar, a currency he was previously unable to forge before. Burger, on the other hand, condemns his acting as a *Kapo* for the Germans, and having his work help the Nazis win the war. He scorns his privileged condition in a concentration camp and threatens to sabotage the operation. Finally, in reality and in the film, he does thwart the production of the American 100 dollar bill.

2. Circular Style and Flashback:
- The circular and flashback technique used by the director is to inform the viewer from the beginning of the film that Sali survives the war. Once we realize that, we can concentrate on the film's themes: What is survival? What does the human being do to survive? What is morality in such a situation? What would we do?
- The first scene of the film shows us Sali in Monte Carlo where he is gambling. He is losing American dollars in the Casino. He meets a glamorous woman who consoles him and when they awaken in bed the next morning, she notices he has a tattoo number on his arm. As his eyes and camera focus on the numbers, there is a flashback telling us his story.

3. Symbols:
- One of the perks that the 142 prisoners of Operation Bernhard receive is a ping-pong table. The scene when Sali and Burger compete against each other while playing table tennis is very telling Their ping-pong game becomes symbolic and personal so they can prove who is stronger: the man who wants to sabotage the scheme and risk his life for the moral cause, or the man who wants to survive and is loyal to himself and his group?
- Both men stop playing ping-pong as they hear beatings and cries on the other side of their fence. Then they hear bullet shots that kill their unknown inmates and fellow Jews next door. They had not heard these sounds before as the classical music the Germans had piped into their barracks while they work, drowned out the screams of reality.

4. Color:
- The film is shot in monochromatic colors of grey and white to emphasize the period and tragedy of the time. However, there is one scene where the grey turns to a reddish hue and we see a prisoner who is bleeding to death. The cinematographer also hand holds the camera and uses natural light as the Scandinavian filmmakers of the Dogma School (See chapter Ten, *In a Better World*). We see how the camera in *The Counterfeiters* moves at times when there are scenes of upheaval and trauma.

Suggested Activities:

- *Ask members of your group to research film reviews of the film and also to write a film review discussing the above cinematographic techniques in their review.*
- *Work in pairs to see other Holocaust films that show the situation in other countries.*

Hints:

- Some holocaust films are: *Schindler's List, Shoah, The Garden of the Finzi-Continis, Sophie's Choice, Europa Europa, etc. See Bibliography at end of this chapter.*

7. Philosophy/Critical Thinking:

a. Moral dilemma:

- Sali is shown from the beginning of the film as a man who survives by his wit and talents. Survival is his principal moral. However, as he befriends the young Russian artist of his group who is dying of tuberculosis, his desire to save his friend, conflicts with his prior code of self-preservation. His loyalty goes to Kolya who is dying and Sali realizes he has the power to help him. We see Sali's moral courage unfold and his sense of humanity takes over. We also witness another scene when Sali does not prevent the German head of the concentration camp, Herzog, from escaping with his family and running away with some forged money. They had agreed to help each other. Sali emerges as a loyal and humane man despite his conflicts. When Burger is sabotaging the production of the American dollar, Sali tells the other members of the group not to denounce Burger: "One doesn't betray one's mate."

Suggested Activity:

- *It has been said by Holocaust survivors that those who survived, may not have been the most moral individuals in the concentration camp. This would make a lively discussion and debate.*

b. What does it take to survive?

- One of the main themes of the film is to pose the question what does it take to survive? Both Sali and Burger represent opposite poles to the answer. The director was fascinated by the metaphysical concept to what degree does an individual abandon human values in order to survive.
- The moral conflict of the film is expressed not only by Sali and Burger but by all the 142 Jewish prisoners who were working on Operation Bernhard. All these

men were told at the out start that they would be saved from extermination if they agreed to work on the forgery project and not sabotage it. In addition, if one person sabotages the operation, the entire group would be exterminated. They also knew that they were *Kapos,* and that the Germans had a policy of killing *Kapos* when they did not need them anymore. Their dilemma was multiple:

- Do they stretch out their work and stall the final production of counterfeit money in order not to accelerate their own death?
- Do they empower the Nazis by printing the foreign currency and help them in war?
- Do they co-operate and become accomplices to defraud the British government and destroy their economy?
- Do they sabotage the entire operation and risk the death of their entire group as was specified in the original deal?
- What is loyalty? To whom? Where should their allegiance go?

Suggested Activity:
- *These are profound questions to discuss. Use a round robin technique to answer one of the above questions. Other Holocaust literature and films discuss the question from different points of view.*

c. Personal Voice: Memoir and Diary

- The film is taken from Adolf Burger's memoir where he emerges as a hero. In the film, the director originally wanted to be true to the memoir but as the character of Sali emerged, the director found Sali's character nuanced with shades of moral conflict and consequently more dramatic for a film. The director focuses more on Sali's character.

8. Music:

a. Argentine Tango:

- In an early scene when we are introduced to Sali, he is preparing an Argentine passport for a beautiful German Jewess who wants to escape Nazi Germany to Argentina. Most likely, she was arrested at the same time when Sali was arrested.
- In real life, Sali goes to Argentina after the war and dies there in the 1960s.

- When Sali is dancing at the beginning of the film in Berlin and at end of the film in Monte Carlo, he is dancing to tango music. The music softens the forefront story of suffering and adds to the background a "life force" element of hope, which is the sentiment of the Tango. We hear the up-beat music as we look at a horror of history that unfolds before our eyes. The juxtaposition is startling.
- Tango music and its associated dance originated in Buenos Aires, Argentina in working-class districts and at the port of Buenos Aires in the 1890s when European immigrants first entered the capital. The music is derived from a fusion of various forms of music from Europe.
- The film's sound track consists of classical tangos that were recorded by Hugo Diaz, an Argentine harmonica player of the 1940s.

Suggested Activities:
- *Share some tango music and/or learn how to dance the tango.*
- *Many film directors have used the Argentine Ballroom tango as background music in their movies. Have your group research which films.*

Hints:
- The following films use tango music as background:
  Last Tango in Paris, Death on the Nile, Never Say Never Again, Scent of a Woman, Strictly Ballroom, Addams Family Values, Schindler's List, True Lies, Evita, Moulin Rouge, Chicago, Frida, Shall We Dance, Mr. And Mrs. Smith, and Rent.

b. Classical music:

- Opera music by Strauss is being played inside the counterfeiters' workplace to drown out the cries and shootings of other inmates of the concentration camps. The SS did this intentionally so as not to depress the counterfeiters and keep them working. It was also a way to appease them. The SS feared sabotage.

9. Technology:

- *Banking in Iceland*
  What happened in Iceland from 2008 to 2011 is regarded as one of the worst financial crises in history. Yet, Iceland, with a population of 320,000, has also

staged an unprecedent recovery. Since 2011, the gross domestic product has been on the rise. Salaries are also rising, the national debt is sinking and the government has paid off most of the billions in loans it received in 2008 from the International Monetary Fund, ahead of schedule.

Iceland's rapid return to health hinged on a series of measures: Allow their ailing banks to collapse; devalue the currency; and introduce capital controls. Practically what helped was: a hard-working populace, healthy democracy, high level of education, tourism, natural resources, and fisheries.

Björk, a very famous Icleandic singer and actress, has saved the banking crisis and helped revived the economy along with several other women of her country with Audur Capital, a Reykjavik-based investment company founded and managed by women. Audur Capital has succeeded by making investments in the country's environmental resources and green energy such as wind, hydro-power and geothermal energy.

Suggested Activities:
- *Ask members of your group to research exactly what happened since Audur Capital implemented new policies. An interesting film to see and disuss is Michael Moore's, Where to Invade Next, and listen to how the women of Iceland analyze their financial success.*

Sidebars:
---

1. Public Response:

- *The Counterfeiters* has been very successful in over 40 countries, winning major prizes, and sub-titled into many languages. But in Austria the audience was mixed in their reception for the Austrians still struggle with issues the film raises. The Austrian government has never apologized for their role in the Holocaust, unlike Germany and France.

2. Actors and Directors:

- Austrian director Stefan Ruzowitzky, whose paternal grandfather supported Fascism and volunteered to join the German army, felt the need to assuage his inherited guilt at the horrors of his past. He was eager to do this film as a way of coming to terms with history and as a "Nazi descendant." While studying theater and history at the university in Vienna, he was searching for a new cultural identity. "We have to tell the stories of the Holocaust and are morally obliged to do it in such a way that we reach as many people as possible." Upon graduation, he made this film.

3. Awards:

- Academy Awards, USA
  2008- Won- Best Foreign Language Film – Austria

- Berlin International Film Festival
  2008- Nominated- Golden Berlin Bear for director, Stefan Ruzowitzky

- German Film Awards
  2008- Won- Best Actor; Won- Best Director for Screenplay Won- Best Cinematographer

---

Bibliography of Films: Filmography
Further Global Study Resources through Film:

Holocaust:

- *Exodus* (U.S.A.)
- *The Garden of the Finzi-Continis* (Italy)
- *The Last Metro* (France)
- *Shoah* (France)
- *The Sorrow and the Pity* (France)
- *Au Revoir les Enfants* (France)
- *Europa Europa* (France)
- *Schindler's List* (U.S.A.)
- *Il Postino* (Italy)
- *Anne Frank Remembered* (United Kingdom)
- *Life Is Beautiful* (Italy)

- *Sunshine* (Hungary)
- *Kadosh* (Israel)
- *Maus* (U.S.A.)
- *Divided We Fall* (Czechoslovakia)
- *Into the Arms of Strangers: Stories of the Kindertransport* (United Kingdom)
- *Nowhere In Africa* (Germany)
- *The Pianist* (France/ Poland)
- *Facing Windows* (Italy)
- *Nina's Tragedies* (Israel)
- *Munich* (U.S.A.)
- *Fateless* (Hungary)
- *Black Book* (Holland)
- *The Boy in the Striped Pajamas* (U.S.A.)
- *A Secret* (France)
- *One Day You'll Understand* (France)
- *Defiance* (U.S.A.)
- *The Reader* (U.S.A./ Germany)
- *Valkyrie* (U.S.A.)
- *Gruber's Journey* (Romania)
- *The Year My Parents Left on Vacation* (Brazil)
- *Hannah Arendt* (Germany)
- *Josef Mengele: The Final Account* (U.S.A.)
- *Adam Resurrected* (U.S.A./ Israel)
- *Good* (U.S.A.)
- *Katyn* (Poland)
- *Flame & Citron* (Denmark)
- *Good Morning Mr. Wallenberg* (Sweden)
- *Paper Clips* (U.S.A.)
- *Shanghai Jews* (China/ U.S.A.)
- *The Port of Last Resort* (U.S.A./ Austria/ China)
- *Dead Snow* (Norway)
- *Inglourious Basterds* (U.S.A.)
- *A Film Unfinished* (Germany/ U.S.A.)
- *Sophie Scholl: The Final Days* (Germany)
- *Sobibor* (France)
- *The Darien Dilemma* (Israel)
- *Night and Fog* (France)

- *Phoenix* (Germany)
- *Labyrinth of Lies* (Germany)
- *Son of Saul* (Hungary)

About the Story of the Counterfeiters:

- *The Great Nazi Cash Swindle* (U.S.A.)
- *Private Schulz* (U.S.A.)
- *Kapo* (Italy)
- *The Odessa File* (U.S.A.)

CHAPTER 9

THE LIVES OF OTHERS (GERMANY)

TITLE OF FILM: "Las Leben der Anderen" ("The Lives of Others")
YEAR OF RELEASE: 2006
COUNTRY: Germany / East Germany
DIRECTOR: Florian Henckel Von Donnersmarck
LANGUAGE: German
RUNNING TIME: 138 minutes
RATING: R
CURRICULUM THEMES:

A.HISTORY AND SOCIAL SCIENCE:

- Chapter's Key Themes: Communism in East Germany; Political activism and fiction
- World History: Stasi; Yalta & Potsdam Conferences; Cold War; Berlin Wall
- Geography: East and West Germany; Cold War divisions
- Economics: Proletariat/ Bourgeoisie
- Civics, Citizenship and Government: Dictatorship; Purity of the party; Surveillance

B. LITERATURE and VISUAL ARTS:

- World Literature: Bertolt Brecht; *Der Spiegel*; Typewriters and typeface
- Media Studies: Film Clips and Scene Discussions; Cinematography Techniques: character foil, circular movement, color and lighting; Symbolism
- Philosophy/ Critical Thinking: Character development; 3rd person omniscient narrator and 3rd person limited narrator; Spying today
- Art/ Music: Beethoven
- Technology: Youtube to hear a concert; virtual field trip to a concert hall

Introduction:

The Lives of Others was directed by Florian Henckel von Donnersmarck; produced by Max Wiedemann, O. Berg and Dirk Hamm; edited by Patricia Rommel; production design by Silke Buhr; music by Gabriel Yared; and distributed by Buena Vista Pictures in 2006. (138 min)

Christa-Maria Sieland ....*Martina Gedeck*
Gerd Wiesl.. *Ulrich Muhe*
Georg Dreyman .... *Sebastian Koch*

The power of *The Lives of Others* comes from two essential sources: first, its accurate depiction of the political atmosphere in East Germany during Communism; and second, its vivid portrayal of human nature and emotions. These elements offer depth to the story about a complicated time period. The combination of a fictional love relationship set in a historic political period helps the viewer understand that circumstances, not differences in human nature, made the Cold War what it was. The depiction of Communism, plagued by unspeakable horrors, may be unknown to most people today. Yet, this film is so powerful that the viewer can easily relate to the storyline's motivating factors of fear and love.

Director and writer Henckel von Donnersmarck saw the importance of portraying the role of human emotions in creating the atmosphere of the film when visiting his family in East Berlin as a child. He said that he had sensed the fear his parents had when subjects of a communist state.

The idea for the film came from author Maxim Gorky's account of a conversation with Lenin, in which the iron-handed dictator said that hearing Beethoven's *Appassionata* weakened his resolve in the revolution. The idea that there are things that can touch even those most imbued with Communist rhetoric and redeem that soul is an important theme of the film. The concept that a man can change parallels that a government can also change.

Pivotal Moments in History:

- **1945** - The Yalta Conference (February 1945) brought together the Allies of World War II in order to decide how Germany would be governed after the war. The principle of dividing the country into 4 parts was established by the victors of war.

- **1945** - The Potsdam Conference (July 16-August 2, 1945) solidified the plan: Germany was to undergo demilitarization, denazification, and democratization. It was to give up all the annexations they had made during the war. And it was to be split into 4 parts: one section going to each of the U.S., the U.K., France, and the Soviet Union. Berlin, too, was to be split up into four parts. And Austria also was split into 4 corresponding parts.
- **1948,** at the London Conference, the U.S., U.K. and France united their parts of Germany to form West Germany, or the Federal Republic of Germany. The part of Germany under Soviet control was called East Germany, later known as the German Democratic Republic. (GDR).
- The Soviets established a Berlin Blockade (**June 1948-May 1949**).The Soviets blocked access to West Berlin.
- The West responded with the Berlin Airlift, using airplanes to fly supplies into West Berlin. This was a huge success and the Soviets lifted the Blockade.
- In October **1949,** four prominent parties in Germany (including the Communist Party) merged to form the Socialist Unity Party of Germany (SED), which came to monopolize political power in the next few decades.
- February 8, **1950,** the secret police, of East Germany known as the Stasi, was founded. The Stasi was "the shield and sword" of the SED.
- In **1989**, The Berlin Wall falls on November 9, 1989 in a series of powerful protests from Eastern European satellite countries. The Stasi are ordered to stop spying on and arresting people considered "enemies of the state." There is a mass exodus from East Germany into West Germany with the fall of the Berlin Wall.
- On October 3, **1990,** East and West Germany are reunited.

Pre-Screening Questions:

- The government of East Germany after World War II is historically referred to as Communist. However, in the movie, Socialism is usually used to describe the system. Furthermore, the party in power was called the Socialist Unity Party of Germany (SED).

Suggested Activities:
- *Ask members of your group to discuss the differences between Communism, Marxism, and Socialism. Which one applied to East Germany? During research, other vocabulary words may come up; keep a running list and look them all up as they come.*

Hints:

- Marxism: a socioeconomic system proposed by Karl Marx and Friedrich Engels in their book, <u>Das Kapital</u> (1867). In a society in which the poor "proletariat" workers own the means of production and the rich "bourgeoisie" benefit from their work, it is inevitable that the workers overthrow the aristocracy and establish a classless society.

- *Communism:* a system of government based on Marxism. It adds the concept of "guardianship," which means that there is a small group of people in charge of the system who know what's best for the people and has the authority to rule them.

- *Socialism:* a way of distributing goods and services in which most are publically owned; unlike Communism and Marxism, which refer to a political system as well as an economic one, Socialism refers only to the economy. Socialism, in which some goods and services publically owned by the government, and some are privately owned, is a milder form of Communism, in which most goods and services are publically owned. The distinction between the two is blurry. Communism has a strong secret police, no personal or human freedoms, no judicial rights, and no human rights.

Suggested Activity:

- *Students can discuss how and when Germany ended up being separated into East and West Germany.*

Hints:

- After WWII, (1948) when the cold war conflict between the Soviet Union and the West escalated, France, the U.S., and the U.K. united their sections of Germany and Berlin forming West Germany (capitalistic and democratic); the Soviet Union's portion became East Germany (communistic) and East Berlin.

Suggested Activity:

- *In small groups, discuss several possible ways in which members of the Stasi justified their actions to the public and to themselves.*

Hints:

- A central element of the movie is the Stasi. The Stasi were the secret police of East Germany that spied on possible enemies of the state (particularly people with influence like politicians, writers, educators, and journalists) and apprehended anyone who directly spoke out against the Communist Party. Very few in positions of power spoke out or took action to stop the horrors that happened under the Stasi.

- The Stasi used the Machiavellian principle that the end justifies the means: inhumane actions were acceptable because in the end it was the only way to protect the people. The Prince advocated that the Prince should be feared, not loved. The Stasi used this as their principle.

Suggested Activity:
- *In groups, discuss why so few people with influence came out against the Stasi.*

Hints:
- Many East Germans did not protest against the government because of:

  1. Futility: knowledge that their words would have little effect and that the party would quickly silence them before they could do any damage.
  2. Fear: people were afraid that speaking out would endanger their lives. Those who had family or lovers were especially reluctant to act out because it would be putting their loved ones in danger as well.

Pivotal Moments in Film:

- A particular reverence in the film is reserved to the role of Art. One of the film's themes is to show that Art has the ability to reach people across socio-economic and ideological levels. We see this film in several scenes:
- Christa-Maria's career as an actress is shown as something that can reach out to audiences and impress them. It is something that Wiesler as a changed man, tells her in order to protect her from making a mistake.
- The piano piece, "Sonata For a Good Man," that Georg is playing is the turning point for Wiesler and marks his change of character. It has the power to reach him despite his lifetime of being brainwashed. Georg says to Christa-Maria, "Can anyone be bad who really listens to this music?" Wiesler is listening to this music through his head-phones. He cries and realizes Georg is right.
- Writing is portrayed as a powerful tool that can change minds and bring political action. It's because of this that Georg is monitored in the first place.
- Summary of Film: In 1984 East Germany, successful dramatist Georg Dreyman and his lover, actress Crista-Maria Seiland, have been among the fortunate few who enjoy the luxury of an unmonitored apartment and private life, thanks to

their apparent longstanding loyalty to the Communist party. However, Secret Service agent Wiesler is soon delegated to bug their home, monitor their activities and bring proof that they are actually enemies of the state. But as Wiesler is drawn deeper into the poignant lives of these two people, he begins to question the communist party. *The Lives of Others* is a believable story about the gradual change in a man's heart that leads him from a loyal supporter of Communism to a disingenuous Stasi agent. In his change of character, he becomes a symbol of the change of government in East Germany and Eastern Europe.

Post-Screening Questions:
A.   History and Social Science:

1. *How did the government maintain control of the population?*
2. *How were "enemies of the state" treated?*
3. *What did the Stasi threaten to take away from suspects until they confessed crimes?*
4. *What happened to suspects who could not be proven to be traitors?*
5. *When did the East German government stop spying? Why?*

Hints:
- The East German government maintained control in two main ways: emotionally and physically. Emotionally, they inspired fear in the population, making them reluctant to talk to others about their thoughts and preventing them from uniting in protest. Physically, the secret police kept society from toeing out of line, through violence, arrests, interrogations, threats, and ultimately loss of one's life, either by the loss of one's position (as wirh Christa-Maria and later Wiesler) or by suicide (as with Jaeger) or imprisonment (as Georg feared.)
- Enemies of the state were often interrogated by extreme methods and kept in custody until they confessed. Often times, the confession wasn't real, only an attempt to escape their ordeal. Arrests and disappearances without charges were common.
- Suspects who couldn't be proven to be traitors were made to disappear from their families and from their work. Wiesler, for instance, was demoted to a boring, useless job in an underground basement where he could no longer pose a threat to the party.

- The Stasi threatened primarily their family and their careers – essentially, their position in society. They could destroy a life without killing anyone and that was why they were particularly dangerous and feared. This was the greatest fear of the Artist, for once they were imprisoned and even if released, they were not able to produce again.
- The government ordered the Stasi to stop spying approximately at the time when the Berlin Wall fell (1989).

Suggested Activities:
- *Students can discuss the following scenes that illustrate Wiesler's change of character:*

Hints:
- Wiesler is in the elevator with a young boy who asks him if he is a Stasi agent and tells him that his father said all Stasi are bad men. Wiesler asks the boy what is his father's name but midway through the question he changes his phrase and asks what is the name of his ball?
- Wiesler steals Georg's book written by Brecht.
- Wiesler talks to Christa-Maria in a bar, knowing about her dilemma if she should meet the Minister of Culture, Hempf. He dissuades her.
- Wiesler hides the typewriter that would doom Dreyman, and thus, risks his own position.
- Wiesler does not write down the conversation between Dreyman and his friends about testing if Georg's apartment is bugged.
- Wiesler does not report that Georg is writing an article for *Der Spiegel*, about suicide in East Germany. Instead he says that Georg and his friends are writing a play to celebrate the 40th anniversary of Communism.

B. Literature and Visual Arts:

- What is it about Georg and Christa-Maria's lives that manage to touch the hardened Stasi agent, Wiesler? Do you think his change of heart is plausible? What scenes in the movie show us the differences between Georg's life and Wiesler's life?
- What significance did Christa-Maria's death have for both the characters and the movie as a whole?
- After the fall of the Berlin Wall, when Georg found out who saved him and tracked Wiesler down, why did he not talk to him? Why did he walk away?

- What instances of character development do you see? Is Wiesler the only one who undergoes a change of character or is his change only the most dramatic and symbolic?
- How does Christa-Maria change? Why?
- Why does Georg agree to write the article about suicides in East Germany?
- Why is the film titled *The Lives of Others*? Is it a good title?

Curriculum Themes:
A. History and Social Science:

Chapter's Key Themes: Communism in East Germany

a. Communism in East Germany:

- The film spans the time period of 1984-1991 to show how East Germany changes and moves from communism to democracy. The majority of the plot is set in 1984, during the height of communist party rule, characterized by oppression and fear. The film then shows the events of 1989, in which the communist party and the Berlin wall fall.
- Characteristics of communism in East Germany were:
  ○ powerful secret police known as the Stasi;
  ○ methods used to inspect and apprehend suspected "enemies of the state"
  ○ constant threat of life, family, and career that terrorized the people;
  ○ youth indoctrination (first scene when Wiesler is teaching a class.)
- From 1945 to 1954, East Germany was under the direct rule of the Soviet Union. After 1954, however, it moved away from Soviet control. Oppression increased with the Berlin Wall (August 15, 1961) and the increasing threat of the Stasi in people's private lives.

b. Political Activism and Fiction

- The party constantly cracked down on society's intellectuals (artists, writers, professors, etc.) In *The Lives of Others,* this is shown by surveillance of dramatist Georg Dreyman. His writing was a threat to the East German government and the Stasi. Georg was one of the few "loyal" East German writers who was appreciated in the West, and if he managed to publish in West Germany any-thing about the real living conditions of East Germans, it could alert the world to oppression taking place in East Germany. This is why Dreyman risked every-thing he had in order to write his article in secret and why it was so important to Wiesler that he would succeed. However, one must note that Georg wrote his article, anonymously, and thus tried to reduce his risk.

Suggested Activity:
- *The group can discuss why literary writing could be so dangerous. Offer evidence from the film or from any other source you know to support your argument.*

Hints:
- In many oppressive regimes, as shown in East Germany, a lot of the fear and power of the party is based on turning people against each other. For instance, in the film there's the opening scene in which the man being interrogated and threatened by the Stasi gives information about a neighbor who escaped to West Germany. The most dangerous thing for a communist regime would be if people gathered together to discuss their discontents, because there is power in numbers. Literary writing allowed respected artists from different places to realize that there are other people who think like them and dislike the regime. It unites people, thus posing a danger to the party. In Totalitarian regimes, it is against the law for more than two people to be meeting together – they can be arrested for holding a "meeting."
- Under Communism, art and literature is to praise and serve the party, to inspire patriotism and loyalty to the state. Most artists and writers made con-cessions and compromises in order to continue their careers and remain "unjailed" so they could create.

1. World History:

a. Stasi:

- *The Lives of Others* opens with two interweaving scenes. In the first scene, Stasi officer Wiesler is interrogating a man who is suspected of helping a neighbor escape to West Germany. In the second scene, Wiesler is using audio from the interrogation to instruct a group of students who are aspiring to be Stasi agents His lecture includes how to detect when someone is lying by using techniques as sleep deprivation. When one of the students asks whether the techniques are inhumane, Wiesler marks an "x" next to his name on the attendance record. We see that this same student is working in the basement with Wiesler. Toward the end of the film, a similar incident occurs, when a little boy tells Wiesler that his father speaks ill of the Stasi's methods. This time however, Wiesler consciously stops himself from asking the boy for his name. This marks the change in Wiesler.

Suggested Activities:
- *The opening sequence introduces Wiesler, a successful and loyal member of the Stasi. It also serves to introduce the rhetoric of the regime as championed by the Stasi, placing the film in its historical context. you can research and discuss the creation of the Stasi, focusing on the following:*
  ° *When was the Stasi created?*
  ° *What was their original purpose? How did that purpose change?*
  ° *What were their goals in the 1980s when the movie is taking place?*
  ° *How did they achieve these goals?*

Hints:
- The Ministry for State Security, better known as the Stasi, was the official state security for East Germany. It is considered historically as one of the more effective and repressive secret police agencies in the world. Their motto was "Schild und Schwert der Partei" (Shield and Sword of the Party).
- The Stasi was founded on February 8th 1950, headquartered in East Berlin, and modeled after the Russian KGB. Originally, their role was to wage a campaign against Jews. Little by little they suppressed anyone who opposed their doctrines.

b. Yalta and Potsdam Conferences:

- The film takes place in an East Germany during Communism. The Stasi and the repressive rhetoric seen in the film are both characteristic of East Germany and the Soviet Union during the Cold War.
- In order to better understand how Germany was divided into democratic and communist sectors, it is important to understand the events following German defeat of World War II. This sets the background of the film.
- World War II started officially in 1939 with the German invasion of Poland, after which France and Great Britain declared war on Germany. The conflict

escalated rapidly, with most of the world divided between what became known as the Allies and the Axis Powers. The main players were divided thus:

- ° *Allies:* France, Great Britain and Commonwealth, U. S, U.S.S.R.
- ° *Axis:* Germany, Italy, and Japan
- World War II ended in Europe once Berlin was captured by Soviet and Polish troops in May 1945. In Asia, the war ended in August 1945, when the U.S. defeated Japan's navy. The Yalta and Potsdam conferences were an attempt by the Allies to settle debates over how Germany should be punished after the War.

Suggested Activities:

- *Divide your group into three small groups and have each group represent one of the following Allies at the end of WWII: the United States, Great Britain, and the Soviet Union. Each group can research and speculate what the leaders of their country believed and wanted during the Yalta and Potsdam conferences. Have the three groups debate what should be done with the defeated Germany, reflecting their own country's interests. At the end of the debate, have the groups research the actual conclusion the three powers reached.*

Hints:

- The Allies' interests were presented at both the Yalta and the Potsdam conferences by "the Big Three": Great Britain (Winston Churchill), United States (Franklin. D. Roosevelt) and Russia (Joseph Stalin).
- The Yalta Conference took place before the war ended while the Potsdam Conference took place afterwards. However, they both resulted in many of the same effects. The most important of these are:
  - ° Demilitarization, denazification, and democratization of Germany.
  - ° The division of Germany and Berlin into 4 areas.
  - ° Reparations paid by Germany to the lands they devastated during war.
  - ° Surrender of all the land Germany conquered during the war.
- Once the tension between the Soviet Union and the West escalated into the Cold War, France, the U.K., and the U.S. joined their sectors to form West Germany, while the Soviet-dominated area became East Germany.

c. The Cold War:

- Generally unspoken of during the film is the fact that much of the oppression illustrated is a result of the Cold War. It is a subtle but essential undercurrent in the plot. The passage from East to West that Georg was seeking with his article symbolizes the barriers of the Cold War itself, whose divisions were as much mental (ideology) as physical (for instance, the tangible Berlin Wall). British Prime Minister Winston Churchill described the Cold War at the time as an "Iron Curtain" clearly separating Europe.

Suggested Activity:
- *Members of your goup can create visual timelines of the major events during the Cold War. You can use color-coding to show different events, for instance:*
  - *Red for major confrontations*
  - *Green for geographical changes*
  - *Blue for significant changes in leaders*
  - *Orange for nonpolitical events*

d. The Berlin Wall

- The Berlin Wall is mentioned several times throughout the film:
  - Georg receives his special typewriter with red ink from West Germany.
  - Georg wanted to write his article about unreported suicides in East Germany for publication in the West, not the East. In this way, the West would learn about oppression and suicide as a consequence.
  - At the end of the film, we see Wiesler abandon his desk and his censoring other people's mail because he hears that the Berlin Wall has fallen.

Suggested Activities:
- *Identify and discuss the scenes of the movie pertaining to the Berlin Wall. When is it used as a symbol for division between oppression and liberty, between socialism and capitalism?*
- *In what ways does having a physical barrier between the east and the west affect people's lives?*
- *Discuss the symbolism of the fall of the Berlin Wall for the characters in the film. What did it mean for Wiesler? For Minister Hempf and others who were loyal to the party?*
- *Discuss the "domino effect" of the fall of the Berlin Wall in Eastern Europe?*

Hints:
- Implementation of the Berlin Wall was August 15, 1961. It cut off West Germany from East Germany, traversing the entire country for 91 miles. The height of the wall was an average of 11.8 feet.

- The Wall was very effective. Before its construction, about 3.5 million East Germans escaped East Germany to the West. However, after its construction, only about 5,000 people attempted to pass the wall, resulting in several hundred deaths.
- In Berlin, it was possible for Westerners to pass from the eastern part of the city to the western part only through strictly controlled checkpoints, as *Checkpoint Charlie.*
- In 1981, a series of changes began to affect the countries in Eastern Europe, as the liberalization of Hungary and Poland. This was a result of a gradual increased freedom advocated by Soviet president, Gorbachev. His policies of *Glasnost* (increased transparency in politics) and *Perestroika* (economic restructuring) allowed the weakening of communism's hold on Eastern Europe. The weakening of communism spread to East Germany, causing civil unrest. In 1989 the Berlin Wall was broken down by Germans from both sides of the Wall.

2. Geography:

a. East and West Germany:

- Throughout the movie we see the atmosphere of how East German citizens lived. The streets are colorless, forbidding, and often empty, never bustling with activity. The film is monochromatic with shades of brown and grey. Lurking behind corners are secrets hidden from the public as well as Stasi agents spying on people. There is mistrust even between friends who are close to each other because they never knew who the Stasi coerced to be an informer. Parents had to keep secrets from their children (what would have happened if Wiesler had asked the little boy who is your father? Would the child have caused his father to be arrested?) Even neighbors can't be trusted. It is only in Georg and Christa-Maria's apartment that there is any warmth and love. Until, she, too, is forced to become an informer.

Suggested Activities:
- *Look at Germany as a whole in Europe. What advantages and disadvantages could its placement offer? In trade? In a war? With the European Union? With migrants and immigration?*

Hints:

- Germany is located in Central Europe, stretching from the Alps in the south to the North and Baltic Seas in the north.
- Compared to other countries in Europe, Germany is relatively large; it is also located in the center of Europe. These two characteristics help make it the great power of Europe, as we see today as leader of the European Union.
- Germany has access to the sea, allowing it to be a naval power during World War ll. This also helped with shipments during trade.

b. Cold War divisions:

- Georg publishes his article in West Germany and it makes the News in the East. The line between East and West Germany continued throughout Europe and effectively divided the world into communist and capitalist countries.

Suggested Activities:

- *Listen to Winston Churchill's "Iron Curtain" speech. What countries were behind the Iron Curtain?*
- *Compare the concept of the Iron Curtain with that of the Berlin Wall. How are they similar? Different?*

Hints:

- The Iron Curtain was a concept that symbolized both the ideological and the physical barrier separating the world during the Cold War. Like the Berlin Wall, it was a geographical manifestation of the fighting. The Iron Curtain literally divided Europe in half, with Western Europe developing capitalism and Eastern Europe developing communism.
- On each side of the Iron Curtain, countries developed their own international economies and alliances (for instance, NATO in the west and the Warsaw Pact in the east). Each side developed independently in terms of economics and politics.
- The Iron Curtain began to break apart in 1989 starting in Poland, then spreading to Hungary, East Germany, Bulgaria, etc. Most of the leading regimes collapsed through civil unrest (velvet revolutions) not violent except for Romania in December 1989 with a bloody revolution.
- Winston Churchill's "Sinews of Peace" address was made on March 5th, 1946. He used the term "iron curtain" to describe the power of the "Soviet sphere"

over the capitals of ancient European countries (Warsaw, Berlin, Prague, Vienna, Budapest, Bucharest, Belgrade, and Sofia). At the time of the speech, many people still considered the Soviet Union to be an ally from WWII, and as such Churchill's words were not well received. As the Cold War progressed however, the term grew in popularity.

3. Economics:

a. Proletariat/ Bourgeoisie:

- The proletariat describes a low social class comprised of relatively poor workers. It is sometimes used to identify people with no wealth. In many societies of the past, the proletariat was the largest social class, with the laborers bearing the burden of pushing society forward, but with much power because of their number. Their work benefitted the bourgeoisie, who had all the power in society.
- In Marxism, the proletariat is the class created by a capitalist society. The proletariats – workers- have no ownership of the means of production. Marx believed that Capitalism is based on the exploitation of the proletariat by the bourgeoisie. Marx believed that a revolution of the proletariat was inevitable in such a society, since they were numerous and mistreated; after their success, they would establish a classless society. This is the original tenet of communism. However, this changed once implemented.

Suggested Activities:
- *Review the definition of communism as presented by Marx. Discuss why a classless society is so much more difficult in practice than in theory.*
- *What is the proletariat? What do they want? What powers do they have in society, and what holds them back?*

4. Civics, Citizenship and Government:

a. Dictatorship

- The plot of *The Lives of Others* is built upon a society that has different rules than a "free" society. Although the official name of East Germany was the

German Democratic Republic, there was nothing democratic about it. East Germany was a dictatorship whose heinous practices destroyed their citizens as we see in the film.

Suggested Activity:

- *Discuss the similarities and differences among the following terms: Marxism, Leninism, Democratic Centralism, Communism, Socialism, Theocracy, Fascism, Totalitarianism, Dictatorship. What are some examples for each? (Be sure to specify not just the country but also the time period)*

Hints:

- A dictatorship is an autocratic form of government, which means government is ruled by an individual or a small group of elites. The rule of the elite is unchecked and unrestrained by a constitution, by law, or by society. Many dictatorships that were strong during the Cold War fell apart in 1989 after the fall of the Berlin Wall.
- Fascism and Communism were similar in their tactics of oppression, lack of human rights, absence of freedom, and a strong secret police.
- A totalitarian state is when the government controls every aspect of a citizen's life through a one party dictatorship. This existed in Nazi Germany under Hitler's Fascism; in Fascist Italy under Mussolini during World War II; and in Communist Russia beginning with Lenin when he seized power after the Bolshevik Revolution in 1917 until 1989 when Gorbachev, the dictator in Russia at that time, introduced *Perestroika* and *Glasnost*, and precipitated the fall of Communism in Eastern Europe's satellite countries. Today, unfortunately, there still exists totalitarian governments in the world.

b. Purity of the party:

- Maintaining the loyalty and "purity" of ideology within the ruling party was very important to communist regimes. Anyone who was suspected of sabotage, or even of not fully supporting the methods and plans of the party, suffered consequences that ranged from demotion or surveillance to imprisonment or death. In the film we see an example of the importance of purity when Wiesler is demoted from being an important Stasi officer to reading mail for censorship.

Suggested Activities:

- *Identify and analyze scenes from the film in which determining loyalty to the party was the main motivator. Why is this so important to dictatorships? Describe the atmosphere created in the film by the pressure of party loyalty, and cite evidence of how it is created in the film.*

Hints:

- The Great Purge (1936-1938) was a series of campaigns in the Soviet Union led by dictator, Joseph Stalin. Fear and paranoia led to increased suspicion of saboteurs within the communist party. The Great Purge involved purges of government officials and the military and the repression of peasants.
- The Anti-Rightist Movement (1950s-1960s) was a series of campaigns in China led by leader, Mao Zedong to purge "rightists" from the Communist Party of China. "Rightists" was vaguely defined. Officially the term referred to intellectuals who appeared to favor capitalism and class divisions, but more often anyone who criticized the government was a target. Approximately 550,000 people were persecuted.
- In 1966 Mao and his allies introduced the Cultural Revolution. This was a major purge of intellectuals in the city by killing them or relocating them to the countryside to "re-educate" them. They were considered dangerous and undesirable to the communist state because they read books, thought, asked questions and criticized the government. This inhuman purge and reign of terror lasted ten years until Mao's death in 1976.

c. Surveillance:

- Early in the film, the Stasi wiretap Georg and Christa-Maria's apartment, and for most of the film their activities are recorded by the Stasi. In reality, this type of surveillance of individuals was very common. It is considered mass surveillance, because a significant portion of the population was subject to it. Furthermore, citizens were aware that they are monitored by the secret police. This creates an atmosphere of mistrust, not just of the government but among citizens as well. A clear example of this in the film is that of Georg's neighbor. She was aware of Stasi bugging of Georg's apartment, and at first it may seem like foreshadowing a moment when she will tell Georg about it, giving him an opportunity to outwit the Stasi. However, once Wiesler threatens her daughter's position at the university, the neighbor is effectively silenced.

- Also to note, the film shows other examples of how citizens knew that their apartment was bugged: they met outside to talk; they blasted music so their words wouldn't be heard; they tried to trick the eavesdropper by giving fallacious information.

Suggested Activities:
- *There are many ways to separate society into groups, such as by class or by ethnicity. Another term is "segments of society," which more flexibly can be used to refer to jobs or role, e.g. students, journalists, or intellectuals. What segments of society to Georg and Christa-Maria belong to? Whom would it be in the best interests of the ruling party to monitor? Which segments of society pose the most threat to a dictatorship?*
- *You can debate the moral and legal arguments against surveillance. Are there any situations in which it would be acceptable? Draw on your knowledge of history.*

Hints:
- The Stasi carried out one of the largest mass surveillance operations in the world during the 20th century. Bugging was done either with small microphones or cameras hidden in apartments and other buildings. Besides technological surveillance, there were other techniques by which the party kept tabs on people. The main targets were intellectuals – professors, writers, lawyers, etc. There were full-time officers in all the major industrial plants of the time; there was one tenant in every apartment building acting as a spy; and the most heavily watched were schools, universities, and hospitals. Surveillance was done by strict official guidelines on how to extract information and how to control those from whom the information came. Stasi agents were also closely monitored by their superiors.
- By 1990, the Stasi had amassed a network of 300,000 civilian/ informants whose job was to report even the smallest hint of political dissidence.

B. Literature and Visual Arts:

5. World Literature:

a. Bertolt Brecht:

- In the film, we learn that Georg is reading Brecht and that Wiesler steals the book. Who was Brecht? Why was his work so important to both men? Bertolt

Brecht was born near Munich before the 20th century. In 1917, at 18 years old he went to study drama at Munich University. At 24 years old, he had already produced several plays and was the most famous voice in German Drama. Brecht spent most of his years living and writing in East Berlin. In 1933 his work was eclipsed by the rise of Fascist rule in Germany. He left Germany for the U.S. where he stayed until after the war. Living and writing in the States, he was questioned by the U.S. House Un-American Activities Committee (HUAC), which believed he was a communist. He returned to East Berlin in 1949, which was Communist, and finished his life there, with his own theatre company and as one of the most important literary figures in Germany. Brecht received the Stalin Peace Prize in 1954.

- Brecht wrote very few plays in his final years in East Berlin, none of them as famous as his previous works. He dedicated himself to directing plays and developing the talents of the next generation of young directors and dramatists.

b. Der Spiegel:

- In the film, we learn that Georg is clandestinely and anonymously writing his article about suicide for the most influential magazine in Germany, *Der Spiegel*. The first edition of *Der Spiegel* was published in Hanover, West Germany in 1947. Since 1952, *Der Spiegel* has been headquartered in its own building in Hamburg. *Der Spiegel* is similar in style and layout to the American news magazines, *Time* or *Newsweek*. It is considered the most important magazine written in the German language. It is known for its distinctive, academic writing style and its large volume—a standard issue may run 200 pages or more. *Der Spiegel*'s circulation rose from its first year in 1947 to 15,000 copies, to 65,000 in 1948, and 437,000 in 1961. By 1990, with German re-unification, readers included East Germans and circulation exceeded one million.

c. Typewriters and typeface:

- *The Lives of Others* takes place before the Digital Revolution and computers, when the main method of writing was with a typewriter. Georg Dreyman writes his article about East German suicides on a small, portable typewriter that is smuggled to him from a friend who lives in the West. The typewriter is unique;

it uses a red ribbon for ink and it has a typeface that is different from the major companies in the east or the west. Therefore, when the article is published and the Stasi are attempting to find its author, they bring in an expert in typeface who can't identify the source.

Suggested Activities:

- *Members of your group can research the historical development of the typewriter. What were some early innovations for the typewriter? When did it become standardized and what does that mean? Is there anything similar to the keyboard of today's computers and laptops with the typewriter?*

Hints:

- A typewriter is a device that can be either mechanical or electromechanical and that prints characters onto paper by pressing keys. There is no single inventor of the original typewriter. Historians believe that some type of typewriter was invented about 50 times before it settled into a standard design in 1910.
- Communist countries used to demand that an owner of a typewriter, would have it registered, so the government could control written literature.

6. Media Studies:

a. Film Clips and Scene Discussions:

- *Spying:* (Scene: 00:02 –> 00:03 minutes)

  The film begins immediately with an example of how the Stasi interrogates someone they want information from: " Sit down. Hands under your thighs, palms down. What do you have to tell us? I haven't done anything. I don't know anything. So you think we just arrest innocent citizens on a whim? No, not... If you think our humane system is capable of something like that, ... that'd be reason enough to arrest you. We want to jog your memory, Prisoner 227. Your friend and neighbor fled the Republic on September 28th. And we have reason to believe he was helped. I don't know anything about it. He never told me, he wanted to leave. I first heard about it at work. The enemy of our State is arrogant."

  Discuss what is the relationship of spying with present-day government surveillance, Wikileaks and cyberattacks.

- *The ending of the film:* (Scene: 02:05 –> 02:06)
  "2 Years Later Georg Dreyman. "The Sonata of Good Men." Dedicated to HGW XX/7, in gratitude. Want it gift-wrapped? No, it's for me."

  The title of the book that Georg Dreyman wrote is, "The Sonata of Good Men."

  What does it mean? Recall the earlier scene and discuss its significance to title.

b. Cinematography Techniques:

1. Character Foil:
- A character foil is a character who contrasts with another character, usually the protagonist, and, in so doing, highlights various facets of the main protagonist's personality. The author may use the foil to highlight the character of the protagonist into sharper relief. In the film, Georg and Wiesler are character foils. At the end of the film, Wiesler changes and as such becomes the character foil for Christa-Maria.

2. Circular Movement:
- The mark of a powerful film or literary work is in its circular movement, and as such, usually highlights the change in a leading character. This is the case with Wiesler, who begins as an anti-hero and then turns into a hero. The anti-hero is generally considered to be a protagonist who is contrary to the hero, or is an antagonist, and is usually not liked by the audience or readers.

3. Color and lighting:
- The director, whose personal experience influenced the making of this movie, sought to replicate not just the political situation in East Germany but also its atmosphere of fear, mistrust, longing, and melancholy of all Totalitarian governments. This atmosphere is brought to life by many subtle techniques, the most effective of which is the manipulation of lighting and color. Most of the film is bathed in grays and browns and dark colors to create that atmosphere of loneliness and fear. We never see bright colors of red or sky blue, even Wiesler's blue jacket is a light, washed-out blue.

Suggested Activities:
- *Take notice of the difference in the colors used for Georg and Christa-Maria's apartment and the colors used for the rest of the film. What does this show?*

- *The dimmest lighting in the movie occurs when Wiesler is alone, listening to what's going on in Georg's apartment. What does this suggest?*

c. Symbolism:

- The most powerful symbols of the movie come in the form of actions and characters rather than objects. This too is an element that adds to the subtlety of the film.
- When Christa-Maria runs out into the street and is hit by a bus, Georg is left to believe that she was the one who moved the typewriter and therefore saved him from arrest. It makes sense that someone who loved Georg as much as Christa-Maria would do that for him if she could. After the revolution, when the Stasi's files were made public, (what actually happened) Georg reads Wiesler's reports, including the omissions and fabrications that saved both Georg and Christa-Maria. However, it's not until Georg sees the red fingerprint on the paper that he realizes the extent to which Wiesler went to protect him. That red fingerprint (from moving the typewriter's red tape) is a symbol not only of the ideological conversion Wiesler went through, but also of the unexpectedness and goodness of the human heart. Wiesler found in him the strength of character to do what he believed was right.
- Wiesler and Dreyman were not friends; they weren't even acquaintances. Nevertheless, Dreyman and Christa-Maria both had a profound effect on Wiesler. Is their relationship then very intimate or very distant? When Georg finally tracks Wiesler down, there is a tension in the film that highlights this strange relationship, as Georg tries to decide whether to talk to him or not. The dedication in Georg's book at the end of the film symbolizes this distant but intimate relationship by acknowledging his sacrifices and thanking him at the same time, all in the same wordless way in which Wiesler himself saved Georg with the red ink of the typewriter.

Suggested Activities:
- *Can you identify any other symbols in the film?*
- *Discuss the symbolism behind Georg's neighbor and her silence. What does she stand for in the context of East German politics?*
- *An essential scene in the film occurs when Georg plays "Sonata for a Good Man." Discuss this scene and the symbolism behind it – what does music represent here?*
- *Research and discuss the differences between a Bildungsroman and character development novel.*

Hints:

- A character development novel is when the author studies the protagonist in depth. A Bildungsroman's emphasis is to show the development of the formation of the protagonist's inner character from early youth to adulthood. "A coming of age novel."

- *Bildungsroman* comes from the German term of which the archetype example is <u>Wilhelm Meister's Apprenticeship</u> by Goethe, meaning "bildung" (development, in German) and "roman" (novel, in German and French). The book's theme is the spiritual, moral, psychological, and social development of the protagonist. These themes are often portrayed in films as well as in novels.

- The Bildungsroman usually contains specific and common elements:
  - Journey motif and structure. The protagonist has a reason to go on this journey. It can be due to a loss or unhappiness that catapults he/she to travel away from the home or family.
  - Struggle to define oneself, consisting of repeated clashes between the desires of the hero and judgments of the protagonist's society.
  - The novel ends with an assessment by the protagonist of himself/herself and his/her new role in society.
  - There are themes of exile or escape.
  - The following works fit into the genre of Bildungsroman:
  - <u>Harry Potter</u> series by J. Rowling
  - <u>Portrait of the Artist as a Young Man</u> by James Joyce
  - <u>The Adventures of Huckleberry Finn</u> by Mark Twain
  - <u>Candide</u> by Voltaire
  - <u>Persepolis</u> by Marjane Satrapi
  - <u>Of Human Bondage</u> by Somerset Maugham
  - <u>Siddartha</u> by Hermann Hesse
  - <u>The Genius</u> by Theodore Dreiser

7. Philosophy/ Critical Thinking:

a. Character development

- Of all the characters in the film, Wiesler is the only one who undergoes a profound change. The relative immutability of the other characters emphasizes this as well; the fact that the other characters react as expected by their character creates a sharp contrast with the surprising conversion of Wiesler.

Suggested Activities:

- *What makes character development in fiction "believable?"*
- *Ask members of your group if there was a moment in their life that they changed. Was there one turning point or was it a gradual change? Was the change due to new knowledge or to an emotional event?*
- *The film intends for its audience to sympathize with Wiesler; he becomes a hero in the film. At the end of the film, it's hard to see him as the cold-hearted Stasi agent we glimpse in the beginning. Do his actions in the case of Georg and Christa-Maria fully redeem him? In post-war Germany, should he be judged in court for wartime crimes? Should Stasi agents who remained loyal to the end be judged in court?*

Hints:

- In *The Lives of Others,* there are two main aspects that make change in Wiesler believable. Firstly, the change is gradual, not sudden. It starts on a small scale, with Wiesler merely omitting information from his reports; then it escalates to fabrications on reports; and the change reaches a peak in which Wiesler physically goes out and speaks to Christa-Maria and also acts on his new beliefs by hiding Georg's typewriter and risking himself.
- During these changes of heart, the emphasis is placed always on emotions. Wiesler was long aware of the intellectual arguments against the Stasi's methods (the film even starts with a student pointing out the inhumanity of their interrogation methods) but it was through his emotions that he began to actually believe in those intellectual arguments. It allows modern audiences to empathize with Wiesler across time and space, because human emotions remain the same.

b. 3rd person omniscient narrator and 3rd person limited narrator

- The film follows Wiesler and shows us East Germany through his eyes, which means that the main point of view (narrator's voice) is used in "3rd person limited" – that is, limited to one character. However, there are moments in which we see the thoughts and actions of characters without Wiesler being present. In these cases, the point of view of the movie is "3rd person omniscient narrator."

Suggested Activities:

- *Define "omniscient" from context clues or from prefixes and suffixes.*
- *Ask members of your group to choose an event in their life and tell it as a short story both in 1st person point of view and in 3rd person. What are the differences? Which one*

is more effective? What are the advantages of each? Are there certain types of stories that work better when told from 1st person and others that are more effective when recounted in 3rd person?

- *Identify the scenes in which 3rd person omniscient narrator is used. When is Wiesler not present not even by spying?*

c. Spying today:

- The Stasi was known for its spying on individuals. After the demise of Communism in 1989, theoretically, there was also the cessation of spying on people. Yet, is this true today? Techniques may have changed, but still, privacy is not assured. Have your group discuss the pros and cons of spying. Why is it done? What are some methods we have today in comparison to the Stasi in East Germany? Who is doing this? Where?

8. Art/ Music:

a. Beethoven:

- The inspiration for the film came from the music of Ludwig van Beethoven's "Appassionata." that touched Lenin. From this theme we see the change of Wiesler and the hope that change is possible to help Humanity.
- "Sonata for a Good Man" is an original piece composed for the film by Gabriel Yared.

Suggested Activities:
- *You can watch an online performance of Beethoven's "Appassionata" and discuss the music. How would you describe the music? Your feelings while listening?*

Hints:
- Lenin said of the musical piece: "I can't listen to music often, it affects my nerves, it makes me want to say sweet nothings and pat the heads of people who, living in a filthy hell, can create such beauty. But today we mustn't pat anyone on the head or we'll get our hand bitten off; we've got to hit them on the heads, hit them without mercy, though in the ideal we are against doing any violence to people. Hm-hm - it's a hellishly difficult office!"

9. Technology:

a. Beethoven composed the Appassionata after he had lost his hearing; discuss the significance of this fact for his music. How can you still "hear" music when deaf?

Suggested Activities:
- *You can watch a video in which a deaf singer or musician demonstrates their love for music. The Italian singer Andrea Bocelli is blind and is very active travelling all over the world. His live performances can be heard and seen on YouTube: https:www.youtube. com/user/andreabocelli.*
- *You can take a virtual trip to a concert as to Carnegie Hall in New York City or the National Opera in Paris.*

Extracurricular Activities:

- Films from a variety of historical conjunctures may shed light on a common experience: that of living in a society undergoing modernization. Citizens in these situations have to cope with the loss of their old, familiar world and the emergence of a new one of hopes and challenges. Such settings are apt to give rise to dramas of existential meaning and to experimental artistic forms that facilitate our learning from such dramas. These are all interesting aspects to make a fascinating film. *The Lives of Others* is such a film – depicting the change of a society from Communist to non-Communist in 1989.

Suggested Activities:
- Divide into small groups and have each group see one of the following films that depicts a society in political, economic and cultural change as the country moves toward modernity:

  Christin Puiu, *Four Weeks, Three Months, Two Days* (Romania)
  Alain Resnais, *La guerre est finie* (France).
  Ingmar Bergman, *Winter Light* (Sweden).
  Jean-Luc Godard, *Two or Three Things I Know about Her* (France).
  Pier Paolo Pasolini, *Teorema* (Italy).
  Andrei Tarkovsky, *Solaris* (Soviet Union).
  Wim Wenders, *Alice in the Cities* (Germany).
  Chantal Akerman, *Jeanne Dielman* (Belgium).

Abbas Kiarostami, *The Wind Will Carry Us* (Iran).
Nuri Bilge Ceylan, *Distant* (Turkey).
Hou Hsiao-Hsien, *Café Lumière* (Taiwan / Japan).
Jia Zhangke, *Still Life* (China).
Lucrecia Martel, *The Headless Woman* (Argentina).
Pedro Costa, *Colossal Youth* (Portugal)
Zhamng Zimoung, *Coming Home* (China)

Sidebars:

1. Public Response:

- The film was received with widespread acclaim by critics and viewers alike, especially for the authenticity of the film's backdrop and atmosphere. East German dissident songwriter Wolf Bierman wrote in a March 2006 article in *Die Welt:* "The political tone is authentic, I was moved by the plot. But why? Perhaps I was just won over sentimentally, because of the seductive mass of details which look like they were lifted from my own past between the total ban of my work in 1965 and denaturalization in 1976."
- In 2010, I, Roberta Seret, screened this film at one of the foreign Missions at the U.N. A German diplomat moderated our post screening Q and A session. As he started talking, he burst into tears, confessing that he "had been the officer in charge of opening up the Stasi's documents to the public and he had witnessed the shock that families experienced while learning that their own family members had spied on them."

2. Director's/ Actor's Role:

- In his "Director's statement," Donnersmarck wrote: "More than anything else, *The Lives of Others* is a human drama about the ability of human beings to do the right thing, no matter how far they have gone down the wrong path."
- Donnersmarck told *The New* York Times about Beethoven's music being his inspiration: "I suddenly had this image in my mind of a person sitting in a depressing room with earphones on his head and listening in to what he supposes is the enemy of the state and the enemy of his ideas, and what he is

really hearing is beautiful music that touches him. I sat down and in a couple of hours had written the treatment."

- The director's parents and family were from East Germany, and as a child he spent some time living in East Germany. This gave him the opportunity to experience first-hand the atmosphere of fear that permeated much of the society. The emotional aspect of the regime struck him more than the political rhetoric, since he was only a child at the time, and it was that particular atmosphere that he sought to recreate in the movie.
- Von Donnersmarck had trouble gaining the funding for creating the movie because of the film industry's reluctance to expose the horrors of East Germany's Communism.

3. Awards:

- Academy Awards, USA
  2007 – Won – Best Foreign Language Film of the Year – Germany

- British Independent Film Awards
  2007 – Won – Best Foreign Independent Film – Germany

- Golden Globes, USA
  2007 – Nominated – Best Foreign Language Film – Germany

- New York Film Critics Circle Awards. 2007 – Won – Best Foreign-Language Film

Bibliography of Films: Filmography
Further Global Study Resources through Film:

German Films:

- *Triumph of the Will*
- *The Marriage of Maria Braun*
- *Lili Marleen"*
- *Lola Lola*

- *Veronika Voss*
- *Aguirre*
- *Beyond Silence*
- *The Boat*
- *Downfall*
- *Goodbye Lenin*
- *Head-On*
- *The Edge of Heaven*
- *Soul Kitchen*
- *The Reader*
- *Nowhere In Africa*
- *Sophie Scholl: the Final Days*
- *Phoenix*
- *Labyrinth of Lies*

Famous German Film Directors:

Rainer Maria Fassbinder:

- *Katzelmacher* (1969)
- *The American Soldier* (1971)
- *Beware of a Holy Whore* (1971)
- *The Merchant of the Four Seasons* (1972)
- *The Bitter Tears of Petra von Kant* (1972)
- *Ali: Fear Eats the Soul* (1974)
- *Martha* (1974)
- *Effi Briest* (1974)
- *Fox and his Friends* (1974)
- *The Enigma of Kaspar Hauser (1974)*
- *Mother Küsters Goes to Heaven* (1975)
- *Chinese Roulette* (1976)
- *The Stationmaster's Wife (1977)*
- *Despair* (1978)
- *In a Year of Thirteen Moons* (1978)
- *The Marriage of Maria Braun* (1978)
- *Berlin Alexanderplatz* (1980)
- *Lili Marleen* (1981)

- *Theater In Trance* (1981)
- *Lola* (1981)
- *Veronika Voss* (1982)
- *Querelle* (1982)

Wim Wenders:

- *Summer in the City (1970)*
- *The State of Things (1970)*
- *The Goalkeeper's Fear of the Penalty (1972)*
- *Paris, Texas (1984)*
- *Wings of Desire (1987)*
- *Until the End of the World (1991)*
- *Buena Vista Social Club (1999)*
- *The Soul of a Man (2003)*
- *Pina (2011)*
- *The Salt of the Earth (2014)*

CHAPTER 10

IN A BETTER WORLD (DENMARK)

TITLE OF FILM: *In a Better World*
YEAR OF RELEASE: 2010
COUNTRY: Denmark
DIRECTOR: Susanne Bier
LANGUAGE: Danish, Swedish, English
RUNNING TIME: 113 minutes
RATING: R
CURRICULUM THEMES:

A. HISTORY and SOCIAL SCI ENCE:

- **Chapter's Key Themes: Bullying; Racial Intolerance**
- **World History: Major religion: Lutheran; Separation between church and state**
- **Geography**
- **Economics: European Union; Euro; Foreign trade**
- **Civics, Citizenship and Government: Constitutional monarchy; Immigration and Relationship with Muslim Community; Schengen Agreement; Attempts to discourage asylum-seekers**

B. LITERATURE and VISUAL ARTS:

- **World Literature: Hans Christian Andersen; Greek influence; Gospel of Matthew; Code of Hammurabi**
- **Media Studies: Dogme 95 cinematography; Cinematography Techniques; Symbols; Title of film and happiness**
- **Philosophy/Critical Thinking: Kierkegaard and Existentialism**
- **Art: Music of Johan Sodergvist**
- **Technology: Recreational Mathematics**

Introduction:

In A Better World was directed by Susanne Bier; screenplay by Anders Thomas Jensen; produced by Sisse Graum Jorgensen; cinematography by Morten Soborg; edited by Pernille Bech Christensen and Morten Egholm; production design by Peter Grant; music by Johan Soderqvist; released by Sony Pictures Classics in 2010. (113 minutes)

Anton ....*Mikael Persbrandt*
Marianne ....*Trine Dyrholm*
Claus ....*Ulrich Thomsen*
Christian ....*William Johnk Nielsen*
Elias...*Markus Rygaard*

What makes a foreign film challenging, is the opportunity to peer into a different world and to form a relationship with characters in that society because of a better understanding and empathy. Such a film is *In a Better World* that gives explicit details about the human condition and how humanity can be paralleled with diverse societies, such as a picturesque town in Denmark and a struggling refugee camp in Sudan.

In a Better World illustrates the friendship of two Danish boys who are bonded together by the presence of strife in their respective families: Christian is coping with his anger over the death of his mother and strained relationship with his father; Elias is consumed by anger against his parents who have divorced and his father's commuting to Sudan to work as a doctor for les Mèdecins sans Frontières. Elias has also become a victim of school bullies.

While the boys fight their battles with their personal lives, the director (Bier) takes the viewer to a refugee camp in Sudan, where Elias' father (Anton) is posted. As the movie starts to unravel, it becomes clear that underneath the poverty and devastation in Sudan's refugee camp, there is a parallelism with Denmark and the human condition. *In A Better World* gives us a picture of revenge and the difficulty of finding forgiveness.

Pivotal Moments in History:

Sudan

- In **1947**, the British decided that northern and southern Sudan should unite to become one country. However, this was very conflicting for the Sudanese people because Northern Sudan is populated by people who practice the Islamic religion, while Southern Sudan is centered on its authentic African culture and Christianity. As a result, the first civil war in Sudan started in **1955.** This war lasted from **1955-1972,** which was Southern Sudan's fight for freedom from Northern Islamic rule. The casualties of this war were estimated to be at least five hundred thousand people, as well as thousands of survivors being forced to leave their homes. This war ended with the Addis Ababa Agreement of **1972,** declaring that Southern Sudan is a single administrative region with various defined powers.

- Civil peace in Sudan lasted ten years until President Gaafar Nimeiry declared that all Sudan is an Islamic state, including the Southern non-Islamic region. This angered the citizens of Southern Sudan, which resulted in the eruption of a second Sudanese civil war. This was a religious battle between Muslim and Christians Sudanese, and similar to the previous civil war, thousands were relocated and an estimated two million Sudanese Christians were killed. Moreover, the northern government ordered their armed forces (also known as the Janjaweed) to attack and raid villages in the South to enslave thousands of women and children. The Janjaweed also killed those who did not support Northern Sudan and destroyed thousands of fields and homes, as well as acquire resources such as oil, water, cattle, and land. Those that were not killed or enslaved, were left hungry and homeless.

- As of August **2015,** South Sudan President Salva Kiir has signed a peace deal with rebels. However, some of the top commanders have split from [rebel leader] Machar, and they say the peace deal means nothing to them. Doctors Without Borders said two of its staff members were killed recently. Thousands of people have been killed. More than 1.6 million people have been displaced. The UN said that young girls have been raped and burned alive. Meanwhile, oil-rich South Sudan's public debt has climbed from zero at its independence in 2011 to $4.2 billion as of June **2015.**

Pre-Screening Questions:

- The film is titled, *In a Better World.* What are some characteristics that attribute to the notion of an utopian society?
- What does it mean to be bullied?
- How do some people respond to being bullied? Respond to the perpetrator? To the victim?
- What does racial intolerance mean?
- Does racial intolerance exist in other parts of the world? Where? Is there a reason?

- What are some attempts or ways to rectify racial intolerance?
- What is Sharia Law?

Hints:

- Sharia Law is a religious code for how Muslims should live, in the same way that the Bible offers a moral system for Christians. It is used to refer both to the Islamic system of law and the totality of the Islamic way of life. Sharia is derived both from the *Koran*, which is believed by Muslims to be the word of God, as dictated to the prophet Muhammad by the angel, Gabriel, and illustrates the exemplary life of the Prophet, Muhammad.

Pivotal Moments in Film:

- Paris, March 1995. Filmmakers around the world gathered at the *Le cinéma vers son deuxième siècle* symposium to celebrate a century of cinema and to discuss its future. Controversial Danish director, Lars Von Trier, presented everyone at the event a manifesto, *The Vow of Chastity*. Its goal was to free filmmakers from high budget films and the excess of visual details. This manifesto entailed a list of rules, which in turned created a new genre of cinema, called Dogme 95. These rules included: location shooting without artificial props or sets, the use of hand-held cameras without special lighting, prohibition sounds and music from being produced apart from the images (meaning that the film is shot the way it would be perceived in real life).
- Susanne Bier, the director of, *In a Better World*, aligns herself with the Dogme 95 group movement.

Curriculum Themes:
A. History and Social Science

Chapter's Key Themes: Bullying; Racial Intolerance

a. Bullying:

- The director illustrates the theme of bullying with multiple scenes as a variation on a theme:
  - Elias is constantly being harassed by one of his classmates;

    °   Anton, his father, is getting slapped in the face over a dispute in a play-
        ground (as well as in the auto shop by the same man);

    °   "Big Man" is terrorizing villages across Sudan as well as bullying Anton,
        who works as the doctor in the refugee camp.

Suggested Activities

- *Ask members of your group to discuss how the director uses the theme of bullying as a parallel to countries that are also bullied in the European community. Has this been part of Denmark's history during World War II?*
  In present times?
- *Start to discuss bullying by using the following headlines that have appeared in newspapers:*
  "Mom sues city after suicide of 12-year-old son, who was harassed by schoolmates."
  "Community gym offers self-defense classes for kids."

Hints:

- Bullying is defined as an act of repeated aggressive behavior to intentionally hurt another person, physically or mentally. Bullying is characterized by an individual's behavior to gain power over another person. There are several types of bullying that span from bullying at school, bullying in the workplace, to bullying through the use of technology, as on the Internet and through social network. One major problem with bullying is that victims of bullying are unable to communicate their suffering and don't know who to turn to for help. Studies have shown that there is a strong link between bullying and suicide in young people. Suicide is the third leading cause of death among young adults in the U.S.

- Today, countries have started to take a stand against bullying, including the U.S. and Denmark. In March 2008, the Danish Ministry of Education launched a campaigned titled "United Against Bullying." This program is aimed at improving the well-being, tolerance and safety of students. Since the start of the campaign, the number of Danish schools that have constructed a plan against bullying has risen to 85 percent.

- Even though there are programs to prevent bullying in schools throughout the U.S., this problem continues. The future of solving this issue is dependent on more recognition that bullying exists and to address it on several levels: with parents, teachers, classmates, and professionals. Bullying takes its toll throughout society and leaves victims fragile forever. The destruction to people and society is high and can be irreparable.

- To discuss bullying with students and bring it into the open is important. Bullying exist and should be stopped. To screen the film, *In A Better World* is a good way to begin the subject.

b. Racial Intolerance:

- In the beginning of the movie at the schoolyard scene, Elias is trying to get through a crowd of bullying classmates, only to find out that his bicycle tires have been deflated. As he is trying to get through the crowd, one of the bullies calls Elias a "Damn Swede" as well as a "mutant." This verbal abuse against Elias' nationality can be seen again when Elias' dad, Anton, a Suede by birth who lives in Denmark, confronts Lars, a mechanic who slapped Anton in a playground. When Anton enters Lars' auto shop, Anton tells one of Lars' employees that he is looking for him. The employee calls out to Lars exclaiming, "Sweden calling." Moments into Lars and Anton's conversation, Lars demands Anton to, "shut the hell up and get your ass back to Sweden." This attack of racial intolerance against Anton's family for being Swedish is a reoccurring theme of the film. Racial intolerance and bullying come together as parallel problems.

Suggested Activities:
- *Discuss racial intolerance and the role it has in countries worldwide. Divide into the following groups for discussion: Fascists in Germany during World War II, Rwandans Hutus and Tutsis; Kurds in Iraq, Syria, Iran and Turkey; Arab Sunnis against Arab Shiites in Iraq; and now Muslim migrants seeking refuge in Europe.*
- *Students can discuss what is the relationship of bullying with intolerance?*

Hints:
- Racial intolerance toward Muslims has been a major issue in Denmark with the migration of Muslims in the past couple of decades. The director chose to include racial intolerance in the film due to the problem in 1995 Denmark about cartoons made by Danish journalists that ridiculed Mohammad in Danish newspapers. The film shows Danes who express racial slurs to other nationalities as Swedes. (This is softer to palpitate and less volatile than directly showing anti-Muslim sentiments). The use of racial intolerance in the script can also be associated with the theme of bullying. This does not mean that all Danes are racially intolerant, but it suggests that people can use race as a weapon of verbal harassment. The director addresses racial intolerance as a way to show that bullying can be without limit and with great consequences on all levels of society.

1. World History: Denmark:

a. Major Religion: Evangelical Lutheran Church

- 95% of Danes practice the Evangelical Lutheran official religion. However, other forms of Christianity are present, in a small percentage, as Protestant and Roman Catholic. In recent years there has been an increase of immigrants following the Muslim religion. Prior to that, Denmark has been a very homogenous country. The Conservative government in Denmark has taken position against Muslims.

Suggested Activities:
- *Research the Evangelical Lutheran church and discuss the role it plays in forgiveness and in death. You can analyze scenes in the film involving characters retaliating to bullying and discuss if the characters' responses are align with religion and prejudice.*
- *You can include in your discussion the relationship between church and state in Denmark and whether there is separation between the two.*
- *Demark is used by the director as one example, but the situation can be traced throughout Europe. Discuss other countries of the E.U. that have such problems of religious and racial intolerance. Which E.U. countries have right wing governments in power?*

Hints:
- Martin Luther was a German monk who went against the Roman Catholic doctrine and began the Protestant Reformation in the early 16th century.
- Martin Luther described the reform movement with the term "Evangelical" and Evangelical Lutherans. This is the name still used by them in Denmark, Scandinavia and Germany. Luther and his followers began to use the term in the middle of the 16th century in order to identify themselves from other groups, such as Calvinists.
- The split between the Lutherans and the Roman Catholics began with the Edict of Worms in 1521, which officially excommunicated Luther and all of his followers. Because Luther had always been a devout Catholic and because he was the first of the Protestants, the Lutheran doctrines did not stray from traditional Catholic doctrines. Most differences tend be in that Lutheranism simplifies Catholic practices.

- Members base their beliefs on the Bible and the Augsburg Confession, written in 1530 and the *Book of Concord,* written in 1580. A strong emphasis is placed on the doctrine that a person is saved solely through their faith and not through any works they might perform.
- Luther's departures from Roman Catholicism were based in areas related to:
  - ° Baptism - Lutherans practice both infant and adult baptism
  - ° Individual Access to God - Luther believed that each individual has the right to reach God through the Scriptures with responsibility to God
  - ° Salvation for All - Luther believed that salvation is available to all humans
  - ° Scripture – He believed the Scriptures contained the one necessary guide to truth
  - ° Worship - No church is bound to follow any set order.

b. Separation between Church and State:

In Denmark, this has been an issue of public concern. The government and tax-payers support the Church of Denmark; however, membership is voluntary for everyone except the Danish Royal family, who are required by law to be members. Polls have shown that less than five percent of the population attends church on a weekly basis, but the church still receives most of its income from taxes. Even if Danes de-register themselves from the church, the state pays the Church in state subsidy, which is equal to approximately 130 kroner per year for every citizen. In recent years, there is declining membership and low church attendance, but still the majority of Denmark's population uses the church for marriages, funerals and confirmations. A major criticism of the church is that it lacks central authority, meaning that there are no official positions in the church that allow clergymen to participate in governmental affairs.

2. Geography:

- The capital of Denmark is Copenhagen.
- The official language of Denmark is Danish, but there are several minority languages spoken throughout the country as German, Faroese (Denmark owns the Faroe islands), English and Greenlandic (Denmark owns Greenland).

- Denmark is located between the North Sea and the Baltic Sea. The landscape consists of fiords, deep inlets of the sea between high mountain cliffs. The coastline stretches to 7,314 km. Denmark has a temperate climate, meaning that the winters are mild and windy and the summers are cool. The country's natural resources include petroleum, natural gas, fish, salt, limestone, stone, gravel and sand. One of the biggest natural hazards of the Denmark is flooding, due to its low land terrain. There are 443 named islands surrounding the mainland and approximately one-quarter of the population lives in the capital. Recent polls have names Danes one of the most happy group of people in the world for 2013, 2014 and 2016.

Suggested Activities:
- *Members of your group can research and compare Sudan's and Denmark's geography by using resources, data and tools as aerial photographs, satellite images, geographic information systems (GIS), map projections and cartography.*
- *You can calculate the commute that Anton has to make from Denmark to Sudan and determine how many countries he has to travel to get to his destination.*

3. Economics:

a. European Union (EU):

- Denmark is a member of the European Union as of 1973. Yet, the EU began in 1958 with 6 original countries: Belgium, France, Italy, Luxembourg, the Netherlands and West Germany.
- In 1993 the Maastricht Treaty established the European Union under its current name and constitution. The treaty established the three pillars of the European Union – the European Community pillar, the Common Foreign and Security Police pillar, and the Justice European Community pillar. The creation of the pillar system to extend the European Economic Community to areas of banking, trade, foreign policy, military, criminal justice, security, and judicial cooperation.
- The EU is an economic and political union of 28 European countries that has as its goal to maintain a single market through a standardized system of laws that apply to all member states. The EU countries form a combined population of over 500 million inhabitants, or 7.3% of the world population.

b. The Euro:

- The European Union is also a single currency monetary union with the Euro as the unifying currency that is used by 17 member countries. The Euro, with its 17 member countries, is the second largest currency in the world.
- The Euro has experienced problems as of late 2009 with Sovereign Debt problems and faulting on their Budgetary requirements. Ireland faltered first, followed by Greece, then Italy, Belgium and Spain. Major discussions in Brussels during December 2011 ensued to save the Euro crisis, where the European Central Bank was empowered to save the Euro and fund financially distressed euro zone governments by overseeing cuts in spending, regulating comprehensive packages, loans and bonds in co-operation with the International Monetary Fund.

Suggested Activities
- *In pairs, define the following financial terms: sovereign debt; sub prime; loans; collateral; inflation; recession; International Monetary Fund; GNP; and bonds.*
- *Members of your group can represent east, west, south and north Europe to discuss which countries are part of the European Union and use the Euro.*
- *Identify which leaders of the European Union had to step down from power because of the Financial Debt Crisis of 2010-2011.*

Hints:
- Money is a technical device, a means of exchange, and symbolizes unity or disunity. Money exists because communities exist. A community in which people live and trade – they exchange freely- creates value. Their money symbolizes that value.
- There are 28 countries that as of 2016 comprise the European Union:
  Austria (1995), Belgium (1952), Bulgaria (2007), Cyprus (2004), Czech Republic (2004), Denmark (1973), Estonia (2004), Finland (1995), France (1952), Germany (1952), Greece (1981), Hungary (2004), Ireland (1973), Italy (1952), Latvia (2004), Lithuania (2004), Luxembourg (1952), Malta (2004), Netherlands (1952), Poland (2004), Portugal (1986), Romania (2007), Slovakia (2004), Croatia (2013), Slovenia (2004), Spain (1986), Sweden (1995), United Kingdom (1973).
- There are 17 member countries that use the Euro:
  Austria (1995), Belgium (1952), Cyprus (2004), Estonia (2004), Finland (1995), France (1952), Germany (1952), Greece (1981), Ireland (1973), Italy

(1952), Luxembourg (1952), Malta (2004), Spain (1986) Netherlands (1952), Portugal (1986), Slovakia (2004), Slovenia (2004).

- From late 2009, a sovereign debt crisis developed among investors concerning rising government debt levels across the globe together with a wave of down-grading of government debt of certain European countries. Concerns intensi-fied in early 2009 and thereafter, making it difficult or impossible for Greece, Ireland, Portugal and Belgium to re-finance their debts. At different intervals in 2011-2012, Europe's Finance Ministers approved rescue packages aimed at ensuring financial stability across Europe.
- The European Central Bank infused $640 billion into 523 European banks as a way to overturn the European Union's debt crisis. The new policy lends capi-tal to commercial banks at a low rate of interest, 1%. The goal is to increase the country's productivity, increase employment, and decrease spending on social projects. The International Monetary Fund has stepped in also, espe-cially helping Greece.
- In a domino-fall occurrence, many European leaders had to relinguish power. After they stepped down, there was also a shift of Parties in control of their government. The following were some victims of the Sovereign Debt Euro Crisis: Greece – George Papandreou; Italy- Silvio Berlusconi; Spain – Jose Luis Rodriguez Zapatero.

c. Foreign Trade:

- The economy of Denmark is greatly dependent on foreign trade. The country's main industries include: food processing, energy, machinery and transporta-tion equipment, textiles, shipbuilding and refurbishment, pharmaceuticals and medical equipment. In 2009, it was estimated that Denmark earned $91 billion dollars in export revenue. The country's high standard of living is shown through the government's strong welfare system that ensures all Danes receive tax-funded health care, child-care and unemployment insurance.

Suggested Activities:
- *Members of your group can analyze different welfare programs around the world and see if there is a correlation with import/export revenue. Scandinavian countries have a strong welfare system. Compare some of the European countries' benefits with America's.*

4. Civics, Citizenship and Government:

a. Constitutional monarchy:

- Denmark has a constitutional monarchy with a parliamentary system of government. It has state-level and local governments. It is a member of the European Union since 1973, but it has not adopted the Euro as its currency.
- The Kingdom of Denmark includes Denmark, Faroe Islands and Greenland.

Suggested Activity:
- *Divide into two groups. One group supporting a constitutional monarchy (Denmark) and the other supporting the two governments in Sudan (North and South). The groups can compare the ideologies and structure of governments, keeping in mind liberty, justice, equality, and the fair rule of law.*

b. Immigration and Relationship with Muslim community:

- The Muslim community in Denmark has become increasingly prominent in the last couple of decades. Since the 1980's, asylum seekers and economic refugees from Iran, Iraq, Syria, Gaza and the West Bank, have immigrated to Denmark. As these individuals made Denmark their new home, more Muslims started to immigrate into the country as a part of family reunification. There is an estimated 200,000 Muslims living in Denmark today. As a result, some Danes fear that Denmark's culture will disintegrate with an increased number of immigrants. Right wing Political parties, such as the Danish People's Party, campaign to strengthen nationalistic and anti-immigration policies with the goal to persuade immigrants from residing into their country and to enforce specific regulations. For example, women cannot wear Muslim traditional head coverings in the workplace; the prohibition of the use of immigrant children's native language in Danish schools; and the barring of forced marriages. These laws have resulted in increased tension between Muslims and Danes.
- On September 30th, 2005, the Danish newspaper, Jyllands-Posten, received major criticism from Muslims around the world when the newspaper published 12 editorial cartoons depicting the Islamic prophet, Muhammad in caricatured format. Danish embassies, as well as stores carrying Danish products,

were bombed and attacked in the Middle East. Right-wing governments in Europe stood up to protect Denmark's Nationalistic position. Still today, there is tension.

Suggested Activities:
- *Members of your group can divide into pairs, supporting the cartoons and criticizing them, and debate if the cartoons were justified.*
- *Compare the use of cartoons in the Danish newspaper with cartoons and caricatures made by the Nazis in their newspapers during World War II.*
- *Discuss how xenophobic movements have influenced conservative governments to abolish the Schengen Agreement as of 2015. Why? Which countries are these?*

Hints:
- Denmark is not the only country in Europe that has vociferous right-wing political parties. Norway's Progress Party, Sweden's Sweden Democrats, Germany's National Democratic party, France's National Front, Italy's Northern League, U.K.'s English Defence League, Hungary's and Holland's conservatives, are also against the multi-cultural diversity of their countries. Hate speech, inflammatory rhetoric, violence, terrorist killings and obsessive hate, have divided societies throughout Europe in the past decade. The tragic death of 77 young people in Oslo, Norway on July 22, 2011, caused by one person, right-wing Norwegian, Anders Behring Breivik, attests to the dangerous fanaticism of Europe's strengthening Right-wing parties.

c. The Schengen Agreement:

- In 1985, the Schengen Agreement led the way toward the creation of open borders without passport controls between most member states and some non-member states. However, in May 2011, Denmark, one of the signatories of the Schengen Agreement, re-imposed border control to check for illegal refugees entering Denmark from neighboring Sweden and Germany. In a similar move, Italy and France, who have had a great influx of refugees coming from Tunisia, Algeria, Libya, Egypt, Syria and Morocco during the Arab Spring of 2011, have tightened their borders. As of 2015, other members of the EU have abandoned the Schegen Agreement.

Suggested Activity:

- *Discuss how the Schengen Agreement has polarized Europe, within the country, and from other countries of the E.U.*

d. Attempts to Discourage Asylum-seekers:

Denmark passed a law in January 2016 requiring that newly arrived refugee-asylum-seekers to hand over valuables, jewelry, gold and money to help pay for their lodging and stay in Denmark. This is a way to discourage migrants from entering and remaining in Denmark. The government has also passed a law stating that any asylum-seeker must wait three years before they can apply to bring their families to Denmark.

Suggested Activities:

- *European countries are trying to find ways to discourage refugees from entering the country. Switzerland requires asylum-seekers to hand over their money that exceeds 1,000 Swiss francs. Germany requires that they contribute to their living expenses. Other European countries are stipulating similar laws. This concept makes an interesting debate. Divide the class into small groups and present reasons for your position.*
- *Discuss what other ways European countries are discouraging migrants?*

Hints:

- The migrant issue is a major problem for Europe. In 2015 more than 1 million asylum-seekers entered Germany. E.U. countries are looking for ways to curtail immigration: Denmark, spurred by the concept of a large influx of migrants, has required that public day care centers and kindegartens include pork for lunches. In Germany's Bavaria, police are allowed to search new arrivals for valuables. Refugees can only keep 700 Euros. Countries are paying transportation fare to dissatisfied migrants to return home.

B. Literature and Visual Arts

---

5. World Literature:

a. Hans Christian Andersen:

- During the funeral of Christian's mother, Christian recites a passage from Danish writer, Hans Christian Andersen, "The Nightingale." The passage illustrates a bargain between Death and a Nightingale over the life of a Chinese Emperor. The deal states that if the Nightingale continues to sing its song, Death will exchange the Emperor's life for treasures. The Nightingale continues to sing its song, keeping death away from the Emperor, allowing the Emperor to live. The Emperor asks what he can do in return for the Nightingale, but the bird states that because the Nightingale's song brought the Emperor happiness, that was the greatest gift of all. While Christian (symbolic use of his name) is reciting this passage, his audio is played over images of children living joyfully in a Sudan refugee camp and images of Sudan's dry landscape. These images dissolve into a shot of Christian using the passage in his eulogy for his mother's funeral. The director uses this passage as a vehicle to connect the despair in Sudan with the events that unfold after the funeral. Both worlds display an outer layer of anguish but when all the pain and suffering is removed, there is an underlying theme of happiness. Behind the motivating forces that keep these worlds in darkness and make these worlds appear different, are human beings. The director's angel is to show that behind Sudan's wars and poverty, and behind Denmark's family conflicts and school bullies, there is a universal homogeneity in human interaction. Ms. Bier shows in her film that the ultimate goal of human relations is to pursue happiness. Our reward will be to find ourselves, *In a Better World.*

Suggested Activities:
- *Analyze and discuss why director, Susanne Bier, chose Hans Christian Andersen's, "The Nightingale." Does the name of the protagonist, Christian, have a symbol?*
- *At the principal port in Copenhagen, there is a statue of "The Little Mermaid." Find photos and discuss the statue's significance.*

b. Greek Influence:

- One of the distinctive features of classical Greek drama is the Greek chorus that consisted of men dressed in similar costumes and hidden under the stage. Their role was to observe and comment on the actions of the actors and help the audience follow the plot. The chorus was the voice and truth of the characters' intentions. This allowed the audience to assimilate themselves into the inner conscious of the drama's characters and achieve "catharsis" – a purging of emotion. In the film, Christian symbolizes a Greek chorus, as he voices his understanding of the world around him. And yet, Christian is only twelve-years-old. One must wonder does the director delegate Truth in the child's voice? Is she telling us that children are our Hope?

Suggested Activity:

- *Discuss the role of a Greek chorus in this movie and how the characters act in relation to this Greek influence. Take into consideration the naive role of Christian. For example, Christian comments that the best way to get revenge on the man who slapped Anton is by blowing up the man's car. Christian does not understand that perpetuating violence will result in more sorrow. When Anton discusses with Elias the adverse effects of retaliation with violence, the reality of their actions becomes clear. Anton has the potential to vocalize the truth and also act as the Greek chorus, but he withdraws from intervening and does not assert justice. Instead, he chooses to act as a bystander until he can no longer remain passive and acts violently.*

c. Gospel of Matthew:

- The Gospel of Matthew is one of the four canonical gospels, and the first book of the New Testament. The Gospel of Matthew expresses themes of life, death, and the resurrection of Jesus of Nazareth. In this Gospel, we find the phrase, "Turning the other cheek." This is found in the teachings of Jesus in the Sermon on the Mount, as Jesus voices, "You have heard that it was said, An eye for an eye, and a tooth for a tooth. But I tell you, do not resist an evil person. If someone strikes you on the right cheek, turn to him the other also. And if someone wants to sue you and take your tunic, let him have your cloak as well. If someone forces you to go one mile, go with him two miles. Give to the one who asks you, and do not turn away from the one who wants to borrow from you." (Matthew 5:38-42).

- The theme of "turning the other cheek" plays a major role in this film, as there are various incidents where characters are forced to decide how they should respond in the presence of bullying. Anton is an example of a man who is pushed to respond to bullying in several different occasions. When Anton goes into the auto shop to confront the man who slapped him in the playground, he chooses to discuss the situation and understand the man's actions. He chooses not to retaliate with violence. As Anton asks why the man did what he did, the man repeatedly slaps Anton in the face until Anton is forced to leave. Anton stands there and lets the man slap him in the face to show his kids and Christian that responding to violence isn't always the solution to prove that you are strong. Later on in the film, Big Man, the Guerilla warfare leader who has been terrorizing Sudan refugee camps, comes into Anton's hospital with the hope that Anton would treat his wounded leg. Anton reluctantly accepts to treat Big Man under the condition that all of Big Man's followers and guns are miles away from the camp. However, Anton realizes that Big Man continues to make offensive remarks about the deceased, and decides to throw him out of his hospital. By doing this, Anton is giving the people in the refugee camp a chance to get revenge. By letting Big Man suffer this fate, he is giving the "bully" what he deserves. Anton fights back by letting the people decide the bully's fate, not him.

d. Code of Hammurabi:

- In opposition to the Christian tradition of "turning the other cheek," is the Babylonian law dating from 1772 B.C., known as the Code of Hammurabi, which can be explained as, "The law of retaliation." This first modern- legal document, dictates that an individual is to be given equitable retribution for their offenses.

  The Code of Hammurabi states: "If a man knocks the teeth out of another man, his own teeth will be knocked out." (An eye for an eye, a tooth for a tooth.) The notion of people being responsible for their actions plays a crucial role in revenge and in forgiveness in this film.

Suggested Activities:
- *Themes from the Code of Hammurabi and the Gospel of Matthew are exemplified throughout the movie. You can debate how these opposing rules influence Anton's behavior. Discuss during which scenes?*
- *Discuss Ghandhi's quote, "An eye for an eye makes the whole world blind."*

6. Media Studies

a. Dogme 95 Cinematography:

- Dogme 95 is an avant-garde filmmaking movement that was started in 1995 by Danish director, Lars von Trier who created the "Dogme 95 Manifesto" and the "Vow of Chastity." In these works, he stated specific rules for filmmaking based on traditional values of story, acting, and cinematographic techniques, excluding the use of elaborate special effects or Hollywood-style budgets.
- Susanne Bier is a member of Dogme 95. She says this about her filmmaking techniques:" I believe in rules. I believe in artistic limitations, and I always

have. I've always thought that setting out a set of rules before you start, and then being completely consistent with them, is the only way to make a really good film. These particular Dogme rules are austerity rules. They force you to deal with the storyline and the characters, and that's it. And I thought it was a real challenge in a positive way."

- One of the rules of the Dogme 95 genre is that the camera must be hand-held. By using this type of camera, filming can take place directly and intimately where the action takes place. This facilitates that the audience can experience what the characters are going through at the same given moment. With this rule in mind, the camera moves around a scene to capture all different angles of a location and action. There are many instances where the camera shifts to the perspective of the characters. When Christian is being introduced to his classmates for the first time, the camera shifts from Christian's perspective of looking at the classroom, to Elias' perspective of observing Christian.

b. Cinematography Techniques

- A cinematic technique that the director uses is panoramic shots with wide angle lenses. When there is a scene where the characters are located in a large open environment, the camera captures the entire environment, even when the actors are in a small portion of the frame. This allows the camera to capture the beauty of the landscape as well as illustrate the relationship between the character's interaction with the location of the shot. An example of this is when Anton and his children are sitting on their deck overlooking the water. When the camera is facing the characters, we can see also the house, the property, and the sun setting through the trees. When the shot is reversed, looking at the characters from behind, we can see the vastness and beauty of the landscape, the grassy fields, and the large body of water. During these shots, the camera is more focused on the landscape then the interactions between the characters. This creates the notion that there is a larger world outside of the problems of the characters and the viewer is only getting insight on one family's turmoil. Also, we feel that the beauty of the setting (external) will heal the internal world of the characters.
- The use of natural lighting is a major component of the Dogme 95 movement. Throughout the film, the natural environment captures the majority of the lighting. During transitions between scenes in the films, the director shows many images of landscape. In these shots, the placement of the sun or

the quantity of clouds that filled the sky, determine the brightness of color in the landscape. In a sunset shot, the camera is pointed directly at the sun, and its brightness overpowers the rest of the shot, leaving only an outline of everything else in the shot that would have been seen if the camera wasn't pointed at the sun. During filming when the sky is cloudy, the images appear dark and grey. The placement of the shots evoke different emotions from the audience. The lighting of the shots captures and parallels the emotions of the characters and action.

- When shots are located indoors, the available lighting sources are used to illuminate the rooms. During the funeral scene, the room is primarily dark except for the windows, which shine a dull white light into the room. The windows are only shining in on one side of the room, exposing half of the actor's faces to light. As Christian recites "The Nightingale," his anger and sadness are captured through the light shining on only half of his face. In another scene, when Marianne and Anton have their cell phone conversation discussing their divorce, the sun had just set. The dark night sky gives the shot a darken blue tint, which exemplifies the sadness that has been absorbed by both characters. (Again a relationship between the external and internal.)
- Dogme 95's quest to capture natural beauty is also shown in the character's costumes. The actors from Denmark wear ordinary clothes that do not highlight wealth or poverty. Their attire can be easily associated with the viewers watching the film. The actors have no make up on and are captured by the camera with their natural appearance. This allows the viewer to feel that the characters can be put in any setting and the viewer would get the same impressions about their appearances. On the other hand, in contrast, the refugees from Sudan wear tattered dirty clothes, which we can presume to be a realistic rendering of their daily attire.

c. Symbols

- *Soccer ball:*
- In the beginning of the movie, when Anton and his colleagues are in a truck heading to the refugee camp hospital, kids are following the truck and yelling, "Hi, hi, hi." Anton throws a soccer ball to the kids and the children cheer and play with the ball. This is the opening scene and introduces Anton and his colleagues as wanting to help the refugees. Africans are passionate about soccer, as it is one of the major sports played throughout the continent. Anton's

act of giving the children a soccer ball represents hope for international support and impending relief in their future. Soccer is a symbol "of and for the people." It makes sense that, Anton, the doctor, should be the person to offer hope to the people.

- *Knife:*
- Christian threatens the school bully with a knife, warning him that if he continues to harass Elias or anybody else, the bully's life will be endangered. After the boys give their testimonies and everything gets resolved with their school, Christian gives Elias the knife. The knife creates a bond between the two boys, which is centered on trust. When Elias' mother finds out about the knife, she tells Christian's dad, who yells at Christian. Without the knife, Elias' persona is perceived as innocent and weak to Christian.
- Elias tries to apologize but Christian rejects him and storms off. Christian eventually forgives Elias when Elias agrees to make a bomb to harm the man who slapped Elias' father. The knife represents the boys liberation from reality, but once taken away, the bond is broken. This bond is healed with Elias' commitment to perpetuate violence by making a bomb.

d. Title of film and Happiness:

In A Better World is an interesting title. The director, Ms. Bier, obviously hopes that society can improve. And if it does, she hopes that people would be happier. Yet, Denmark, in 2013, 2014 and 2016, was crowned the happiest country in the world by "The United Nations' World Happiness Report." The six factors for a happy nation were:

- a large GDP per capita
- healthy life expectancy at birth
- lack of corruption in leadership
- social support
- freedom to make life choices and
- a culture of generosity

However, the film does not show that the characters are happy until the end. The symbolic ttle of the film gives us the opportunity to discuss, what is happiness?

Suggested Activities:

- *The human goal is to be happy. But what is happiness? How can each person define it, strive to attain it, and achieve it? Take time with your students to have each student think about this question and then to discuss some possibilities. Ask them to consider the importance of finding a balance between professional and personal goals.*

- *Students can write down their thoughts and then analyze the group's opinions. What factors repeat? Is there a pattern? Is there a list of priorities?*

- *Ask students to research which countries in the world have been voted to be the "happiest"? Discuss why? Has this list of countries changed in the past 5 years? Why?*

7. Philosophy/ Critical Thinking:

a. Philosophy of Kierkegaard and Existentialism:

- Søren Kierkegaard (1813-1855), a Danish philosopher, has been called the "Father of Existentialism." He was critical of intellectuals and philosophers of his time. He was also critical of the practice of Christianity in his lifetime, primarily the Evangelical Lutheran Church of Denmark. Much of his philosophical work deals with the issues of how one lives as a "single individual," giving priority to concrete human reality over abstract thinking, and highlighting the importance of personal choice and commitment. What was important to him was how one acts and how one exists.

- *Themes in his philosophy:*

a. Alienation:

Kierkegaard was one of the earliest philosophers to write about Alienation, a term that applies to: any feeling of separation from, and discontent with, society; feeling that there is a moral breakdown in society; feelings of powerlessness in the face of the solidity of social institutions; the impersonal, dehumanized nature of large-scale and bureaucratic social organizations.

b. Ethics:

Kierkegaard supports that God exists but God does not necessarily create human morality: it is up to us as individuals to create personal morals and values.

c. Individuality:

For Kierkegaard, individuality is called selfhood. Becoming aware of one's true self is the true task and endeavor in life. It is an ethical imperative, as well as preparatory to a true religious understanding. To have a direction, we must have a purpose that defines for us the meaning of our lives. And it is the individual who can create and define his own life. "Life is not a problem to be solved, but a reality to be experienced."

Quote from Kierkegaard:

> *"What I really need is to get clear about what I must do, not what I must know, except insofar as knowledge must precede every act. What matters is to find a purpose, to see what it really is that God wills that I shall do; the crucial thing is to find a Truth which is truth for me, to find the idea for which I am willing to live and die."*

- The authors and philosophers that lived after Kierkegaard and were influenced by him, claimed as their central argument that in an absurd world that lacks meaning, every individual gives his/her life meaning through his/her actions. One of the central concepts, that "existence precedes essence," means that we are defined only by what we choose to be and to do. There is no predetermined meaning to our lives but what we choose as our purpose.

- *Some major Existentialist figures are:*
- *Fyodor Dostoyevsky* (philosopher and writer, 1821-1881). His personal life was an example of Existentialism: "I used to imagine adventure for myself. I invented a life, so that I could at least exist somehow." (Art and storytelling is an act of defining oneself.)
- *Jean-Paul Sartre* (philosopher, 1905-1980): "Man is condemned to be free; because once thrown into the world, he is responsible for everything he does." (Man is rersponsible to create his own life and he is free to do so.)

- *Albert Camus* (philosopher and writer, 1913-1960): "Basically, at the very bottom of life, which seduces us all, there is only absurdity, and more absurdity. […] You will never live if you are looking for the meaning of life."

  Yet, for Camus, despite the absurdity of life, man must continue to live; for it is living that gives essence to our existence. Camus' protagonist Meursault, in *The Stranger,* is symbolic to Existentialism: Meur (to die) sault (alone). Before this happens, we must live life to its fullest. "There is not love of life without despair about life. There is scarcely any passion without struggle."

Suggested Activities:
- *Take one of the philosophical concepts that Kierkegaard and his followers wrote about and discuss their philosophies.*
- *The Existentialists that followed Kierkegaard were not religious like him.*
- *Consider why Anton is a character that Kierkegaard would have liked. It is no coincidence that Danish director, Susanne Bier, has used Kierkegaard's philosophy to create her characters.*

8. Art

a. Music of Johan Sodergvist:

- Throughout the film, we hear the music of Johan Sodergvist. Director, Susanne Bier, and Johan Sodergvist have been collaborating with each other since Bier's 1991 film, *Freud Flyttar Hemifran (Freud's Leaving Home)*. In this film, Sodergvist composed all of the music and made very specific decisions on which instruments to use. The most prominent instrument is the African instrument, mbira, which is the national instrument of Zimbabwe and is commonly known as the "voice of the ancestors."
- A typical mbira consists of between 22 and 28 keys constructed from forged metal affixed to a hardwood soundboard in three different registers—two on the left, one on the right. This instrument can be described as a thumb piano that produces intimate sounds that resembles bell glass. Sodergvist also uses vocal solos ranging from Kurdish mourning to a countertenor to a reconciling African voice that is placed in opportune moments to evoke emotions from the viewers.
- According to the Dogme 95 movement, a director cannot have music that has been produced apart from what is being captured on film. Bier uses African music when she is filming the Sudan sections.

Suggested Activity:

- *Students can research the mribi and discuss why the composer chose that instrument for this film.*

9. Technology:

a. Recreational Mathematics:

- Math is more than a tool. It is a challenging means to discover puzzles, invent objects and encourage math as a means of decipher problems. *Scientific American Magazine* has a series of math games. Encourage your members to form pairs to go to the magazine's site and recreate recreational math puzzles in the format of "Sudoku" and "KenKen."
- There is another website, "Project Euler," whose problems require not just math insight but also programming skills for more advanced students.

Sidebars:

---

1. Public Response:

- The idea for the film originated when Susanne Bier and screenwriter, Anders Thomas Jensen, had discussions about the perception of Denmark as a very harmonious society. They then wanted to write a story where dramatic turns of events would disrupt the image of a place perceived as blissful. The development of the narrative started with the doctor character, Anton, and the idea of an idealist who becomes the victim of an assault.
- Director Susanne Bier said: "Our experiment in this film is about looking at how little it really takes before a child, or adult, thinks something is deeply unjust. It really doesn't take much, and I find that profoundly interesting. And scary."

2. Actors and Directors:

- As the film jumps back and forth between Africa and Europe, it raises similar questions in each location about the nature of revenge and the difficulty of finding forgiveness. Director Susanne Bier, explains, "The whole point is to communicate that the conditions of living in Africa in a refugee camp and in a privileged part of Denmark couldn't be more different, but the actual human nature is so similar," she says. "It's kind of, in a way, showing the same story but in two different shapes."

- Bier has long told stories that explore how people behave during crisis situations. Though none of her movies are autobiographical, Bier says she tends to be drawn to themes that have also played a role in her family's history. "I'm Jewish, and my family is Jewish, and I've always had a very distinct recognition of war being an imminent catastrophe, of being a real thing," she says. "So I think it's been very natural for me to place some of my movies in a warlike situation."

    In 1943, Bier's relatives fled Denmark after the Nazi invasion. Sailors helped them cross a narrow sea into Sweden. Bier says hearing the story of how her parents escaped has stayed with her for many years and continues to play a theme in her films.

- Actor, Mikael Persbrandt, who plays Anton, is actually a Swedish actor. Why do you think the director used a Swedish actor instead of a Danish actor?
Hint: he has an accent when speaking Danish.

3. Awards:

- Academy Awards, USA
2010- Won- Best Foreign Language Film

- Golden Globe Award:
2010- Won – Best Foreign Language Film

- Rome International Film Festival 2010; Marc'Aurelio Audience Award for Best Film Marc'Aurelio Grand Jury Award

---

Bibliography of Films: Filmography
Further Global Study Resources through Film:

Racial Discrimination:

- *Sarafina!* (U. K. / South Africa)
- *Cry, the Beloved Country* (U.K./South Africa)
- *Remember Mandela* (South Africa)

- *The Stick* (South Africa)
- *Long Walk to Freedom* (South Africa)
- *Place of Weeping* (South Africa)
- *Mapantsula* (South Africa)
- *Skin* (South Africa)
- *Invictus* (U.S.A.)
- *Marooned in Iraq* (Iran/Iraq)
- *No Where in Africa* (Germany)
- *Before the Rain* (Macedonia)
- *Rabbit Proof Fence* (Australia)
- *The Pianist* (Poland/France)
- *Europa Europa* (France)
- *Fateless* (Hungary)
- *Caché* (France)
- *Days of Glory* (Algeria/Morocco/ France)
- *The Killing Fields* (Cambodia)
- *Paradise Now* (Palestine)
- *Divided We Fall* (Czech Republic)
- *The Color Purple* (U.S.A.)
- *Mississippi Burning* (U.S.A.)
- *Beloved* (U.S.A.)
- *Do the Right Thing* (U.S.A.)
- *Under the Same Moon* (Mexico)
- *The Class* (France)
- *A Secret* (France)
- *Skin* (South Africa)
- *Waltz with Bashir* (Israel)
- *Darfur Now* (U.S.A.)
- *Marooned in Iraq* (Iran/Iraq)
- *The Killing Fields* (U.S.A./Cambodia)
- *Carla's List* (Switzerland, Yugoslavia)
- *Fateless* (Hungary)
- *Exodus* (U.S.A.)
- *The Garden of the Finzi-Continis* (Italy)
- *Shoah* (France)
- *Europa Europa* (Holland/ France)
- *Schindler's List* (U.S.A.)
- *Anne Frank Remembered* (U.K.)

- *Life Is Beautiful* (Italy)
- *Sunshine* (Hungary)
- *Kadosh* (Israel)
- *Bloody Sunday Bloody* (Hungary)
- *Divided We Fall* (Czechoslovakia)
- *Into the Arms of Strangers: Stories of the Kindertransport* (U.K.)
- *Nowhere In Africa* (Germany)
- *The Pianist* (France/Poland)
- *Marooned in Iraq* (Iraq)
- *Philomena* (Ireland)

ANTARCTICA

CHAPTER 11

MARCH OF THE PENGUINS (ANTARCTICA)

TITLE OF FILM: *March of the Penguins*
YEAR OF RELEASE: 2005
COUNTRY: France/ Antarctica
DIRECTOR: Luc Jacquet
LANGUAGES: French, English
RUNNING TIME: 80 minutes
RATING: G
CURRICULUM THEMES:

A. HISTORY and SOCIAL SCIENCE:

- Chapter's Key Themes: Climate change: Environment
- World History: Survival of the Fittest; Intelligent design vs. evolution; Environmental problems in the 21st century
- Geography: Map studies: Antarctica; Environmental problems: Decline of Emperor Penguins' population; Climate change influences migratory behavior
- Economics: Multinational corporations and the environment
- Civics, Citizenship and Government: Communal society; Gender roles; Animal and human behavior

B. LITERATURE and VISUAL ARTS:

- World Literature: Public Speaking and Speech Communication; Media presentations
- Media Studies: Film Clips and Scene Discussions: for allegory, journey motif and point of view; Film and Cinematography Techniques: Use of camera; Voiceover

- **Philosophy/Critical Thinking: News and Magazine articles; Oral storytelling; Analyze the winning team**
- **ART: Photography**

Introduction:

March of the Penguins was directed by Luc Jacquet; screenplay by Luc Jacquet and Michel Fessler; produced by Yves Darondeau, Christophe Lioud and Emmanuel Priou; co-produced by the National Geographic Society and Bonne Pioche; cinematography by Laurent Chalet and Jerome Maison; edited by Sabine Emiliani; music by Emilie Simon and Alex Wurman; distributed by Warner Independent Pictures, Lionsgate, Maple Pictures, and Alliance Films; (80 minutes)

March of the Penguins is a documentary film about nature in animated style. The first screening was at Sundance Film Festival in the U.S. (2005) and one week later it was released in France. There are multiple versions to the film. The American version features a third-person narrative with a professorial voice by Morgan Freeman. The original French version, as the German, Danish and Hungarian, uses a first-person narrative voiceover technique as if the penguins are telling the story themselves. Another difference between the American and European versions involves the music. The original French version uses experimental electronic music by Emilie Simon while the American version uses an instrumental score by Alex Wurman.

Pivotal Moments in History:

- In the past several years, the ice caps and glaciers in Antarctica have been reduced to an unparalleled historic retreat. Scientists are studying the cause and effects of natural environmental forces that have exposed one million square miles to melting as well as to "ice moving." This area, spreading into the ice fields of Canada, the North Pole, Antarctica, Russia, the U.S., Greenland and Scandinavia, is the size of 6 Californian states.
- Scientists have shown that due to greenhouse gases and global warming, there have been unprecedented winds that have pushed huge amounts of thick ice out toward Antarctica and Greenland. Older, thicker sea ice has been replaced by thinner ice.
- This causes a loss of sea ice that is dangerous to animal life, as the film, *March of the Penguins* demonstrates. The Emperor penguins need thick and strong ice to hold the weight of hundreds of penguins at their breeding grounds.

- Scientists have cited that the ice meltdown has been caused in part by human activity. Scientists agree that Antarctica waters are forming rings of water instead of ice during summer. They also report that there is global warming in Greenland; glaciers near the coast, break off. They empty 20 billion metric tons of water annually. And scientists estimate that 150 billion metric tons of glaciers and ice vanish each year.
- In the North Pole, the Arctic Ocean has shown new areas of open water instead of solid ice. Scientists attribute these findings to:
  - Warm air temperature from north-eastern Siberia that has pushed melted ice from the Siberian coast;
  - An increased rate of heat on open water which causes a slowing of winter freeze and the formation of new, thinner ice;
  - High pressure and gases that create a clear sky over Antarctica and allow more sunlight to heat the ocean and retain less ice.

Pre-Screening Questions:

a. The film, March of the Penguins, is filmed in Antarctica. Where is Antarctica? Which countries own territories there? What is a continent? Locate them on a map.

- Antarctica is the name of the continent that is comprised mostly (98%) by ice mass. Climate conditions are the coldest there on earth. The South Pole is at the center of Antarctica.
- Antarctica territories are owned by 7 countries: Argentina, Chile, France, New Zealand, Norway, United Kingdom, and Australia. *March of the Penguins* was filmed at the French scientific base of Dumont d'Urville in Adélie Land (*Terre Adélie*), in the French territory.
- A continent is one of several large landmasses on Earth. There are 7 areas known as continents. They are, from largest in size to smallest: Asia, Africa, North America, South America, Antarctica, Europe, and Australia.
- Antarctica is the 5th largest continent; it is 1.3 times larger than the continent of Europe.

b. What is Darwin's Theory of Survival?

- In the 5th edition of Charles Darwin's The Origin of Species (1869), he uses the phrase, "*Natural Selection or the Survival of the Fittest.*" Natural selection signifies the preservation of favored races to survive in the struggle for life. The term survival of the fittest is used to apply to principles of competition and to the characteristics of an animal or human that improves its chances of survival. As humans and animals reproduce, there is a natural selection – those who are the best suited to the environment. Those are the ones who will survive.

c. What is a documentary film? What is the difference between a documentary film and a feature film?

- The term documentary was not coined until 1926. It was used initially by the French to refer to any nonfiction film, including travelogues and instructional films. This *genre* tends to document reality and it is a filmmaking process that has expanded to include video and digital productions. *March of the Penguins* is a documentary about nature.
- In recent years, the documentary as an art form has become very popular and creative in its format. Computer Generated Imagery (CGI) is used to increase realism in documentaries.
- A feature film is based on fictional elements, not reality; yet, it may use some realistic elements to make the details appear more credible. The viewer must be careful not to believe everything the director says, for the director films from his point of view. His goal is to sway the viewer to accept his position. While viewing a feature film that uses history or realistic subjects for its premise and theme, the viewer must be aware of the difference between fact and fiction. CGI is also used a lot in feature films to make them more realistic: *Revenant, Life of Pi, Avatar.*

Pivotal Moments in Film:

a. Every year in autumn, all the Emperor Penguins of breeding age (five years old) leave their habitat near the ocean to walk inland to their ancestral breeding ground. There, the penguins participate in a courtship that if successful, results in the hatching of a chick. The aim of their voyage is to survive and to ensure the survival of their chick so the voyage can be repeated generation after generation.

b. Emperor penguins are birds, not mammals. And yet, they do not fly. They swim or walk or even slide on their belly when they are tired. They are four feet tall and weigh 45-100 pounds. They can go under the water for as long as 22 minutes and dive to the depths of 1400 feet in ice water. They can withstand winds of 100-150 miles per hour and live in freezing temperatures of -58 degrees Fahrenheit. They can march 70 miles to search for food while they are starving. They are without a doubt, the strongest species on earth, living in the coldest area of the world.

c. The Emperor penguins exemplify Darwin's theory of the survival of the fittest where the animal's cyclical journey is so harsh, that not all the penguins of the community survive. For the baby chick to survive, both parents must make arduous journeys between the ocean and the breeding grounds.

d. Luc Jacquet, the director and screen script author, spent 13 months with his crew in French Antarctica to film one complete breeding cycle of the Emperor penguins. When they had to edit their footage and shoot more scenes, they filmed in Patagonia (Argentina and Chile) for Antarctica was just too harsh for another year of filming and one of the cameramen fell victim to frostbite.

e. Luc Jacquet and cameramen Laurent Chalet and Jerome Maison, achieve a great feat in filming. We don't see them but we know they are there, working in frigid conditions as they document the penguins' behavior. They capture all the important moments. They attached cameras to a balloon to get aerial shots of the males as they huddle together to get warm. They were on the spot when the chicks pecked their way out of the egg and then huddled under their father's belly for protection. And they witnessed predators as they were ready to prey on the new chicks. There was a separate diving crew that filmed under the sea to capture the mothers as they hunted for fish and squid.

f. In the film's opening, the narrator, Morgan Freeman, tells us as we watch thousands of Emperor penguins march in a single file, appearing so human-like, that this is a "story of life over death, a story of survival, a story about love." But it is also the story of choosing a mate, breeding, protecting the chick, and the mother and father working together to assure continuation of the species. We watch in awe as the mothers march 70 miles to sea to find fish for their infant and the father withstands sub-zero conditions for 125 days to protect the chick. We witness the penguins' precise, synchronized cooperation to procreate their species despite the innumerable risks. A mistake of one second freezes the egg, kills the chick and ends the life cycle of that family. All of this is filmed in ethereal beauty under dire conditions.

Post-Screening Questions:
A. History and Social Science:

1. *Describe the seasons in Antarctica:*
- Antarctica is in the southern hemisphere; therefore, their seasons are opposite to our seasons in North America, in the northern hemisphere. Their winter is our summer.
- There are basically two seasons. Summer consists of October to February, when the sun never sets and there is constant light; yet, the temperature is still on the average, 50 degrees Fahrenheit. Winter is brutal with no light at all and it is from March to September.

B. Literature and Visual Arts:

1. Discuss which scenes in the film show role reversals of traditional gender role and behavioral patterns among the Emperor penguins.
2. Discuss which scenes in the film show the penguins to have human-like qualities. Describe them.

Hints:
- Emperor penguins are monogamous during each breeding season. Both parents are responsible for their chick's survival. Both parents teach the chick how to recognize their voice and how to walk. The penguins also express human qualities as love and jealously.

Curriculum Themes:
A. History and Social Science:

Chapter's Key Themes: Climate Change; Environment

a. Climate change:

- We see in the film that when the penguins march, they travel in a single file and take care to follow a path that is thick in ice, for thin ice cannot withstand the group's massive weight. As summer brightens Antarctica, we are told by the narrator, that the ice thins and cracks. The ocean becomes closer and the parents can go back and forth more quickly to get fish to feed their family. In November, the beginning of their summer, the ocean is close to the breeding ground where the penguins can feed in open waters.

- As the ice melts, the new family goes their separate ways, ending their 9 months together. For the next 3 months (December, January and February), the males and females will feed and get stronger. By March, the beginning of autumn and winter, they are ready to repeat their breeding cycle and find another mate. In this cycle of breeding and life, there is a precise correlation with the seasons because the path of their march depends on the ice's thickness. But in recent years, it is not only the seasons that effect Antarctica's climate.

Suggested Activities:
- *Students can begin a discussion of global warming and make a list of environmental problems.*
- *Discuss the following questions: What is the "ozone hole" and what are its effects? How does global warming affect Antarctica and how does this influence the rest of the world? What types of pollution threaten Antarctica?*
- *Students can use their answers from the above questions to create an "environmental fact sheet" - graphic organizer for Antarctica describing the causes, effects and predictions for environmental problems. Students can use this graphic organizer as a prewriting activity before writing a newspaper article for their school and/or community newspapers.*

Hints:
- Global warming, the gradual rise in the earth's temperature, is a consequence of industrialization and the burning of fossil fuels, as oil, coal and natural gas, which release large amounts of carbon dioxide into the air. This excess

of CO2, traps more heat near the earth. An increase in CO2 means a thicker blanket over the Earth's atmosphere, which might cause the temperature of the atmosphere to rise. (Global warming)

- During the 1990s, scientists noticed an "ozone hole" – a large hole developed seasonally in the ozone layer over Antarctica. Most ozone is produced naturally high up in the atmosphere. The largest concentration of ozone occurs at an altitude of between 10-15 miles above the Earth's surface. Without this layer of ozone-rich air, it would be difficult for us to live on Earth. Ozone acts as our planet's sunscreen. It provides an invisible filter that protects humans and all life from the sun's damaging ultraviolet rays. Therefore, the "hole" in the ozone layer can result in not protecting us and could cause a possible increase of people suffering from skin cancer.

- A rise in temperature in the Antarctica will impact the entire world: rise in ocean and sea levels; changing ocean currents; changing shorelines; reducing ice sheets; and killing off penguins who need ice sheets to navigate to breeding grounds. The Arctic Ocean could be ice free in 2050; consequently, more than a million species worldwide could be driven into extinction.

- International scientists are studying pattern shifts of ice and climate change in Antarctica as an indicator to other environmental problems of the world: shifts in ecosystems; change in weather patterns; deaths and diseases to animal and plant life.

b. Environment:

- The Emperor Penguins use a specific area for their breeding ground because the ice there is solid year round and there is no danger of the ice becoming too soft to support the heavy weight of the penguin colony. At the beginning of the summer, the Antarctica breeding ground is less than 1,000 feet from the open water where the penguins can feed. Yet at the end of the summer, when they begin their voyage, the breeding ground is 62-70 miles away from the water. It is this great voyage that begins their story.

- *March of the Penguins* describes the importance of the Arctic Ocean's ice fields for the continuation of the Emperor Penguins' breeding. This film is an excellent point of departure to discuss global warming and the world's environmental problems. Most scientists are convinced that greenhouse gases are warming the Earth. If temperatures do rise globally, the most important result would be that some portion of the Arctic and polar ice fields would melt, raising global sea levels. The rise in sea levels would cause havoc in some islands as flooding, displacements of human populations and destruction of animals and farmlands.

- Some scientists blame human behavior, claiming levels of gases covering the Earth have increased due to industrialization, increased populations and use of dangerous gases.

1. World History:

a. Survival of the Fittest:

- In the introductory scene of the film, narrator Morgan Freeman tells us that, "this is a story of survival… These souls live in the darkest, driest and coldest continent on earth." For them to breed and have the next generation survive, they have practiced for thousands of years, specific behavioral patterns.

Suggested Activities:
- *Students can discuss how Darwin's theory of the Survival of the Fittest applies to the Emperor penguins in their breeding and life cycles.*
- *Create a chart of the specific behavioral patterns of the Emperor penguins and another chart with the behavioral patterns of humans.*
- *In pairs, choose other animals that have survived thousands of years like the crocodile, alligator and giraffe. List why these animals and others have survived while animal species like dinosaurs became extinct. Include physical characteristics, type of habitat and climate conditions that help animals survive.*

Hints:
- Some behavioral patterns are learned; others are instinctive. This is the case for animals and humans. The Emperor penguins practice innate behavioral patterns as well as learned. For the latter, the parents teach the chick their sounds. Penguins recognize each other by their unique sound, their voice. The mother teaches the young chick how to walk by planting his feet on her feet as she walks. She also teaches the chick how to march in a group, because after four years, the chick will go on the march with his community and begin his cycle of breeding.

b. Intelligent Design vs. Evolution:

- Intelligent design refers to certain features of the universe and of living things that are best explained by an intelligent cause, not an undirected process such as natural selection. It is an argument for the existence of God and that God created the universe and the first humans.
- Evolution is the opposite belief that refers to the creation of the universe due to natural selection and the change in the inherited traits of a population through successive generations. During natural selection there are traits that vary from one generation to another that aid reproduction and survival. Over many generations, inherited traits are filtered by natural selection and the positive changes are retained genetically.

Suggested Activities:
- *Students can discuss if the Emperor Penguins' survival is an example of intelligent design or evolution. In small groups, work together to give examples to support your position.*
- *Some viewers believe that the film has similarities with, and even lessons for, human society. This would make a lively classroom debate.*

c. Environmental Problems in the 21st Century:

- In the 21st century, we are becoming aware of the urgency for all individuals to address environmental problems. As globalization continues and becomes even stronger, the earth's problems become problems for all people around the world. Few countries will be untouched by the earth's problems. Some of the greatest issues are: global warming, air pollution, acid rain, smog, ozone depletion, hazardous waste, overpopulation, water pollution, and deforestation.
- In the United States, air pollution is an environmental problem that affects all people. Among the many types of air pollutants are nitrogen oxides, carbon monoxides and organic compounds that can evaporate and enter the atmosphere. Forest fires, volcanic eruptions, wind erosion, pollen dispersal, evaporation of organic compounds, and natural radioactivity are also causes of air pollution.

Suggested Activities:
- *Divide students into groups representing each of the 7 continents and report on what environmental problems the countries in that continent have experienced in the last*

decade. Have them make a chart listing country and environmental problems. Then have them discuss what the local, state and federal governments, as well as individuals of that country, are doing to address the problem.

- *In 2015, the government passed the "Clean Power Plan" that requires all 50 states to cut carbon energy which would reduce gas emissions and pollutants. However, such efforts have been slow. Ask the class to research why?*

2. Geography:

a. Map Studies: Antarctica

- The narrator begins the film by telling us that thousands of years ago "Antarctica used to be tropical. However, the continent drifted south and the forest turned to ice. The former inhabitants died. Only one tribe stayed behind."
- He is referring to the *tribe* of the Emperor penguins. It is on this continent, where 98% of the land is covered by ice sheets that average one-mile thick and yet, is always moving. It is on this bulk of ice that thousands of penguins can march for the ice can hold their weight. (Some of them weigh up to 100 pounds.) It is the location of thick ice that determines their path as they journey in a group to their breeding ground.

Suggested Activities:
- *Students can make a map of Antarctica and chart the penguins' journeys over a nine-month period, from March to November. Color coordinate each journey and specify if the journey is for the male or female and specify the months.*
- *Discuss in a group the following details of the penguins' journeys: Why do the penguins' path vary each year? Why is their path different during the winter and summer months? Why do the penguins march at the ice's edge near the ocean? What is the relationship of the thinning of the ice in September, October and November, and the penguins' journey?*

   Begin by introducing Antarctica and its extreme climate. Explain how penguin life survives these extremes. Suggest ways in which you think penguins have adapted to survive.

Hints:
- Antarctica is the Earth's most southern continent, situated in the southern hemisphere and south of the Antarctic Circle. It is surrounded by the Pacific,

Atlantic and Indian Oceans. It is the coldest, driest and windiest continent with very little precipitation. Only penguins and fur seals can live in such brutal conditions. There is no plant life.

- Navigation and discoveries on the continent were not made until 1820 by the Russians, and Antarctica remained neglected because of its hostile environment.

- The Antarctica Treaty of 1959 signed by 45 international countries, prohibits military activities, nuclear explosions, radioactive wasted disposal, and mineral mining on the continent. It supports scientific research and protects the continent's eco-zone. Ongoing experiments are conducted by more than 4,000 scientists from the 45 countries.

- Antarctica has 90% of the world's ice, which is comprised of ice sheets, glaciers, floating ice forms, and ice walls. This represents approximately 70% of the world's fresh water. If all this ice would melt, the ocean levels surrounding the continent would rise about 200 feet and cause massive flooding to towns and cities near the coast.

b. Environmental Problems: Decline of Emperor Penguins' Population

- Former Vice President, Al Gore, says in his book, <u>An Inconvenient Truth</u>, that "… one fact left out of *March of the Penguins* is that the population of Emperors has declined by an estimated 70% over the past 50 years – and scientists suspect that the principal reason is global warming."

- Narrator, Morgan Freeman, tells us that warmer temperature causes the sea ice to become thinner. But in addition, Mr. Gore tells us that in order for the sea ice to be stable enough to nest on, it must also be attached to the land. Yet, as climate changes, the thin ice separates from the land and creates more sea. There is a decline in the population of Emperor penguins as they struggle to survive in theses conditions.

Suggested Activities:
- *Students can analyze, discuss and describe how the physical system throughout the world has changed in the past decade, using as examples: seasons, climate, the water cycle, natural resources, and population.*
- *Discuss if your community has changed with regards to land configuration.*
- *Divide into groups to research and describe an environmental problem that you would like to address for your neighborhood, home or school.*

c. Climate Change Influences Migratory Behavior:

- According to the research project that Dee Boersma directs on Magellanic penguins in Punta Tomba, Argentina (which is the world's largest colony of Magellanic penguins, totaling 200,000) climate change has affected their migratory behavior. In an article in <u>The New York Times</u> (March 31, 2009), she gives us the following information:

    "Through the tagging we've been able to show that in the last decade, the birds are swimming about 25 miles further in search of food. They're having trouble finding enough fish to eat... Of the 17 different penguin species, 12 are suffering rapid decreases in number."

Suggested Activities:
- *Using this primary source, students can discuss why there is a change in migratory behavior of Magellanic penguins. Is there anything that can be done? Encourage students to form groups to work on their ideas.*
- *Research, analyze and discuss the role of technology in evaluating climate change and environmental problems.*

Hints:
- There is a decline in population for the Magellanic penguins because of a reduction in fish for them to feed on. This is due to commercial fisheries in these waters. It is also due to pollution, due to oil spills and dumping from ships.

3. Economics:

a. Multi-national Corporations and the Environment:

- Traditionally, the goals of business have been cost effective and profit-driven so as to satisfy shareholders with profitable quarterly reports. But corporations are now being forced to include other goals. National and global corporations are becoming more aware of their responsibility to connect their goals with social and environmental programs.

Suggested Activities:
- *Students can research and discuss corporate roles in the following areas: conservation; genetically engineered foods; biodiversity; waste disposal; greener corporate buildings*

and sites; technologies that help preserve the environment; executive-educational pro-
grams; and outreach environmental programs.

- *Introduce and discuss the role of international not-for-profit organizations (NGOs).*
  Research their role in the global environmental arena.
- *Compare and contrast the economic effects of environmental changes and crises result-*
  ing from disasters as floods, storms, droughts, etc. Divide into pairs to research specific
  crises: New Orleans, Galapagos Islands, tsunami, water droughts, volcanic eruptions,
  earthquakes, forest fires.

Hints:

- In the past few years, corporations are being forced to change their corporate philosophy of profit-only for a more compromising position toward society and the environment. Some of the reasons for this change are the following:
- There has been a shift in "macro-economic" forces that are driving corporate stock ownership. In earlier times, a limited number of wealthy individuals owned corporate shares. But today, many stock funds are owned by pension funds, which are represented by working people as investors. In addition, media, public pressure and other factors are requiring corporations to be more accountable to their communities and society.
- National tax structures are changing. In the forefront are countries like Germany, the United Kingdom, France, and Scandinavian countries that tax pollution and waste and offer tax benefits for the following: energy efficiency and substitutions; development of renewable energy products and services; public transportation programs; recycled goods; greenhouse gas reduction; research and development projects.
- Local, state and federal governments are getting more involved in regulating corporations' responsibility to the environment in the form of laws, international agreements, regulations, subsidies, and rules that determine profitability of a product or service.

4. Civics, Citizenship and Government:

a. Communal Society:

- In the opening scene of *March of the Penguins,* we see the Emperor penguins march and they do so in a group community, called a "rookery." The penguins are a clan, a tribe. The females, as well as the males, stay with their group as they go through all the stages of the cycle of life: they march in a single file, incubate the egg, feed the chick, and assure the survival of the next generation. When a penguin tries to steal the egg or the chick of another, the group goes to protect the victim and ostracizes the kidnapper. The Emperor penguins' survival is not only based on a cooperative relationship between the father and mother, but among all the members of the group. Emperor penguins live comfortably in their group community. When one penguin leaves the group, he falls prey to a predator or loses his way as he marches alone.

Suggested Activities:
- *Divide students into groups. Ask each group to choose an animal that lives in a "community" similar to the way the Emperor penguins live in a rookery. Have the students research the following for their animal community:*
- *Do the animals have assigned roles for their activities? Who cares for the young? How do the animals interact with each other? Do they have any rituals like the emperor penguins? Are there any roles in the animal community that does not exist in the human community?*
- *Ask students to imagine that they are on assignment to spend time with these penguins.*
- *Ask students to write a journal entry that explains their experience as a penguin, describing the role they played, and how they "fit in" with the other penguins as part of their community. What did they learn about being a community member?*

Hints:
- A community is different from a neighborhood. A neighborhood is a physical place where people live. A community is a group of people or animals who are interdependent. The members of the community rely on each other and help each other in some way by sharing roles and responsibilities to make the community safe and successful.

b. Gender roles:

- March of the Penguins shows the viewers that the Emperor penguins share human characteristics.
- Emperor penguins are monogamous like humans. Both species have one mate at a time, but the penguins have one mate per mating season. The next year, they find another mate.

- Both the mother and father penguins feed and protect the egg and chick but they do so in a reversal of roles from humans. The mother penguin produces one egg per mating season fertilized by the male, but it is the mother who treks 70 miles in freezing conditions to find food while the father stays home, incubating the egg in a flap of his belly skin. He plants his feet on the ice in such a position to protect the egg from the wind and cold. He stands like this for 125 days without food or water, in howling storms and total darkness, sometime huddled together with the other fathers as a community for warmth. It is under the protection of the father's belly that the egg is hatched. And it is perfectly timed to match the return of the mother. If she is a day or two late, the father continues to protect his young chick by instinctively, coughing up a milky liquid that serves as food that he gives his new born until the mother returns.

Suggested Activities:
- *Students can chart the responsibilities of the male and female Emperor penguins. Have them also chart the male and female responsibilities for humans.*
- *Research which societies and cultures have different gender roles than our society. (Refer to anthropologist, Margaret Meade's work as a source.)*
- *Discuss the changing gender roles in our society, comparing your grandparents' generation with your parents' generation and your own. Discuss the reasons for the change and the implications for our society.*

Hints:
- Unlike sexual roles, which are based on biology, gender roles are based on culture and the society's traditions. Women, in the majority of societies, statistically, have a lower status than men. But the gap between the sexes varies according to historical time, society and culture.
- As early as the <u>Old Testament</u> in Levicticus, God told Moses that a man is worth 50 sheikels (the name of their currency) and a woman is worth 30. (Today, this corresponds approximately to salary differences of the sexes in the U.S.)
- In 1980, the United Nations summed up and defined gender inequality: Women, who comprise half the world's population, do two-thirds of the world's work, earn one tenth of the world's income, and own one hundredth of the world's property.

c. Animal Behavior Reflects Human Behavior:

- The director, Luc Jacquet, negates a comparison between penguins and humans in his film. When asked by the *San Diego Union Tribune* to comment on the film's use as a metaphor for family values, Jaquet responded, "I find it intellectually dishonest to impose this viewpoint on something that's part of nature. It's amusing, but if you take the monogamy argument, it's different... The monogamy of penguins only lasts for the duration of one reproductive cycle. You have to let penguins be penguins and humans be humans."

Suggested Activity:
- *Students can write an essay on what similar behavioral patterns exist between penguins and humans that they learned from seeing this film.*

Hints:
- The penguins walk upright. They are curious. They're social. They live together in a harmonious society with rules. They help each other but they also compete with each other. They mate, are devoted to their mate and their offspring, but during the next breeding season, they find another mate.

B. Literature and Visual Arts:

5. World Literature:

a. Public Speaking and Speech Communication:

- Rachel Louise Carson (1907-1964) was an American marine biologist and nature writer whose landmark book, <u>Silent Spring</u> is often credited with having launched the global environmental movement. <u>Silent Spring</u> had an immense success and effect in the United States, where it spurred a reversal in national pesticide policy. Ms. Carson's work was centered on documenting the environmental effects of pesticides. She believed that chemicals have an impact on the entire ecosystem.

- Ms. Carson explored the subject of *environmental connectedness:* although a pesticide is aimed at eliminating one organism, its effects are felt throughout the food chain, and what was intended to poison an insect ends up poisoning larger animals and humans.

Suggested Activities:
- *Students can research, analyze, report and discuss the concept that chemicals have an impact on the entire ecosystem. They can use pesticides as an example.*
- *Divide the class into three groups and have each group present a public speech to their class and school about the fate of "environmental connectedness."*

b. Media Presentations:

- Former Vice President, Al Gore, has made public the imminent dangers of global warming in his book, <u>An Inconvenient Truth</u> (2006). He brings together in a lecture and media presentation format, the scientific research from scientists around the world as well as photos, graphs and charts that environmental dangers are not just about science or politics, but about morals and values. He believes that global warming is due to human negligence. Then he pleads to the reader to help address the problems and resort to human surveillance.
- From the book's success came the film of the same name. In the film, Al Gore gives a lecture and shows us by using charts, diagrams, slides, statistics, and visual information, about environmental changes in multiple countries and continents.

Suggested Activities:
- *Divide students into groups. Have each group research a problem-related issue of the environment and report on it to the class by using a media presentation.*
- *Students can begin understanding the book, <u>An Inconvenient Truth</u>, by analyzing the following quotation from the introduction:*
  "... What we are facing is not just a cause for alarm; it is paradoxically also a cause for hope. As many know, the Chinese expression for *crisis* consists of two characters side by side. The first is the symbol for *danger.* The second is the symbol for *opportunity.*"

Hints:
- In the film's slideshow, Mr. Gore reviews the scientific options on climate change, discusses the politics and economics of global warming, and describes

the consequences he believes global climate change will produce if the amount of human-generated greenhouse gases is not significantly reduced in the near future.

- The film includes many segments intended to refute critics who say that global warming is insignificant or unproven. For example, Mr. Gore discusses the risk of the collapse of a major ice sheet in Greenland or in West Antarctica, either of which could raise global sea levels by approximately 20 feet, flooding coastal areas and producing 100 million refugees. Melted water from Greenland, because of its lower salinity, could halt the Gulf Stream current and quickly trigger dramatic local cooling and flooding in Northern Europe.

6. Media Studies:

a. Film Clips and Scene Discussions:

- The film is an *allegory* and the narrator gives us this information in the beginning of the story: (Scene: 3:47-3:57 minutes)

The following words describe this: "So in some ways this is a story of survival. A tale of life over death. But it's more than that. This is a story about love."

The narrator reinforces the allegory by comparing the penguins to humans: (Scene: 12:52-13:39)
Such key words are: "Hostilities among the ladies are inevitable ... They pout. They bellow. They strut."

- *Journey motif:* (Scene: 4:30-4:39)

Students can analyze and discuss these thoughts: "Each year around the same time, he will leave the comfort of his ocean home and embark on a remarkable journey. He will travel a great distance."

- *Point of view.* (Scene 2:22-2:28)

All films, even documentaries, are not totally objective. They contain a point of view (POV). Students can enjoy discussing this concept with the following dialogue: "There are few places harder to get to in this world. But there aren't any where it's harder to live."

Suggested Activities for Allegory:

- *To discuss an allegory, students can indicate and analyze the scenes where the Emperor penguins behave like human beings. They can make a chart with the examples.*

Hints:

- An allegory is a literary and/or artistic technique in which characters or events are used to represent other things and thus, symbolically offer another level of meaning.
- In *March of the Penguins* when the narrator speaks, we realize he is explaining the Emperor penguins in terms usually associated with humans. These *souls* live in the darkest continent. We see their determination to *breed, love, and protect* – all human qualities. We see how they live together as a *clan*.
- The photographers emphasize the human qualities in the first scene. They use long distance lenses to photograph the penguins as they walk and we think at first that they are men dressed in black suits. The photographers also show the penguins' negative human-like qualities as possessiveness and jealousy. The narrator tells us that the female fights for her male. "She pouts, bellows, struts, and uses contact force." And the cameras also get the personality of the penguins when they are affectionate to each other.

Suggested Activities for Journey motif:

- *To discuss the journey motif, discuss the concept that animals have an innate sense of direction. Research and study different animals and their abilities and techniques to navigate their migratory routes, their nesting grounds and their habitat location. Include birds, fish, ants, butterflies, and seals.*
- *Compare a human being's sense of direction with an animal's. Do all people have the same sense of direction? What do people do to find their way? Can they rely on their own navigational capabilities? Discuss what innate navigational techniques an individual would use in the desert, at sea, in the mountains, in a new city, and in the forest.*
- *Winged Migration is another excellent film made by a French crew that depicts the migratory patterns of birds. Students can watch this film and compare the journey motif of the many different species of birds with the Emperor penguins.*

Hints:

- The film, *March of the Penguins,* takes us on a journey to Antarctica where we spend 13 months with the Emperor penguins to follow their life cycle. We begin our journey as the penguins march to begin their breeding. We finish our journey when the chicks are strong enough to be left on their own and the parents go their separate ways to begin another year of breeding with another mate. This cycle of life is a journey that contains elements of love, family life, community behavior, and survival. It is a voyage that is circular as well as cyclical. It begins at the mating ground and it ends there, and then begins again at the mating ground. The narrator tells us that, "the destination is always the same but each year their path is different because of the ice configuration that shifts." Stars and sun guide them as an invisible compass.

  In *Winged Migration,* (2001) the viewer is shown different migratory paths of birds. We see how geese, storks, cranes, ducks, and all kinds of birds migrate southward for thousands of miles and navigate instinctively by the stars, moon, sun, and the Earth's gravitational field. We see their life cycle and we see them become victims of predators. As we watch them fly, we ask ourselves, how did the photographers get such unique footage? Some footage was made with cameras in airplanes. Some footage was taken from cameras attached to hot air balloons. And some footage was made in the editing room with computers. The birds' journey to recreate and survive is very similar to the Emperor penguins' journey and we see how birds and penguins resemble men in the most important journey of all - the procreation of life.

Suggested Activities for point of view:

- *Students can analyze and discuss what is the director's and narrator's, point of view in the film. Is their point of view the same as their thesis? What is the aim of the film? Why did the crew live and work under such harsh conditions for more than a year? What lessons do they want to communicate?*
- *This film has many layers of interpretations and goals. Have the students divide into groups and discuss these layers of meaning. Students can also discuss the role of the cameras to establish point of view.*

Hints:

- Every film as well as literary work, has a point of view. It may be obvious or not, but it expresses the thesis of the creator. Art is created not only for "art's sake" but also for a reason. That reason is the thesis – what the creator wants to prove or show.

- An omniscient narrator in literature, and also in cinema, witnesses all events, even some that a character cannot witness. The omniscient narrator is privileged to all things past, present and future - as well as the thoughts of all characters. As such, an omniscient narrator offers the reader a birds-eye view about the story. The third-person omniscient narrator is usually the most reliable narrator. The story line therefore depends on the point of view of this omniscient narrator.

- *March of the Penguins* is structured without live characters, so we need some device to present the story line and to explain and comment on the characters' behavior. This is the role of the omniscient narrator. In telling the story, and being the only live voice in the film, Morgan Freeman becomes one of the protagonists and we listen to what he tells us. We accept his point of view.

- Filmmakers often use the concept of "spatial perspective" when shooting their film. One method is P.O.V. or Point of View when the camera sees a scene as if the camera's lenses are the eyes of a protagonist. Being there are no actors in *March of the Penguins,* the cameras take the roles of the actors and show us what the filmmaker wants to show us.

- Spatial perspective takes on a corollary interpretation as we apply it to a broad picture of environment. If we use our eyes as a wide-angle lens, we can see a big picture. Then we begin to focus and move closer to the subject and use different shots like a close-up and an establishing shot.

- Another method of spatial perspective relates to the distance the camera lens is from the subject. A far shot is used in the beginning as we see black figures wobbling in a long straight line. At first, we think they are human beings, but as the far shot becomes a close-up, we realize they are penguins.

- An establishing shot, as a P.O.V., is an initial reference shot used to frame the setting of a scene. From the beginning of the film, this is Antarctica with ice sheets, ice blocks and glaciers.

- Distance, angle, lighting and position all affect our perception of an image or concept.

b. Cinematography Techniques: Use of camera:

- The camera may function like our eyes, but the camera does not see the world exactly the way the human eye sees it. Lenses allow the filmmaker to put a shape to the space between characters and the screen and manipulate distance, angle and light. The camera has the choice of long shot, medium shot, close-up, and/or high angle shot. In the opening scene when we see the penguins march, the camera distance is precise, using a long shot (emphasizing the human quality of the penguins as well as the smallness of both man and animal in this arctic world), and then the camera moves slowly to a close up (to allow viewer to focus on the animal's face and character.) A camera's placement can influence how a viewer perceives character, events and objects on the screen. The camera introduces ideas and creates mood.

c. Voiceover:

- The term voiceover refers to a production technique where a disembodied voice (a voice coming from someone who cannot be seen) is broadcast live or pre-recorded in film, television, radio, or broadcasting.
- Voiceover is a direct vocal address to the viewer that may come from a character or narrator. It is a storytelling technique that links the viewer to the character/animal and human narrator.
- This device of using well-known celebrities for voiceovers is to enhance the personality and human quality of the characters.
- Voiceover shapes the audience's response to the story. In the American version of this film, the academic voiceover from narrator Morgan Freeman, explains and teaches about the penguins' behavior, and even links it to humans. In the original French version, the penguins themselves "speak" which gives the film a more family-oriented adventure style. American audiences probably would not have felt comfortable with the French interpretation about a story of life and death handled in a light tone.

7. Philosophy/Critical Thinking:

a. News and Magazine Articles:

- At the closing of *March of the Penguins,* the narrator tells us that, "the new family goes their separate ways. For nine months they've been together and will part. The tribe returns to their home." The mother and father will separate. Their monogamous relationship for one breeding season is over and they will look for another mate. For the next 3 months the chicks will feed at the sea's edge. For 4 years, they will live with the other chicks. On the 5th year, the chicks will be fully developed and begin their march just like their ancestors did. But scientists fear that if the ice sheet melts or gets too thin, these grown up chicks will not be able to march. They can become victims of global warming.

This information is similar to a news or magazine article but we do not read it, we see it visually in a "film."

Suggested Activities:
- *Encourage students to discuss how they can get involved to stop global warming and prepare for the future. One of the ways is to inform the public is by writing a magazine article. Begin the article by citing specific pollution problems in the community.*
- *Encourage students to take photos or create a 30-second video in the format of a Public Service Announcement (PSA), to point out problems of environment in their community. Incorporate these visual proofs in their magazine articles.*
- *Research where to send the article. Begin by going to UNICEF's web site for suggestions and to youth magazines.*
- *Write an Opinion-Editorial (Op-Ed) in the local newspaper. This is another way to apprise the public about the imminent dangers of global warming. Perhaps your class can list suggestions of how citizens at home and at work can start getting active in the fight to "think green."*
- *Another vehicle to create citizens' awareness about the dangers of environment is by writing as a group, a newsletter about different topics related to "save the environment." Then follow through what to do with the newsletter to make the concerns public.*

b. Oral Storytelling:

- Mr. Freeman is telling us a story as if we were children. He begins by saying, "This is a story…"
- Storytelling is the oldest form of teaching. Traditions, legends, rituals, customs, religious beliefs are passed down from one generation to the next by an oral narration. The older, wiser person of the clan or group, takes a subject and tells it in the form of an interesting story with the goal to educate the younger members of the group and to transmit the group's heritage.

Suggested Activities:

- *Telling a story is an effective way to teach. The subject of environment can also be put into a story. Words can be our action and medium to teach others to act. It is a way to go into people's imagination to find other means of actions to save the environment.*

- *Encourage students to visit younger children in their school and community and tell them stories about the environment to encourage their awareness. Students can use animals as their protagonists and they can encourage the younger children to tell stories about their pets or favorite animal characters from books and television. All the time, students can relate their stories and lessons to the environment.*

Hints:

- A common and beloved form of storytelling to children has been "fables," stories about animals that are personified as characters to represent human beings' behavior.

- Aesop, a storyteller who lived in ancient Greece (620-560 B.C.), introduced fables as a way of teaching children about morals and values. ("The Tortoise and the Hare," The Boy Who Cried Wolf.")

- La Fontaine, in 17ᵗʰ century France, adopted the same format of using animals that resemble men to teach morals.

- The Grimm Brothers in Germany (1780s-1860s) used the same technique in their fairy tales: "Little Red Riding Hood," "Hansel and Gretel," "Cinderella," "Snow White," and "Sleeping Beauty."

- One of the lessons we can derive from *March of the Penguins* is rooted in the perils animals and modern men share about the world's environmental future. There have been animals who lived in previous centuries but are now extinct. They were not able to readapt to their new environment.

c. Analyze the winning team:

- A century ago in 1911-1912, two teams of Arctic explorers, one British led by Captain Robert Scott, the other Norwegian, led by Roald Amundsen, competed to be the first men to reach Antarctica and the South Pole. No human being had ever been before this date to the coldest place in the world. Only one team would win; one team would stake their country's flag; and one team might not return home.

Suggested Activity:

- *The class can form two groups: British and Norwegian. Have each group present how they prepared their exploration. Discuss tools, animals, sleds, skis, clothing, food, scientific instruments, and other equipment needed to survive for 3-5 months in Antarctica.*

8. Photography:

- At the end of *March of the Penguins,* we see the movie's credits on half the screen; on the other half of the screen, we see how the camera crew worked while filming. Dressed in special red suits, similar to astronauts, they move on skis and sleds as they position their camera equipment. The penguins come close to them, friendly and curious, and the photographers interact with the colony.
- Luc Jacquet and his crew spent 13 months in Antarctica in order to film one complete breeding cycle. The difficulty of filming this subject was not only due to the climate, but to the animal's acceptance of the photographers. This was a necessary pre-requisite in order for the animals to continue their behavior despite human intruders. The photographers were able to shoot extraordinary details. We see the chicks pecking their way out of the egg as well as their eyes peeking out of their father's caring belly. We even see the teeth of the predators preying on the swimming female penguins. The photographers filmed every detail of the journey by dividing the crew to cover the males and the females, and an underwater crew to film the ocean as the penguins fed on fish.
- The photographers also filmed Antarctica. We experience unique sunsets and sunrises, the different shades of white and ice, and the beautiful seasons of the year
- The photographers have instilled a human-like quality to the penguins by concentrating on their emotions that are so similar to a human mother and father.

Suggested Activities:

- *In a round-robin format, encourage students to make believe they would ask questions to the camera crew, if they could, about behind-the-scene filming.*

- *If some students are familiar with a movie camera, encourage them to take films of their pets or animals that show unusual animal behavior. Encourage them to submit their films to on-line web sites.*
- *Photo essay. Students can take photos about a topic in the environment and write a five-paragraph essay about the photo.*

Extracurricular Activities:

1. Power Point Presentation: one of our teachers, asked her students to prepare a power point presentation to illustrate an environmental problem that occurs around the world. Two students worked together to illustrate how "Global Water Shortage" is a problem in India, China, Egypt and Israel. They showed pictures and wrote text to answer the following topics: how did it become a problem; what is being done; possible solutions; consequences of ignoring the problem; costs of the problem; and questions to ask. They even included a bibliography.

2. Another group of students chose the topic, glaciers. Their power point presentation with photos and text, illustrated how melting glaciers around the world are becoming a problem.

3. Other students investigated what animals are part of an "Endangered Species." Several students researched pandas and their power presentation included text and photos about why pandas are becoming extinct; what some countries are doing about the problem; and suggestions on how to address the situation.

4. Students can mimic how penguins keep warm by performing a science experiment. Fill plastic buckets with ice cubes and cold water. Have students place rubber gloves on each hand. Students will cover their left hand with petroleum jelly and leave their right hand without. Record start time and have students place both hands in the bucket of ice water. Time how long they can keep each hand in the water. Compare how penguins keep warm with how humans keep warm. Ask students to speculate how the crew kept warm while filming *March of the Penguins.*

5. Students can work in groups or with a partner to create a visual timeline showing key events in the life cycle of an emperor penguin.

6. Students can create a series of simple drawings illustrating the process of transferring the egg from the female penguin to the male penguin. They can

plan their illustrations so they can use them to create a flipbook or a comic that shows the egg transfer process.

Sidebars:

---

1. Public Response:

- Former Vice President Al Gore has done a great deal to promote public awareness. His book and documentary, have catapulted the following:
  ◦ He has trained 1,000+ volunteers to give the presentation of his film including celebrities.
  ◦ Several countries have required their high school students to view the film: U.K., Norway and Sweden.
  ◦ Organizations like "Share the Truth" are distributing free DVDs of the film to community centers across the U.S.
  ◦ Al Gore won the Nobel Peace Prize (2007) jointly with the United Nations Intergovernmental Panel on Climate Change.

2. Production:

- National Geographic Society is the co-producer of the film.
- There was an original French language release featuring "dubbed" dialogues among the penguins as if they were speaking to each other. The Hungarian and German versions were similar, but dubbed in the country's language. The English language release did not use the dubbing techniques of the penguins conversing, but a straight-forward narration by Morgan Freeman. The Dutch and Indian versions used their own native-speaking narrator.
- The sound track also varied according to the country of distribution.

3. Awards:

- Academy Awards, USA
  2006- Won- Best Documentary Feature

- Writers Guild of America, USA
  2006- Nominated- Documentary Screenplay Award

- Cannes Film Festival, France
  2006- Won- Best Sound
  2006- Nominated- Best Editing
  2006- Nominated-Best First Work
  2006- Nominated- Best Music Written for a Film

- American Cinema Editors, USA
  2006- Won - Best Edited Documentary Film

Bibliography of Films: Filmography
Further Global Study Resources through Film:

About Antarctica and Nature:

- *Mermaid* (Hong Kong / China)
- *An Inconvenient Truth* (U.S.A.)
- *Shakelton's Antarctica Adventure* (U.S.A.)
- *Arctic Tale* (U.S.A.)
- *Microcosmos* (France)
- *Happy Feet* (U.S.A.)
- *The Sea Around Us* (U.S.A.)
- S*kroner* (Denmark)
- *Expedition Sirius 2000* (Denmark)
- *Arktika: The Russian Dream that Failed* (Russia)
- *Serious Arctic* (United Kingdom)
- *Immortals of the Arctic* (Canada)
- *Antarctica: An Adventure of a Different Nature* (Australia)
- *Pole to Pole* (U.S.A.)
- *Tales from Earthsea* (Japan)
- *The Antarctica Challenge* (Canada)
- *The Polar Explorer* (Canada)
- *Arctic Mission* (Canada)

- *With Byrd at the South Pole* (U.S.A.)
- *90 Degrees South* (United Kingdom)
- *Encounters at the End of the World* (U.S.A.)
- *Antarctic Antics* (U.S.A.)
- *Great Adventurers: Ernest Shakelton* (U.S.A.)
- *Great Adventurers: Robert Scott* (U.S.A.)
- *Cool It* (Denmark)
- *Nankyoku Tariku (Antarctica)* (Japan)
- *Pingu* (Switzerland)
- *The Chef of the South Pole* (Japan)
- *Antarctic Journal* (South Korea)

Other Types of Documentaries:

- *The Fog of War* (U.S.A.)
- *Fahrenheit 9/11* (U.S.A.)
- *Lost in La Mancha* (U.S.A.)
- *Air Guitar Nation* (U.S.A.)
- *Grizzly Man* (U.S.A.)
- *An Inconvenient Truth* (U.S.A.)
- *The Act of Killing* (Indonesia / (U.S.A.)
- *The Missing Picture* (Cambodia)
- *Bowling for Columbine* (U.S.A.)
- *Hoop Dreams* (U.S.A.)
- *Super Size Me* (U.S.A.)
- *Man on Wire* (U.S.A./ France)
- *Enron: The Smartest Guys in the Room* (U.S.A.)

AFRICA

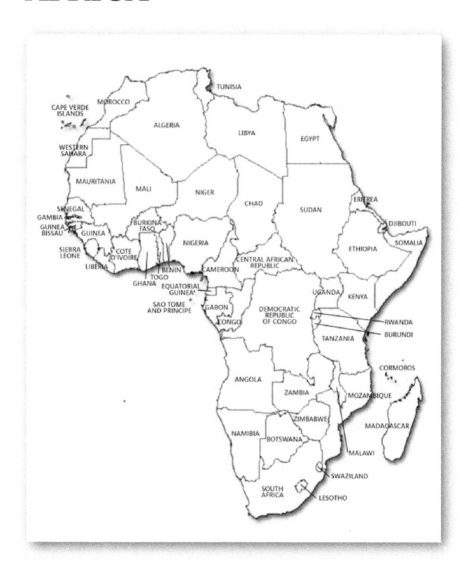

CHAPTER 12

MADAGASCAR (MADAGASCAR)

TITLE OF FILM: *Madagascar.*
YEAR OF RELEASE: 2005
COUNTRY: Madagascar
DIRECTOR: Eric Darnell, Tom McGrath
LANGUAGES: English
RUNNING TIME: 86 minutes
RATING: G.
CURRICULUM THEMES:

A. HISTORY and SOCIAL SCIENCE:

- **Chapter's Key Themes:** City Life; Identity; Survival
- **World History:** The early Beginnings; Imperialism in Africa
- **Geography:** Map studies; Habitat
- **Economics:** Trade and Shipping
- **Civics, Citizenship and Government:** Madagascar Today: What is life like for a student your age? Housing, schools, shopping, food, sports, animal life, and nature.

LITERATURE and VISUAL ARTS:

- **World Literature:** Hainteny poetry; Ohabolana proverbs
- **Media Studies:** Film Clips and Scene Discussions; Computer Generated Imagery (CGI); Escape from Madagascar
- **Philosophy / Critical Thinking:** Personal essay; Vocabulary words; Collective nouns
- **Music:** Hiragasy Troupe
- **Technology;** Animated digital storytelling; comic strips; animated videos

Introduction:

Madagascar was directed by Eric Darnell and Tom McGrath;
produced by Mireille Sorian; screenplay by Eric Darnell and Tom McGrath;
music by Hans Zimmer; distributed by Dreamworks Animation; 86 minutes.

Alex ....Ben Stiller
Marty ....Chris Rock
Melman ....David Schwimmer
Gloria ....Jada Pinkett Smith

Madagascar is an animated film that tells the story of four Central Park Zoo animals who have spent their lives in blissful captivity there, but are bored. Wanting adventure, they are unexpectedly transported back to Africa, getting shipwrecked on the island of Madagascar. And then they want to return home to Central Park, NYC.

Pivotal Moments in History:

- The written history of Madagascar began in the seventh century A.D., when Arabs established trading posts along the northwestern coast. European contact began in the 1500s, when Portuguese sea captain, Diego Dias, sighted the island after his ship became separated from a fleet bound for India.
- In the late 17th century, the French established trading posts along the east coast. From about 1774 to 1824, it was a favorite haunt for pirates, including Americans, one of whom brought Malagasy rice to South Carolina.
- Beginning in the 1790s, Merina rulers succeeded in establishing control over the major part of the island. In 1817, the Merina ruler and the British governor of Mauritius concluded a treaty abolishing the slave trade, which had been important in Madagascar's economy. In return, the island received British military and financial assistance. British influence remained strong for several decades, during which the Merina culture and people were converted to Presbyterianism, Congregationalism, and Anglicanism.
- The British accepted the imposition of a French protectorate over Madagascar in 1885 in return for eventual control over Zanzibar (now part of Tanzania) and as part of an overall definition of spheres of influence in the area.
- French control over Madagascar was established by military force in 1895-96, and the Merina monarchy was abolished.

- Malagasy troops fought in France, Morocco, and Syria during World War I. After France fell to the Germans, the Vichy government administered Madagascar.
- British troops occupied the strategic island in 1942 to prevent its seizure by the Japanese.
- The Free French received the island from the United Kingdom in 1943.
- In 1947, with French prestige low, a nationalist uprising was suppressed after several months of bitter fighting. Ten years later, Madagascar moved peacefully toward independence.
- The Malagasy Republic was proclaimed on October 14, 1958, as an autonomous state within the French Community. A period of provisional government ended with the adoption of a constitution in 1959 and full independence on June 26, 1960.
- As of elections in 2014, the new President is Hery Rajaonanmampianina.

Pre-Screening Questions:

- Where is Madagascar located? What makes it so exotic?

Hints:
- Madagascar is an island in the Indian Ocean, which is located off the Southeastern coast of Africa. It is located in the Indian Ocean directly across the African country, Mozambique. Islands surrounding Madagascar are:
  In the North: The Seychelles
  In the East are: Mauritius and Reunion
  In the North West are: Comoros and Mayotte

- Madagascar has a population of 22 million people. It is considered one of the most exotic countries in the world. It has bright green rice paddies like in Asia and pristine beaches like Tahiti. It is home to 3,000 species of butterflies, half the world's chameleons 90% of all known Lemur species and over 90% of its wildlife is found no where else on Earth.

Pivotal Moments in Film:

- A the Central Park Zoo, Marty the zebra is celebrating his tenth birthday, but longs to see the rest of the world from outside his protected life in the zoo. Believing that he can find wide-open spaces to run around in, like Connecticut, Marty's best friend, Alex the lion, attempts to cheer up his friend. Marty gets some tips from the zoo's penguins: Skipper, Kowalski, Rico and Private. The penguins are similarly trying to escape the zoo. Marty's friends—Alex the lion, Melman the giraffe and Gloria the hippopotamus—realize Marty's folly and try to follow him. The four, along with the penguins and the chimpanzees, Mason and his silent friend Phil, eventually find themselves at Grand Central Station, but are quickly sedated by tranquilizer darts when Alex's attempt to communicate with humans is mistaken for aggression. The zoo (under pressure from animal-rights activists) is forced to ship the animals, by sea, to a Kenyan wildlife preserve. During their travels, the penguins escape from their enclosure and take over the ship, intent on taking it to Antarctica. Their antics on the bridge cause the crates containing Alex, Marty, Melmen, and Gloria to fall off the boat and wash ashore on to the island of Madagascar.

- The animals are soon able to regroup, initially believing themselves to be in the zoo at San Diego, California. Upon exploring, however, they come across a pack of lemurs led by King Julien XIII, and quickly learn of their true location. Alex blames Marty for their predicament and attempts to signal for help to get back to civilization. Marty, on the other hand, finds the wild to be exactly what he was looking for, with Gloria and Melman soon joining him in enjoying the island. Alex eventually comes around, though his hunting instincts begin to show; he has been away from the pampered zoo life of prepacked steaks for too long. The group is accepted by the lemurs, though King Julien's adviser, Maurice, cautions them about Alex's predatory nature.

- Marty attempts have been made to convince the now grizzled, starving Alex to return to New York. And so the four friends voyage back to New York's Central Park zoo.

Post-Screening Questions:
A. History and Social Sciences:

B. Literature and Visual Arts:

1. Describe the environment in Madagascar and its natural resources.
2. Discuss how the characters struggle to adapt to the new environment and how they overcome it.
3. Compare the population in New York and Madagascar.

Hints:

- Madagascar is a country rich in nature with a tropical climate. The natural resources of Madagascar are graphite, coal and bauxite. The current issues in Madagascar are soil erosion resulting from deforestation and several endangered species that are facing extinction.
- The population in Madagascar is 23,201,926 and New York has the population of 19,465,197, including the 5 boroughs of Manhattan, Bronx, Brooklyn, Queens and Staten Island.

Suggested Activities:

- *Discuss which scenes in the film show the difference between living in Madagascar and New York City.*

Hints:

- The film, *Madagascar,* portrays how the animals must survive on their own "in the wild." In Madagascar, they are surrounded by wilderness and nature. Several scenes show how the animals struggle to adapt to the new environment. In New York City, the animals were given food and water daily; however, in Madagascar, they have to hunt for their food in order to survive. The animals learn to overcome their fears by using their survival instincts.

Curriculum Themes:
A. History and Social Science

Chapter's Key Themes:

a. City Life:

- We see in the film that the characters were experiencing some difficulties adapting from their city life in New York City to the wild life in Madagascar. The city lifestyle has pampered these wild animals. They were given shelter, food and water to survive. Since they were taken care of by humans, they lost their natural animal instincts to survive in the wilderness.

b. Identity:

- In the movie, the animals experience identity crises when they escaped from Central Park Zoo to Madagascar. Marty, the zebra, always had the feeling that he belonged somewhere else, in the jungle, where the wild animals roam free. Their time in Madagascar was confusing because they didn't know how to properly act like the other wild animals.

c. Survival:

- Having to live in the zoo for most of their lives, Alex, Marty, Melman and Gloria didn't have to hunt for their food like other wild animals in the jungle. They had to learn how to survive like the other wild animals in Madagascar. Their survival instincts kicked in when they learned that they are not being fed in the jungle. The survival instincts in animals is natural, but when animals are caged in a zoo, their survival instincts tend to weaken.

- *Survival of the Fittest:*
- In the movie, they showed that the main characters are struggling to adapt to the jungle life after having to live in the Central Park Zoo. When the animals got to Madagascar, they learned that they have to fight other animals for food and shelter in order to survive.

Suggested Activities:
- *Students can discuss how Darwin's theory of Survival of the Fittest applies to the wild animals in their survival in the jungle.*
- *Create a chart of the specific behavioral patterns of the wild animals and another chart with the behavioral patterns of humans.*
- *We are becoming more aware of the urgency for all individuals to address the extinction problems that endangered animals are going through in the 21st century. Students can discuss how we, as humans, can help prevent the extinction of endangered species as rhinoceros, elephants, etc. In pairs, work together to give examples to support your position.*

1. World History:

a. The early Beginnings:

- Let's go back in a Time Capsule to 88 millions of years ago when a piece of land split from India and became an island off the coast of Africa.

- About 2,000 years ago, the first human settlement in Madagascar began when immigrants from Borneo, Indonesia arrived in Madagascar. Their language was similar to Indonesian.
- Africans, Europeans and Polynesians followed.
- Until the 19th century, Madagascar was ruled by many noblemen and aristocrats from 18 ethnic groups that make up their Merina culture.

Suggested Activities:
- *Merina is a word that describes the early ethnic group and culture of the people in Madagascar. Malgas is a word that describes today's ethnic groups in Madagascar. Have students write a definition paragraph about each term.*

Hints:
- The Merina is the dominant ethnic group in Madagascar, and one of the country's 18 official ethnic groups. Their territory where they live corresponds to the former Antananarivo Province in the center of the island. However, during the 17th and 18th centuries, the Merina ethnic group dominated the entire island and governed all Madagascar. In 1895-96, the French colonized Madagascar and abolished the Merina monarchy in 1897.
- The Malgasy are today's ethnic groups that represent nearly the entire population of Madagascar. They are subdivided into sub groups depending on where they live: on the coasts, highlands, or inland, and what their professions are: agriculture, fishing, hunting,

b. Imperialism in Africa:

- As the world approached the 19th and 20th centuries, many Imperialistic powers in Europe conquered countries in Africa. This began a flurry of imperialistic activity from France, Great Britain, Belgium, Spain, Portugal, Germany and Italy.
- The Europeans wanted African territories as well as their diamonds, gold, oil, copper, and phosphorus. But as the European Empires continued to control the African countries, there were rebellions.

The Africans Wanted Freedom and Independence:

- Portugal lost their colonies in 1973 and 1975
- Belgium lost their colonies in 1960, 1967 and 1997
- Germany had to give freedom to their colonies in 1961 and 1966

- Italy lost Libya in 1947
- Spain gave up their colonies in 1958, 1968 and 1976
- Great Britain lost 23 countries from 1952 to 2011
- And France lost their Empire of 22 countries from 1810 to 1977

Suggested Activity:
- *Have students make a large map with color coordinated Empires to show how Africa was controlled by many Empires over the centuries. Include all the countries of Africa, which number more than 50. All are presently independent.*

2. Geography:

a. Map Studies

- On the eastern coast of Madagascar there are dense tropical rainforests. Along the western coast of the island, there are lands with dense swamps and mangroves that give way to deep bays. Madagascar—an island off the coast of Africa—also has some of the world's most interesting animals. About 75% of the animal species found in Madagascar live nowhere else on the planet.

Suggested Activity:
- *Students can make a map of Madagascar and chart the animals that are currently facing extinction in the area.*

b. Habitat

- Habitat means where we live. The habitat of the zoo was different than that in Madagscar. Our friends, the animals, had to re-adapt to survive in their new habitat.

Suggested Activities:
- *Let's discuss and think about where we live. How can you describe your habitat? Is it urban or rural? What sort of climate do you have? Describe your geographical location.*
- *In small groups, make a poster with photos to display the information you find out about your habitat as your town, city, state, and region.*

- *Use different headings and pictures of natural products and animals as well as words. Use magazine articles to find photos that resemble your habitat and past them on your posters. Compare with the other groups.*
- *In the film, Alex, Marty, Gloria and Melman are friends even though they are from different species. Discuss in your groups, if you think the 4 animal characters would have known each other if they had not lived in the zoo? What kind of habitat would they live in? Discuss where these 4 animals would live in real life, if not in the zoo, and what they'd eat there.*

3. Economics:

a. Trade and Shipping:

- Madagascar primarily exports agricultural products as coffee, vanilla, shell-fish, sugar, and fiber. It is also a producer of cotton textiles, minerals, and gemstones (though it is believed most gems are smuggled out of the country illegally).

    In 2002, 39% of trade exports went to France, nearly 20% to the U.S., and 5.5% to Germany. Lesser trade partners include Japan and Singapore. In 2003 Malagasy export were worth about $700 million and the country's trade deficit was around $220 million.
- As of June 2014, the U.S. government has reinstated preferential trade status that will help their undeveloped economy.

Suggested Activities:
- *Students can analyze, discuss and speculate about the economic effects of environmental changes and crises resulting from natural disasters.*
- *Research on what is a "preferential trade status" for a country doing trade with the United States. Are there specific products that are listed?*

4. Civics, Citizenship And Government:

a. Madagascar Today:

- What is life like for a student your age? Housing, schools, shopping, food, sports, animal life, and nature.

- *Housing:* a typical house in Madagascar is a single-family bamboo house, simple, built in the middle of farming land. Families are large, with the average of 6 children; and yet, they all live in one or two rooms. Most people live in the country, and build their own houses from bamboo or wood.
- *Schools:* in Madagascar schools are small, just one or several rooms. Students wear uniforms. Education is mandatory from 6-14 years old. Elementary school is for students aged 6-11. There is a junior secondary school for those 12-15 and a senior secondary school for those 16-18 years old. In the capital, there are also private schools and several universities.
- *Shopping:* in Madagascar this is done at outdoor markets.
- *Food:* in Madagascar food is different from what we know in the U.S.
  Rice is served sometimes three times a day, but is varied, as in stews and fish. Sweets, like Koba is wrapped in banana leaves and mixed with peanuts. Mofo is sweet rice flavored with fruit and wrapped in balls of dough and fried. Coconuts, the island has so many, supplies milk, and the food is also cooked in the milk as well as sweet desserts.
- *Sports:* in Madagascar sports take on a beach activity like surfing, kayaking, snorkeling, and fishing. They also enjoy the same sports as we do, as: volleyball, football, their soccer, boxing, judo, tennis, and basketball.
- *Animals and wildlife:* are unique in Madagascar. They are found nowhere else. Why? Because the island is so isolated, the animals could not go off the island and travel to other continents as the elephant bird, now extinct. There are so many lemurs and so many different types.
- To protect these animals, the government has created 9 million acres of protected parks as: Stone forest where lizards live and Limestone Towers in the western section of the island.
- *Nature:* Originally, the island was all rain forests. Over the years, the forests have been destroyed and the wood stolen and sold, as in the Avenue of the Baobabs where so little remains. Now, citizens are replanting one million trees every three years.

Suggested Activities:
- *Students can write an essay on how they would react if they were to live in a completely different country. They can use as examples differences based on language, environment and culture. They can also compare their life style with that of students from Madagascar and discuss several differences using the topics above.*
- *Food varies from country to country as well as from species to species. People and animals also eat different foods. Using the film as a point of departure, form small groups*

to discuss the 4 animals in the film and what they like to eat? For example, Alex likes eating steaks. Make the point that Alex, Marty, Gloria and Melman live in captivity at the zoo so they don't have to hunt/look for food as they would have to do in the wild.

Discussion questions can include: What kinds of food did the zoo keepers feed them? Do you think the animals would have been able to find their own food if they were set free?

- *As people we have different tastes and enjoy different foods. What do you like to eat? How about your classmates? Divide the class into groups. Ask them to record what each member of the group usually eats for different mealtimes. Ask students to compare their findings with the other groups. Discussion questions could include: Are there any similarities/differences? Do we all like the same foods? Does anyone have a special diet? (e.g. vegetarian) Is there a difference between the foods we like to eat, and the foods we need to eat to stay healthy?*

- *An interesting assignment is to compare lunches that are served in school cafeterias around the world.*

B. Literature and Visual Arts:

5. World Literature:

a. Hainteny poetry:

- Hainteny, Malagasy for "knowledge of words," is a traditional form of Malagasy oral poetry, incorporating the use of metaphors. It is associated primarily with the Merina people of Madagascar. The Ibonia is an epic poem, spoken and performed for centuries, and offers insight into the diverse mythologies and beliefs of traditional Malagasy communities.

b. Ohabolana proverbs:

- Hainteny often incorporates ohabolana, which are proverbs, famous oral sayings that are handed down from one generation to another in Madagascar. They express daily life where they are spoken and used at weddings, funerals, and births and constitute an essential component of performances and comments on life from a philosophical perspective. They also include folktales, *angano,* and historical narratives, *tantara,* and riddles, *ankamantatra.* The use of this in today's present culture was started by famous poets from Madagascar.

- Their form persists unchanged from ancient times even when grammar and syntax of contemporary speech have since evolved because altering an ohabo-lana would constitute disregard for the venerated ancestors who are their orig-inators. Ohabolana are characteristically brief, metaphorical and symmetrical. Some examples are:

- *Manasa lamba be tseroka; na madio aza, mangarahara.*—Washing a very dirty dress: even though it gets clean, it becomes full of holes.

- *Ny tsiny toy ny rivotra: mikasika ny tena, fa tsy hita tarehy.*—Blame is like the wind: felt but not seen.

- *Aza asesiky ny fitia tanteraka, ka tsy mahalala ny ranonorana ho avy.*—Don't be so much in love that you can't tell when the rain is coming.

6. Media Studies:

a. Film Clips and Scene Discussions:

- *Create one's life* (Scene 00:02 –> 00:03 minutes)

It's just that another year's come and gone and I'm still doing the same old thing. I see your problem. You just need to break out of that boring routine. How? Throw out the old act Get out there. Who knows what you're gonna do. Make it up as you go along. Ad lib. Improvise. You know, make it fresh."

Discuss how and when one can create one's life. What about risks, responsibili-ties, obligations? Consider how you would change your situation at school, at home, with your friends?

- *Routine:* (Scene 01:179 –> 01:19)

"What do you guys think? Should we head back to New York? I don't know Marty. I mean, this is your dream. You sure you want to leave? I don't care where we are. As long as we're together, it doesn't matter to me. Well, in that case… Just smile and wave, boys. Smile and wave."

What are the benefits of a daily routine? Discuss how a routine can give you strength.

b. Computer Generated Imagery (CGI)

- The animation used in Madagascar has been a result of Computer Generated Imagery, an application that has been used for *Life of Pi, Avatar, Revenant* and many animated films.
- Computer-generated imagery is 3D computer graphics to achieve special effects. CGI is used in movies, television programs and commercials, and in printed media.
- CGI is used because it is often cheaper than physical methods, such as constructing elaborate miniatures for effects shots or hiring extra actors for crowd scenes. It also allows the creation of images that would not be feasible using any other method. And it is safer when working with a tiger or bear.
- In 1995, the first fully computer-generated feature film was Pixar's *Toy Story*.
- In the early 2000s, computer-generated imagery became the dominant form of special effects.

b. Escape from Madagascar:

- In the film we see that our 4 animal friends want to escape from Madagascar. The question is how do they achieve their goal?

Suggested Activity:
- *Students can pretend they want to escape an island by using a boat or vessel. As a group, discuss and design the escape vessel. What materials will float? How can you hold them together? Which size would float best? Consider the following materials to build your escape vessel: plastic tubs, cartons, food trays or lollipop sticks, glue, lego, small pieces of light wood, etc. Draw some ideas first. And then have fun testing them.*

7. Philosophy / Critical Thinking:

a. Personal essay:

- Sometimes we do not appreciate what is near us, like our family, our friends, our school. We think someone else has a better life. Or life is better somewhere else. Our characters in Madagascar were bored in Central Park's zoo and wanted to go "into the Wild."

Suggested Activity:

- *Discuss in your group what the characters in the film learned from their adventures and if you ever learned a similar lesson? Write a five paragraph personal essay using as your subject a wish for an adventure or for a change of lifestyle.*

b. Vocabulary:

- The film contains new vocabulary words: shipwreck, survival, predator, hunting, camouflage, instincts, lemur, and fossa.

Suggested Activity:

- *Have students take these new vocabulary words and define them, and then use them to tell an oral story to the group. Each student can have a turn of giving their interpretation. Do this as a round robin project.*

Hint:

- The word, camouflage involves disguising something in order to hide it. A zebra, like Marty in Madagascar, has markings that run off its edges into the background. This allows the zebra to fade into the background so it is difficult to see it. What other animals use their camouflage for protection and survival?

c. Collective nouns:

- Animals live in groups and there are adjectives that correspond to a group of animals, for example, a group of birds is called a flock of birds. Words that describe a group or family of animals are called collective nouns. Look at the list of animals below on left. Match the animals with their collective nouns on rig

ANIMAL	**COLLECTIVE NOUN**
- A…….. of lions	pride
- A …….of zebras	herd
- A……… of giraffes	tower
- A……… of hippos	huddle

- A ....of penguins   gaggle
- A ....of geese   school
- A......... of whales   colony
- A.......... of ants   caravan
- A ....of camels   litter
- A.......... of pups   herd

8. Music:

a. Hiragasy

- The hiragasy (hira: song; gasy: Malagasy) is a musical tradition in Madagascar and particularly among the Merina ethnic group in the regions around the capital of Antananarivo. The hiragasy is a day-long spectacle of music, dance, and oral public speaking performed by a troupe (typically related by blood or marriage and of rural origin) or as a competition between two troupes.
- The tradition in its contemporary form began in the late 18th century when the Prince first used musicians to draw a crowd for his political speeches; these troupes became independent, and began to incorporate political commentary and critique in their performances. The audience plays an active role at hiragasy events, expressing their satisfaction with the talent of the troupe members and the message they proclaim through applause, cheers or sounds of disapproval.
- After independence from France in 1960, the hiragasy troupe was held up as an icon of traditional Malagasy culture. Aspiring politicians routinely hire hiragasy troupes to attract a crowd for their political speeches while campaigning. While most troupes remain apolitical, some have opted to throw their support behind particular candidates.
- The performance of the hiragasy follows a number of conventions, such that there are certain similarities between the 80+ troupes currently performing in Madagascar. Among these are the order in which songs, dances and oratory are performed; how troupes are named; what costumes are worn (men typically wear straw hats, red coats and pants inspired by 19th century French military garb, and matching sashes; women wear identical dresses.
- The most common instruments are violins, trumpets and drums.

Suggested Activity:

- *Students might find it fun to recreate a Hiragasy Troupe celebration. They can find photos of costumes that they can use for their own. Perhaps they can find some music and accompany the songs with their own instruments to create a festive event. Preparing food, in the style of Malagasy culture would add to the festive flavor.*

9. Technology:

- Animation uses computer generated imagery. Students can create their own digital stories in the classroom by using the Microsoft website: www.microsoft.com/windowsxp/using/digitalphotography/PhotoStory/default.mspx

Suggested Activities:

- *Students can create digital stories by scanning and/or photographing with their own camera, as well as collecting pictures from animated sources and graphic novels, In groups, they can write a storyboard and narration.*
- *Students can also create a comic strip story by using Make Beliefs Comix (www.makebeliefscomix.com) and create an animated video at Flux Time Studio (www.fluxtime.com). They can save their videos and present them to other classes and grades.*

Sidebars:

1. Public Response:

- *Madagascar,* the movie, had amazing reviews by Entertainment Weekly, Washington Post and USA Today. Not only it is a family friendly movie, but it is also very educational to the youth. It teaches young children the themes of survival, and at the same time, shows the beauty of Madagascar. Although it is an animated film, children would get the idea of Madagascar being a very beautiful, diverse and jungle-like country.

2. Awards:

- AFI's 10 – Nominated – Category: Animated
- Annie Award, U.S.A., 2006 – Nominated – Best Animation – Animated Effects – Character Designed in an Animated Feature Production – Music in an Animated Feature Production – Production Design in an Animated Feature Production – Storyboarding in an Animated Feature Production.

- Kids' Choice Award, U.S.A., 2006 – Won – Category: Favorite Animated Movie

Bibliography of Films: Filmography
Further Global Study Resources through Film:

About Madagascar:

- *Natural History of Madagascar* (U.S.A)
- *The Separation of Madagascar and Africa* (U.S.A)
- *The Palms of Madagascar* (U.S.A)
- *Relationships and Traders in Madagascar* (U.S.A)
- *Penguins of Madagascar* (U.S.A.)

Animal Extinction Issues:

- *Lemurs of Madagascar* (U.S.A)
- *A Field Guide to Mammals in Africa* (U.S.A)
- *Mammals of Madagascar: A Complete Guide* (U.S.A)

MIDDLE EAST

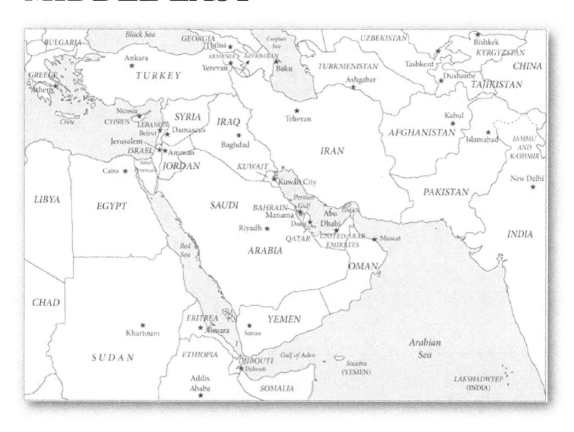

CHAPTER 13

WADJDA (SAUDI ARABIA)

TITLE OF FILM: *Wadjda*.
YEAR OF RELEASE: 2012
COUNTRY: Saudi Arabia
DIRECTOR: Haifaa al-Mansour
LANGUAGE: In Arabic with English Subtitles
RUNNING TIME: 98 minutes
RATING: PG
CURRICULUM THEMES:

A. HISTORY AND SOCIAL SCIENCE:

- **Chapter's Key Themes: Gender Discrimination; Girls' Rights**
- **World History: Religion: Islam and Wahhabism**
- **Geography: Riyadh**
- **Economics: Oil**
- **Civics, Citizenship and Government: Theocracy; Women's Rights; Education**

B. LITERATURE AND VISUAL ARTS:

- **World Literature: Saudi Arabian Writers and Resistance**
- **Media Studies: Film clips and scene discussions; Cinematography Techniques: Symbols; Cinema as a reflection of culture; Foreign influence**
- **Philosophy/ Critical Thinking: What constitutes Happiness?**
- **Art**

Introduction:

Wadjda was written and directed by Haifaa al-Mansour; produced by Razor Film and Gerhard Meixner and Roman Paul; cinematography by Lutz Reitemeier; edited by Andreas Wodraschke; production design by Thomas Molt; music by Max Richter; and released by Sony Pictures Classic. 98 minutes.

Wadjda:...Waad Mohammed
Wadjda's mother: ....Reem Abdullah
Ms. Hussa: ....Ahd

The first feature film directed by a Saudi Arabian woman, and the first film ever to be entirely shot in Saudi Arabia, *Wadjda* is about a tenacious and rebellious ten-year-old girl challenging the constraints of her society, a society in which girls and women face severe restrictions on what they can and cannot do. Wadjda has her heart set on having a bicycle and saving up her money to buy the green one she falls in love with after seeing it roll up off of a car and into her local toy store. Until 2013 in Saudi Arabia, girls were not allowed to ride bicycles—"A bicycle is not a toy for girls," Wadjda is told– it's dangerous for her virtue.

That director, Haifaa al-Mansour as a Saudi Arabian woman now living abroad, was able to tell this ground-breaking and deeply humanistic coming-of-age story on her own terms, parallels the resourceful resilience of Wadjda, a character the director says she based on her niece. Viewers know from the opening shot at school that Wadjda is a rebel—she's wearing black Converse sneakers, unlike the black shoes the other girls wear. And her best friend is a boy with a bicycle who teaches her how to ride one.

Though not particularly interested in Islam at first, Wadjda, who makes bracelets for money as well as doing all sorts of enterprising endeavors to earn money to buy her own bicycle, is motivated to study the Koran to win the prize-winning contest money. And when she wins, to the consternation of her teacher, she announces she will buy a bicycle. She is publicly told at school that she absolutely will not do that, what she will do with her money is to give it to "her brethren in Palestine." Thanks to her loving and supportive mother, Wadjda does indeed get her wish.

Pivotal Moments in History:

- Saudi Arabia is very rich in oil, and is ruled by a king.
- Home to Mecca and Medina, two of the holiest and most sacred Islamic cities, Saudi Arabia is where the prophet Mohammed was born, lived and buried.

The country has long practiced *Sharia*, Islam's moral code and religious law, but it became more strictly enforced by the government after the 1979 Iranian Revolution and subsequent Grand Mosque Seizure in Saudi Arabia. Before 1979, Saudi women didn't have to cover their faces and bodies; they were allowed to drive a car and allow men who weren't their relatives, into their homes, as long as they left the door open. This is no longer true.

- Fifteen of the nineteen al-Qaeda hijackers who flew the planes into the World Trade center on September 11, 2001, were Saudi Arabian citizens, including Bin Laden.

- Today in Saudi Arabia there are initiatives that suggest changes are moving away from strict Fundamentalism.

Pre-Screening Questions:

1. How does the film *Wadjda* show gender discrimination and how one girl fights quietly against it?

    Discrimination against a person because of her race, religion, age, sexual orientation, or gender, violates human rights.

2. What's the difference between the way girls and women behave in public and in private?

    Women and girls' behavior and restrictions in public are intensely scrutinized; however, in private they are more free to act and dress as they please. (We see this in the film.) Women have to fully cover themselves with abayas when they're outside, but they don't cover themselves at home. Girls aren't allowed to polish their nails; and so many things are forbidden. Women have drivers as they're not allowed to drive. Wadjda's mother fears that her husband will seek a second wife to bear him a son as she hasn't been able to do.

Pivotal Moments in the Film

- Because women have to hide from men when there's a gathering or when men enter a public space, director Haifaa al-Mansour, intent on filming in Riyadh, shot *Wadjda* while she was inside a van using walkie-talkies, computers, and cell phones to direct her male actors.

- It is also important to note that in 2014 Saudi Arabia nominated *Wadjda* for the country's first film entry for the foreign language category of the Academy Awards.

Post-Screening Questions:
History and Social Science

1. Did the film influence authorities to allow girls to ride bicycles and change that ruling?
2. How are Saudi women fighting to get the right to drive cars?

Suggested Activity:
- *Divide into groups to research on the Internet about rights for Saudi Arabian women.*

Hints:
- As a result of the film, girls were given the right to ride bicycles in parks and recreational areas, provided they're dressed in a full black abaya and they have a male adult to accompany them. The official law says, "Women may not use the bikes for transportation but only for entertainment,' and that they should shun places where young men gather to avoid harassment." This change came when King Abdullah was alive.
- Although women are legally not allowed to drive cars in Saudi Arabia, women in some rural areas outside cities are able to drive cars. Many Saudis believe that allowing women the right to drive could lead to Western-style openness and a rejection of traditional values; however, Saudi women are staging protests and driving in some cases in cities, challenging and protesting against this law.
- Prior to 2008, women were not allowed to enter hotels and furnished apartments without a male relative or chaperon. That changed in 2008 when a decree issued by King Abdullah that stated the only requirement needed to allow women to enter hotels are their national ID cards, and the hotel must inform the nearby police station of their room reservation and length of stay. However, this happens with everybody who stays at the hotel, not just women. Currently, Saudi women are not allowed to work in a mixed sex workplace, as shown in the film with Wadjda's aunt in a hospital.
- A report published by Human Rights Watch (http://www.hrw.org), stated that Saudi Arabian women have been denied many rights, including the right to freedom of movement, equality before the law and equality in marriage. In the past, Saudi women also were denied education and employment equality; however, today, education is mandatory for females. Women make up 58% of university students. And, today, many women work and own businesses in Saudi Arabia.

Post-Screening Question:
Literature and Visual Arts

1. Discuss which scenes in the film show women being denied basic human rights. How do they deal with mistreatment?

Suggested Activity:

- *The word "forbidden" comes up many times in the film. Students can create a list of what things are forbidden and discuss how and why the theocracy categorizes them as such.*

Curriculum Themes:
A. History and Social Science

Key Themes: Gender Discrimination; Girls' Rights

a. Gender Discrimination:

- In an early scene, Wadjda gets called out by her teacher for wearing black Converse sneakers. Another girl gets chided for laughing. Ms. Hussa, the Headmistress, tells her "A woman's voice is her nakedness."

Suggested Activities:

- *Discuss what Ms. Hussa means by, "A woman's voice is her nakedness." What are the consequences of limiting girls' self-expression?*
- *Ask members of your group to watch trailers from the Iranian film, Offside, and the Turkish film, Mustang to compare and contrast the portrayal of girls who want to go to a soccer game. Why do these societies place such strict and unfair restrictions on girls?*

Hints:

- When leaving the house, Saudi women need to be accompanied by a 'mahram' who is usually a male relative. Such practices are rooted in conservative traditions and religious views that hold giving freedom of movement to women might make them vulnerable to sin.

b. Girls' Rights:

- There are still a lot of child marriages for girls in Saudi Arabia that are pre-arranged by male relatives, as shown in the film. Wadjda's mother promises her she will not marry her off. Children, especially girls, do not have free choice to whom they want to marry or on how they want to direct their life.

   In an interview, Al-Mansour was asked:

Q. In Wadjda, it feels as though one of the messages is that women must take responsibility for their own independence. Do you think that's true?
A. Absolutely. I don't think women who are aggressive and fighting with everyone will achieve it. I think it is about women being assertive and having a career and pursuing a dream. That is what will change things in Saudi Arabia. Saudi Arabia is a very tribal and conservative place. If women go out there and are aggressive and screaming, "I want to do this," they will be shunned. People will not hear them. It is better to take a long road, and work day by day, to slowly change the situation.

1. World History:

Religion: Islam and Wahhabism

- In 622 A.D., Saudi Arabia becomes homeland to the Arab people. Islam's two holiest places, Mecca and Medina, are there. The prophet Mohammed was born in Mecca and he founded Islam in Saudi Arabia. His power based was in Medina, where he is buried.
- Saudi Arabians practice Wahhabism, a form of Sunni Islam that is Fundamentalist and ultraconservative. While both Wadjda and her mother question the parity of some of their religion's practices and beliefs, they are devout followers. There are scenes in which the camera stops over mother and daughter at prayer together, showing that their faith is a part of their womanhood and femininity and that they are not against this.

Suggested Activities:
- *Ask members of your group to discuss how Islam is practiced in various parts of the world, including Iraq, Iran, Turkey, Libya, Tunisia, and Nigeria, focusing on the role of women and women's rights in these countries.*

- *Create a chart dividing the Islam religion into Sunnis and Shiites and showing which countries practice the specific domination. (See chart in chapter 14)*

2. Geography:

Riyadh

- Riyadh, where the film is set, is the capital city. Saudi Arabia is rich in oil. A self-appointed king rules this country whose population is 27 million people. Saudi Arabia is the largest Arab country in western Asia. Jordan and Iraq are to the north, and Yemen is to the South. It's the only country that borders the Red Sea and the Persian Gulf. Jordan and Iraq are to the north, Kuwait is in the northeast, Qatar and Bahrain to the east, and United Arab Emirates, and Oman and Yemen are to the south.
- After establishing Riyadh as his headquarters, Abdulaziz captured all of the Hijaz, including Makkah and Madinah, in 1924 to 1925. In the process, he united warring tribes into one nation. On September 23, 1932, the country was named the Kingdom of Saudi Arabia, an Islamic state with Arabic as its national language and the Holy Qur'an as its constitution.

3. Economics:

Oil

- Saudi Arabia is rich in oil. The Saudi reserves are about one-fifth of the world's total oil reserves. Saudi Arabia has traditionally been regarded as the world's most important *swing producer of oil*, which means that the Saudi government could and would increase or decrease oil production to maintain a stable global price. For example, to weaken their number one adversary in the Middle East, Iran, and Iranian oil production, Saudi Arabia has lowered its price per barrel, and thus, reduces the amount of money that Iran can sell its oil, if Saudi oil is cheaper. This is a form of price control that's used.
- However, as of 2016, Iran will be able to export its oil legally. Iranian oil will compete with Saudi exported oil. This is dangerous for Saudi Arabia, for their economy is a petro-economy and low oil process will lower their budgetary surplus and increase their global debt. As Fundementalism spreads in Yemen and

in the area, and there is war in Yemen, Saudi Arabia's economy is weakening and can strain the country's politics. They will need to find other economic sources that the Prince is investigating.

- As of 2015, Saudi Arabia has led a coalition of mostly Gulf Arab countries (from Bahrain and the United Arab Emirates) with Yemeni fighters, in a military campaign to drive out Iranian-aligned rebels, known as Houthis, who seized the capital, Sanaa, in Yemen. Saudi Arabia is the region's Sunni Muslim powerhouse and fears that Shiite Iran is using the Houthis, who are also Shiites, as proxies to take control of Yemen.

Suggested Activities:
- *There is a strong relationship between economics and politics. Discuss this and give examples of how throughout the Middle East, a country's economics has affected its politics. What comes first? Economics or politics?*
- *Why are Saudi Arabia and Iran competitors economically and why are they antagonists? Religion (Sunnis vs Shiites) can begin to explain this. To be the leader of the geo-political region also influences this competition.*

Hints:
- Saudi Arabia is mainly a Sunni nation while Iran is a Shiite country. The Wahabis, an extreme form of Sunnism, is strongly represented in Saudi Arabia.

4. Civics, Citizenship, and Government:

a. Theocracy

- Saudi Arabia is a Theocracy. A country's rule of law is based on religion, the Koran for Saudis. Non-Muslims are not allowed to have Saudi citizenship. (We see this with Wadjda's mother's chauffeur.)
- In 1902 King Ibn Said took over and declared himself leader, he began to modernize the country. Accompanied by only 40 followers, he staged a daring night march into Riyadh to retake the city garrison, known as the Masmak Fortress. This legendary event marks the beginning of the formation of the modern Saudi state. Saudi Arabia joined the Arab League of Nations and took part in the war against Israel in 1948. A king took over in 1953 and fought against Egypt. In 1996, King Abdullah took over and worked to achieve balance. Abdullah in some respects did modernize his country. In 2009, he

established the first coed university, modern hospital, and gave women some rights.

- The world's most absolute monarchy, Saudi Arabia is known as a gerontocracy, a form of an oligarchy in which a country is ruled by leaders who are "significantly older than most of the adult population." At the death of King Abdullah in 2015, King Salman took over; yet, he, is also aging. His son, Mohammad Bin Salman Al Saud, is deputy-King.

Suggested Activities:
- *Research other Monarchies: United Kingdom, the Netherlands, Denmark, Sweden, Norway, Belgium, Lichtenstein, Luxembourg, Monaco, Spain, and Morocco.*
- *How was King Salman appointed, and in what ways are his policies similar and different from King Abdullah? Who will lead the country after him? How old is this son?*
- *Ask students to discuss which aspects of Saudi Arabian society King Salman should address? What changes to existing laws should be changed and why? Would changes reflect the philosophy of the country? Would changes be better or worse for the society?*

b. Women's Rights

- Some progress is being made for Saudi women. In 2012, the first delegation of women athletes competed in the London Olympics. In 2013, girls were allowed to participate in sports in school. In 2015, women for the first time, had the right to vote and to present female candidates for governmental office. In 2016, women won and gained political positions in towns and cities throughout Saudi Arabia.

- However, women still face a lot of separation from men. Wadjda's mother complains that she needs a driver to take her places, and when her driver quits, she's severely limited. Wadjda sets out to correct this wrong. Also, in a subtle act of defiance against discrimination of women, Wadjda tapes her name onto an actual family tree in her living room when she sees for herself that women are not considered a part of the family tree.

Suggested Activities:
- *Ask members of your group to research and talk about why fundamentalist Muslims give privilege to boys and men, and exclude women. Are there any other cultures or religions that do the same?*

- *Discuss whether our culture has expectations of how women should act and dress in public compared to how they act and dress in private. Does it vary according to city?*
- *Research the book, <u>In the Land of Invisible Women: A Female Doctor's Journey in the Saudi Kingdom</u> by Qanta Ahmed (Sourcebooks, 2008); <u>I Am Malala: The Girl Who Stood Up for Education and Was Shot by the Taliban</u> (Little, Brown, 2013). There is also from the book, the film, He Called Me Malala. (2015)*

Hints

- Wadjda's friendship with Abdullah is innocent and charming; however, it is also against the rules. And yet, he doesn't treat her differently because she's a girl. Is the director trying to tell us something about the future?
- There are unusual restrictions for women in Saudi Arabia, including entering a cemetery and working in a lingerie shop. Some lingerie stores and department stores have recently begun hiring female employees, but the majority are still staffed by men. (As in the film when Wadjda's mother buys a dress and tries it on in the bathroom.)

c. Education

- In Saudi Arabia, girls and boys are separated in early education. We see this in the film for Wadjda attends an all girls' school where education is focused on Religion.
- In the first half of the 20th century, reading was acceptable for women, but not writing, as "writing is an accomplishment regarded as unsuitable in a woman, though not forbidden. " The reason, according to the men, was that "If our wives knew how to write, how could we prevent them from writing to other men." Letters had to be written by a male relative or a paid scribe.
- In 2009, Nora bint Abdullah al-Fayez, an American-educated former teacher and an expert on girls' education became the first woman minister in Saudi Arabia when she was made deputy education minister in charge of a new department for female students. Saudi Arabia now offers female students one of the world's largest scholarship programs. Thanks to this program, thousands of women have earned doctorates from Western universities as well as from King Abdullah's University in Riyadh, where women can attend classes and earn degrees, especially in science, math, and technology.

Suggested Activity:

- *Research the difference between girls and boys education in Saudi Arabia. What is a madrasah and its curriculum? (Young Abdullah goes to a different school than Wadjda.)*

5. World Literature:

Saudi Arabian Writers and Resistance

- In 2011, a Saudi Arabian novelist, Raja Alem, became the first woman to win the International Prize for Arabic Fiction, which she shared with a Moroccan poet. Alem's novel, *The Doves' Necklace,* is set in Mecca, and explores crime, religious extremism and the exploitation of foreign workers by a "mafia" of building contractors, which is destroying the historic areas of the city. Now living in Paris, Alem, whose writing has been compared to Nabokov's, also writes stories and plays on the same subject.

- Turki Al-Hamad was born in 1953. His coming-of-age trilogy entitled *Phantoms of the Deserted Alley* is about a young man in Saudi Arabia. It is set between the Six Day War (1967) and the oil boom (1973). Four fatwas were issued against Al-Hamad when his first book was published because as he says, "Where I live there are three taboos: religion, politics and sex. It is forbidden to speak about these. I wrote this trilogy to get things moving." He was arrested in 2012 for tweeting.

- Abdulrahman Munif (1933-2004) was one of the most important Saudi writers, and his novel *Cities of Salt,* originally published in Beirut in 1984, was banned in his own country as well as other Arab countries. It exposes the social injustice and inequality of the oil boom's dividing of the country into the very wealthy and the very poor.

- The classical favorite is <u>One Thousand and One Arabian Nights,</u> a collection of folk tales first compiled in Arabic during the 8ᵗʰ century. The work was collected over many centuries by various authors and in turn relied partly on Indian, Arabic and Persian oral elements. The story concerns Shahryar, whom the narrator calls a king ruling in "India and China." He is shocked to discover his wife's infidelity and has her executed: but in his bitterness and grief decides that all women are the same. He begins to marry a succession of virgins only to execute each one the next morning. Eventually his assistant cannot find any more virgins. The assistant's daughter, Scheherazade, offers herself as the next bride and her father reluctantly agrees. On the night of their marriage, Scheherazade tells the king a tale, but does not end it. The king is thus forced to keep her alive in order to hear the conclusion. The next night, as soon as she finishes the tale, she begins, but only "begins" another tale. And so she continues for 1,001 nights.

6. Media Studies:

c. Film clips and Scene Discussion

- *Change of roles:* Scene: (01:03 –> 01:04)

"Interested in your father's family tree. You aren't on it. It only includes men's names. Clean up when you've finished. Hide the traces of your crime. I don't want to make him upset with us again."

Suggested Activity:
- *Ask members of your group to discuss if they ever wondered if their life would be different if they were born another gender? Ask them to role-play and switch their gender for the activity and imagine how their life would be different in Saudi Arabia.*

- *Pre-arranged marriages:* Scene: (01:05 –> 01:06)

"Give me the picture! I said give me the picture! What's going on? Salma just got married and brought pictures of her wedding. Congratulations! Can I see the pictures? Are these of your wedding? Is this your husband? How old is he? 20. Pictures are forbidden at school. Let's get started."

Suggested Activity:
- *In some countries, parents arrange the marriages of their children. Discuss in your group this concept. Are these marriages successful? Are they different from our American way? Compare the rate of divorce.*

b. Cinematography Techniques:

- *Symbols:*
  Converse sneakers – Wadjda is the only girl in the film who wears Converse sneakers. The camera takes us to view the girls' feet; they're all wearing black flats.

Converse is an American brand, and Wadjda's sneakers represent that she's a rebellious non-conformist, and that she's fond of Western culture.

- *Mixed tapes* – Western music is banned in Saudi Arabia. Wadjda sells mixed tapes to make money, and even to make "friends" as with the merchant of bikes.

c. Television as a Reflection of Culture:

- There are very few movie theaters in Saudi Arabia, but television is popular. Research what kind of TV shows are on the air. Also, are movies shown today? Where?

Hints:
- In the 1970s, there were many movie theaters in Saudi Arabia and they were not considered un-Islamic. But in the 1980's the government closed all cinemas and theaters. Currently, the only theater in Saudi Arabia is an IMAX cinema located in Khobar in the Scitech complex, a science and technology center offering exhibits that deal with varying science and technologies, as well as an astronomic observatory. This IMAX cinema is showing documentaries, mostly produced in the United States during non-prayer timings. The documentaries are shown in Arabic and headphones are available with English audio.

d. Foreign influence:

- The final scene of Wadjda while riding her bicycle is an exhilarating ending reminiscent of Francois Truffaut's *The 400 Blows*.

7. Philosophy/ Critical Thinking:

a. What constitutes Happiness?

Neighboring country, United Arab Emirates, has nominated (2016) a Minister of Happiness and Minister of Tolerance. The people of Dubai will have leaders to help them find "social good and satisfaction."

Suggested Activities:
- *The human goal is to be happy. But what is happiness? How can each person define it, strive to attain it, and achieve it? Take time with your students to have each student think about this question and then to discuss some possibilities. Ask them to consider the importance of finding a balance between professional and personal goals.*
- *Students can write down their thoughts and then analyze the group's opinions. What factors repeat? Is there a pattern? Is there a list of priorities?*
- *Ask students to research which countries in the world have been voted to be the "happiest"? Discuss why?*

8. Art:

- The art from Saudi Arabia is a rich one that has been shaped by its Islamic heritage, during its historical role as an ancient trade center and its Bedouin traditions. Ivory, carpets and silk are important products that Saudis use in their artistic expressions.

    In ancient times, these works of art were indications of how wealthy a family was, especially those from the Royal family.

Suggested Activities:
- *Some museums have Saudi art and can be found through the Internet.*
  Was this country part of the ancient silk road? Salt road? Is ivory trade outlawed today in Saudi Arabia as it is in China and Africa for being an "endangered" species?

Hints:
- Located at the center of important ancient trade routes, the Arabian people were enriched by many different civilizations. As early as 3,000 BC, Arabian merchants were part of a far-reaching trade network that extended to south Asia, the Mediterranean and Egypt. They served as a vital link between India and the Far East on one side, and Byzantium and the Mediterranean lands on the other.
- The introduction of Islam in the 7th century AD further defined the region's art and culture. Within a century of its birth in the Arabian Peninsula, Islam had spread west to the Atlantic Ocean and east to India and China. It fostered a dynamic period of great learning in culture, science, philosophy and the arts known as the Islamic "Golden Age."

- And every year for the past 14 centuries, Muslim pilgrims from around the world travel to holy sites in Mecca and Medina, further enriching the region's culture. The pilgrims brought ivory from Africa and carpets from the East, and took local goods back to their homelands.
- When the Kingdom of Saudi Arabia was formed in 1932, King Abdulaziz bin Abdulrahman dedicated himself to preserving Arab traditions and culture, and his sons and successors have done the same.

Sidebars:

1. How things have Changed or not Changed Since the Period Covered by the Film:

- The former 89 year-old King Abdullah had a mixed record in terms of women's rights and human rights. In many ways, he was considered a "modernizer" and reformer:

    He gave give women the right to vote. He also allowed women for the first time to consult on his high-level council as well as allowing and encouraging them to study with men at the university that carries his name. 15% of the students are women there.

    Human rights activists are urging Abdullah's 70 year-old successor, King Salman, to work harder at protecting freedom of speech and women's rights. Many fear that King Salman is more conservative than his late predecessor.

2. Public Response:

- Although the director, Al-Mansour, sought and found financing and producing partners outside of Saudi Arabia, she ultimately received validation by her Saudi cultural compatriots. "We are proud of the film as an authentic representation of our country and culture and are pleased to see the themes of the film resonate with audiences well beyond our borders," said Sultan Al Bazie, the head of the Saudi nominating committee. It is due to her excellent film that there developed a film industry for the first time in Saudi Arabia and that female directors were also encouraged to work and receive government financing for their work. It is also the first time the nation has received awards for a film and had a film selected to compete for the Academy awards; unfortunately, the film ultimately wasn't nominated.

- All this shows the power of film, and a film director's voice, to make changes.

3. Actors and Directors:

- Al Mansour grew up in Saudi Arabia as the daughter of the poet, Abdul Rahman Mansour. Her father introduced her to films by video as there were no movie theaters at that time in Saudi Arabia. She majored in comparative literature at the American University in Cairo and then went to film school in Sydney, Australia. After directing three short films, she directed the documentary *Women without Shadows* (2006), which deals with the contrast between contemporary Saudi women's lives and their counterparts in the recent past. It was shown at 17 international festivals.

- The actress, Ajd, plays Wadjda's teacher, Ms. Hussa. She is also a Saudi filmmaker, and is the first Saudi Arabian ever to get a degree in directing in the U.S. She received her degree from the New York Film Academy. The beautiful Reem Abdullah who plays Wadjda's mother is also famous in Saudi Arabia. She starred on the hit television comedy "Tash Ma Tash," a Saudi comedy series known for its liberal criticism of intolerance and reactionary societal views.

- The challenge of casting Wadjda is that many Saudis don't think acting in films is appropriate for girls. Not only was the 12-year old (at the time) Waad Mohammed perfect for the role, but Al Mansour noted she came in "wearing jeans and Chuck Taylor sneakers, hair curled, listening to Justin Bieber; she looked exactly like a teenager in London." Obviously, she was in her role from the beginning.

Director's Statement:

"I'm so proud to have shot the first full-length feature ever filmed entirely inside the Kingdom. I come from a small town in Saudi Arabia where there are many girls like Wadjda who have big dreams, strong characters and so much potential. These girls can, and will, reshape and redefine our nation. It was important for me to work with an all-Saudi cast, to tell this story with authentic, local voices. Filming was an amazing cross-cultural collaboration that brought

two immensely talented crews, from Germany and Saudi Arabia, into the heart of Riyadh. I hope the film offers a unique insight into my own country and speaks of universal themes of hope and perseverance for all people."
Haifaa Al Mansour

4. Awards:

- Alliance of Women Film Journalists, 2013. Won—EDA. Female Focus Award, The Year's Outstanding Achievement by a Woman in the Film Industry for challenging the limitations put on women in her culture.
- Los Angeles Film Festival, 2013. Won—Best International Feature.
- National Board of Review, 2013. Won—Freedom of Expression Award.
- Boston Society of Film Critics Award, 2013. Won—Best Foreign Language Film
- Palm Springs International Film Festival, 2013. Won—Directors to Watch.
- Rotterdam Film Festival, 2013. Won– Dioraphte Award.
- Women Film Critics Circle Award, 2013. Won—Best Foreign Film by or About Women.
- Vancouver International Film Award, 2013. Won– Most Popular International 1st Film
- Durban International Film Festival, 2013. Won—Best First Feature.
- Guild of German Art House Cinema, 2013. Won—Foreign Film.
- Venice Film Festival, Interfilm, CinemAvvenire and C.I.C.A.E. Awards, 2012
- Dubai International Film Festival, 2012. Won—Muhr Arab Award, Best Film and Best Actress—Waad Mohammed.

Bibliography of Films: Filmography
Further Global Study Resources through Film:

Women's Rights:

- *Baran* (Iran/Afghanistan)
- *Offside* (Iran)
- *The King of Masks* (China)
- *Whale Rider* (New Zealand)
- *Moolaadé* (Senegal)

- *Bend It Like Beckham* (United Kingdom)
- *Camille Claudel* (France)
- *Whale Rider* (New Zealand)
- *Zanzibar Soccer Queens* (Zanzibar)
- *Water* (India)
- *Fire* (India)
- *The Lady* (Myanmar/ Burma)
- *4 Months, 3 Weeks, and 2 Days* (Romania)
- *The Flowers of War (China)*
- *The Circle* (Iran)
- *The Day I Became a Woman* (Iran)
- *Rabbit Proof Fence* (Australia)
- *The Magdalena Sisters* (Ireland)
- *Winter Sleep* (Turkey)
- *Mustang* (Turkey)

CHAPTER 14

THE OTHER SON (ISRAEL)

1. TITLE OF FILM: *The Other Son*
2. YEAR OF RELEASE: 2012
3. COUNTRY: France
4. DIRECTOR: Lorraine Lévy
5. LANGUAGE: French, English, Arabic
6. RUNNING TIME: 105 minutes
7. RATING: Unrated
8. CURRICULUM THEMES:

A. HISTORY AND SOCIAL SCIENCE:

- **Chapter's Key Themes:** The Conflict; Parties Engaged in Direct Negotiations; Arab League; Attempts at Peace
- **World History:** Dateline
- **Geography:** Neighbors and Problems: Iraq, ISIS, Syria, Egypt, Saudi Arabia, Iran, Jordan, Lebanon
- **Economics:** Kibbutz; Oil drilling in the Mediterranean Sea
- **Civics, Citizenship and Government:** Knesset - Israeli Parliament; internal divisive issues

B. LITERATURE AND VISUAL ARTS:

- **World Literature:** Early writings; Theodor Herzl.
- **Media Studies:** Film Clips and Scene Discussions; Is this a true story? Personal identity; Artistic and cultural boycotts
- **Philosophy/ Critical Thinking:** Debates
- **Architecture:** Israel's antiquities: Massada, the City of David, Tzippori
- **Technology**

Introduction:

The Other Son was directed by Lorraine Levy; produced by Virginie Lacombe and Raphael Berdugo; production company by Rapsodie Production; music by Dhafer Youssef; distributed by Haut et Court (France) and Cohen Media Group (U.S.A.);

Orith Silberg .... *Emmanuelle Devos*
Alon Silberg .... *Pascal Elbe*
Joseph Silberg .... *Jules Sitruk*
Yacine Al Bezaaz... ....*Mehdi Dehbi*
Leila Al Bezaaz.. .....*Areen Omari*
Said Al Bezaaz.. .....*Khalifa Natour*

The Other Son is more than a story about Israeli and Middle Eastern politics. It is a story about human error and heartbreak, a story that could happen to anyone. And yet, it is also a movie of Hope. If an Israeli and Palestinian could "learn" to love the enemy, as shown by director Lorrain Levy, then why can't we? Why can't they?

The story begins with a Polemic, similar to a philosophical debate a professor presents in class: "What would you do if…?" As the viewer watches this heart-rendering problem unfold, the entire history of the Middle East is symbolized on the screen. We empathize and hope the director or actor or someone, can find a solution.

Spoken mostly in French with some Arabic, Hebrew, and English, the four languages make the situation appear more universal. We are transported out of the Middle East and into our own home to ponder if we could eradicate prejudice and love another son?

Curriculum Themes:
A. History and Social Science:

Chapter's Key Theme:

a. The Conflict:

- The ongoing Israeli-Palestinian conflict has formed the core part of a wider Arab-Israeli problem since the creation of the State of Israel. Palestinians and Israelis have failed to reach a peace agreement on key issues: mutual recognition; borders; security; water rights; control of Jerusalem (holy city for both Islam and Judaism); Israeli settlements; Palestinian freedom of movement; two-state solution; Arabs living in Israel – integration, identity and citizenship; and resolving Palestinian claims of a right of return for their refugees.

Many attempts have been made to create a two-state solution in which there would be the establishment of a state of Palestine alongside the state of Israel. There is also the question of Jerusalem to be the capital for both nations. Neither side, as of 2016, has agreed to these issues despite numerous attempts.

Instead, there is continuous violence in the region. Casualties have not been restricted to the military, but also to the civilian population on both sides. Fighting is conducted by regular armies, and paramilitary groups, terrorists and individuals.

b. Parties Engaged in Direct Negotiations:

- The two sides engaged in direct negotiations are the Israeli government and the Palestine Liberation Organization (PLO). The official negotiations are mediated by an international contingent called the Quartet of the Middle East.

c. Arab League:

- The Arab League is another important factor in the conflict between the Arabs and Israelis. After Israel was declared a state on May 14, 1948, the Arab League decided to intervene on behalf of Palestinian Arabs, and marched their forces into former British Palestine, beginning the main phase of the 1948 Arab-Israeli War. This conflict led to approximately 15,000 casualties but ended with armistice agreements. Israel would hold much of the Mandate territory (Palestine), Jordan would occupy the West Bank, and Egypt would take over the Gaza Strip.

d. Attempts at Peace:

- Three main events characterize peace attempts between the Palestinians and the Israelis: the Oslo Accords in 1993, the Camp David Accords in 2000, and the Taba Summit in 2001:

- ° *Oslo Accords:* The U.S. brokered the Oslo agreement that Israel would gradually cede control of the Palestinian territories over to the Palestinians in exchange for peace. The agreement failed after the assassination of Yitzhak Rabin, the Israeli Prime Minister involved in the peace-making process.
- ° *Camp David Accords:* Israel offered a deal to the Palestinians: a non-militarized Palestinian state split into 3 to 4 parts containing 87-92% of the West Bank, including parts of East Jerusalem, and the entire Gaza Strip. The offer was rejected by Arafat, leader of the Palestinians. He did not provide a counter-offer and no peace agreement was reached.
- ° *Taba Summit:* A new map was proposed that both sides agreed on: Palestinians would gain sovereignty over the Temple Mount Al Aqsa sanctuary and the Israelis would have control over the Western Wall. Both holy sites are located next to each other in Jerusalem. Israel would also provide compensation for refugees and acknowledge the pain caused to the Palestinians in 1948 when the State of Israel was created. However, Ariel Sharon defeated Ehud Barak in the Israeli elections and the new Prime minister, Sharon, decided not to resume high-level talks. A settlement was therefore not reached.

- In 1995, Prime Minister Rabin, from the liberal Labor party, was assassinated by a radical Israeli extremist, in part because of the Oslo Agreement. Right wing radicals and conservative Likud members, thought Rabin was a traitor in his peace negotiations. Since then, there has been an overt schism in internal issudes dividing the nation. These relate to domestic policies regarding: construction and retention of settlements; peace agreements and territories; two-state concept; right of return for Arab refugees; place of Arab-Israelis within Israeli society.
- *PLO (Fatah & Hamas):* After 2007, the territory recognized as the State of Palestine was split between Fatah in the West Bank and Hamas in the Gaza Strip. In 2014, both groups formed a coalition government.
- *Hezbollah:* This is a terrorist group located in Lebanon, giving support to the official governments in Iran and Syria.

Suggested Activities:
- *Cause/Effect Chart – In 2006, the terrorist group, Hezbollah from Lebanon, attacked Israel in a bloody war.*
- *Ask your group to to create a chart of effects pertaining to the Lebanon War.*

- *In 2012, the United Nations recognized the Palestinian territories of the West Bank and Gaza Strip, Fatah and Hamas, as a non-member observer state. As of 2015, the United Nations flies the Palestinian flag outside N.Y. Headquarters, as well as the Vatican flag, also a non-member observer state.*
- *What rights are given to the Palestinians as a result of this status? What does this imply for the future of the Palestinian state and for Israel? What are both sides doing with this new status?*
- *Peace in the Middle East has been difficult to achieve. Leaders on all sides have been assassinated because of their attempts, either by their own dissatisfied people or by those from the opposing side. Divide into pairs to research who was assassinated.*

Hints:
- The following leaders have been assassinated while trying to achieve peace:
  - Egyptian President, Sadat, was killed in 1981 after he signed the Camp David Accords and Peace Treaty with Prime Minister Begin of Israel in 1979. Both leaders received the Nobel Peace Prize. However, the treaty was not recognized by Egypt or Israel. Prime Minister Rabin of Israel was assassinated in 1995 at a peace rally in Tel Aviv by a right-wing Israeli fanatic.

1. World History:

a. Dateline:

- 1909: Tel Aviv is founded as a Hebrew-speaking Jewish city.
- 1917: Britain issues the Balfour Declaration, viewed as a U.N. endorsement for a national Jewish homeland in Palestine.
- 1919-1939: More than 100,000 Jews arrive from Russia and Poland to settle in Palestine. Arabs protest and riot.
- 1947: The United Nations proposes an establishment of two separate states for Jews and Arabs.
- 1948: Establishment of the State of Israel.
- 1964: The Palestinian Liberation Organization (PLO) is established by the Arab League. Their goal is the liberation of Palestine through armed struggle, and the right of return for Palestinians to Palestinian territories.
- 1978: Wars continue since 1919. In 1978, the Camp David Accords' Peace Treaty is signed between Israel and Egypt.

- 1979: For this, Prime Minister Begin of Israel and President Sadat of Egypt are awarded the Nobel Peace Prize.
- 1981: Egyptian President Sadat is assassinated while he was watching the annual military parade commemorating the 1973 war with Israel. He is succeeded by Mubarak who remained president until 2011.
- 1995: Israeli Prime Minister Rabin is assassinated at a peace rally in Tel Aviv by a right-wing Israeli fanatic. His assassin opposed Rabin's peace initiative, particularly the signing of the Oslo Accords.
- 2000: Camp David Summit in the U.S. with President Clinton, Arafat from Palestine, and Barak from Israel. They fail to agree on a peace treaty.
- 2005: Israel withdraws from the Gaza Strip under Israeli Prime Minister Ariel Sharon.
- 2006: Members of the Military wing of Hamas attack the Israeli border at Gaza Strip. The group, Hezbollah from Lebanon, also attacks Israel.
- 2012: November 30, The United Nations General Assembly upgraded U.N. status for the Palestinian Authority, The resolution elevates their status from "non-member observer entity" to "non-member observer state," the same category as the Vatican.
- 2014: Israel releases Palestinian prisoners in an effort toward peace negotiations.
- 2015: June 25, The Palestinian Authority made its first submission of evidence of alleged Israeli war crimes to the International Criminal Court, trying to speed up an ICC inquiry into abuses committed during the 2014 Gaza conflict. Israel will decide either to cooperate with the ICC investigation or find itself isolated as one of a few countries that have declined to work with its prosecutors.
- 2015-2016, Israel is critical of U.S.-Iran deal of Iran's anti-nuclear development program.

Suggested Activities:
- *As a result of Fatahs' and Hamas' coalition, Israel has taken steps to fortify and protect their state: increased construction of the dôme, destruction of tunnels, increased use of drones.*
- *Form small groups to discuss the relationship between politics and economics. Include: Arab countries that have financially supported the Palestinians.*
- *Create a flowchart to visualize the relationship between politics, economics, and financial support.*
- *It might be interesting to write an answer to the question, "Who are the enemies of Israel?" You may want to include background information that explains the nature of their animosity with Israel. Include: Lebanon, Hezbollah, Fatah, Hamas.*

Hints:

- Saudi Arabia and Qatar, two wealthy oil-producing countries, have supported Hamas and Fatah. One of the Five Pillars of Islam requires that Muslims donate their money to those in need. As of 2014, Saudi Arabia and Qatar have helped Palestinians in many ways: schools, hospitals, army, etc.

- Some enemies:
- LEBANON – Hezebollah's Shiite leader, Nasrallah, supports and helps arm, the governments of Syria, Iran and Iraq.
- FATAH – previously known as the PLO's, with their Founding leader, Yasser Arafat until his death in 2004, maintains power in the West Bank.
- HAMAS – is the opposition Palestinian party, maintaining power in the Gaza Strip. The United States, Canada, the European Union, and Japan classify Hamas as a terrorist organization while Iran, Russia, Turkey, and Arab nations do not.

2. Geography

a. Neighbors and Problems:

1. Iraq:
Modern Iraq was created after the Treaty of Sevres and placed under British control in 1921. Baghdad is the capital of Iraq and is located in the center of the country. The kingdom of Iraq gained its independence from Britain in 1932 and became the Republic of Iraq in 1958. Iraq was controlled by the Ba'ath Party and Saddam Hussein until the U.S. invaded Iraq in 2003, known as the Iraq War. The U.S. allegedly had evidence that Iraq had weapons of mass destruction (WMDs) and asked the U.N. Security Council to authorize an attack. When the U.N. Security Council refused, the U.S., the U.K. and 29 other countries in a "coalition of the willing" launched an invasion against Iraq in March 2003. There were a large number of casualties from all sides in this war. Majority of Iraquis are Sunnis.

2. ISIS:
ISIS (Islamist State of Iraq and Syria) also known as ISIL or Daesh, is a Sunni terrorist group that is the biggest threat to peace as of now in the Middle Eastern Region. Its aim is to establish a caliphate - a single, transnational Islamic state based on Sharia, the Islamic law. Much of their money comes form oil production from their territories. Kurds have joined the U.S. to fight against ISIS in Syria, Iraq and Libya.

3. Syria:

Peace has not yet been established between Syria and Israel as the Golan Heights issue is still being disputed. (As of 2016) After the 1967 Six Day War, Syria lost the Golan Heights to Israel. Major negotiations since then have been pushing for a "land for peace" agreement entailing that Israel will return the Golan Heights to Syria if Syria recognizes Israel and establishes peaceful relations with it. Israel has not returned the Golan Heights.

4. Egypt:

Egypt and Israel have had tense relations in the past especially after Egypt's attacks on Israel in the 1948 Palestine War and the 1967 Arab-Israeli War. However, ever since the 1979 Egyptian-Israeli Peace Treaty, mediated by U.S. President Jimmy Carter, full diplomatic relations between Israel and Egypt have been established and continue to exist today. The economic ties between Israel and Egypt are very strong; in 2011 the exports between Israel and Egypt totaled $236 million. This economic alliance has strengthened the political relationship.

5. Saudi Arabia:

Saudi Arabia and Israel work together for they share common interests: they both oppose the expansion of Iran's influence in the region and are both strategic allies to the U.S. Their King, Salman, and his son, Mohammad, rule Saudi Arabia.

6. Iran:

Iran originally voted against Israel's admission to the United Nations and showed solidarity to the Arab states during the 1948 Palestine war. However, Iran was the second Muslim-majority country to recognize Israel as a state after Turkey. These diplomatic relations did not last long. After the 1979 Iranian Revolution that ousted the pro-Western Shah Pahlavi, Iran broke all diplomatic and commercial ties with Israel and stopped recognizing Israel as a legitimate state. Currently, Iranian President Rouhani has negotiated and agreed to the limitations of his country's nuclear energy program for 15 years, in exchange for a cessation of U.N. and Western economic sanctions, which are expected to come to fruition in 2016. However, after 15 years, a nuclear-armed Iran represents again a major threat to Israel and region, especially because Iran was found guilty by the U.N. of supplying to Gaza and Hamas longer-range missiles that were used against Israeli civilians.

7. Jordan:

Before 1994, Jordan and Israel had territorial issues and non-diplomatic relations as Jordan supported the Arab expulsion of Israel from the region. However, after the

1994 Israel-Jordan peace treaty, relations between Israel and Jordan normalized. This peace treaty resolved territorial disputes as well as water sharing and led to positive outcomes, such as increased economic growth and Israel helping to establish a modern medical center in Amman, Jordan. Today Jordan is in charge of maintaining the Blue Dome, Al Aqsa mosque, in Jerusalem as a holy site for Muslims and relations between the two nations are not antagonistic.

8. Lebanon:

Lebanon and Israel do not have economic or diplomatic relations. Hezbollah is the dominant political party and overrules the Christian Democratic Party. Hezbollah's Shiite leader, Nasrallah, supports and helps arm Syria, Iran and Iraq and the Shiites of the region.

Suggested Activities:

- *All the countries in the Middle East except Israel, share the Islamic religion. Yet, some are Sunnis and others are Shiites.*
- *Divide into small groups to collaborate and identify the percentage of Sunnis and Shiites in each country in the Middle East.*
- *Divide into pairs, each with an assigned Middle Eastern country. Research the religion, traditions, politics, and economics of each country.*
- *Israel has a population of 8 million people. 6 million are Jewish and 2 million are Arabic and Druze.*
- *Discuss the following:*
  - *Who are the Druze in Israel? What rights do they have in Israel?*
  - *Who are the Arabs in Israel? What rights do they have in Israel?*

Hints:

- The Islamic Religion is divided throughout the world into 2 branches: *Shiites and Sunnis.*
- There are more than a billion Muslims in total. 85-90% are Sunnis.
- 10-15% are Shiites, also pronounced as Shia's.
- The number 5 is important for Muslims: There is a call to pray five times a day; Five Pillars are needed to be considered a devout Muslim.
- There are five things that are necessary in an Arabic village: mosque; madrasah (school); Hamma (public bathing); water fountain; and a public oven to bake bread.
- The Muslim religion is divided into Sunnis and Shiites:

- Despite many common beliefs and their shared obedience to the Koran, their differences make coexistence difficult. We find the different representation in the following countries:

Country	Sunnis	Shiites & Offshoots
Afghanistan	84%	15%
Bahrain	30%	70%
Egypt	90%	1%
Iran	10%	89%
Iraq	32-37%	60-65%
Kuwait	60%	25%
Lebanon	23%	38%
Pakistan	77%	20%
Saudi Arabia	90%	10%
Syria	74%	16% (Alawites)
Turkey	83-93%	7-17%
United Arab Emirates	81%	15%
Yemen	70%	30%

3. Economics:

a. Kibbutz:

- A kibbutz is a voluntary democratic community where people live and work together on a non-competitive basis. Its aim is to generate an economically and socially independent society founded on principles of communal ownership of property, profit, social justice, and equality.
- A kibbutz is a unique economic system based on socialism and Zionism in Israel which involves a collective community that is traditionally based on agriculture, but has now expanded to also incorporate the manufacturing of military equipment, household appliances, electronics, and furniture. The first *kibbutzim* (plural) were developed in the early 1920's by young Zionists. As of 2010, there were 270 kibbutzim in Israel; yet, only 2.8% of Israel's population live on kibbutzim. One of the most prolific kibbutzim, the Kibbutz Sasa, generated $580 million in annual revenue from its military-plastics industry.

b. Oil drilling in the Mediterranean Sea:

- There was a discovery in late 2010 of the Leviathan Natural Gas Field, a large underwater reservoir of natural gas off Israel's northern Mediterranean shores, at approximately 130 km west of Haifa. It is estimated that this field contains 122 trillion cubic feet of natural gas and 1.7 bn barrels of oil, worth approximately $240 billion. Oil extraction companies such as Noble Energy Inc. and Israel's Delek Group believe there is enough gas to supply the Jewish state for as much as 150 years at the current rate of consumption and still have enough to export.

Suggested Activities:
- *Oil has caused wars throughout the Middle East for decades. However, Israel is using their new oil wealth for peaceful purposes. They have started to export petrol and natural gas to Egypt and Jordan, neighbors and allies, at a reduced rate. Discuss the benefits of using oil to make allies rather than enemies.*
- *All citizens of Israel must go into the Army after high school and before college, including women and Druze. Divide into two groups to debate the question of an Army for all.*
- *The formation of the State of Israel as a Socialist state entails a high tax rate for all citizens. Divide into small groups to discuss the following:*
  ° *What are the ramifications of high taxes?*
  ° *Where does the tax money go?*
  ° *What other countries have a high tax rate?*
  ° *What do these countries share in common?*
  ° *For what is the tax money used?*

Hints:
- Sweden, Norway, Denmark, Finland, France, Switzerland, and Iceland have high tax rates.

4. Civics, Citizenship and Government:

a. Knesset:

- There are 34 Parties that participate In Israel's Parliament, the Knesset.
- The 3 main parties are:

    °   Likud – right wing conservatives and ultra Orthodoxs
    °   Labor – center-left
    °   Kadima - more left and more liberal

Suggested Activities:
- *Political parties are very important in Israel. As part of the Israeli constitution, no single political party can govern alone. There must be a coalition government comprised of at least two different parties. Discuss, the following:*
  - ° *Why is it important to have a coalition government in Israel?*
  - ° *What do the 3 main political parties stand for?*

b. Internal divisive issues:

- Orthodox Rabbis in Israel have strong political power due to their influence in voting. They control juridiction in marraiges, deaths, praying locations at the holy Wailing Wall, and even schedules for stores in Jerusalem. The Rabbis' ultra-conservative positions have divided the society among Reformed and Conservative Jews.

Suggested Activities:
- *Students can research the above examples of divisive practices and present arguments pro and con in a debate*

Hints:
- The Orthodox rabbinate does not recognize Reform or Conservative Judaism in Israel or throughout the Diaspora. Jewish newcomers to Israel who do not qualify as «fully Jewish» under religious law, cannot get a mariage License. Many of them go to Cyprus to get married.
- There has been a new wall space built at the Wailing Wall (known in Hebrew as the Kotel) for men and women to pray together, or for women alone. Previously, women were not allowed to pary there. The Wailing Wall is a remnant of the retaining wall that surrounded the Temple mount, revered by Jews as the location of their ancient temples and the holiest site in Judaism. It is located next to the Blue Mosque, Al Aqsa.
- There has been a decree that all citizens should display «Loyalty in Culture.» Law requires that an NGO in Israel must disclose funding they receive from foreign countries. In addition, Israeli law does not want Jewish artisits, writers, scholars, filmmakers, etc to criticize Israeli governmental practices regarding

settlers, settlements, Arabs in Israel and as neighbors, right of return for Palestinians, etc.

5. World Literature

a. Early Writings

- Early Jewish writings consist of the Old Testament, the Torah, and the Ten Commandments.
- Islam's early writings comprise the Koran.

Suggested Activities:
- *Divide into 4 groups, and assign each group an early writing (Old Testament, Torah, Ten Commandments, Koran) to research and present evidence (historical facts, events, persons, excerpts) citing and exemplifying the writing's cultural and historical significance, both past and present.*

Hints:
- The Old Testament is the Jewish Bible. It is considered basis for Jewish oral and written law. It has been studied, practiced and treasured by Jews throughout the world for more than 3,000 years.
- The Torah, Jewish Law, laid the foundation for monotheism (there is only one God) and laid the foundation for the subsequent religions of Christianity and Islam that has also as its basic tenet, monotheism.
- Ten Commandments, Jewish Law, lists ten rules of law and morality.
- The Koran is the Holy book for all Muslims. The Koran contains the teachings of Muhammad, who was born in 570 A.D. He is believed by Muslims to be the messenger for God, Allah. Muhammad taught that God, Allah, should be worshipped through prayer. Muslims are called to prayer 5 times a day and a good Muslim should pray at least once a day. The Dome of the Rock, Al Aqsa Mosque in Jerusalem, was designated by the prophet, Muhammad, for pilgrimage. It is at the Al Aqsa Mosque where Muhammad ascended into Heaven and was given the 5 Pillars of Islam from Allah.

b. Theodor Herzl

- Herzl is considered the father of the Jewish Homeland – Israel.

- At the end of the 19th century in 1896 in Leipzig, Germany, Theodor Herzl, a journalist and author, wrote <u>The Jewish State (Der Judenstaat)</u> in which he proposed and outlined the re-establishment of a Jewish state to be located in Jerusalem. Herzl envisioned a Jewish state that combined modern Jewish culture with European Jewish heritage.

Suggested Activities:
- *Discuss Herzl's vision for the new state of Israel as an "open," and "utopian socialist" society.*
- *Think of other famous visionaries and how Herzl's ideals compared to these others.*

Hints:
- Herzl's premise was that Palestine is the unforgettable historic Jewish homeland. He wrote, "The plan would seem mad enough if a single individual were to undertake it; but if many Jews simultaneously agreed on it, it is entirely reasonable, and its achievement presents no difficulties worth mentioning. The idea depends on the number of its adherents. Perhaps our ambitious young men, to whom every road of advancement is now closed, and for whom the Jewish state throws open a bright prospect of freedom, happiness and honor, perhaps they will see to it that this idea is spread."
- Herzl envisioned the future Jewish state to be a "third way" between capitalism and socialism, with a developed welfare program and public ownership of the main natural resources. Industry, agriculture and trade were organized on a cooperative basis. He called this economic model, "Mutualism" which he envisioned from the French utopian-socialist thinking. It is not surprising, based on the original Socialist premise of the political structure of the Jewish state, that Russia was the first country to support the creation of Israel after World War ll.

6. Media Studies:

a. Film Clips and Scene Discussions:

- *Empathy:* Scene: (00:53 –> 00:54 minutes)

"How did you feel when you heard? Same as you, I imagine. I'm tying to make sense of it all. So I don't go under. Does Bilal know? He knows he has a brother and it isn't me. Is that why he didn't come? He doesn't want to come? Does he hate us? How's it feel to be Palestinian? Do you feel hatred? No, really, I don't. You never hated? No. You? I live in Paris, a long way away."

What is empathy? How does it help us understand other people's problems? How would you feel if you'd learn for the first time that your biological parents are not the parents you live with? How would you feel if your biological parents came from a country you did not like?

- *Peace:* Scene: (01:40: –> 01:41)

"You know what I thought when I learnt that my life should have been yours? I thought, Now I've started this life, I have to make a success of it so you'll be proud of me. Same goes for you. You have my life, Joseph."

The goal of the film is to give a suggestion on how the people in the Middle East can make peace. Discuss the possibility and give concrete suggestions on how you and your group would make peace. Discuss how the ending of the film offers hope.

b. Is this a True Story?

- Director, Lorrain Levy, says that the screen script is not based on a book or one true story. Instead, it is based on what *could* have happened. She uses the question as a polemic, a philosophical discussion and debate, to extrapolate whether it is possible to learn to love one's enemy in the same way that two families could love a son who is not theirs biologically.
- The concept of a switch at birth between two enemy families in Israel, Arab and Jewish, is used to explore that it is possible to have a peaceful, two state society. Art and film are the mediums through which the director strives to answer the philosophical and political questions that plague the Middle East crisis for generations.

b. Personal Identity:

- To further her thesis, the director uses Film to discuss the philosophical question - what is identity? The Rabbi tells Josef that he is no longer Jewish because his biological mother is not Orith, but a Palestinian woman. Yet, Josef cannot believe that the *other one* is more Jewish than him, even though the *other one* was raised an Arab.

Suggested Activities:
- *Using the film as a point of departure to discuss personal identity, ask members of your group to imagine that they have been raised in a different type of family - in regards, to race, religion, and gender. Discuss if they would think of themselves differently:*
  - *Would their personal identity change? Their self image? Their ego? Their life style?*
  - *Discuss the role of environment vs. biology, Nature vs Nurture. Share examples of how the environment and biology work together. Ex. Darwin's Finches, the evolution of the Peppered Moth, the importance of the education system, domestic animals vs. wild animals*
  - *How does our environment shape our personal identities?*
  - *What does it mean to have natural attributes and characteristics; where do these come from?*

c. Artistic and Cultural Boycotts

- A spoken or unspoken rule is that Arab artists and academics, do not want to participate in exhibitions or conferences in Israel. They "boycott" Israel. This is a form of protest or punishment against the state of Israel because they are considered an "Occupier state."

Suggested Activity:
- *Divide into pairs to identify other groups, or prominent individuals, such as, British artists, lecturers, and athletes, who "boycott" Israel.*
- *What does this mean? How does it affect Israel?*

7. Philosophy / Critical Thinking:

Debates: The following can be used for debates and philosophical discussions:

a. Religious intolerance has caused wars throughout history. After World War ll in 1948, the United Nations was created with the hope that differences of intolerance could be resolved through diplomacy and not war. Unfortunately, this has not always been achieved. Research, compare and debate where religion today has torn people apart who live in the same country. Is there a relationship between their religious and philosophical perspectives?

b. Israel is the home and philosophical center to many religions. Jerusalem is the nuclear core for the beginning of Judaism, Christianity and Islam. Israel is also the home to other religions as the Armenian Orthodox Church, the Coptic Church, the Latin Church, and the Bahai Faith. Research, compare and debate if Israel is the optimum location for these religious headquarters?

Hints:
- Jerusalem has been the holiest city in Judaism and the spiritual homeland of the Jewish people since the 10th century Before Christ. The first temple was built by King Solomon in 950 B.C. The Torah, which contains Jewish Laws, laid the foundation for monotheism, Judaism, Christianity and Islam.
- Christianity was born in 1 A.D., in the year of the Lord, when Jesus Christ, son of God, was born in Bethlehem. Jesus was born and raised Jewish. The Temple Mount in Jerusalem is also important to Christians because it was the site where Jesus Christ preached and healed the sick. It was also in Jerusalem where he created disturbances that led to his Crucifixion.
- Jerusalem is considered a sacred site also for the followers of Islam. The Islamic prophet Muhammad visited the city in the year 610 A.D. and he designated the blue Al-Aqsa Mosque for pilgrimages. This is where Muhammad ascended into heaven and was given the 5 pillars of Islam from Allah, which is still used today.
- The Bahai Faith is also a monotheistic religion emphasizing the spiritual unity of all humankind. The Bahai Faith was founded by Bahaullah in 19th century Persia. He was exiled for his teachings. Today, there are more than 5 million Bahais around the world in more than 200 countries. The center of the Bahai religion (I-Bah Haifa) can be found in Haifa, Israel.
- Many other religions have strong origins to Israel as:
  - The Russian Orthodox Church had members visiting the Holy Land as early as the 11th century,
  - The Armenian Orthodox Church dates from the year 301 and the Armenian community has been present in Jerusalem since the 5th century.
  - The Coptic Church flourished as early as the 13th century when their Patriarch was first represented in Jerusalem.
  - The Latin Church of Jerusalem had their Patriarchate in Israel since 1099. Today, the Latin Church of Jerusalem has a strong community in the West Bank and Gaza.

8. Architecture:

- Israel's archeologists work on more than 300 excavations every year. The best ones are turned into national parks. The Israel Antiquities Authority, IAA, supervises annual excavations, accounting for about 95 percent of all the archeological digs in Israel. The digs usually take place at a *mound*, composed of the remains of ancient settlements. Most of them are UNESCO Heritage Sites.

Suggested Activity:
- *Divide group into three divisions to research and collect facts and interesting anecdotes about each of the following famous sites of antiquity in Israel: Massada, City of David and Tzippori.*

Hints:

a. Massada:

- Herod the Great — the Roman king who built the Second Temple in Jerusalem and the port of Caesarea was also responsible for Masada, an ancient fortress overlooking the Dead Sea. This is the site of a popular revolt against the Romans by a band of Jewish families.
- The Northern Palace, built on three rock terraces, included bedrooms, bathhouse, storerooms, hundreds of clay pots, 12 gigantic cisterns, ritual baths and a stable-turned-synagogue (one of the earliest synagogues in the world).
- Archeologists found skeletons and more than 5,000 coins, mostly minted during the five years of the rebellion, along with scroll fragments.

b. City of David:

- Dating back more than 3,000 years, when David conquered a narrow hill south of today's Old City of Jerusalem, this area was once the Israelite capital and spiritual center. Surrounded by valleys, the city was fortified against attack with walls and towers. Taking advantage of the nearby Gihon Spring, the ancient builders made a sophisticated water system.
- However, archeological finds show that the city was already inhabited more than 5,000 years ago, a small but significant walled city in the Middle Bronze Age at the time of the biblical Patriarchs.

- The City of David affords great views of Mount Zion and the Temple Mount. Guides take visitors into the underground tunnels through which the city was conquered and residents fled, down into the hidden spring where kings were coroneted, and into the dark flowing waters of Hezekiah's Tunnel.

c. Tzippori:

- Tzippori, the traditional birthplace of Mary, was an important scholarly city in the hills of Lower Galilee, west of Nazareth. Herod conquered it in 37 BC, but 33 years later it was destroyed by the Romans following rebellions there. However, Herod Antipas restored it to become "the ornament of all Galilee," and it served as the seat of the Sanhedrin (the Jewish high court) and a preferred residence for Talmudic sages until the mid-fourth century.
- The city was rebuilt and settled by an unusual mix of Christians and Jews in the fifth century. Today, one can see there a 4,500-seat Roman theater; a restored third-century villa in which a mosaic depicts scenes from the life of wine god Dionysus and the so-called "Mona Lisa of the Galilee"; a synagogue with a restored mosaic floor; and a 250-meter-long, first-century underground water system.

9. Technology:

a. Israel is a favorite touristic spot for its study of religious sites and antiquities. All this can be found from computers in a virtual tour format.

Suggested Activities:
- *Enjoy a virtual tour of Christ's Stations of the Cross and the Via Dolorosa in Israel and retrace the steps Christ took before his crucifixion. Then travel with a virtual tour to Israel's antiquities. Share your findings with other groups and schools in your community.*

———————
Sidebars:
———————

1. Public Response and Directors' Response:

What makes this film unique, is the opportunity it offers to ask the question, Who am I? Am I what my DNA pre-defines me, or am I a product of my environment? In the film, it catapults the plot and becomes the pivotal point. It raises a philosophical as well as a religious question. And, thus, offers the opportunity for dialogue and introspection. We are, perhaps the director concludes, who we love and who loves us. If that is the case, as the film depicts, then we are offered a road map for Peace in the Middle East.

2. Awards:

- Tokyo International Film Festival
  2012– Won - Best Director, Lorraine Levy
          Won - Tokyo Gran Prix, Lorraine Levy

Bibliography of Films - Filmography:
Further Global Study Resources through Film:

Holocaust Theme:

- *Exodus* (USA)
- *The Garden of the Finzi-Continis* (Italy)
- *The Last Metro* (France)
- *Shoah* (France)
- *The Sorrow and the Pity* (France)
- *Europa Europa* (France)
- *Schindler's List* (USA)
- *Anne Frank Remembered* (United Kingdom)
- *Life Is Beautiful* (Italy)
- *Sunshine* (Hungary)
- *Kadosh* (Israel)
- *Maus* (USA)
- *Divided We Fall* (Czechoslovakia)
- *Into the Arms of Strangers: Stories of the Kindertransport* (United Kingdom)
- *Nowhere In Africa* (Germany)
- *The Pianist* (France/Poland)
- *Facing Windows* (Italy)
- *Nina's Tragedies* (Israel)

- *Fateless* (Hungary)
- *Black Book* (Holland)
- *The Counterfeiters* (Austria)
- *The Boy in the Striped Pajamas* (USA)
- *A Secret* (France)
- *One Day You'll Understand* (France)
- *Defiance* (USA)
- *The Reader* (USA/ Germany)
- *Gruber's Journey* (Romania)
- *Katyn* (Poland)
- *A Film Unfinished* (Germany/U.S.A.)
- *Night and Fog* (France)
- *Ida* (Poland)
- *Sarah's Key* (France)
- *Sobibor* (France;
- *Hannah Arendt* (Germany)
- *Phoenix* (Germany)
- *Labyrinth of Lies* (Germany)

Printed in the USA
CPSIA information can be obtained
at www.ICGtesting.com
LVHW081758071224
798595LV00006B/239